The Values of Educational Administration

T0386188

This book is for Marilyn and Laurie

The Values of Educational Administration

Edited by

Paul T. Begley and Pauline E. Leonard

RoutledgeFalmer
Taylor & Francis Group

LONDON AND NEW YORK

First published 1999 by Falmer Press
2 Park Square, Milton Park, Abingdon, Oxon, OX14 4RN

Transferred to Digital Printing 2004

Simultaneously published in the USA and Canada
by Garland Inc., 19 Union Square West, New York, NY 10003

Typeset in 10/12 pt Times by Graphicraft Limited, Hong Kong

Jacket design by Caroline Archer

British Library Cataloguing in Publication Data
A catalogue record for this book is available from the British Library

Library of Congress Cataloging in Publication Data
A catalogue record for this book has been requested

ISBN 0 7507 0937 5 (hbk)
ISBN 0 7507 0936 7 (pbk)

Table of Contents

List of Figures   vii
Acknowledgments   viii
Foreword   ix
Peter Ribbins, University of Birmingham, UK

Introduction   1
Paul T. Begley, OISE/UT, Canada

Part I: Perspectives on Values and Educational Administration   5

Chapter 1   The Triumph of the Will   6
Christopher Hodgkinson, University of Victoria, Canada

Chapter 2   Moral Dimensions of Leadership   22
Robert J. Starratt, Boston College, USA

Chapter 3   Against Leadership: A Concept Without a Cause   36
Gabriele Lakomski, University of Melbourne, Australia

Chapter 4   Academic and Practitioner Perspectives on Values   51
Paul T. Begley, OISE/UT, Canada

Chapter 5   Complexity, Context and Ethical Leadership   70
Colin W. Evers, Monash University, Australia

Part II: Research on Values and Valuation Processes   83

Chapter 6   Inhibitors to Collaboration   84
Pauline E. Leonard, University of Saskatchewan, Canada

Chapter 7   The Value of Language and the Language of Value in a
Multi-ethnic School   106
James Ryan, OISE/UT, Canada

Chapter 8   Context and Praxis in the Study of School Leadership:
A Case of Three?   125
Peter Ribbins, University of Birmingham, UK

Chapter 9   Leadership From A Distance: Institutionalizing Values
and Forming Character at Timbertop, 1951–61   140
Peter Gronn, Monash University, Australia

Table of Contents

Part III: Value Praxis and Other Ethical Issues   169

Chapter 10   The Meaning of Time: Revisiting Values and
Educational Administration   170
Clay Lafleur, OISE/UT, Canada

Chapter 11   Leadership and Management in Education: Restoring the
Balance in Pursuit of a More Just and Equitable Society   187
*Paul Carlin, Australian Principals Centre and Helen Goode,
Catholic Education Office, Ballarat, Australia*

Chapter 12   Poietic Leadership   201
Don Shakotko and Keith Walker, University of Saskatchewan, Canada

Chapter 13   Values, Leadership and School Renewal   223
Clive Beck, OISE/UT, Canada

Chapter 14   The Future of Public Education   232
*Lynn Bossetti, University of Calgary and Daniel J. Brown,
University of British Columbia, Canada*

Chapter 15   Future Directions for the Study of Values and
Educational Leadership   246
Pauline E. Leonard, University of Saskatchewan, Canada

Notes on Contributors   254
Index   256

List of Figures

2.1   Mapping school practices by structural scaffolding   30
3.1   A generic leadership model   45
4.1   Syntax of value terms   55
4.2   Arenas of value action   57
4.3   Mapping theories and conceptions of values using a linguistic
      metaphor (Begley, 1996b)   58
4.4   Integrating cognitive information processing theory and values
      theory (Begley, 1996b)   63
5.1   A three-layer net with some connections shown   76
10.1 Typology of time in the lives of educators   174
12.1 A trinity of human operations   202
12.2 A tripartition model of art   203
12.3 An aesthetic model of leadership   203
12.4 A poietic model for leadership   204
14.1 Three values behind educational governance   239

Acknowledgments

We are grateful to Anna Clarkson, Senior Editor at Falmer Press for her patience and support throughout the preparation of this book. Thanks also to our associates at the Centre for the Study of Values and Leadership at the Ontario Institute for Studies in Education, University of Toronto (OISE/UT), its affiliate the UCEA Center for the Study of Leadership and Ethics (University of Virginia), and the various manuscript reviewers for their support and helpful comments. With your advice we have produced a better book.

Chapter 1: The Triumph of the Will was originally a paper given at the Toronto Conference on Values and Educational Leadership, OISE Centre for the Study of Values and Leadership, University of Toronto, October 1996, by Christopher Hodgkinson. It has since been published in *Educational Management and Administration* (1997) *BEMAS* **25**, 4, pp. 381–94.

Material relating to the linguistic metaphor presented in Chapter 4: Academic and Administrative Perspectives on Values is taken from BEGLEY, P. (1996) 'Cognitive perspectives on the nature and function of values in educational administration' in LEITHWOOD, K.A. (ed.) *International Handbook on Educational Leadership and Administration*, Boston: Kluwer Academic. Material presented in Chapter 4 relating to applying cognitive perspectives to values and leadership was excerpted from a more detailed account originally published in BEGLEY, P.T. (1996) 'Cognitive perspectives on values in administration: A quest for coherence and relevance', *Educational Administration Quarterly*, **32**, 3, pp. 403–26.

Foreword

Harold Bloom, in his elegiac defence of *The Western Canon*, identifies 26 authors who, for their 'sublimity and their representative nature' (1996, p. 2) are, for him, canonical. Amongst them, one is central. Shakespeare, for Bloom, is 'the largest writer we will ever know . . . his powers of assimilation and of contamination are unique and constitute a perpetual challenge to universal performance and criticism'. But, in modern times, the canon as a whole, and Shakespeare in particular, is under attack – 'I find it absurd and regrettable that the current criticism of Shakespeare . . .' is in 'full flight from his aesthetic supremacy and works at reducing him to the 'social energies' of the English Renaissance, as though there were no authentic difference in aesthetic merit between the creator of Lear, Hamlet, Iago, Falstaff and his disciples such as John Webster and Thomas Middleton (pp. 96, 3). Such a development represents a collapse of 'aesthetic value' in which 'things have . . . fallen apart, the centre has not held and mere anarchy is in the process of being unleashed . . .' (p. 1). In attempting to describe and account for this collapse, Bloom draws upon Giambattista Vico's notion, in *New Science* of 'a cycle of three phases – Theocratic, Aristocratic, Democratic . . . Vico did not postulate a Chaotic Age before the *ricorso* or return of a second Theocratic Age; but our century, while pretending to continue the Democratic Age, cannot be better characterised than as Chaotic' (pp. 1, 2).

In proposing this last judgment, Bloom appears to have in mind a collapse which is not restricted to the literary and aesthetic. In this context, the fear that 'ethics', along with all other forms of knowledge which rest ultimately upon claims and statements about values, is not what it was, has been voiced at more or less regular intervals over the last two and a half thousand years. In this century, the growing hegemony of ideas drawn from modern, modernist and, most especially, post modernist thinking has ensured that it is being heard once again. And so it should be because there is a very real possibility that the extent, quality and nature of the discourse on values will, as the new age of chaos works its way through the contemporary historical epoch, be further diminished and trivialized. To illustrate the danger, I would point to three developments which have influenced thinking about values, and their place in the theory and practice of educational administration, over the last 50 years.

1. That values are not fit subjects for meaningful discourse

This and related claims are usually justified in terms of the 'verifiability principle' which is at the heart of logical positivist thinking. Briefly, according to this principle, we can never have knowledge as opposed to opinions about matters which turn on values. In its most rigorous forms, logical positivism asserts that propositions which are not, in principle at least, objectively verifiable by appropriate observation are not to be regarded as either true or false but as meaningless. As such, attempts to offer evidence or argument either for or against such propositions are pointless. At best ethical, and aesthetic, propositions can be regarded as pseudo-propositions, which amount to statements of preference.

Such thinking was mediated to the field of administration, and subsequently to educational administration, by Herbert Simon; initially through his book, published in 1945, *Administrative Behaviour*. Simon did not deny the place of values in the world but, for the kinds of reasons identified above, believed that they were not susceptible to objective verification. As such, they were not proper subjects for study for social scientists and should therefore as far as possible be removed from the concern of administrators. Such a perspective entailed that students and practitioners alike should restrict their attention to the worthwhile and realistic task of producing objective, value-free knowledge of what worked in the administration of organizations, rather than in the pursuit of a self indulgent, and ultimately, vain search for subjective and value-laden prescriptions of what ought to be done.

The influence of these and related ideas, found their way into educational administration in the 1950s, mainly through the work of the group of scholars, notably Campbell, Getzels, Halpin and Griffiths, who came collectively to constitute what has sometimes been labeled as the 'Theory Movement'. As Hughes (1985) puts it, this approach entailed 'a determination to rely exclusively on a natural science methodology' and its consequence was that 'concepts used were to be defined operationally, i.e. their meanings were to correspond, as Herbert Simon had insisted, 'to empirically verifiable facts or situations'. Value judgments as to the desirability of policies and behaviours were therefore to be firmly resisted in the new studies being initiated, which would concentrate on determining what *is* rather than what *ought to be* (Culbertson, 1965, p. 4).

These approaches seem to share two beliefs. First, that educational administration is properly a science and, as such, to do with what 'is', and not with what 'ought to be'. Second, that propositions about what 'is' and what 'ought to be' are logically different and cannot be deduced one from the other (a view sometimes known as the 'naturalistic fallacy'). Whilst most members of the theory movement accepted the validity of the notion of the naturalistic fallacy, many also had high hopes for science. More recently, some contemporary students of administration, and of educational administration, whilst rejecting the notion of the naturalistic fallacy, have nevertheless harboured similar and, indeed, in some respects, much grander hopes for science than ever did Dan Griffiths or Andrew Halpin.

2. *That science will eventually tell us all we need to know about values*

Hughes in his account of the theory movement, has argued that it was characterized by 'a significant infusion of new ideas, propagated by a new breed of able enthusiasts [including Jacob Getzels, Andrew Halpin, Ronald Campbell and Dan Griffiths] whose expertise in educational management was derived more from study and research in the social sciences than from long practitioner experience' (1985, 11). They believed that the field should turn away from the study of practical problems and focus on research into theoretical issues. Theory, in this context, was to be closely defined. Halpin, for example, advocated Fiegl's definition of theory as 'a set of assumptions from which can be derived by purely logico-mathematical procedures a larger set of empirical laws. The theory furnishes an explanation of these empirical laws . . .' (1951, p. 182). From this beginning, some eagerly anticipated a great leap forward. As Hughes (1985, p. 11) notes, 'The ideal which Griffiths enthusiastically envisaged was the development of a general theory of human behaviour, within which the theory of administrative behaviour in education would be a sub-system. The natural sciences, and particularly physics, would provide the model, Kepler's Laws of Planetary Motion being the prototype of the yet undiscovered laws of Educational administration (Griffiths, 1957, p. 388)'.

With the advantage of hindsight, it is easy to exaggerate the extent to which the ideal of a hard science of educational administration, based upon a single and overarching grand theory, ever fully achieved paradigm status. In the United Kingdom, for example, and, indeed, in many other parts of the world, it found few adherents. Even within the United States there were always sceptics. By the mid 1960s, critics like Schwab were already arguing that 'contrary to the burden of recent literature on administration, the pursuit of one sufficing theory of administration is a manifest impossibility in the foreseeable future, and an uncritical aping of the wrong model' (1964, p. 47). Shortly afterwards, key members of the theory movement also began to voice their disillusion with what had been achieved and doubts about what was possible. Andrew Halpin was in the first of these categories. In 1969, 1972 and 1977 he published a series of papers which seemed to suggest that in the history of the theory movement it was people who had failed theory rather than that the theory had failed the people. Dan Griffiths was in the second. By 1966 he was already warning that 'the search for one encompassing theory (if anyone is searching) should be abandoned . . . We have learnt that a more modest approach to theory pays off' (quoted in Baron, Cooper and Walker, 1969, p. 166).

Griffiths, was later to acknowledge that the final demise of these early hopes 'came at the 1974 meeting of the IIP in Bristol . . . The *coup de grâce* was delivered by Greenfield who made an across-the-board denunciation of every aspect of the theory movement' (1988, p. 30). Some years later, Griffiths was to qualify this first assessment. In doing so he suggested that whilst Greenfield's critique of the theory movement was 'clear, strong, consistent and emotional' his attack 'was actually on a narrow segment of the movement – that is, the handful of theories developed by American scholars in the late 1950s' (p. 152). He also argued that although Greenfield's 'critique deepened over the years . . . it did not broaden . . . It started as an attack on the Theory Movement . . . and that is what it remained' (p. 152).

Evers and Lakomski take a different view. Having attested to the power and importance of the arguments which Greenfield had presented in 1974, they claim that in the years after Bristol, he had 'broadened and deepened his critique. In an impressive set of papers . . . he has sought to develop a systematic view of social reality as a human invention, in opposition to the systems scientific perspective of social reality as a natural system. He has constructed strands of argument on the nature of knowledge, on administrative theory and research, on values, on the limits of science, of the importance of human subjectivity, truth and reality . . . the magnitude of his undertaking and a corresponding elegance of argument make his work the most important theoretical development in recent educational administration' (1991, p. 76).

The papers to which Griffiths and Evers and Lakomski refer, appeared at regular intervals in the 19 years after Bristol and revised versions of several of them are collected together in Greenfield and Ribbins (1993). In 1980, Greenfield published 'The man who came back through the door in the wall: Discovering truth, discovering self, discovering organizations' which he came to believe summarized authoritatively key aspects of his thinking. The paper took the form of a *prolegomenon* for a new study of organization. This, he stressed, was not presented as 'a blueprint of organizational reality or as hypotheses that can be confirmed or disconfirmed by empirical facts alone. The claim for them is only that they weave together what some people have defined as the limits of knowledge with what others have experi-enced as the reality of organizations'. They attempt to 'forge a coherent but necessarily incomplete argument about the nature of organizations and the possibility of inquiry into them'. The prolegomenon has *nine propositions*: That organizations are accomplished by people and people are responsible for what goes on in them; that organizations are expressions of will, intention and value; that organizations express becoming and not being; that facts do not exist except as they are called into existence human action and interest; that man acts and then will judge the action; that organizations are arbitrary definitions of reality woven in symbols, expressed in language; that organizations expressed as contexts for human action can be resolved into meaning, moral order and power; that there is no technology for achieving the purposes which organizations are to serve; and, that there is no way of training administrators other than by giving them some apocalyptic or transcendental vision of the universe and of their life on earth (1993, pp. 103–113). Such a statement represents a powerful affirmation of the place of values in the theory and practice of educational administration. In making it, Greenfield was committed to defending the notion of the naturalistic fallacy and to contesting the view that science, traditionally conceived, represented the way forward for the field.

In this context, and notwithstanding the generous acknowledgment of Greenfield's achievements, Evers and Lakomski, whilst rejecting what they regard as its foundationalist preconceptions, do appear to share some of the key aspirations of the theory movement. Their views, sometimes known as Australian naturalism or naturalistic coherentism, have been developed at length (1991, 1996). They claim to be able to offer a solution 'to the current stand off' in the field of educational administration which entails 'neither a return to traditional science [as advocated by the members of the theory movement], not the acceptance of multiple paradigms with their many world views [as advocated by Greenfield and his allies] which fragment the research enterprise, but to develop a new science of administration. Our new science is justified by a coherentist epistemology that is the best available alternative to foundational theories of knowledge . . .' (1996, p. xiv). Underpinning such a conception of new science are some sweeping claims about the possibilities of neuro-science in the years to come. On this Evers and Lakomski's express some surprise that 'while there seems little disquiet over neuro-scientific explanations regarding more mundane human activities, the level of scepticism rises sharply where such issues as human subjectivity and culture are included as contenders for neuro-scientific explanation' (p. xvi) and are puzzled that 'at a time when scientists are beginning to unravel many of the traditional mysteries of what goes on inside a person's head, that is, beginning to find causal accounts for human action, our naturalistic programme is considered to be 'reductionist' in the sense of de-humanizing' (p. xvii).

If such ideas can be regarded as a prolegomenon for a new 'Ionian Enchantment', Evers and Lakomski are by no means alone in advancing them. Thus, for example, Edward Wilson, the American biologist, who has been described as one of the world's greatest living scientists, has called for consilience. This postulates the existence of an underlying and fundamental unity to all knowledge – of the natural sciences, social sciences and humanities – in which everything in our world, indeed within our universe, is shaped by a small number of fundamental natural laws that comprise the principles underlying every branch of learning. As Wilson puts it, 'the central idea of the consilience world view is that all tangible phenomena, from the birth of stars to the workings of social institutions, are based on material process that are ultimately reducible, however long and tortuous the sequences, to the laws of physics' (p. 266). Wilson's claims, like those of Evers and Lakomski, are presented essentially in the form of an undated promissory note. He is at pains to acknowledge the enormity of the task involved if the project he envisages is to be brought to a successful conclusion. He recognizes, like Evers and Lakomski, that 'such reductionism is not popular outside the natural sciences' (p. 227). It is certainly not popular in the social sciences and is even less so in the humanities.

3.   That values are not respectable topics for sophisticated modern discourse

Some commentators have claimed that the spirit of the contemporary age is characterized by a reluctance to engage in discourse, serious or otherwise, about values and when such talk does take place it is often impoverished. Why this should be so is described and explained in a variety of different ways.

James Wilson, in *The Moral Sense*, describes the spirit of the age as deeply sceptical. It is an age in which 'science has challenged common sense'; one theory of science holds that we can never have knowledge, as opposed to mere opinion, about morality. Anthropologists have shown how various are the customs of mankind. The dominant tradition in modern anthropology has held that those customs are entirely the product of culture, and so we can conclude that man has no nature apart from his culture. Philosophers have sought to find a rational basis for moral judgements; 'the dominant tradition in modern philosophy asserts that no rational foundation can be given for any such judgement' (1997, p. viii). With this in mind, Wilson asks 'whether the mirror that modern scepticism has held up to mankind's face reflects what we wish to see?' (p. x). He believes most 'ordinary men and women . . . wish to make moral judgements but their culture does not help them to do it. They often feel like refugees living in a land captured by hostile forces. When they speak of virtue, they must do so privately, in whispers, least they be charged with the grievous crime of being "unsophisticated" or, if they press the matter, "fanatics" [. . .] Our reluctance to speak of morality and our suspicion, nurtured by our best minds, that we cannot "prove" our moral principles has amputated our public discourse at the knees' (pp. x, xi).

Wilson draws upon his experience of discussions with college students asked to make and defend moral judgments to illustrate and explain what he means. Many, he suggests, 'will act as if they really believe that all cultural practices were equally valid, all moral claims were equally suspect, and human nature is infinitely malleable or utterly self-regarding . . . If asked to defend their admonitions against "being judgmental", the students sometimes respond by arguing that moral judgements are arbitrary, but more often they stress the importance of tolerance and fair play' (pp. 6, 7). As an attack on the deficiencies of 'cultural relativism', these views echo those advanced a decade earlier by Allan Bloom. In *The Closing of the American Mind*, Bloom acknowledges that 'men are likely to bring what are only their prejudices to the judgement of alien peoples. Avoiding that is one of the main purposes of education. But trying to prevent it by removing the authority of men's reason is to render ineffective the instrument that can correct their prejudices. True openness is the accompaniment of the desire to know, hence the awareness of ignorance. To deny the possibility of knowing good and bad is to suppress true openness' (1987, p. 40). He identifies two kinds of openness: 'the openness of indifference – promoted with the twin purposes of humbling our intellectual pride and letting us be whatever we want to be, just as long as we don't want to be knowers – and the openness that invites us to the quest for knowledge and certitude, for which history and the various cultures provide a brilliant array of examples for examination' (p. 41). Sadly, whilst 'openness used to be the virtue that permitted us to seek the good by using reason. It now means accepting everything and denying reason's power. The unrestrained and thoughtless pursuit of openness, without recognizing the inherent political, social, or cultural problem of openness as the goal of nature, has rendered openness meaningless' (p. 38).

What are the implications of all this for the future of discourse on values? Wilson claims that 'Most of us have a moral sense but have tried to talk ourselves out of it' (1997, p. ix). Given the intolerance of the new age of tolerance, people tend to 'flinch . . . at least in public' from addressing fundamental questions about values (p. xi). As commonly used today, the 'word "values" finesses all the tough questions. It implies a taste or preference and recalls to mind the adage that there is no disputing taste' (p. xi). This is a bleak conclusion but, as Wilson also stresses, 'we don't really mean that our beliefs are no more than tastes, because when we defend them – to the extent that we can – our muscles tighten and our knuckles grow white. Arguments about values often turn into fights about values . . . That is not the way we discuss our taste for vanilla ice cream' (p. xi).

Does such passion have a relevance to educational administration? On this, and for once, the views of my own most influential mentors are not easily compatible. Thomas Greenfield was not altogether optimistic. Reflecting upon the training of educational leaders he noted that:

'One of the things I have sensed in speaking to leaders in education, is how impoverished their real world is. They don't see beyond a narrow horizon. They don't see the problems of education, except in rather technological terms, or if they do see it, if they talk about it in larger terms, they are sentimental and platitudinous. We need leaders in education who can think about the larger issues . . . But it will be an uphill struggle to bring them to such a contemplation . . . The headlong pressure to act, to do, to be the leader militates against a reflective attitude – a stance that is need for the growth of worthwhile values, of character. That is what I see as the ultimate in the nurture of leaders through training. It would be aimed at . . . fostering awareness of values and of the value choices that face them, and thereby perhaps assisting character growth.' (Greenfield and Ribbins, 1993, pp. 258, 259)

This account does not square with Christopher Hodgkinson's experience of training administrators in educational or other fields. As he notes: 'From the beginning I have had an obsession with administrative man and the concept of values. Real life administrators are often thought to have a minimal attention span, a contempt for all things intellectual and a pride in their tough images, but I have found that when you start talking about values you can establish an instant rapport with them. Values are the key to their interests. They know what you are talking about. You are onto something which is important to them' (Ribbins, 1993, p. 15).

My sympathies lie with Hodgkinson. Many years of involvement with school principals and other educational leaders have taught me that values are important to them. Almost all those I have interviewed for my books on headteachers and headship in primary, special and secondary schools (Pascal and Ribbins, 1998; Rayner and Ribbins, 1999; Ribbins, 1997; Ribbins and Marland, 1994) talked fluently and enthusiastically about their efforts to achieve a shared vision for their schools, and of the struggle to clarify and apply their values as leading educators in practice. One example must suffice, particularly as it is located somewhere between the views of Greenfield and Hodgkinson and since it speaks to so much of the rest of what I have had to say earlier. In my discussion with him, Brian Sherratt, headteacher of the largest school in the United Kingdom, stressed that

'building the ethos of the school and . . . working it daily' was absolutely crucial. Such an ethos, he emphasized, must be expressed in the values and procedures of the school. It is 'because we have these values, this is the way we do these things . . . On the whole teachers are not very happy with philosophical talk. They tend to say "That is philosophy, it's nothing to do with . . . the realities of the job"; but it can be, and if they can see the principles which drive the institution the way the institution wants to do things, and this can be broken down into the things they

do in the classroom and the yard . . . they will accept that this stress on values can
be helpful'. (Ribbins and Marland, 1994, p. 170)

In summary, given the paucity of published texts which focus specifically and
in depth, on values, or even on ethics, morals, or politics, in educational administration it probably invites hubris to speculate upon the status of the canon. Even
so, a growing number of scholars, many of whom have attended the conferences
on 'Values and Leadership in Education' and are represented in this book and
its accompanying volume, have made an important contribution to thinking on
these and related topics. It might also be widely accepted that at least one of these
scholars, Christopher Hodgkinson, in what I think of as his 'Victorian Quartet' –
Towards a Philosophy of Administration (1978), *The Philosophy of Leadership*
(1983), *Educational Leadership: The Moral Art* (1991), and *Administrative Philosophy: Values and Motivations in Administrative Life* (1996) – may already have
achieved canonical status.

What is surely certain, is that the field owes an considerable debt to Paul
Begley, and to his colleagues at the Centre for the Study of Values and Leadership
at the Ontario Institute of Studies in Education of the University of Toronto, and its
affiliate the University Council for Educational Administration Centre for the Study
of Leadership and Ethics of the University of Virginia, for organizing the series
of conferences from which this collection and its companion volume *Values and
Educational Leadership* have been derived. Such events are important vehicles for
enabling and encouraging discussion about the meaning and relevance of values in
the study and practice of educational administration. Their importance should not
be underestimated; without them, as Bloom puts it, 'the shadows lengthen in our
evening land, and we approach the second millennium expecting further shadow-
ing' (1994, p. 16). On the last day that I spent with him, Thomas Greenfield said to
me, as the long series of conversations which prefaced our preparation for his only
book drew to a close, 'a more balanced judgement of my work will surely be
possible after the results of the program we are engaged in here appear . . . After its
publication, I would hope to hear the opinions of those who may bring an open-
mindedness to the issues and ultimately a balanced appreciation of them. *De quistibus
non est disputandum*. I am willing to let the matter rest with a "trial by what is
contrary" as Milton has described the process of truth making' (Greenfield, T. and
Ribbins, P., 1993, 267). Such a hope expresses exactly my expectations for *The
Values of Educational Administration*.

Peter Ribbons
University of Birmingham, UK

References

Bloom, A. (1987) *The Closing of the American Mind*, New York: Simon and Schuster.
Bloom, H. (1996) *The Western Canon*, London: Papermac.

CULBERTSON, J. (1965) 'Trends and issues in the development of a science of administration', in *Perspectives on Educational Administration and the Behavioural Sciences*, Oregon: Centre for the Advanced Study of Educational Administration.

EVERS, C. and LAKOMSKI, G. (1991) *Knowing Educational Administration*, Oxford: Pergamon.

EVERS, C. and LAKOMSKI, G. (1996) *Exploring Educational Administration*, Oxford: Pergamon.

FIEGL, H. (1951) 'Principles and problems of theory construction in psychology', in *Current Trends in Psychological Theory*, Pittsburgh: University of Pittsburgh Press.

GREENFIELD, T. (1988) 'Writers and the written: Writers and the self', in *Curriculum Inquiry*, **19**, 1, pp. 1–9.

GREENFIELD, T. and RIBBINS, P. (1993) (eds) *Greenfield on Educational Administration: Towards a Humane Science*, London: Routledge.

GRIFFITHS, D. (1957) 'Towards a theory of administrative behaviour', in CAMPBELL, R. and GREGG, R. (eds) *Administrative Behaviour in Education*, New York: Harper.

GRIFFITHS, D. (1978) 'Contemporary theory development and educational administration', in *Educational Administration*, **6**, 2, pp. 2–8.

GRIFFITHS, D. (1979) 'Intellectual turmoil in educational administration', in *Educational Administration Quarterly*, **15**, 3, pp. 43–65.

GRIFFITHS, D. (1995) 'Review of Greenfield on educational administration: Towards a humane science', in *Educational Administration Quarterly*, **31**, 1, pp. 151–58.

HALPIN, A. (1957) 'A paradigm for research on administrative behaviour', in CAMPBELL, R. and GREGG, R. (eds) *Administrative Behaviour in Education*, New York: Harper.

HALPIN, A. (1969) 'A foggy view from Olympus', in *The Journal of Educational Administration*, **VII**, 1, pp. 3–18.

HALPIN, A. (1970) 'Administrative theory: The fumbled torch', in KROLL, A. (ed.) *Issues in American Education*, New York: Oxford, pp. 156–83.

HODGKINSON, C. (1978) *Towards a Philosophy of Administration*, Oxford: Blackwell.

HODGKINSON, C. (1983) *The Philosophy of Leadership*, Oxford: Blackwell.

HODGKINSON, C. (1991) *Educational Leadership: The Moral Art*, New York: SUNY.

HODGKINSON, C. (1996) *Administrative Philosophy: Values and Motivations in Administrative Life*, London: Pergamon.

HUGHES, M. (1985) 'Theory and practice in educational management', in HUGHES, M., RIBBINS, P. and THOMAS (eds) *Managing Education: The System and the Institution*, London: Cassell, pp. 3–39.

PASCAL, C. and RIBBINS, P. (1998) *Understanding Primary Headteachers*, London: Cassell.

RAYNER, S. and RIBBINS, P. (1999) *Headship and Leadership in Special Education*, London: Cassell.

RIBBINS, P. (1993) 'Conversations with a condottiere of administrative value', in *The Journal of Educational Administration and Foundations*, **8**, 1, pp. 13–29.

RIBBINS, P. (1997) (ed.) *Leaders and Leadership in the School, College and University*, London: Cassell.

RIBBINS, P. and MARLAND, M. (1994) *Headship Matters*, London: Longmans.

SCHWAB, J. (1964) 'The professorship in educational administration', in WILLOWER, D. and CULBERTSON, J. (eds) *The Professorship in Educational Administration*, Columbus OH: UCEA.

SIMON, H. (1945) *Administrative Behaviour*, New York: Macmillan.

WILSON, E. (1998) *Consilience: The Unity of Knowledge*, New York: Alfred Knopf.

WILSON, J. (1997) *The Moral Sense*, New York: Free Press Paperbacks.

Introduction

Some might ask why study values or, why connect values and educational leadership at all? Christopher Hodgkinson's answer to the values question is,

> ... educational administration is a special case within the general profession of administration. Its leaders find themselves in what might be called an arena of ethical excitement – often politicized but always humane, always intimately connected to the evaluation of society ... it embodies a heritage of value on the one hand, and is a massive industry on the other, in which social, economic, and political forces are locked together in a complex equilibrium of power. All this calls for extra-ordinary value sensitivity on the part of educational leaders. (1991, p. 164)

There are other pioneers of the field equally convinced that a values perspective is essential to educational administration. These include Starratt (see Chapter 2) and Willower (see Begley, Chapter 4), and although it would be safe to say that all the contributors to this book agree on the importance of values as a topic for inquiry, beyond that, some quickly part company. Evers (Chapter 5) and Lakomski (Chapter 3) propose coherentist perspectives as a comprehensive and epistemologically justifiable foundation for a philosophy of educational administration. Willower (see Begley, Chapter 4) is more in favour of Deweyan pragmatism. Hodgkinson (Chapter 1) believes scholars should be studying the problems of emotions, ethics and ego. Ryan (Chapter 7) reminds us that it is a post-modern world. Finally, those with practitioner orientations (i.e. Begley, Chapter 4; Gronn, Chapter 9; Leonard, Chapter 6; Shakotko and Walker, Chapter 12) prefer a situated problem-based approach, or to focus on the resolution of value conflicts in specific contexts. The overall effect is to illustrate that theory and research about values and leadership are still very much works in progress. The field remains fragmented at this time, and although many academics are now actively engaged in dialogue with each other, there is still no strong consensus on the nature and function of values as influences on administration.

Newcomers to the literature on values may find this on-going academic ferment intimidating and complex. To help initiate readers to the debates, it may be helpful to table several propositions. While not all the contributors to this book accept these propositions as true, they nevertheless highlight some of the key issues. Proposition one is that organizations are essentially social constructions, not necessarily perceived by all individuals in the ways intended by organizational leaders and managers, or those with vested interests in that organization. Furthermore, these social constructions we call organizations are driven, animated or operated by people, often a small number of people whose interests the organization serves. Proposition two states that as interesting as it is to analyze and describe the values manifested by organizations, inevitably the organizational meta-values of growth, profit, maintenance and survival will prevail, often at the expense of individuals who become pawns or are treated as expendable resources. People and their well-being ought to be treated as ends not merely as organizational resources, a tendency that probably started with the Industrial Revolution when labour and identity began to be traded for wages on a large scale – and a pattern which continues today despite our frequent rhetoric about collaboration and increasing concerns for the development of moral or good organizations. Proposition three, perhaps the most hotly debated, states that as wonderful as the advances of science may be, particularly in the area of mind-brain studies, they will only in the end explain the *how* not the *why* of human enterprise, and they will never be capable of 100 per cent prediction of human intentions or actions. There is one final proposition, and on this most of the contributors would agree. It states that the transcending agenda of theorists, researchers and practitioners of educational administration should be to do the following: promote reflection by individuals on personally held values (the examined life); followed then and only then by promoting a sensitivity to the value orientations of others, individuals and groups; and thirdly encouraging a sustained dialogue among all people as the only hope of reconciling certain tragically persistent values conflicts between and within societies. Otherwise people are doomed to keep repeating the mistakes of the past over and over again.

This book is organized in three sections totalling 15 chapters. To summarize briefly, the first section of the book, comprised of five chapters, is devoted to theoretical and conceptual perspectives. Both the traditional debates as well as several intriguing new perspectives are presented. Four of the chapters in Section One are authored by giants of the field; Hodgkinson, Starratt, Lakomski and Evers. Hodgkinson (University of Victoria, Canada) is best known for his subjectivist orientation to administration, something he has termed 'the moral art'. Starratt (Boston College, USA), a well-known American scholar, writes prolifically on the subjects of moral, ethical and visionary leadership. Evers (Monash University, Australia) and Lakomski (University of Melbourne, Australia) are best known for their coherentist contributions towards the formulation of an epistemology of educational administration. The fifth contributor to this section is Begley (OISE/ UT), co-editor of this book, a mid-career academic and relative newcomer to the field. He contributes a strong practitioner orientation to the theoretical and conceptual debate on values and valuation processes.

The second section of the book, composed of four chapters, is devoted to reporting the findings of recent research on values and valuation processes in educational settings. The contributors include two respected international scholars, Peter Ribbins (University of Birmingham, UK) and Peter Gronn (University of Melbourne, Australia). Their two chapters (8 and 9 respectively) reflect the ethnographic perspectives for which they are best known. Ryan (OISE/UT), like his Values Centre colleague Begley, is a mid-career academic who is concerned with issues of equity, minority culture issues, and language (see Chapter 7). Leonard (University of Saskatchewan), a newcomer to the field and co-editor of this book, contributes a chapter based on her ground-breaking research on the culture and values of school communities (see Chapter 6).

The third and final section of the book is devoted to a more highly focused discussion on particular topics and issues. In many respects the discussion in these chapters reflects the intersection of theory and practice, hence the adoption of the word praxis in the section title. A total of six chapters make up this concluding section. The contributors are several promising young scholars as well as established authorities. The newcomers to the field with important things to say are Lafleur (Chapter 10), Carlin and Goode (Chapter 11) and Shakotko (Chapter 12). The other contributors – Walker (Chapter 12), Beck (Chapter 13) and Bossetti and Brown (Chapter 14) – are all established academics. A concluding chapter by co-editor Leonard speculates on an agenda for future theory building and research in the field.

The chapters that make up this book began as papers delivered at the annual Values and Educational Leadership Conference which, since 1996, has alternated between Toronto, Ontario and Charlottesville, Virginia. This conference, usually held in October, is sponsored by the OISE/UT Centre for the Study of Values and Educational Leadership in Toronto, and its University Council for Educational Administration (UCEA) affiliate, the Centre for the Study of Leadership and Ethics, based at the University of Virginia. Both research centres were established in 1996 and are devoted to the promotion of theory development and research on the subject of values and valuation processes in educational leadership situations. The 1996 Values and Educational Leadership Conference was an inaugural event that brought together an impressive international team of philosophers, theorists and researchers in the field of values, ethics and leadership. This original group, as well as an expanding network of associates, has continued to meet annually and the annual conference is rapidly becoming an institution. This book presents the outcomes of these most productive gatherings in the form of updated, expanded and synthesized versions of the best among the original papers.

It is the hope of the authors that this book will satisfy the primary audience for which it was intended: university faculty, graduate students and experienced educational administrators. The book is highly recommended as a text in support of the increasing number of graduate level courses focused on the topics of values, ethics and moral leadership. Finally, Begley and Leonard, representing the contributors, wish to express their thanks and appreciation to the editors of the Falmer Press for accepting this book for publication. The authors count themselves privileged to be associated with this very fine publishing house.

Paul T. Begley, OISE/UT
December 1998

Reference

HODGKINSON, C. (1991) *Educational Leadership*, Albany, NY: SUNY Press.

Part I

*Perspectives on Values and
Educational Administration*

1   The Triumph of the Will: An Exploration of Certain Fundamental Problematics in Administrative Philosophy

Christopher Hodgkinson

> *An incompetent leader – a value judgment*
> *An impotent leader – an oxymoron*

These semantics are instructive. Innumerable assertions, laudatory or pejorative, can be made about the executive, the administrator, the leader – but what cannot be said is that the office, the role or its incumbent is without power. This drives home to us what we already know at the deepest level, even though it may take some semantic conjuring to raise it to the surface of consciousness. What is then revealed is the absolute necessity for power in administrative affairs. *Power is the first term in the administrative lexicon* (Hodgkinson, 1982, prop. 6, p. 2).

Without defining, or confining, this primal concept of power, it may be said that it is the human analogue of the physical science term energy, that is, the ability to do work, to accomplish ends. But in administration, in human affairs as opposed to the simplicities of physics and mechanics, power is much more. It is above all else the ability to impose one's will. Here the contrast with natural science is revealing. In physics power is equivalent to force and is measurable in quantitative terms such as watts, joules, ergs, or pounds per square inch. But physical events are not human events. At most they are only components of human events. In science one presumes a determinism, a mechanism, a law of causation – notwithstanding that at the quantum level of analysis (that is, subatomic particle physics) strange paradoxes and 'irrationalities' are observable that seem to defy our ordinary understanding of cause and effect. In human events a new factor appears. In addition to the mechanistic-deterministic laws of cause and effect to which human beings are themselves subject, there is now introduced a concept of will or voluntarism. Thus the human agent in the total equation of determining forces is felt to possess a freedom of choice – whether that sense of freedom is illusory or whether or not it is an epiphenomenon, a psychological by-product of unconscious vectors that are the real determinants. Administration cannot exist without either the reality or the illusion, and science itself stops short at the edge of voluntarism, at the frontiers of conscious choice. For this reason a distinction between administration and management is essential (Vickers, 1979, p. 229): the former opening upon the limitless horizons of philosophy, the latter upon the restricted field of vision right and proper to science and technology.

It follows that administration is a form of life in which wills enter into a complex domain of conflict, reconciliation and resolution. In other words, administration is politics: the creating, organizing, managing, monitoring and resolving of value conflicts, where values are defined as concepts of the desirable (Hodgkinson, 1991, pp. 94–6). In principle or in theory the accomplishment of administrative ends, goals, targets, aims, purposes, plans and objectives is no more than the imposition of a putative collective will upon the resistant and countervailing forces of matter, circumstances, materials, resources and contending *wills*. To be without will would be to be without power and, conversely, to have power is to have the ability to *impose* will. And here for the tender of heart and the already disaffected it may be allowed that 'to impose' can also be rendered as 'to change'.

The Will to Power

At this point one may consider a deeper motivational concept: the will to power. This formulation is central to the philosophy of Friedrich Nietzsche[1] although its origins can be traced through his mentor Schopenhauer (the will to life) back to Vedantic Indian philosophizing about the life-force and the eternal dynamic of creation, preservation and destruction.[2] Less metaphysically and more simply, in administrative terms it can be said to refer to the primal maxim; self-preservation is the first law of nature. I have represented this elsewhere as the first of the metavalues (Hodgkinson, 1982, pp. 180ff.).

How does the will to power bear upon administration? It does this in obviously fundamental ways. For example, inasmuch as administration is an attempt *via* organization to control the future, it is a *philosophical* activity:

> *Genuine philosophers, however, are commanders and legislators:* they say, '*thus it shall be!*' ... With a creative hand they reach for the future, and all that is and has been becomes a means for them, an instrument, a hammer. Their 'knowing' is *creating*, their creating is a legislation, their will to truth is – will to power. (Nietzsche, 1976, p. 211, author's emphasis)

Conway expands upon the theme in this way: 'As commanders and legislators, they must introduce order and discipline into the formless economy of Nature, thus "correcting" for Nature's profligacy. Toward this end philosophers legislate a hierarchy of values that both promotes the flourishing of certain forms of life and excludes other forms . . .' (Conway, 1995, pp. 39–40). This point is directly relevant, we may note, to postmortem and politically correct conceptions of inclusion. The *will* referred to here is, of course, despite the totalitarian nuance, the nomothetic will, the will of the collectivity. Corporations, organizations and nations can in this sense be said to be imbued with the will to power.

But now the problem of will has ramified. It can be seen as deriving from the individual, from the group and, as Weber made specific, from the environment, culture and *Weltanschauung* (Weber, 1948, pp. 120–1; Roth and Wittich, 1968, pp. 24–5). In essence Weber argues that, on the one hand, the administrator takes cultural values as given and is, for example, 'politically correct' in the contemporary sense. This would allow the administrator to assume the mantle of self-righteous 'responsibility' and to steer a satisficing course to given ends as per the doctrine of H.A. Simon (Simon, 1965, pp. 38–41, 240–4). On the other hand, the administrator may embody convictions (and commensurate will) towards ends which may or may not be either cultural or those of the corporate entity he represents. This leads to the potential for 'irresponsibility' or bureaupathology, as when the interpretation of orthodoxy (*Weltanschauung*) is appropriated by the leader.[3] Will to power here acts as an administrative countervailing force to the downward impress of cultural and organizational dictates. Yet even in the case of the administrative factotum-administrator as Simonian agent *simpliciter* – will to power as a depth motivation is a powerful determinant in the overall collective equation.

Grand Assumptions

Granted that administration is the very business of power, that power is its pre-eminent characteristic, it is somewhat curious that (with a few exceptions, notably Machiavelli) the standard literature glides so smoothly and blandly over the problematics of power. Two very deep-seated assumptions seem to underlie this phenomenon; assumptions so entrenched and buried that they might be regarded meta-assumptions,[4] or assumptions at the unconscious level that pass without question, scrutiny or examination. Before we examine them, however, it should be repeated that these are assumptions in the literature, in the theory of administration, in the conventional wisdom and orthodoxy. It should also be noted that the assumptions selected for critique are only two examples of presumptive error in administrative thought and praxis; others such as the naturalistic, homogenetic, militaristic and excisionistic fallacies have been dealt with elsewhere (Hodgkinson, 1996). The first of these meta-assumptions or presumptive fallacies is that 'We are all honourable men' (and/or women, to satisfy the politically correct). The second is that authority and leadership in and of themselves legitimize power. Taken together these two unspoken assumptions effectively divorce the administrator from problems of ethics, morals, values, axiology or philosophy – leaving in their place only problems of technique, of managerial efficacy and efficiency; problems in decision-making and implementation that can in principle be solved by the application of rationality and technology. Systems theorist MacNamara's belated apologia for the Vietnam War is a case in point (MacNamara, 1995). Flowing from these assumptions is the concept of power as neutral instrumentality; a means to righteous ends (derived from outside the system) which means are also the professional property of a managerial elite. Thus honourable men and women pragmatically muddle through to resolve the ongoing problems of their particular organizational interest – making a profit, breaking even, delivering quality services, satisfying educational demands, winning the war against crime, or drugs – whatever it might be. Or else the same honorati apply the full force of rationality, systems theory, technocracy, bureaucracy and quantitative methodology to produce pro tem solutions that satisfy or satisfice the stakeholders and constituencies involved. Either way, ends are achieved and our leaders rise above their earthbound followers, escaping the bonds of gravity by means of their virtue, home aloft on the wings of these grand assumptions, and falling from grace only with failure to maintain the proper altitude and attitude for airborne manoeuvring.

Alas! neither assumption withstands the light of conscious scrutiny. The first assumption can be rejected not on the grounds that fools and knaves assume the administrative mantle – fools and knaves know no boundaries of role or occupation – but on the simple logic of universal self-interest. Self-interest, when it takes the form of egoism, vanity and careerism, is often (but not always) antagonistic to the organizational and higher interests. But more subtle considerations compound the potential for pathology. For example, consider, as Nietzsche does, the feeling of power, the affective quality of power. Nietzsche's analysis in *The Gay Science* dissects this in ethical terms:

> By doing good and doing ill one exercises one's power upon others – more one does not want! By doing ill upon those to whom we first have to make our power palpable [. . .] By doing good and well-wishing upon those who are in some way already dependent upon us [. . .] Whether we make a sacrifice in doing good or ill does not alter the ultimate value of our actions; even if we stake our life, as the martyr does for the sake of his Church – it is a sacrifice to our desire for power or for the purpose of preserving our feeling of power. Certainly, the condition in which we do ill is seldom as pleasant, as unmixedly pleasant, as that in which we do good – it is a sign that we still lack power . . . (Nietzsche, 1974, s. 13)

This analysis hardly needs explication for the practicing administrator. It is a matter of simple experience, even if that experience goes unscrutinized and unexamined. It penetrates and permeates the affective life and insidiously subverts the claim to honour. It is at the root of Lord Acton's aphorism that power corrupts, and its little known corollary: 'Great men are almost always bad men' (Acton, 1960, Appendix).

The second assumption, the assumption of formal legitimacy, falls even more calamitously and precipitously into the pit of decadence. This is because it is entirely a dependent function of a special perception, namely, the perception of the common good, the common interest, of, in a word, the *commons*. Before legitimacy can be assigned to the formal role of leader there must be agreement upon the collective purpose or the public interest or, simply, the *larger* interest. But what is this legitimizing interest in a neo-feudal (Hodgkinson, 1983, Ch. 4), corporatist (Saul, 1995) social structure where everyone is obliged to defend the *parochial* interest of some organization or subset of an organization, the interests of which may well be antagonistic to the whole? This is a system wherein the first duty of each administrator is to 'fight his own corner'; where everyone and anyone is a 'stakeholder'; and where devices for litigation and conflict resolution and power equalization (ombudspersons, equity and harassment officers, quotas, commissars for this and that perceived abuse) proliferate *ad absurdum*. In all of this is there somewhere a commons, a source of legitimacy, or has it nihilistically gone to the wall in the general pandemonium of postmodernism? Is it not fair to say that our present condition is one wherein the *sense* of commonality tends to dwindle to the vanishing point among contending ideologies? In this condition, paradoxically, the demand for conformist orthodoxy and political correctness frustrates the use of reason and speech and inhibits dialogue and dialectical examination of values (Saul, 1995, 38–71, gives an independent treatment of this problem). Surely any experienced academic or politician would vouch for the resultant bad faith and loss of community? Surely also every practising administrator knows the meaning of political expediency and has faced the choice between personal welfare and the common good on some occasion?

And yet the myth remains. The leader represents and embodies the good of the whole and thus has the authority and power of a legitimized will. *L'état, c'est lui, c'est elle.* But, despite the assumptions and presumptions of the textbooks, administrative reality is less a field of honour than a battleground of wills, a domain of confused, confusing and conflicting values and, as often as not, a 'darkling plain . . . where ignorant armies clash by night' (Arnold, 1961).

Will, Affect and Circumstance

On the darkling plain victory is a function of will. Will and power, the will to power, these concepts are correlative, they are aspects of one another. In Nietzsche's view, and he was as much psychologist as philosopher, there is nothing *simple* here. Willing goes beyond both feeling and thinking; it transcends the affective and the cognitive faculties. But it is essentially an experience of *commanding* – whether this be of others or of oneself.

What is called 'freedom of will' is essentially the emotion of superiority over who must obey: 'I am free, "he" must obey' – this consciousness adheres to every will, as does that tense attention, that straight look which fixes itself exclusively on *one* thing, that unconditional evaluation 'this and nothing else is necessary now', that inner certainty that one will be obeyed, and whatever else pertains to the state of him who gives commands. A man who *will* – commands something in himself which obeys or he believes obeys . . . (Nietzsche, 1976, s. 19).

Here, it seems to me, Nietzsche is alluding to what I have elsewhere described as a Type 1 level of valuation (Hodgkinson, 1983, 1991, 1996). In the face of this charismatic quality of will, lesser individual wills are, as it were, psychologically disempowered. Resentfully or otherwise one either submits or, aligning with the leader, gains force from a psychological identification with the stronger 'freer' power.

> . . . he who believes with a tolerable degree of certainty that will and action are somehow one – he attributes the success, the carrying out of the willing, to the will itself, and thereby enjoys an increase of that sensation of power which all success brings with it. 'Freedom of will' – is the expression for that complex condition of

pleasure of the who wills, who commands and at the same time identifies himself with the of the command – who as such enjoys the triumph over resistances involved who thinks it was his will itself which overcame these resistances. (Nietzsche, 1976, s. 19)

There is enough in these enucleated Nietzschean insights to preoccupy the reflections of the administrator for a long time, but it must be noted that what they are pointing towards is the triumph of the will, not its defeat, not its failure nor its *décadence*.[5] The will derives its exuberance and its power from a clarity of interest and a commitment to values – whatever the content of those values. Technical competence or expertise does not enter into it.

But the will, free or unfree, always encounters circumstance. For the most part we delude ourselves about the freedom of our will because we are not conscious of the extent to which we are mechanistically determined or programmed by external, subjective and objective, factors. Our capacity to shape events, for ourselves and others, is much less than we might think. Nothing new in this. The Romans said it: *Fata viam inveniunt*, things happen by themselves. In complex circumstances things just *happen* and consequently the honorific of leadership (or administration) is often falsely attributed to an actor who is simply in the right place at the right time. Fate has smiled upon him. His plan has worked out. His enterprises have been successful. All of which, pace Nietzsche, speaks nothing to either his virtue or his will.

'Yes. But he brought this great matter to a successful conclusion.' – That means something, but not enough; for we rightly accept the maxim which says that plans must not be judged by results. The Carthaginians punished bad counsels in their captains even when they were put right by a happy outcome. And the Roman people often refused to mark great and beneficial victories because the qualities of leadership of the commander were inferior to his good luck. In this world's activities we often notice that rivals Virtue: she shows us what power she has over everything and delights in down our presumption by making the incompetent lucky since she cannot make them wise. She loves to interfere, favouring those performances whose course has entirely her own. That is why we can see, every day, the simplest amongst us bringing the greatest public and private tasks to successful conclusions. (de Montaigne, 1995, p. 57)

To sum up: will is one thing, affect is another, and fate and accident are always administrative parameters.

Malaise

Let us move now from the Renaissance and classical allusions to our own postmodern times. The practical wisdom of de Montaigne has long since been forgotten. Nowhere are fate, accident, affect and will explicated or seriously discussed in the management literature our day. The managerial technopundits have no vocabulary to comprehend or cope with such untidy concepts. In the dialectic between the philosophy of administration and science of management the latter has achieved a salience unthought of or undreamt of in earlier epochs. Thus today the president of a Canadian bank can confidently assert that 'The manager's principal aim is to remove uncertainty' (Courville, 1994, pp. 33, 38). MacNamara in his apologia still maintains, 'To this day, I see quantification as a language to add precision to reasoning about the world' (MacNamara, 1995, p. 6).

Paradoxically this very modernist orientation occurs in a condition of post-modernity and questions arise as to whether it is a triumph or a failure of the will. Is it victory or defeat, affirmation or negation, health or pathology? Is this tacit administrative philosophy – one could call it managerialism – an aspiration towards the ultimate Apollonian ascendancy over the Dionysian forces of passion, violence and unreason which might threaten it?

To answer such questions or to try to is to engage in philosophy, more precisely, in axiology: the problem of values. Doing philosophy and doing axiology can be demanding – such efforts require will. The line of least resistance is to retreat into managerialism, to stick to the book and the numbers, to become a functionary, a factotum. To abdicate will in the face of complexity is all too understandable, if not entirely forgivable.

This malaise or failure of the will is a pathology. Its therapy requires some understanding of the morphogenetics of value. The distinctive value dimensions bearing upon administration can be visualized as a series of concentric spheres of influence. These descend from a cultural level (V_5) through subcultural (V_4), organizational (V_3) and group (V_2) levels to the irreducible level of the individual (V_1). This whole constitutes the morphogenetic field, a complex of value forces, an ecology of interests and will, which forms the axiological context of practical administration (praxis). This schema allows us to identify the central value conflict and source of contemporary malaise. It points to the hypothesis that the root conflict is not the conventional idiographic contest between V_1 and V_3 but rather a dual. There is first the tension between individuals (V_1) and their organizations (V_3), the orthodox idiographic-nomothetic dissonance. Second, there is the conflict between the state as representative of (V_5) culture and its component corporate units (V_3), where the tenons of interest conflict can be specified in economic terms: the greed of the parts being in opposition to the welfare of the whole. This in turn leads us to the idea of neo-feudalism.

As society becomes *organizational*, with large, complex, bureaucratic corporate entities increasingly dominant and increasingly international and global in scope, so the phenomenon of the individual deriving psychological *identity* from the organization which dominates that individual's life as the source of livelihood becomes more and more the norm. Saul has defined 'corporation' as

any interest group: specialized, professional, public or private, profit-oriented or not. The one characteristic assured by all corporations is that the primary relationship of individual members is to the organization and not to society at large. In a corporatized society the group replaces the individual and therefore supersedes the rule of democracy. In their own relationship with the outside world corporations deal whenever possible with other corporations, not with individuals. The modern corporation is a direct descendant of the medieval craft guild. (Saul, 1994, p. 74)

To whom then is one beholden as liege lord? The more one is beholden in a hierarchical structure, the more one is in the power of one's immediate superiors, as well as one's peers!

Such dependency throughout the working life is not necessarily to be condemned out of hand. This is exemplified by the Japanese experience but theirs, of course, is a culture of the East and Japan, we must acknowledge, can lay considerable claim to having been the modern world's first police state. Neo-feudalism is also familiar to the West in all its forms of *military* organization. But its scope and ramification, its penetration of the public mind at the unconscious level, is a novel aspect of contemporary rational-legalistic, bureaucratized, scientific-technological mass society. Those who have such neo-feudal affiliations – that is to say, *we* – are the fortunate. Those without liege lords, the unemployed for example, are the unfortunate. Such *ronin* suffer economically but worse, they find no modality for self-identification, for self-worthiness, for life-meaning, save perhaps insofar as they can accept the label of victim and alleviate their resentment through political action.[6]

In Saul's view, corporatism represents the triumph of fascism over democracy; democracy in the romantic Athenian or practical Swiss sense, fascism in its proper original sense as a collectivity of V_3, interests bound together by the State – the emblem of which was the bundle of sticks (*fasces*) bound together around an axe and earned before the Roman senators by the lictors as a symbol and reminder of the common good. One can easily break one stick but the bundle of them is invincible. (It is interesting to see how Greece and Rome part company.) Examples of contemporary sticks (and feudal identities) are the professions, the bureaucracy, the corporations of industry, trade, commerce and entertainment. Rather thick sticks, one must admit, but by them we come to identify ourselves to ourselves not as individuals, as persons, but rather as doctors, or lawyers, or civil servants, or educators or administrators. Thus we leach our individuality, our wills and our very consciousness into the roles provided by the organizational forms.

The administrative implication of this malaise is that it tends to exacerbate the imperative to fight one's own corner, whatever that might be: the department or section or company or corporation or private practice. The larger good is always decided elsewhere and, increasingly, *if at all*. Our eyes are on the next prize and prizes are bestowed close to home. One is *not* rewarded for blowing the whistle in the greater interest. In this state of affairs our consciousness of ourselves is defined and limited by our roles and our wills are weakened by corporatist and subcorporatist myopia. What is good for General Tobacco may be good for the nation or not but it is certainly good for a GT chief executive officer. As to democracy, with respect to the greater good of the commonwealth, what difference does one-man-one-vote make in a mass electorate? What is one vote among a million? What power attaches to a drop in the ocean? What is one will against the will to power?

Again, and at a larger level of generality than the organizational, there is a V_5 examination or value impress stemming from the *Zeitgeist*, the spirit of the times.

To this can be assigned the descriptor postmodernism.[7] For administrative purposes, postmodernism can be described simply as that condition where a loss of value coherence typifies the overall culture. Its hallmarks are, variously: pluralism, relativism, nihilism, multiculturalism, *bien-pensant* liberalism, identity politics, anomie, alienation, victimology, ecoactivism, terrorism, meaninglessness, *ressentiment*, political correctness. One merely peeks beneath the lid of the Pandora's box before snapping it shut, remarking only that Nietzsche predicted such outcomes a century ago, not least as a consequence of his most famous utterance that God is dead.[8] This selective catalogue may seem like a vision of hell and the worst of worlds but it must be remembered that it is simply a partial assortment of value ills associated with the postmortem condition and, in any event, it is 'where we are at'. Each epoch has its own 'worst of times' and this is merely ours. Our concern here is not with the putative glories of our era, which are surely many, but with its malaise, with those aspects that confront the will to power and that dissipate and enervate the will to lead.

The point for administrators is that, to the extent that postmodernism constitutes a discernible condition of organizational context, they have the onus to become aware of the issues it entails, of the philosophical arguments and of the postmortem polemic itself. Failure to take up this onus again means loss of consciousness, loss of meaning, submission to mechanical determinism, failure of nerve, and weakening of the will to power. The outward manifestation of this weakening appears in the declension of leadership towards pragmatic mediation of interests, in pandering to designated minorities and vocal activists, in the compulsive search for consensus, in the reluctance or inability to say no, in the endless oiling of squeaky wheels, in meek surrender to group-think or politically correct orthodoxy. The postmortem administer harbours a fear of violating any norm. In the words of the Comte de Mirabeau, 'There go the mob and I must follow them for I am their leader.'

Recuperation

Restoration, reclamation of the will, the justification and recovery of power, *consciousness*: what can be done to achieve such aims?

First of all let us acknowledge the administrative–managerial distinction (Hodgkinson, 1982, p. 4 and *passim*; see also Allison, n.d.). It can then be asserted that in the preparation of administrators generally the managerial side of things is fairly well taken care of. We can even commend ourselves on this. Managerial science (or *proto*-science), systems theory, quantitative methods, rational problem-solving and inquiry, research methodology and so on, are with varying emphases well covered in the curricula of our professional schools. The administrative side is more open to critique but even here commendation is possible. Sampling only from the subset of educational administration there is a quite respectable endowment. One need only consider the highly sophisticated common sense of Willower and Sergiovanni[9] or the highly sophisticated uncommon sense of Evers and Lakomski.[10] To these can be added the ethnological work of Gronn and Ribbins[11] and, of course, the radical insights into the social construction of organizational reality of the late T.B. Greenfield.[12] One could go on and still leave many contributors to this side of the equation unacknowledged. Indeed the temptation is to say that, as compared with other disciplinary subsets, educational administration is in the van of curricular progress. In any rigorous comparison, however, the differential emphases of subsets would have to be taken into account.[13] Nevertheless, what falls short generally, or at least what tends to receive cavalier treatment, is what might be called administrative philosophy or the humanities insofar as they exceed or transcend conventional social science and social psychology. So-called human relations, group dynamics, personnel 'management' and the like are *de rigueur*. Even 'leadership' in a sort of *reductio ad absurdum* to anecdotage or pencil-and-paper tests is often a required study. But what I have been talking about and reaching towards is conspicuously absent. By philosophy I do not mean what goes on by and large in academic departments of philosophy, but rather those aspects of practical wisdom, including logic and rhetoric, and focusing above all on the nature and problem of value, which are directly relevant to administration and leadership praxis. Such an administrative philosophy would also subsume every aspect of *Realpolitik* of bureaupathology and of contemporary polemic. Begley has recently expressed in succinct and persuasive form the practitioner argument for axiology in leadership training and preparation (Begley, 1996). The case for the components of logic and rhetoric is equally cogent, while the case for the education of the will has, so far as I am aware, not even been thought of in any serious manner. Curricular change in these directions, while it cannot of itself bring about rebirth, or the rejuvenation of a flagging and failing will, could hypothetically provide a preparatory educational context that would be supportive of recovery, simply because its manifest function is to enhance and deepen understanding. The ability to understand and penetrate issues, to reveal fallacies and to lay bare faulty reasoning and indefensible sentiment is a prerequisite to the health of the will to power.

Yet in the end we are inexorably returned to V_1, the value-phenomenology of the individual, and to the character of the leader. This is the elusive central vital element in the entire complex of mysteries conjured up by the terminology of will, power, value, consciousness and leadership.

The Education of the Will

The will to power is an abstraction. Nietzsche himself refused to advance positive characterizations of the will to power. It was simply that which 'resides at the most basic level of intelligibility' (Lingis, 1977, pp. 37–63; see also Nietzsche, 1968, s. 1067), in other words, the primal motivation. It becomes reality as it is embodied and manifested in the individual. Moreover it must be understood that, at the individual level, will (intention) is a faculty distinct from either thinking (cognition) or feeling (affect). What commonly passes for will is not that at all but simply an unconscious resultant of competing affective preferences or vectors (impulses) in which the strongest wins out and is thereafter rationalized (if it is thought about at the conscious level) as an 'act of will'. Actually it is the act of an automaton. 'Thus I chose' could be translated 'Thus *it* chose for me'. Let us discriminate then between apparent will and real will, between mechanical will and *free* will. The question before us then becomes: is it possible to acquire the free will, to become free? To put it another way, can one achieve self-mastery?

The general answer to this question is yes. But the education or training necessary to achieve this affirmative is unlikely to be found in the schools of leadership, management and administration in the West.[14] The military disciplines of leadership training practised in officer schools of both West and East, while they clearly confront part of the problem through ego-submission techniques and anti-akrasia do not thereby educe *freedom* of the will. On the contrary, it could be argued that such education is moral programming or conditioning rather than any induce-ment to Socratic examination of self or questioning of authority. With reservations, much the same might be said of elite schools of administrative preparation gener-ally. Indeed, short of adopting Oriental, monastic or Zen principles of character development and training, all that can be reasonably said or done is to hypothesize the psychological sequence implicit in these more esoteric methods of training and offer them up for reflection and consideration.

The essential central and primary element in all such methods would appear to be introspection. In our society, the administrative leader, man or woman, is engaged continually in action, in affairs, in gossip, in the hurly-burly and the rough and tumble of politics, calendars, schedules, meetings, conferences and human contacts which, if not always abrasive, are always demanding of energy. In con-sequence, the psyche is drained. Any spare time is occasion for guilt that there *is* spare time. Such time is not generally conceived as retreat, as space for solitary reflection, or for the inward look of contemplation. (Vampires do not like looking in mirrors either!) Such time is more generally regarded as an opportunity for well-earned egoistic self-indulgence (and possibly more wear and tear). Now from the standpoint of the emergence of true will I would like to plead that, whether action and contemplation are conceived of as being at opposite ends of a psychic con-tinuum, or whether they are just plain dichotomous, either without the other is insufficient. I would go further and assert that the one without the other is a vanity and a futility.

Let us return to the hypothetical psychological sequence implicit in will devel-opment. Such an hypothesis would be verifiable not in the empirical scientific mode but in the sense of individual experience or personal experimentation. Reflection or introspection or self-observation is then assumed to lead to an inner understanding which is accompanied by increased awareness or consciousness of one's being and of one's actions. This sensibility is then directly transferable to others because it increases the capacity for *Mitfühlung*, for empathy and insight into the motiva-tions of one's fellows. One becomes a *Menschenkenner*; one senses or knows what makes people 'tick', and this knowledge is power. But power also comes from another direction, from the hypothesis that consciousness and will are correlative (Hodgkinson, 1983, p. 229). The increase of the former creates at least the potential for a corresponding increase of the latter.

None of this is novel. It takes us back a very long way, to pre-Socratic times when the Delphic oracle answered seekers after power with the maxim, 'know thyself'. This may be called the ultimate leadership imperative (Hodgkinson, 1991, p. 153). It is quite safe because in truth we actually know so little of ourselves – we do not see ourselves as others see us, for example – and indeed we tend to avoid or shy away from such knowledge even if we firmly believe in the maxim that knowledge is power. The education of the will is then inseparable from the revelation of the self. The approaches to this have been alluded to above but, in the West at least, it appears to be something of a lost art.

At a minimal level any new curriculum with the radical objective of the independence of the will would have to aim at self-discipline and self-mastery in the domain of emotion, particularly *negative* emotion. The assumption is that one *can* control one's emotions, one can be detached or indifferent. In the vernacular, one can keep one's cool, or as Kipling puts it so perfectly, keep one's head while all about are losing theirs.[15]

Of course, there is a great caveat here. In all of this there must be authenticity or else it is mere dramaturgy, and dangerous contemptible dramaturgy at that. Sartre, who had an exaggerated and in my view fallacious notion of the degrees of freedom in human will, nevertheless followed his existential logic through from a false premise to a true conclusion.

> Sartre emphasized that man must never disclaim the responsibility for his actions. Nor can we avoid the responsibility of making our own choices on the grounds that we 'must' go to work or we 'must' live up to certain middle-class expectations regarding how we should live. Those who slip into the anonymous masses will never be other than members of the impersonal flock, having fled from themselves into self-deception. On the other hand our freedom obliges us to make something of ourselves, to live 'authentically' or 'truly'. (Gaarder, 1996, p. 458)

To live authentically and truly would be to have acquired sufficient strength of will to be 'unimpressed' (literally so) by all value levels above V_1. Such a degree of freedom does not mean that those levels would be disparaged but that the leader would use the levels V_2–V_5 to the end of the common or organizational good without being used by *them*. That is, the leadership agenda would be neither unconscious nor reactive. It would be a function of a value system which is itself a reciprocal function of will and consciousness. It would imply at least the embodiment of some Type I values in the leadership.[16] Does this prospect distress the more managerial amongst us? *Tant mieux!* Such leadership may also be, is likely to be, politically incorrect. Again *tant mieux!* This follows because it is the manifestation of an authentic Socratic individualism; this kind of leadership would always be a challenge to social norms and hence it is not without risk. Ideally one could imagine a full comprehension and sensibility of the entire V_2–V_5 range, yet with an independent V_1 interpretation which, while often held in restraint to subserve the consensus, nevertheless at its greatest moments becomes in truth a triumph of the will.

This is clearly what we do not have today and so the question is, can such an authentic integrity of will and praxis be taught? It probably cannot, save by osmosis and, perhaps, mimesis; by the coming into contact and communion with an exemplar. The education of the will may of course happen by chance; by some happy accident or through association with a mentor or patron or peer, or by some inherent personal quality of natural charisma that achieves this consummation autonomously. Such patterns are not only informal but they are improperly understood and far from being transparent in nature. They can as well have outcomes contrary to the notion of freedom of the will: for example, in the crystallizing of a learner's will in the image of the teacher or in the Christian and Islamic paradoxes of 'In His service is perfect freedom' and '*Inshallah!* (As God wants!)' Once again it becomes important to remember the distinction between training and education. That these two pedagogical strategies can run at cross-purposes is always a hazard to any educative project of the will. If the will is free then it cannot be said to be trained, only to be *educated*. But are these strategies independent or symbiotic?

Even if these problematics remain intractable that does not mean that they are imponderable. Surely we can, and should, teach *about* them. Surely we could include them within the compass of our total research effort? Is not administration a specially important part of the general search for meaning? Axiology, value analysis, value auditing: all deserve a better place in the professional sun. The gods of passion also deserve to be restored to the administrative pantheon. Dionysus and Apollo are brothers after all.

What I have crudely sketched here is but a prolegomenon to potential years of labour in the academic vineyard. Such a tentative reconnaissance of the territory probably does not warrant any pointed conclusion. Nevertheless, in the spirit of the text one might essay a latter-day postmodern Nietzscheanism:

The Song of the Herd is
We shall overcome.
The Song of the Leader is
I have overcome . . .
Myself!

Dare one, could one, ought one then add the words 'For them'?

Endlogic

The point of this exploration has already been made: to repeat the peculiar onus upon the leader to acquire self-knowledge and self-mastery. This is not an ethereal or impractical conclusion but rather an *ultra*-practical or even *hyper*-practical suggestion. That it is avoided as often as not is merely the mark of malaise, of the flight into reason rather than beyond it. The more pedestrian practical inferences to be drawn can be summarized as follows:

- There is never any shortage of leadership positions.
- There is never any dearth of aspirants for those positions.
- Therefore the problem is now, as it was in Plato's time, *curricular.*
- The administrative curriculum is lifelong.
- The managerial side of this curriculum is currently adequate, the administrative or leadership side inadequate.
- The inadequacies are axiological not epistemological.
- Axiology is defined as: The philosophical theory of value in general, embracing ethics or the philosophical theory of morality, but extending far beyond it to include aesthetic, technical, prudential, hedonic, and other forms of value. Any field of human discourse in which the general value-terms 'good' and 'ought' figure falls within the range of axiology, even that of scientific method with its principles about the degree of belief we *ought* to give to a hypothesis in the light of a given body of evidence.[17]
- Hence, the emergent curriculum would include consideration of the problem of the will, the problem of the commons, Realpolitik, social critique and bureaupathology in all its forms.
- At a minimum, the emergent curriculum would incorporate practical training in the arts of common-sense logic, rhetoric and polemic.
- Administration proper is a high-risk, high-reward vocation.

Notes

Paper given at the Toronto Conference on Values and Educational Leadership, OISE Centre for the Study of Values and Leadership, University of Toronto, October 1996. Also published October 1997. *Educational Management and Administration* (1997) BEMAS **25**, 4, 381–94.

1 Considering the administrative theorists' concern with power, it is curious that Nietzsche is so rarely cited or referred to in the literature. A text in English exists – Nietzsche, 1968 – and it can be noted that this concept recurs throughout all the Nietzschean opus as a dominant leitmotif or threnody in his philosophy.

2 Nietzsche sees it as an ultimate driving force in the economy of life and nature going beyond merely human affairs: 'Life itself is *essentially* appropriation, injury, over-powering of what is alien and weaker; suppression, hardness, imposition of one's own forms, incorporation and, at its mildest, exploitation ... Life simply is will to power.' Nietzsche, 1976.

3 See Note 8 and Nietzsche, 1976, s. 46.

4 See Note 5.

5 Nietzsche preferred the French term. Cf. Kaufmann, 1974, p. 73 and *passim.*

6 While this led to outlawed status and brigandage in Japan, its correlation with crime and violence, with sabotage and terrorism, is not unknown in the West either.

7 For an extensive scholarly treatment see McGowan, 1991; for a compendium that is itself postmortem see Anderson (ed.) 1995.

8 Nietzsche claimed to have been 'born posthumously' (Nietzsche, 1972). The origin of the graffiti, 'God said to Nietzsche / That'll Tietzsche / You irritating little Krietzsche', is unfortunately unknown.

9   Representative examples are Willower, 1994a, 1994b, 1996. See also Sergiovanni, 1992.
10 Most notably Evers and Lakomski (1991) and also special edition of *Educational Administration Quarterly*, **32**, 3 (August 1996). For an incisive critique see Barlosky, 1995.
11 Gronn, 1986, 1993. Illustrative examples are: Ribbins, 1995 and Ribbins and Marland, 1994.
12 Most accessible in Greenfield and Ribbins, 1993.
13 I have been impressed, for example, by the military employment of the history of philosophy, business administration's concern with ethical practice and public administration's experimentation with social equity.
14 The Matsushita School of Government and Management, Tokyo is, from the author's experience, a clear illustration of the contrary. Cf. PHP Institute, Osaka, Japan.
15 Rudyard Kipling, 'If –'; more fully: 'If you can keep your head while all about you/ Are losing theirs and blaming it on you?'
16 For a discussion of Type I values see Hodgkinson, 1983, 1991, 1996, *passim*.
17 The definition, with which I entirely concur, is that of Lord Quinton (1988) *Dictionary of Modern Thought*, 2nd edn, London: Fontana.

References

ACTON, LORD (1960) *Historical Essays and Studies*, in COHEN, J.M. and COHEN, M.J. *Penguin Dictionary of Quotations*, Harmondsworth: Penguin.
ALLISON, D. (1989) 'Assessing principal assessment centres', *The Canadian Administrator*, **28**, 6, pp. 1–8.
ANDERSON, W.T. (ed.) (1995) *The Truth about the Truth: De-confusing and Re-constructing the Postmodern World*, New York: Putnam.
ARNOLD, M. (1961) 'Dover Beach', in WOODS, R.L. (ed.) *Famous Poems*, New York: Hawthorne.
BARLOSKY, M. (1995) *Curriculum Inquiry*, **25**, 4, pp. 441–74.
BEGLEY, P. (1996) 'Cognitive perspectives on values in administration: A quest for coherence and relevance', *Educational Administration Quarterly*, 32, **3**, pp. 403–26.
CONWAY, D.W. (1995) 'Nietzsche' Gotterdammerung', in SEDGWICK, P.R. (ed.) *Nietzsche: A Critical Reader*, Oxford: Blackwell.
COURVILLE, L. (1994) *Piloter dans la Tempete*, Montreal: Québec/Amérique.
EVERS, C. and LAKOMSKI, G. (1991) *Knowing Educational Administration: Contemporary Methodological Controversies in Educational Administration Research*, Oxford: Pergamon.
GAARDER, J. (1996) *Sophie's World*, New York: Berkley Books.
GREENFIELD, T. and RIBBINS, P. (eds) (1993) *Greenfield on Educational Administration: Towards a Humane Science*, London: Routledge.
GRONN, P. (1986) 'The boyhood, schooling and early career of J.R. Darling, 1919–30', *Journal of Australian Studies*, **19**, pp. 30–42.
GRONN, P. (1993) 'Psychobiography on the couch: character, biography and the comparative study of leaders', *Journal of Applied Behavioral Science*, **29**, 3, pp. 343–58.
HODGKINSON, C. (1982) *Towards a Philosophy of Administration*, Oxford: Blackwell.
HODGKINSON, C. (1983) *The Philosophy of Leadership*, Oxford: Blackwell.
HODGKINSON, C. (1991) *Educational Leadership*, Albany, NY: SUNY Press.
HODGKINSON, C. (1996) *Administrative Philosophy*, Oxford: Pergamon.

KAUFMANN, W. (1974) *Nietzsche*, 4th edn, Princeton, NJ: Princeton University Press.

KIPLING, R. (1961) 'If', in WOODS, R.L. (ed.) *Famous Poems*, New York: Hawthorne 1961: **3**, 117.

LINGIS, A. (1977) 'The will to power', in ALLISON, D. (ed.) *The New Nietzsche*, New York: Delta, pp. 37–63.

MACNAMARA, R.S. (1995) *In Retrospect: The Tragedy and Lessons of Vietnam*, New York: Random House.

MCGOWAN, J. (1991) *Postmodernism and its Critics*, Ithaca, NY: Cornell University Press.

DE MONTAIGNE, M. (1995) *Four Essays*, SCREECH, M.A. (transl.), London: Penguin.

NIETZSCHE, F. (1968) *The Will to Power*, KAUFMANN, W. and HOLLINGDALE, R.J. (transl.), New York: Vintage.

NIETZSCHE, F. (1972) *Ecco HomoU*, London: Penguin.

NIETZSCHE, F. (1974) *The Gay Science*, KAUFMANN, W. (transl.), New York: Random House.

NIETZSCHE, F. (1976) *Beyond Good and Evil*, KAUFMANN, W. (transl.), New York: Penguin.

RIBBINS, P. (1995) 'Understanding contemporary leaders and leadership in education: Values and vision', in BELL, J. and HARRISON, B. (eds) *Visions and Values in Managing Education: Successful Leadership Principles and Practice*, London: David Fulton.

RIBBINS, P. and MARLAND, M. (1994) *Headship Matters: Conversations with Seven Secondary School Head Teachers*, Harlow: Longman.

ROTH, G. and WITTICH, C. (eds) (1968) *Economy and Society*, New York: Bedminster Press, pp. 24–5.

SAUL, J.R. (1994) *The Doubter's Companion: A Dictionary of Aggressive Common Sense*, Toronto: Viking.

SAUL, J.R. (1995) *The Unconscious Civilization*, Concord, Ontario: Anansi.

SERGIOVANNI, T.J. (1992) *Moral Leadership: Getting to the Heart of School Improvement*, San Francisco, CA: Jossey-Bass.

SIMON, H.A. (1965) *Administrative Behavior*, New York: Free Press.

VICKERS, SIR G. (1979) *Public Administration*, **57**, p. 229.

WEBER, M. (1948) 'Politics as a vocation', *From Max Weber*, London: Routledge and Kegan Paul.

WILLOWER, D.J. (1994a) *Educational Administration*, rev. edn, Lancaster, PA: Technomic.

WILLOWER, D.J. (1994b) 'Dewey's theory of inquiry and reflective administration, *Journal of Educational Administration*, **32**, pp. 5–22.

WILLOWER, D.J. (1996) 'Inquiry in educational administration and the spirit of the times', *Educational Administration Quarterly*, **32**, p. 3.

2   Moral Dimensions of Leadership

Robert J. Starratt

In introducing me to a group of fellow urban superintendents, to whom I was to make a presentation on the moral dimensions of leadership, a superintendent wryly called attention to the 'obvious oxymoron' in the title of my presentation. Indeed, in the present academic and political climate, attempts to propose such an orientation to leadership may indeed qualify one for membership in the looney bin. The times, however, are filled with contradictions and paradoxes. At a time when the public would seem to be willing to settle for political leaders of questionable moral qualities, there are simultaneously calls for leaders of school systems to engage in the seemingly impossible task of restructuring school systems for the twenty-first century. This seemingly universal and insistent call for educators to transform schools from their apparently present state of anomie and mediocrity gives a certain legitimacy, nay, urgency, to an attempt to speak of the moral leadership of schools (Beck, 1994). While some would see the transformation of the schools as primarily a technical task of introducing new efficiency and productivity standards, others would readily assert that the task requires a profoundly moral resolve to tap into, nurture and unleash the moral as well as the intellectual energy of communities of parents, teachers and students to create whole new approaches to schooling (Beck and Murphy, 1994; Henderson and Millstein, 1996; Hodgkinson, 1991; Purpel, 1989; Sarason, 1996; Selznick, 1992; Sergiovanni, 1992; Sizer, 1996).

Moral educational leadership takes place in a context of schools and school systems; that context, in turn, is nested in a larger political, cultural and historical context which deeply affects the assumptions, beliefs and actual possibilities of the players in the drama of schooling. Furthermore, the educational context of schooling is further conditioned and influenced at present by a specific national agenda: the agenda of restructuring schools to make them more responsive to the social, economic and cultural conditions of the twenty-first century. The restructuring agenda provides the context for this discussion of moral educational leadership, for it is this context which provides the specific moral and professional challenges for educational leaders today. With the challenge of restructuring schools as the context of educational leadership, I wish to suggest some frameworks for thinking and for acting as moral educational leaders in response to this agenda.

The Restructuring Agenda

The restructuring agenda did not simply fall from the sky. Rather, it has emerged from a complex interaction of politics, advances in understanding due to the cognitive and cultural sciences, changing demographics, international comparisons of student achievement, geopolitical and environmental futuristics, and a vocal plurality of parental demands for schools that are more responsive to the needs of their children. Some of the major shifts that are energizing the restructuring movement are the following.

- The economic need for productive schools. As nations look toward their futures in the world of international trade and geopolitics, they recognize that the primary commodity will be knowledge (Giddens, 1991; Hesselbein, Goldsmith and Beckhard, 1997; Zohar, 1997). Healthy economies will require a greater foundation in knowledge than in raw material; knowledge workers are replacing factory workers; knowledge is the capital that will define a country's wealth and competitive abilities in the global marketplace (Drucker, 1995). Schools, therefore, must contribute their part to the formation of knowledge workers by developing students with scientific, linguistic, computer, social and cultural understandings and skills that are needed for such a knowledge-based economy (McDonald, 1996; Schlechty, 1997). This will require schools to graduate students who not only know more, but who know how to continue learning and how to produce new knowledge (Newman and Wehlage, 1995).
- Advances in the cognitive sciences suggest that learning is much more an active process of incorporating new knowledge into previous knowledge and experience, and into previous knowledge frameworks, rather than a passive acceptance of pre-packaged knowledge which the learner takes in without any taint of personal distortion and can repeat on tests, perfectly free of the learner's dispositions and life history. This suggests that students, not teachers, are the primary workers in the school. Theirs is the work of sense making, of producing the knowledge suggested by the curriculum, of performing that knowledge in a variety of assessable products, of explaining how those performances and productions reveal their understanding, and indeed, the process by which they arrived at their understanding of the material in the curriculum (Brown and Palinscar, 1987; Newman and Wehlage, 1995; Perkins 1992; Shapiro, 1994; Tharp and Gallimore, 1988). This knowledge will *always* be colored by their personal history, by the quality of past learning experiences, and it will always be partial, limited and, indeed, distorted and distorting (Berger and Luckmann, 1966; Bruner and Haste, 1987; Goodman, 1978). The more constructivist approach to learning does not negate the need for knowledge of important factual information. Rather, it argues that factual information requires an interpretive framework to provide its meaning, significance and usefulness.
- Advances in the cultural sciences of literary criticism, of hermeneutics and of the sociology of knowledge point to a new understanding of the social construction of the self (Bandura, 1995; Freeman, 1993; James and Prout, 1990). Knowledge, meaning, language and learning are inextricably

bound up in learning who you are and who we are. New knowledge always *re*-places me in the world, places me in new relationships to my social, physical and cultural world, and therefore alters, however slightly and tacitly, my definition of myself. In one sense, this understanding of how knowledge creates the mind as well as the self, argues against the model based on the analogy of the mind and the computer – the mind as simply an information processing mechanism (Bruner, 1986). Culturally, I am what I know, and conversely, I know by what I am. That is to say, my cultural biography, my language, my prior world view (however accurate or distorted) shape the way I take in new knowledge. What creates *public* knowledge is the dialogue among learners to come to an agreement on a common understanding of what they are studying. (This, of course, is how the scientific community arrives as public, scientific knowledge.)

• As the United States and Canada continue their tradition of building a society out of immigrant communities, the public conversation about the role of the school in responding to children from diverse communities has become more explicit and politically charged. In the past, the public school was seen as the place where children from exotic (in the eyes of the second and third generations of prior immigrants) cultures were shaped into 'Americans', or 'Canadians' with a common language and common cultural values and a common political agenda. Today, there is an attempt to balance the need for a common social, economic and political agenda with an honoring of the cultural wealth of diverse races and cultures of the citizenry. This is an attempt to support a society that is both one and many, unified and diversified. This new respect for diversity, not only among culturally different communities, but also among communities of youngsters with handicapping conditions, places new demands on the schools. These demands not only call for specific programs (bilingual programs for the whole school, special education arrangements) that attend to specific linguistic or learning arrangements, but they call for the intentional development of a more sensitive school wide community that works consistently on breaking down racial, ethnic, gender or any other dehumanizing stereotypes, and works on the positive agenda of creating bonds or respect and caring.

• The above changes in some basic understandings about the student as worker, the student as the active agent in his or her own self-construction, the value of diversity and the effort to balance both inclusion and nurturance of specialness – these contribute to a necessarily more complex understanding of the purposes of schooling. Teaching in these schools will be very, very different, as teachers move from reliance on recitation and drills to the collaborative engineering of complex learning projects that require students to use their prior learning as the scaffolding for constructing new knowledge. This context of restructuring schools points to the moral and professional leadership challenges for educators.

A Process of Leadership for Restructuring Schools

I want to suggest a process whereby educational leaders may move from where they currently find themselves to where the restructuring agenda is calling them to travel. All the research on change and managing change (see, for example, Fullan and Stigelbauer, 1991), suggests that organizational change cannot happen overnight, that it cannot be mandated from the top without the endorsement and commitment of those throughout the organization. This research instructs us, furthermore, that change must proceed in some orderly fashion that entails dialogical exploration of assumptions, building trust and listening abilities, addressing cultural as well as structural issues within the organization, managing time and work loads of people so that the change process is humanly manageable, and integrating the changes into all the essential functions and structures of the organization so that the changes become deeply embedded into a coherent and mutually supporting system that nurtures and expresses the institutional mission of the organization. This is what is called second order change, deep change, organizational transformation. This is what the restructuring agenda will entail.

I want to suggest that leading this change will require a leadership process that moves from transactional leadership, to a transitional leadership, and then to a transformational leadership. As we explore this leadership process, we will simultaneously attempt to surface the intrinsically moral challenges embedded therein.

The political historian James MacGregor Burns (1978) strongly influenced the field of leadership studies with his distinction between transactional and transformational leadership. Transactional leadership usually involves a self-interested exchange of some kind, a granted request here for a future request there, a vote on this in return for a vote on that. These transactions, though self-serving, are nonetheless governed by instrumental values such as fairness, loyalty, contractual commitments, honesty and trust. The transactional leader ensures that procedures by which people enter into these transactions are clear, above-board, and take into account the rights and needs of the people involved (Starratt, 1993). Transactional activity often involves a bargaining, sometimes unspoken, by people whose individual interests and claims serve their own goals primarily, and only secondarily, if at all, serve the interests of the organization.

Transformational leadership, on the other hand, seeks to unite people in the pursuit of communal interests. Motivating such collective action are large values such as community, excellence, equity, social justice, brotherhood, freedom. Transformational leaders often call attention to the basic values that underly the goals of the organization, or point to the value-laden relationships between the organization and the society it serves. Transforming leadership attempts to elevate members' self-centered attitudes, values and beliefs to higher, altruistic attitudes, values and beliefs.

This chapter employs Burns' categories and adapts them to the restructuring change process. To those two categories, I add a third, intermediate category, what I call leadership for the transitional stage of change, or simply, transitional leadership. These categories suggest a leadership approach that moves from status quo transactions to a transitional stage upon which the school can move toward its transformation. Each of these stages present intrinsically moral challenges to the leader. I will try to illustrate this leadership response to the school restructuring agenda by describing a hypothetical, 'ideal-type' leader who respects the pace and organizational dynamics of significant second order change.

Transactional Leadership

Let us assume a newly appointed principal, Mary Doe, at the Blue Sky School. She arrives with a mandate from the superintendent and the school board to take the school community through a thorough-going school restructuring 'aimed at enhanced learning for all children in conformity with the state curriculum standards and the community's expressed desire to prepare their children for life and work in the twenty-first century'.

Mary Doe's initial efforts involve an organizational audit of the school; that is, she wants to learn how the school works, where it does not work, who is responsible for what, how people go about their work and how they interpret and feel about that work. She assumes that the school community has some sense of purpose, some standard operating procedures, some rules and policies that govern expectations and contracts entered into by the teachers and students.

Looking first at the students, she discovers that as many as 22 per cent are labeled special education students, 28 per cent are second language learners, 34 per cent qualify for the free lunch program, and 25 per cent of the students are scoring below grade level on standardized tests of reading. Of those students below grade level in reading, 60 per cent of them are second language learners, and 90 per cent qualify for free lunch.

Her audit of the faculty finds a distrustful, isolated and cynical group of predominantly veteran teachers. Almost none of the new teachers who have been hired in the past five years have stayed. There are no minority teachers on the staff, although minorities make up 38 per cent of the student body. The teachers tend to blame the students and their parents for the school's mediocre academic record. A glance through teacher classroom evaluations from the past five years indicates a perfunctory and almost uniform set of comments about superficial behaviors of teaching. Past arrangements for two annual professional development days were dictated by the central office.

The condition of the teachers' lounge says a lot about the morale of the teachers: faded curtains on curtain rods that no longer work, a floor of worn-out, stained linoleum tiles, a dropped ceiling with water-stained ceiling tiles and a blackened air circulation vent, a pair of sagging, chipped formica tables surrounded with an assortment of plastic or folding chairs, the standard coffee brewer, plastic cups, and noisy, miniature refrigerator and a bulletin board cluttered with last year's notices.

Clearly, Mary Doe has more than enough to do at the transactional level of leadership. After her audit, she shows the superintendent her report and requests supplementary funds for paint, new bulletin boards, for a thorough refurbishing of the teachers' lounge, including new furniture, drapes and kitchen equipment, and in addition, two new computers to be installed. Secretaries were to be issued new computers and trained in data base management systems. She wanted better backup from the central office business and facilities manager to evaluate the condition of the building and classroom furnishings, and prepare a five-year budget for updating and replacement of equipment. She also arranged for a follow-up meeting with the facilities manager to review the evaluation procedures for the building maintenance crews. She conferred with the assistant superintendent for curriculum and instruction and received permission to work first with the teachers to explore what they saw as their professional development needs before any central office decisions about that year's programs were to be enacted.

She told the superintendent that she would need to attend to very basic needs in her building before she could begin to marshall the energies needed to tackle the restructuring agenda. She also informed him that she was planning a series of open-house meetings with parents, in order to establish lines of communication with them.

Mary Doe then began an extended series of one-on-one interviews with her teachers. She wanted to hear their stories, to get a sense of the human beings she was supposed to work with. If they were to have a chance to engage in school renewal, they had to work from a sense of basic trust. Mary needed to know what and whom she could count on. Besides the listening, there had to be attention to the ordinary daily transactions – the use of space and time (who had the worst schedules and the worst classrooms, and how could they be compensated or rewarded for having to put up with those), the communication and feedback systems (did information flow in all directions, how were people thanked, how do people complain or seek assistance when inconvenienced, how do teachers have a say in school decisions that directly affect them, etc.), the amenities needed to build up a sense of cooperation, appreciation, gratitude, loyalty (thank-you notes, birthday treats in the teachers' room, faculty monthly breakfast meetings, finding out what teachers do well and talking with them about it, etc.).

Beyond the everyday transactions, Mary had to check over the systems, policies and structures that controlled the ordinary transactions of the school: policies and procedures for teacher supervision and evaluation, the way grades were computed and reported, the procedures for settling grievances, the way parents were notified of problems their children were having, the way students were assigned to teachers, etc. In other words, well before Mary could restructure the school, she had to at least see that the way the school worked now was fair and functioned according to basic transactional values of honesty, loyalty, responsibility and integrity. If she could not convince the teachers, students and parents that they were all in this together, that she would do her best to see that the present agreements that people made to one another were upheld and respected, then she could not convince them to take up the much more daunting task of restructuring the school.

From one perspective, the attention to making things work reasonably well could be seen simply as good professional administration. Yet there is more to it than simple professional logic. The members of Blue Sky School have to believe

Mary Doe; they have to believe in her, believe that she is personally committed to their welfare, is morally a partner with them in the enterprise. This implies a quality of moral presence to one another, beyond the agreement to behave 'professionally' toward one another. Beyond that level of transaction, we can, however, point to a level of transaction that is personal, that involves a level of respect and caring and loyalty that reflects a moral integrity. This is the kind of transactional leadership that Mary Doe has to establish with her teachers, students and parents. As this kind of transactional leadership matures, it will begin to move toward the second stage of the leadership process, toward transitional leadership.

Transitional Leadership

Transitional leadership has as its focus individual and communal empowerment. This means much more than the inclusion of teachers in the site-based decision-making process, although it may and usually does include that. Empowerment involves the gradual embracing of responsibility for one's actions. It involves autonomous individuals in the choice to be active, rather than passive, to claim aegis over their own lives and their own work. The ultimate power in our posses-sion is our power to be ourselves, to claim ourselves. The exercise of that power is, ultimately, what agency is all about. Providing psychological space and support for people to act on that power is basically what empowerment is all about.

Added to the power to be oneself, moreover, is the power of competence, the power of competent practice. All teachers need the empowerment that comes from developing greater competence in their teaching, whether that involves deeper and broader understanding of their subject matter, or greater versatility in motivating youngsters and connecting the subject matter to their lived experience. Mary Doe had begun to probe the levels of competence within the staff during the transac-tional stage. Conversations with and observations of the staff revealed basic beliefs about and evaluations of their competence. She had initiated small group discus-sions of faculty ideas on ways to upgrade their skills and understandings. From these discussions surfaced the kind of growth opportunities the staff desired. As she moved into the transitional phase, Mary determined to provide opportunities for the staff to increase their power as professionals and to embrace the power of their own personalities.

Mary Doe recognized that she had to plan very carefully for the transition from the status quo to a restructured school. She had identified the nucleus of a faculty and parent steering committee. That committee would initially act as a sounding board and consensus building group. As the work of building a culture of empowerment, collaboration and community took shape, the steering committee would coordinate the work of smaller committees focused on particular aspects and extensions of the work, such as a parent communication committee, or a school spirit committee. Mary Doe began to spell out, initially for herself and subsequently for her steering committee, the ideas and activities that would move the school into the transitional phase.

She realized that what is said of the empowerment of the faculty applies equally to the empowerment of the students. They need to be encouraged to personally appropriate the knowledge they are expected to learn. Performance assessments, portfolio assessments, authentic assessments are all vehicles for both demonstrating public understanding of the material under study, and also for adding the personal imprint to the work produced.

Beyond the empowerment of individuals to express their personal stamp on their work, and the empowerment of learning, lies the more challenging task of empowering teachers and students for individual and communal self-governance. This level of empowerment means that teachers and students will have taken more and more ownership of the work of the institution, to the end that they can write the rules by which they will agree to carry on the work of the institution – in this case, the work of high quality learning by all.

Becoming a community means that members take responsibility for their membership in that community. They internalize the meanings and the values of the community. They intentionally act out the agreed upon work of the community, seeking to reach or exceed the levels of excellence set by the community. They desire the fellowship and personal satisfactions that accrue to being members of a community. In the real world of Blue Sky School, she realized, membership would be a more ambiguous and ambivalent experience. Levels of commitment or of self-interest would vary, personal agendas would assert themselves, differing understandings of community norms and goals would lead to disagreements and conflicts over appropriate means to pursue those goals and norms.

She realized how hard she would have to work during this transitional period to help members learn how to pool their talents, share ideas, negotiate differences, set short term goals, assess achievements and align accountabilities. This transitional stage would involve cultural restructuring. Building a new culture will mean getting agreement on the overall mission of the school, on its core values, on short-term plans and the long-term vision of who they want to be. Culture building is only partially a rational process; it is also an affective process that employs symbols and rituals for negotiating and expressing values. It involves helping people feel comfortable with new working relationships, appreciating the intrinsic rewards accruing from their working together, working at the realignment of their work relationships, gaining an intuitive sense for joint expectations and tacit agreements.

This stage will take anywhere from two to four years. Mary Doe, the transitional leader, has to be both patient and impatient at the same time. The patience derives from her conviction that people need time to learn the lessons of a healthy community. They need to trust, to know that it is all right to disagree with someone's ideas while at the same time respecting the integrity of the person putting forth the idea. They need to become convinced that nothing will really change unless they collectively take responsibility for their future. They need to believe Mary Doe when she assures them that consensus over important decisions affecting the whole community is absolutely required before any official decisions will be adopted. For people whose professional lives (and careers as students) have exposed

Figure 2.1   Mapping school practices by structural scaffolding
(Adapted from Nixon et al. 1996, p. 57)

School Beliefs and Practices Inventory

Extrinsic/Instrumental	**Values**	Intrinsic
Isolated Individuals	**Mythical social origins**	Community
Self-seeking	**Orientation**	Service, relationships
Tracking	**Grouping**	Mixed ability, inclusion
Didactic	**Teaching**	Designing activities
Memorization	**Methods**	Enquiry
Controlled, pre-packaged	**Content**	Negotiated, constructed
Routine	**Tasks**	Complex, creative
Restricted, Controlled	**Relationships**	Collaborative
Inflexible	**Organization**	Participative
Monolinear	**Curriculum**	Multilinear
Subject	**Focus**	Student
Outcomes	**Orientation**	Process and performance
Ethnocentric	**Referent**	International
Information, right answers	**Aims**	Understanding
Summative	**Assessment**	Formative
Outcome	**Differentiation**	Task
Fixed	**Criteria**	Uncertain
Classification	**Purpose**	Diagnosis
Standards	**Achievement**	Progress
Exclusionary	**External Relations**	Partnership

them to entirely the opposite experiences, it will take time to believe that they are collectively in charge, and that the work truly belongs to them.

Mary Doe, however, will be internally impatient, for she knows that there remains in front of them the important work of rebuilding the structures and procedures by which they carry out the work of the school. Her impatience leads her quietly to begin the work of critical analysis of the school's shortcomings, and the initial mapping of the structural roots of the problems. Important as it is to build community, the work of bringing about high quality learning for all remains in front of them.

As Mary Doe continues a deeper audit of the school's institutional practices, she may draw up a critical map such as Figure 2.1 (adapted from Nixon, Martin, McKeown and Ransom, 1996, p. 57). The crucial category is in the middle, with the undesirable descriptors on the left and the desirable descriptors on the right. Moving from the left to the right points to the restructuring tasks ahead of her.

Transformational Leadership

Mary Doe's initial plan begins to stretch into the time beyond the school's transitional phase. By attempting a preliminary scheme of the projected restructuring of her school, she will have a better idea of what she needs to do in the present to create and nurture those capacity building conditions that will facilitate the transformational phase of the change process. Her conversations with the superintendent and his staff, for example, will have to enter a fairly intensive planning phase, so that, while the immediate work of empowering the faculty is going on, the budgeting of resources for the coming years, planning for potential redesign of some instructional spaces and faculty work spaces, the necessary building of parental and community collaboration, initial courting of supportive media sources, alignment of political coalitions, etc., will begin to be addressed. In one sense, the transitional phase of the change process has to anticipate some of the large patterns and processes of the transformational phase (for example, curricular attention to the multicultural communities that make up the student body, active student learning, relating the curriculum to the realities of the knowledge workplace and to the cultural and civic life of the community, etc.) without, at the same time predetermining the exact changes of the transformational phase. Those specifics will be worked out by the working committees.

Mary has begun to jot down her initial brainstorming ideas on a legal pad. In no particular order, these are what she put down.

- While work on the below-grade performance of the students has already begun, this concentration on basic language and mathematics competencies will need to continue.
- Initiate a program of parents and older children reading at home to the youngsters.
- Initiate evening classes for second-language parents.
- Initiate a newsletter written by parents for parents.
- Initiate outreach to social agencies in the community to encourage a greater integration of services for families who need those services: health, employment, housing, welfare issues, alcohol counselling, etc. Put some local parents in charge of coordinating the communication between parents and these agencies.
- Initiate a comprehensive electronic support system for instruction and learning, coordinated both horizontally across grade levels, and vertically between grades; engage in electronic networks, both local and international, to deal with ecological and economic curriculum issues.
- Initiate conversations with artists, actors, musicians, and dancers in the community to enrich the creative arts curriculum in all grades of the school, and to integrate arts across the curriculum.
- Initiate extensive and continuous staff development for teachers; collaboration between teacher unions and local universities to upgrade the science and math backgrounds of the teachers; provide workshops that encourage teachers to try out many of the newer strategies for engaging student active learning, second order thinking, project centered activities, etc.
- Initiate two year-grade clusters to provide for more continuous faculty contact with the same students, initially on an experimental basis.

- Initiate pot-luck dinners for parents; train and hire parents, when feasible, as teacher aides.
- Explore the possibility of a day care center attached to the school, and train and hire parents to staff it.
- Initiate a big brother/big sister program; encourage peer teaching and tutoring.
- Explore block scheduling as a vehicle for promoting project-centered learning, and for providing flexibility for off-campus learning experiences.
- Design daily and weekly schedules that provide teachers with 10 hours a week of professional collaboration and curriculum development time within the regular schools hours; involve administrators in the school and from the central office in some classroom instruction, to help free the teachers for these hours.

As Mary Doe's list lengthened, she sensed a growing excitement over the many possibilities for turning her school into a community resource humming with energy and commitment. Her reading of the research on change has convinced her of the necessity of linking participation protocols with curriculum development and with classroom teaching, learning and assessment. Since the bottom line for the restructuring agenda is enriched student learning, everything must somehow be linked to that. She also realized that all of this would involve very sophisticated planning and coordination, as well as commitment from the teachers, the teachers' union, the school board, the central office staff, the parents and many people in the community. That commitment and effort must be energized by an uplifting and exciting vision of what is possible, and she must play a crucial part in generating and fashioning that vision.

Commentary

While the above description of our hypothetical moral educational leader is sketchy and incomplete, we should begin to get a sense of the moral quality of the three modes of leadership. In the transactional stage, Mary Doe establishes a moral presence. She works out of and communicates very basic moral values of trust, fairness, respect and loyalty. She works hard to get the basic transactions between the school system and her school community, and between the members of her school community to be not only 'effective and efficient', but also to be morally grounded in basic human values.

As she moves into the transitional stage, her leadership moves beyond managing the status quo, however justly and caringly, to the more demanding task of creating a morally fulfilling environment of empowerment and a culture of community. This type of leadership involves a deeper risk-belief in the talents and goodness of every person in the community (Starratt and Guare, 1996). Her transitional leadership calls forth the human resources in each person, both teacher and student – the resources of their own humanity, their unique personalities, and also the resources of their share of talents and potentialities. By freeing individuals to personalize their work, and building up their potential to be even more productive and effective, she is creating that kind of morally fulfilling environment whereby the members of the community participate in the enrichment and building up of the whole community.

By empowering the school community to do what they are supposed to be doing, but now in more effective and fulfilling ways, Mary has built up their capacity for the next stage of the work, the transformation or restructuring of the school. At that stage, her leadership involves the morally challenging work of engaging people in the recreation of their work and their work environment, and indeed in the more intentional work of the continuous creation of themselves as individuals and as a community. It is at that level that the transformational values of achievement of high ideals and new levels of performance, the sense of contributing to the common good of the larger community – when all these values engage the energies of school community. This kind of leadership seeks not simply the value of being number one, or being the most efficient, or winning a competitive contest. Rather, this kind of leadership seeks the moral fulfillment of engaging in humanly significant work.

It is unlikely that Mary Doe has articulated her leadership agenda according to the logic and vocabulary of this model. More than likely, her leadership moves easily back and forth, weaving the transactional mode with the empowering mode and moving into the transformational mode in short intuitive bursts, and then stepping back to attend to transactional issues. If we were to use the vocabulary of transactional, transitional and transformational in conversation with her, she would probably not know what we were talking about initially. On the other hand, I am suggesting that we think about leadership as involving these three modes because the logic of the restructuring agenda and what we know about the change process suggests the need for all three types of leadership, and suggests a greater concentration of one leadership mode for each stage of the change process of restructuring schools. Furthermore, I do not want to suggest that as the restructuring process unfolds that the transactional mode of leadership can be discarded. Rather, the transactional mode and the transitional mode of leadership will be folded in to the more expansive transformational mode as the work progresses. The point of separating them conceptually is to highlight the different skills and the different moral challenges present in each type of leadership.

For those of us involved in preparing the next generation of school leaders, such an analysis enables us to work on some of those discrete skills and moral perspectives with our students and to shape the content of our courses accordingly. For those conducting research on the leadership roles of principals and superintendents in the restructuring process, these distinctions may prove helpful. The moral dimension of leadership is not simply a sugar coating on the professional work of leadership. When examined up close, the work of leading a community of educators in the demanding work of restructuring is simultaneously both professional and moral. When working at work of this depth and significance, the professional work is *moral* work; the moral work is *professional* work.

Robert J. Starratt

References

BANDURA, A. (ed.) (1995) *Self-efficacy in Changing Societies*, Cambridge: Cambridge University Press.

BECK, L.G. (1994) *Reclaiming Educational Administration as a Caring Profession*, New York: Teachers College Press.

BECK, L.G. and MURPHY, J. (1994) *Ethics in Educational Leadership Programs: An Expanding Role*, Thousand Oaks, CA: Corwin Press.

BERGER, P. and LUCKMAN, T. (1966) *The Social Construction of Reality*, Hammondsworth: Penguin.

BROWN, A.L. and PALINSCAR, A.S. (1987) 'Reciprocal teaching of comprehension strategies: A natural history of one program for enhancing learning', in DAY, J.D. and BORKOWSKI, J.G. (eds) *Intelligence and Exceptionality: New Directions for Theory, Assessment and Instructional Practices*, New York: Ablex Publishing.

BRUNER, J. (1986) *Actual Minds, Possible Worlds*, Cambridge, MA: Harvard University Press.

BRUNER, J. and HASTE, H. (1987) *Making Sense: The Child's Construction of the World*, New York: Methuen.

BURNS, J.M. (1978) *Leadership*, New York: Harper Torchbooks.

DRUCKER, P.F. (1995) *Managing in a Time of Great Change*, New York: Truman Talley Books/Dutton.

FREEMAN, M. (1993) *Rewriting the Self*, London: Routledge.

FULLAN, M. and STIEGELBAUER, S. (1991) *The New Meaning of Educational Change*, 2nd edn, New York: Teachers College Press.

GIDDENS, A. (1991) *Modernity and Self-identity: Self and Society in the Late Modern Age*, Stanford, CA: Stanford University Press.

GOODMAN, N. (1978) *Ways of Worldmaking*, Indianapolis, IN: Hackett Publishing.

HENDERSON, N. and MILLSTEIN, M. (1996) *Resiliency in Schools: Making it Happen for Students and Educators*, Thousand Oaks, CA: Corwinn.

HESSELBEIN, F., GOLDSMITH, M. and BECKHARD, R. (eds) (1997) *The Organization of the Future*, San Francisco, CA: Jossey-Bass.

HODGKINSON, C. (1991) *Educational Leadership: The Moral Art*, Albany, NY: State University of New York Press.

JAMES, A. and PROUT, A. (1990) *Constructing and Reconstructing Childhood: Contemporary Issues in the Sociological Study of Childhood*, London: Falmer Press.

McDONALD, J.P. (1996) *Redesigning Schools: Lessons for the Twenty-first Century*, San Francisco, CA: Jossey-Bass.

NEWMAN, F.M. and WEHLAGE, G.G. (1995) *Successful School Restructuring*, Madison, WI: Center on Organization and Restructuring of Schools.

NIXON, J., MARTIN, J., McKEOWN, P. and RANSOM, S. (1996) *Encouraging Learning: Toward a Theory of the Learning School*, Buckingham: Open University Press.

PERKINS, D. (1992) *Smart Schools: From Training Memories to Educating Minds*, New York: Free Press.

PURPEL, D. (1989) *The Moral and Spiritual Crisis in Education: A Curriculum for Justice and Compassion in Education*, New York: Bergin and Garvey.

SARASON, S. (1996) *Revisiting the Culture of the School and the Problem of Change*, New York: Teachers College Press.

SCHLECHTY, P.C. (1997) *Inventing Better Schools: An Action Plan for Educational Reform*, San Francisco, CA: Jossey-Bass.

SELZNICK, P. (1992) *The Moral Commonwealth: Social Theory and the Promise of Community*, Berkeley, CA: University of California Press.

SERGIVANNI, T. (1992) *Moral Leadership: Getting to the Heart of School Improvement*, San Francisco, CA: Jossey-Bass.

SHAPIRO, B. (1994) *What Children Bring to Light: A Constructivist Perspective on Children's Learning in Science*, New York: Teachers College Press.

SIZER, T.T. (1996) *Horace's Hope: What Works for the American High School*, Boston, MA: Houghton Mifflin Co.

STARRATT, R.J. (1993) *The Drama of Leadership*, London: Falmer Press.

STARRATT, R.J. and GUARE, R.E. (1996) 'The spirituality of leadership', *Planning and Changing*, **26**, 3/4, 190–203.

THARP, R.G. and GALLIMORE, R. (1988) *Rousing Minds to Life: Teaching, Learning and Schooling in Social Context*, New York: Cambridge University Press.

ZOHAR, D. (1997) *Rewiring the Corporate Brain: Using the New Science to Rethink how we Structure and Lead Organizations*, San Francisco, CA: Berrett-Koehler Publishers.

3   Against Leadership:
A Concept Without a Cause

Gabriele Lakomski

The Leadership Phenomenon

It is hardly controversial to observe that leadership-as-a-good-thing is deeply entrenched in our common culture. Much is expected of leaders and leadership when economic, managerial or other crises have to be met. The solutions to restructuring for purposes of greater efficiency and effectiveness, whether in private or public sector organizations such as schools, for example, are widely sought in better leadership or 'strong leaders' who are believed capable of steering the organization in desired directions.

While there is no doubt that there have been, and are, strong individuals who by dint of their abilities and personalities were and are able to have a positive impact on organizations, the concept of leadership has acquired a privileged status which seems to have removed it from critical purview. Leadership is commonly, and apparently universally, accepted as really existing in the world, as an essential human quality. This is not to say that there is no critical literature of leadership, there is and it is voluminous, but the debates mainly proceed on the assumption of its unquestioned essence which somehow has to be captured so that we finally know how to create good leaders.

In this chapter I would like to raise some doubts about the purported essence of leadership, the claims advanced in terms of its efficacy and scope and the methodology used by researchers of leadership. I have organized my comments around a number of key theses which will indicate the flavour of the argument to be put. It is also fair to indicate that these issues provide the outline of a longer-term research agenda which is currently evolving. Some of the arguments indicated here are more in the nature of promissory notes in need of fulfillment than polished arguments. The reasons will become clear in the following.

Central Theses

- The concept of leadership is without a referent. There is no natural object or kind in nature to which leadership refers. It is essentialist.
- As a folk-psychological and functionalist concept, leadership is massively disconnected from causation.

- The various findings of descriptive-quantitative (and qualitative) leadership studies, employing instruments such as the LBDQ (see Hemphill and Coons, 1973, pp. 6–38), are artifacts of methodology rather than scientific accounts of empirical phenomena.
- The functionalist framework of most leadership studies, methodologically supported by hypothetico-deductivism, inappropriately sums specific, context-dependent results across all organizations regardless of difference. It thus fails to account for specificity of context and practice.
- Organizational practice is always interpreted practice. Interpretations of leadership are context-dependent, specific, and thus cannot be generalized universally. The concept of leadership fragments at the local level.
- As linguistic abstractions (sentential representations) from specific action contexts, leadership theories systematically fail to account for organizational practice – the 'how' of leadership whose representational structure is a matter of neuonal not sentential organization.
- A causal account of leadership, offered by naturalistic coherentism, contains an empirically defensible account of human learning and all cognitive activity including linguistic ability. It thus offers an account of effective administrative practice.
- From a naturalistic-coherentist perspective, there may be as many different accounts of leadership as there are organizational contexts. Law-like statements about leadership, as postulated by empiricist theories of leadership, are not to be had. Generality, insofar as it can be obtained, would be a matter of the coherence of accounts in a specified context. We may develop modular rather than system-like accounts.
- Effective practice causally depends on the activation of appropriate neuronal patterns of 'leader' and 'followers'. Since these do not follow hierarchical structures, the potential for effective practice resides throughout the organization.
- Organizational learning is thus the key to effective administrative practice with the consequence of creating appropriate web-like organizational structures which maximize the local production of knowledge and facilitate the correction of error through feedback mechanisms.

Leadership and Effectiveness: The Current State of Play in Educational Administration Research

Hallinger and Heck (1996, p. 5) begin their recent review of empirical research about the principal's role in school effectiveness with the following words: 'The belief that principals have an impact on schools is long-standing in the folk wisdom of American educational history. Studies conducted in recent decades lend empirical support to lay wisdom.'

They also add in their opening paragraphs that 'this relationship is complex and not easily subject to empirical verification' (Hallinger and Heck, 1996, p. 6), an assessment shared by, amongst many others, the reviews conducted by Bridges (1982), Bossert, Dwyer and Lee (1982), and Howe (1994). Hallinger and Heck's reassessment is important both in terms of their conclusions and in terms of presenting the kinds of conceptual approaches which have characterized research in the field of educational leadership and effectiveness since 1980. The reason why conclusions and presentation of research models are important is that they are indicative of a stagnant research program which is markedly under-theorized, as will be shown in the following. This strong conclusion, of course, is mine and not the authors. Their own criticisms are softened by a belief that some progress can be noted insofar as greater emphasis has been placed, conceptually and empirically, on the complex interplay of (school) internal, environmental and personal characteristics of the principal. In their view, '. . . the principal's role is best conceived as part of a web of environmental, personal and in-school relationships that combine to influence organizational outcomes' (Hallinger and Heck, 1996, p. 6). However, they also concede that at present '. . . the specific nature of these complex interactions across sets of variables within a model of principal effectiveness remains unclear' (Hallinger and Heck, 1996, p. 38). Practically all the studies they analyzed used cross-sectional and correlational designs with surveys and interviews as the preferred data collection techniques. In the authors' view, such non-experimental studies are less well equipped to draw causal inferences than are experimental studies since independent variables are not manipulated. Determination of causation is thus much more difficult because all relevant independent variables must be controlled which, in a theoretically weak model, may not be specifiable or specified, and thus elude control and create a major threat to validity.

A related and most important concern is that any interpretation of the complexity of the relationships depends on the sophistication of the theoretical model itself. If the model is overly simplistic, then analyses may be simplistic. In this case, results are ambiguous or lack validity leading the authors to conclude that '[i]n the absence of an explicated theoretical model, the researcher often cannot be sure what has been found' (Hallinger and Heck, 1996, p. 17). A further issue are the analytical techniques used themselves. More rigorous techniques would lead to stronger conclusions than the ones reached in the studies examined.

As for models or conceptualizations of the principal's role in school effectiveness, Hallinger and Heck adapted a classification scheme originally developed by Pitner (1988) which needs to be outlined just briefly. These models are defined as (i) direct-effects (Model A); (ii) mediated-effects (Model B); (iii) antecedent-effects (Model A1, B1); and (iv) reciprocal-effects (Model C).

The direct-effects model tests the principal's effects on school outcomes directly without intervening variables, is very common in the literature but is also no longer considered useful because of its 'black box' approach: an empirical relation is tested without having any knowledge about the process of achieving an impact. Leadership itself remains unexplained, and the purported impact remains a mystery.

The mediated-effects model assumes that whatever impact the principal has is achieved by interaction with, or manipulation of, organizational features of the school. Leadership thus works through others.

The antecedent-effects model postulates that the principal's role may be both a dependent or independent variable. This means simply that principals influence, and are themselves influenced by, other variables in the school environment. As a result the principal's actions may be seen as both the outcome of direct or mediated effects. In the author's view, this model presents an advance because it offers a more comprehensive picture of the principal's role in school effectiveness.

The reciprocal-effects model emphasizes the interactive relationship between the principal and organizational features of the school and its environment. Principals learn to adapt to the organization in which they work and subsequently change their behaviour and presumably thus also the impact they have on the school's effectiveness. Leadership is considered as an adaptive process rather than a unitary and fixed feature.

The conclusions Hallinger and Heck draw are illuminating. They believe that unlike Bridges' scathing comments 'that studies of school administrators are intellectually random events' (Bridges, 1982, p. 22), there has been a conceptual advance in that 'virtually all of the studies could be classified as theoretically informed' (Hallinger and Heck, 1996, p. 33). They mean by this that researchers defined their constructs and gave reasons for their choice of variables. However, there is also an advance in terms of explicitly linking studies to theoretical positions both in terms of the relationship of variables to those positions and in terms of the relationship of the leadership construct to a broader theoretical framework.

On the methodological side there is also progress to report, especially in terms of applying more sophisticated analytical tools, such as more powerful versions of structural modelling, which were more appropriate to the theoretical orientations proposed. However, the interpretation of data generated by correlational studies is still limited because of an absence of longitudinal research of both quantitative and qualitative kinds. Hallinger and Heck also note the emergence, since the 1980s, of new leadership constructs potentially useful in explicating leadership effects such as instructional and transformational leadership, as well as models of leadership inspired by the work of Bolman and Deal (1991) and Sergiovanni (1992).

As for that most important question, Do principals make a difference?, the authors advise that 'considerable caution' needs to be applied to the results of the studies they examined. Their qualifications are important to note:

- Theoretical model type made a difference in what was found; the more sophisticated models (Model B, B1) showed more positive albeit still weak relation between leadership and effectiveness;
- while leadership can make a difference, attention must be paid to context, to the conditions under which the effect is achieved, i.e. socioeconomic environment; but studies are too disparate in their ideas of leadership and context variables to be able to specify the relevant contingencies;
- where there was a positive difference, it related more to internal school processes which were in turn linked to student learning;
- studies with positive findings consistently show up goal orientation as a significant factor which, however, is also influenced by environmental factors. Hence this finding needs to be qualified as well.

Hallinger and Heck conclude that one need not be unduly pessimistic about this motley array of qualified research results since much has been gained by acknowledging positive indirect leadership effects, mediated through in-school variables. This, they claim, in no way diminishes the principal's importance since 'achieving results through others is the essence of leadership' (Hallinger and Heck, 1996, p. 39).

However, and although they couch their conclusions in more placatory language, they do agree with Bridges' (1982, p. 25) (as well as Bossert's, Dwyer's and Lee's) conclusions: '. . . there is no compelling evidence to suggest that a major theoretical issue or practical problem relating to school administrators has been resolved by those toiling in the intellectual vineyards since 1967'. Bridges drew a further conclusion from his investigation which is worth repeating: 'If the intellectual sterility and marginal utility of this work is characteristic of research in educational administration, the profession is in difficulty. Studies of 'no significance' are patently more troubling than studies with 'no significant difference' (Bridges, 1982, p. 17).

Leadership and Effectiveness: Early Conceptual and Methodological Criticisms

The old adage that those who do not know their history are condemned to repeat it, is only too true of the history of research on leadership and effectiveness, in particular, the absence of any knowledge of the parent discipline of organizational theory and especially the debates surrounding leadership and effectiveness which arose in the wake of the human relations movement which made leadership the most prominent organizational theory concept to be studied. This is not the place to rehearse the history of the human relations movement, nor to examine the enormous bulk of empirical studies conducted, but to draw attention to perennial problems as they were already visible and acknowledged at the origins of researchers' concern with the phenomenon of leadership. These worries continue, and are clearly evident in Hallinger and Heck's reassessment of leadership and effectiveness in educational administration.

The importance of leadership, as evidenced in a truly voluminous literature, has apparently never been in doubt in terms of being able to shape and give direction to social organization. Hemphill (1949, p. 3), an early advocate, made the case in favour of leadership quite clear when he noted that, 'Both laymen and scientists agree that if we can understand the selection and training of leaders we can begin to take adaptive steps toward controlling our own social fate.'

Heavily influenced by social psychology, the study of leadership at the beginning of this century first concentrated on identifying a unitary trait or personal characteristic which would clearly mark a person as a leader. No such trait has been found, and the unitary trait theory was replaced by a constellation-of-traits theory (Gibb, 1959, p. 914). Although this theory permitted a pattern of traits which could differ between leaders and situations, the 'why' of leadership was still conceived of as a function of personality (e.g. Stogdill, 1948) and is thus a mere variant of the former unitary trait theory. Because of the difficulties of identifying leaders – people formally or informally designated as such are not necessarily 'leaders' – it has been suggested that person is the leader who exerts influence over group members where both influence and its direction are agreed upon by the group members/ followers. However, a more objective approach still was deemed to be attention to leader behaviour occurring in a group. 'Leadership acts may then be defined as the investigator wishes, and leaders are to be identified by the relative frequency with which they engage in such acts' (Gibb, 1959, p. 916). Thus, while personality characteristics continued to be important, the emphasis had shifted to the impact of leadership on groups' performance or satisfaction.

Underlying the focus on leadership since the human relations school and the Hawthorne studies is what Bowers and Seashore describe as a 'commonly accepted theorem':

> Leadership in a work situation has been judged to be important because of its connection, to some extent assumed and to some extent demonstrated, to organizational effectiveness. Effectiveness, moreover, although it has been operationalized in a variety of ways, has often been assumed to be a unitary characteristic. These assumptions define a commonly accepted theorem that leadership is always salutary in its effect and that it always enhances effectiveness. (1973, p. 445)

Indeed, following Perrow's (1986, p. 85) classification, the human relations school has two branches. The first is concerned with morale and productivity and is by far the most empirically researched, while the second, still closely related branch, is more interested in the structuring of groups. A basic premise, especially of the first, is as follows: Good leadership is generally described as democratic rather than authoritarian, employee-centred rather than production-centred, concerned with human relations rather than with bureaucratic rules, and so on. It is hypothesized that good leadership will lead to high morale, and high morale will lead to increased effort, resulting in higher production. While these assumptions seem so eminently commonsensical and true, Perrow sums up his investigation by stating that 40 years of consolidated research only managed to find that human behaviour is far too complex to allow any simple kinds of conclusions to be drawn which characterized the hopes of the human relations theoreticians. Even more importantly, Perrow claims that all empirical studies conducted on the relationship between attitude and performance simply set out to prove that 'happy employees are productive employees' and that the findings were not robust enough to support the assumptions. In fact, the presumed direction of causality could be reversed, as was argued by Lawler and Porter (1967) in their important analysis of 30 empirical studies. In other words: high productivity creates high satisfaction.

Although Lawler and Porter agree that there is a low but consistent relationship between these two variables, they note that it is not all clear why the relationship exists. This raises the problem of whether job satisfaction is indeed important, and if so, whether organizations should take steps to maximize it. In their view, it seems organizationally more prudent to reward high performance by satisfying employees' 'higher needs', i.e. provide them with more autonomy and avenues for self-actualization, which, in turn, has positive outcomes in terms of lower absenteeism and turnover which are positively related to productivity. Of importance is thus the relationship between the two variables, and not just 'satisfaction' as a single feature, as considered in the human relations mode. Furthermore, however, as Perrow (1986, p. 87) notes, some jobs leave no room for high performance, and productivity depends more on technological changes or economies of scale than human effort. (According to Lawler and Porter, 1967, there were few studies reported in the literature regarding the relationship between satisfaction and performance post-1955.)

The study of the effects of leadership behaviour/style on group performance began in earnest in about 1945 and is commonly identified with the Ohio State Leadership Studies. They left a far-reaching legacy which still characterizes much contemporary educational leadership research: the development of the Leader Behavior Description Questionnaire (LBDQ) (see Hemphill and Coons, 1973, pp. 6–38), the Leadership Opinion Questionnaire (LOQ), a leader self-assessment instrument, and the two-factor theory of leadership described by the concepts of (1) 'consideration' (C), and (2) 'initiating structure' (S) (Halpin and Winer, 1973; see also the studies reported in Stogdill and Coons, 1957). Developed in interdisciplinary discussions with psychologists, economists and sociologists, the LBDQ was designed to 'be adaptable to studies in widely different frames of reference. This would make it possible to include such an instrument in each individual research design, thereby contributing to an integration of research findings that would not be possible otherwise' (Hemphill and Coons, 1973, p. 7). Arrived at through various factor analyses, the two remaining factors 'consideration' and 'initiating structure', are similarly entrenched in organizational-administrative folklore. C describes leader behaviour which is warm, shows mutual trust, respect and friendship, while S refers to leader behaviour which 'organizes and defines relationships or roles, and establishes well-defined patterns of organization, channels of communication, and ways of getting jobs done' (Bowers and Seashore, 1973, p. 442). Unlike the earlier human relations view, according to the Ohio Studies, these two factors were not seen as opposites – leaders who are either good on human relations or managed to get jobs done – but both appeared to be equally important. Despite their immense popularity in industrial psychology, management and organization theory, where they have become articles of faith, 'consideration' and 'initiating structure' are variables whose predictive powers regarding organizational or group effectiveness are simply not proven (Korman, 1966, p. 360) .

There is no clear support for the background assumption that leaders high on C, for example, cause better performance in subordinates; rather, Korman notes, causation might well be the other way round; leaders may show more consideration toward already well-performing subordinates, or they may show more C to those who support them. Alternately, supervisors might be higher on S in case of low performing groups. All these possibilities need to be tested experimentally, but have not been. Furthermore, supervisor ratings might be affected by variation in organizational size and climate. Importantly, however, Korman (1966, p. 355) argues that we need to be able to provide 'a systematic conceptualization of situational variance as it might relate to leadership behavior . . .' rather than merely acknowledge its importance, as had been the case in the studies he analyzed.

Amongst the various attempts to broaden this two-factor theory of leadership, Fiedler's 'contingency' theory (Fiedler, 1967) shall be mentioned briefly because it introduces considerably more complexity by adding 'group climate' as a central feature believed to affect leadership effectiveness. Fiedler's (1973, p. 468) model postulates that 'the performance of interacting groups is contingent upon the inter-action of leadership style and situational favorableness'. He thus reinforces the notion that group effectiveness is a feature of leader attributes as well as situational factors. He claims that task-oriented leaders do well in very favourable as well as very unfavourable situations while people-oriented leaders do better in situations of intermediate favourableness. The predictor measure used is his least-preferred co-worker score (LPC). Suffice it to say that while Fiedler has gathered a lot of supporting data, there are more complexities involved in terms of defining the non-leadership variables, i.e. 'situational favourableness' changes, and so do interpersonal perceptions of followers and leaders. Yet the important insight derived from this melding of leader characteristics and situational factors is, as Hemphill (1949, p. 225) put it, that '. . . there are no absolute leaders, since successful leadership must always take into account the specific requirements imposed by the nature of the group which is to be led, requirements as diverse in nature and degree as are the organizations in which persons band together'.

The sheer complexity and contingency of these factors led Perrow to state that,

> If leadership techniques must change with every change in group personnel, task, timing, experience, and so on, then either leaders or jobs must constantly change, and this will make predictions difficult. At the extremes, we can be fairly confident in identifying good or bad leaders; but for most situations we will probably have little to say. We may learn a great deal about interpersonal relations but not much about organizations. (1986, p. 92)

Leadership and Effectiveness: A Regressive Research Program

So what have we learnt from looking back to the origins of leadership studies? The kinds of problems and results Hallinger and Heck report in their latest assessment of leadership and effectiveness in the context of school leaders have typically been reported in the parent discipline – a good 20 years earlier, if not more. But there seems to be no recognition of that history, and the current state of conceptualizing leadership as evidenced in the empirical work reported, is as limited as that reported and variously critiqued in the field of organizational studies. The question which has fascinated and motivated researchers from the beginning, whether leaders make a difference or not, has to date not been answered satisfactorily. The best we can say – on the basis of the empirical studies carried out – is that we think so – somehow! The major point to make here is that our preoccupation with leadership and its impact, while understandable in terms of its commonsense and possibly political appeal, is a preoccupation which we should not pursue in this form because it is epistemically unproductive.

There are specifically two points which emerge from the accumulated history of leadership research which, for present purposes, are important. The first is the inconclusiveness of empirical research results, and the second, the oft-repeated observation that specific requirements and the diverse natures and degrees of organizations studied makes a difference in determining leadership effects; the importance of situational 'contingent' factors, as they arise in the empirical studies, seem to point to the fact that there is no essence to leadership, that leadership means different things to different people in different contexts. In other words, the 'why' of leadership remains a mystery, and this is not surprising given the empiricist hypothetico-deductive framework within which the bulk of leadership studies were conducted.

Consider the structure of a typical study, suggested as more appropriate by Bowers and Seashore (1973, p. 447) than the earlier behavioural ones. What the authors suggest has become standard fare also in studies of leadership in education, and contains the following features: (a) measures reflecting a theoretically meaningful conceptual structure of leadership; (b) an integrated set of systematically derived criteria; and (c) a treatment of these data, which takes account of the multiplicity of relationships and investigates the adequacy of leadership characteristics in predicting effectiveness variables (Bowers and Seashore, 1973, p. 447). 'A theoretically meaningful conceptual structure of leadership' denotes a leadership construct made up of whatever variables the researcher hypothesizes as important. For present purposes, the structure and associated difficulties of such a hypothetico-deductive model can be shown in Figure 3.1.

As a central feature of logical empiricism, this hypothetico-deductive account of scientific theory and practice, no longer accepted as valid in philosophy of science and epistemology, postulates that empirical evidence consists of singular observations, i.e. observation reports of behaviours which are hypothesized to be representative of whatever construct is being tested. These individual claims (observation reports) are at the bottom of the hierarchy, they form the foundations for claims to leadership at the top of the hierarchy. These claims are believed to be empirically testable, and the process of deduction and testing makes up the so-called hypothetico-deductive account (see Evers, 1995, p. 2; and Evers and Lakomski, 1991, 1996, for more detailed examination). In addition, an important feature of this empiricist (positivist) account of scientific theory is the notion of operational definition. Since empiricist theory prescribes that its foundation is based on observation reports, every claim made – whether about 'observable' or 'theoretical' entities – has to be amenable to empirical definition (e.g. Fiedler's account). Now this appears to be straightforward with regard to observable physical objects, but seems problematic in relation to non-observable, theoretical entities, like 'leadership', for example, or any type of value such as 'good citizenship', 'equality' or 'justice'. The way out for logical empiricists was to operationalize them, that is, to develop some measurement procedure which would 'capture' the elusive entity in

Figure 3.1   A generic leadership model

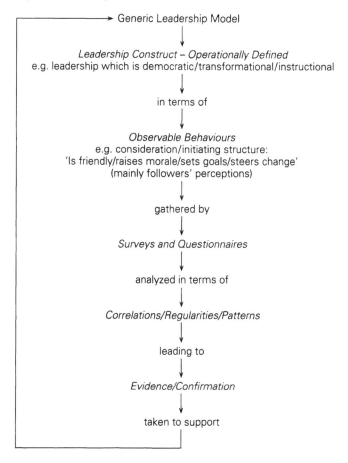

the absence of the possibility of direct observation. Operational definitions played a large part in the traditional scientific account of leadership, as seen in the discussion above, as well as in educational administration (i.e. the Theory Movement), and is still found in the work of Hoy and Miskel (1991).

The history of leadership studies, at least in the early empiricist tradition, seems to be driven by the ongoing effort to find more appropriate factors/variables which can be taken as representative of its true nature: from single trait to multiple traits, to increasingly complex postulated interrelationships between such things as organizational and group structure and environmental factors, commonly subsumed under the umbrella term of the 'situational factor'. Operationalizing these variables by means of designated observable administrative behaviours reported in surveys or questionnaires such as the LBDQ, and gathering and analyzing these via increasingly complex statistical-quantitative methodology was believed to provide appropriate empirical support which would then lead to proper generalizations about leadership across organizational contexts. If that could be achieved, leaders could be trained and organizations be made more efficient.

It seems to be assumed, without argument, that whatever leadership constructs are composed, that they do refer to a phenomenon in nature, and that by re-conceptualizing the constructs/theories, we get closer to its essence. On the face of it, why should we not presume that there is such a thing as leadership since leaders are ubiquitous amongst baboons, birds and bees, just as they are amongst other card-carrying members of the animal kingdom: humans. So where is the rub? Just because we have a vocabulary, or conceptions, i.e. linguistic representations of leadership does not entail that there really is such a thing in nature to which they refer. Following the argument put by Churchland (1993, pp. 284), it is more than likely that all of our commonsense frameworks may be 'unconnected to the world by way of reference of its singular terms and the extension of its general terms'.

This point is easily appreciated when we consider that it is possible to employ a false scientific theory which guides our observations, such as 'caloric fluid' or 'phlogiston', or 'ether'. We can express our observations in the theory's terminology although we know it to be false. Another way of putting this is to say that a false theory can be empirically adequate but referentially empty. Nevertheless, it remains causally connected to the world in the sense that we act on it, learn from it, and construct better theories. For a theory to function, then, it does not have to be true. If it turns out to have referential connections with the world, then that is an additional and rare bonus. So, to put the matter boldly: conceptions of leadership, whatever the specific constructs they contain, may turn out to be massively discon-nected from the world and yet we can continue to talk as if they pointed to some-thing real in terms of leaders 'turning the organization around'.

Take the example of leadership studies' best-known construct: initiating struc-ture and consideration. These constructs were derived from an initial pool of 1790 items, were further reduced to 9 dimensions (Hemphill and Coons, 1973), and eventually to the two remaining (Halpin and Winer, 1973). These were considered the two smallest and most basic dimensions of leader behaviour, and continue to be seen as such to this day. For brevity's sake, S leadership was assumed to be in evidence, represented by a set of descriptive items, when a leader exhibited a requisite behaviour such as, for example, 'defines his role and those of subordinates'; 'sets clear goals'; 'directs group activity through planning, communication, sched-uling'. C leadership, in contrast, was properly expressed in behaviours such as 'expresses appreciation for a job well done'; 'stresses the importance of high morale'; and 'is friendly' (Argyris, 1979, p. 55). These sets of behaviours were seen as extensions of the relevant leadership conception and were believed to be unambigu-ously identifiable as per descriptive item.

Here it is important to remember the familiar point that what is taken to be as a relevant observable behaviour is in part determined by our implicit, explicit or commonsense theory of leadership. What counts as an extension/reference depends upon the embedding framework or assumptions in which it is contained. But, most importantly, human behaviour is always interpreted behaviour. Put differently, it is human cognitive activity which holds the key to what is or is not counted as an extension, given an individual's 'cognitive economy' (Churchland, 1979, p. 287) and the organizational (or other) context in which they find themselves. Put simply, what we believe to be a true reference regarding democratic or C leadership, for example, is a function of our theory of leadership which, in turn, is part of our changing, or ever developing, global theory of the world.

This does not mean to indicate that we have any kind of firm or secure grasp on leadership as a natural object. Reference is tied to our theories and assumptions and these can change, which means reference changes. So rather than beginning by wanting to prove or find evidence of presumed natural objects, or essences, such as leadership, we are better off by beginning from 'the ground up' by comparing the sentences of various leadership theories to see whether any of them answer to anything in the world. (Whether or not there are such things is a matter of our ontology and what evidence we can summon up by way of our epistemological resources.)

Returning to the point of specified behaviours as indicative of certain leadership styles, it becomes clear that these generic behaviours, supposed to be universally applicable and thus context-invariant, take on different meanings depending literally on in whose brain they appear. In other words, leadership constructs as conceptualized in empiricist science which employs a hypothetico-deductive form of reasoning, fragment at the local level. For instance, the item 'expresses appreciation' does not map onto one specific interpretation of behaviour but is open to a multitude of possible interpretations which may all be empirically adequate. This is where the category fragments because people just see things differently and in often widely discrepant ways, as demonstrated in studies Argyris (1979, p. 55) has conducted: 'In one study, "Friendly and easily approachable foremen" (upon observation) turned out to be foremen "who left the men alone and rarely pressured them" ... In another study "friendly foremen" were those who took the initiative to discuss "difficult issues" with the men.'

The category 'expresses appreciation' does not represent the local variance of interpreted behaviour, it rather abstracts from the specificity of the local context. This is to be expected given that much of leadership research is based on the assumption of a functionalist framework. Recall Gibb's (1959, p. 917) most economical version: '. . . leadership is a function of personality and of the social situation, and of these two in interaction'; Hallinger and Heck's (1996, p. 6) more expansive yet compatible definition (which, however, simply identifies leadership with the principal's role, the formal office-holder), and an even more expansive description offered by Yukl. His 'linkage model' proposes to investigate the following:

> Leader behavior variables, intermediate variables, situational variables, subordinate preferences, criterion variables (i.e., satisfaction and productivity), and relevant leader traits. . . . [add] Situational variables [such as] the organizational limiting conditions for participation . . . the structural variables found to be associated with leader decision behavior . . . the situational variables in Fiedler's model, the situational variables cluster-analyzed by Yukl . . . and Woodward's (1965) system for classifying production technology. (1973, p. 465)

Given such complexity, Yukl (1973, p. 465) advises that the predictive power of his model would be improved if one could identify which components of the behaviour variables are the most important determinants of each intermediate variable.

Stipulating functional relationships between such abstract concepts as 'situational, structural, and personal variables' begs the question since any empirical-material content fits the bill in that it can be subsumed under the abstractions. Since different situational and other factors obtain in different contexts, a functional explanation which posits causal relations between individual relations, explains nothing. The point is not that functionalist explanations are merely abstract, the point is that they are vacuous, as well as pretentious (Evers and Lakomski, 1991). This is another way of saying that the concept of leadership is causally massively disconnected from the world, and that no amount of sophisticated quantitative methodology makes any difference in its attempt to secure empirical results.

Leadership Naturalized

The reason that the use of functionalist explanation and empiricist hypothetico-deductive theory obscures, abstracts from, and thus fails to capture the local and specific situations of leadership, resides in its limited view of human cognitive activity. All cognitive activity is identified with linguistic representation, and linguistic representation, in turn, is equated with knowledge, our scientific theories being the most austere examples.

Leaders' and followers' accounts of what they are doing, duly recorded in surveys and questionnaires, are such sentential representations. But language, as everyone knows, first has to be learnt, and learning itself is not primarily linguistic but is determined by chemical brain activity. What we are able currently to represent in linguistic form, then, is only a relatively small part of all the cognitive activity which goes on in our brains. Much, or perhaps even most of our cognitive activity, i.e. things we know how to do, cannot be represented linguistically because it is embedded in the fine-grained neuro-chemical circuitry of the brain, and is in part organized in neuronal patterns.

Given my preceding comments, it seems more productive to discontinue leadership studies that appear to reduce quite readily to the study of effective administrative practice. If conceptions/theories of leadership fragment at the local level subject to organization members' individual interpretations, which, in turn, are a function of their shifting cognitive global economy, then theorizing about leadership/effective practice, at the deepest level, becomes a matter of explaining how the relevant neuronal patterns are activated which facilitate organizational (or any other) action. Several consequences would follow.

Leadership/effective administrative practice is a matter of local and highly specific factors which cannot in principle be universalized as postulated by empiricist theory. This means that large-scale prediction is not possible (Evers and Lakomski, 1991). Whether or not there are general features in common between different organizational contexts would be a matter of empirical investigation, to be determined after the event by use of the coherentist criteria developed in Evers and Lakomski's (1991, 1996) naturalistic coherentism, rather than a priori, as was the case in hypothetico-deductive accounts. It may turn out to be the case that there is not one theory of leadership, but many, modular accounts.

A further consequence relates to organizational structure. If knowledge is not to be identified with the leader/or position, and presumed to flow from the top down, as traditionally assumed, then organizational functioning is much enhanced by gauging the knowledge of all organization members and structuring the organization appropriately to feed it through all levels. Correction of possible error is thus to be emphasized since humans are fallible learners, and structure should prudently reflect human capacity.

These initial forays into a vast and complex field of study serve well to indicate the direction and magnitude of a challenging research agenda which promises spectacular and wide-ranging benefits: a naturalized account of leadership which explains effective organizational practice in schools and non-school organizations alike.

References

ARGYRIS, C. (1979) 'How normal science methodology makes leadership research less applicable', in HUNT, J.G. and LARSON, L.L. (eds) *Crosscurrents in Leadership*, Carbondale and Edwardsville, IL: Southern Illinois University Press.

BOLMAN, L.G. and DEAL, T.E. (1991) *Reframing Organizations: Artistry, Choice and Leadership*, San Francisco, CA: Jossey-Bass.

BOSSERT, S.T., DWYER, D.C. and LEE, G.V. (1982) 'The instructional management role of the principal', *Educational Administration Quarterly*, **18**, 3, pp. 34–64.

BOWERS, D.G. and SEASHORE, S.E. (1973) 'Predicting organizational effectiveness with a four-factor theory of leadership', in SCOTT, W.E. and CUMMINGS, L.L. (eds) *Readings in Organizational Behavior and Human Performance*, Homewood, IL: Richard D. Irwin.

BRIDGES, E.M. (1982) 'Research on the school administrator: The state of the art, 1967–1980', *Educational Administration Quarterly*, **18**, 3, pp. 12–33.

CHURCHLAND, P.M. (1979) *Scientific Realism and the Plasticity of Mind*, Cambridge, MA: Cambridge University Press.

CHURCHLAND, P.M. (1993) *A Neurocomputational Perspective: The Nature of Mind and the Structure of Science*, Cambridge, MA: MIT Press.

EVERS, C.W. (1995) 'Recent developments in educational administration', *Leading and Managing*, **1**, 1, pp. 1–14.

EVERS, C.W. and LAKOMSKI, G. (1991) *Exploring Educational Administration: Coherentist Applications and Critical Debates*, Oxford: Pergamon.

EVERS, C.W. and LAKOMSKI, G. (1996) *Knowing Educational Administration: Contemporary Methodological Controversies in Educational Administration Research*, Oxford: Pergamon.

FIEDLER, F.E. (1967) *A Theory of Leadership Effectiveness*, New York: McGraw-Hill.

FIEDLER, F.E. (1973) 'Validation and extension of the contingency model of leadership effectiveness: a review of empirical findings', in SCOTT, W.E. and CUMMINGS, L.L. (eds) *Readings in Organizational Behavior and Human Performance*, Homewood, IL: Richard D. Irwin.

GIBB, C.A. (1959) 'Leadership', in LINDZEY, G. (ed.) *Handbook of Social Psychology*, Reading, MA and London, Addison-Wesley.

HALLINGER, P. and HECK, R.H. (1996) 'Reassessing the principal's role in school effectiveness: A review of empirical research, 1980–1995', *Educational Administration Quarterly*, **32**, 1, pp. 5–44.

HALPIN, A.W. and WINER, B.J. (1973) 'A factorial study of the leader behavior description', in STOGDILL, R.M. and COONS, A.E. (eds) *Leader Behavior: Its Description and Measurement*, Columbus, OH: College of Administrative Science, The Ohio State University.

HEMPHILL, J.K. (1949) *Situational Factors in Leadership*, Columbus, OH: Ohio State University Personnel Research Board.

HEMPHILL, J.K. and COONS, A.E. (1973) *Development of the Leader Behavior Description Questionnaire*, Columbus, OH: College of Administrative Science, The Ohio State University.

HOWE, W. (1994) 'Leadership in educational administration', in HUSEN, T. and POSTLETHWAITE, T.N. (eds) *International Encyclopedia of Education*, 2nd edn, Oxford: Pergamon.

HOY, W.K. and MISKEL, C.G. (1991) 'Educational administration: Theory, research and practice', New York: Random House.

KORMAN, A.K. (1966) '"Consideration", "initiating structure", and organizational criteria – a review', *Personnel Psychology*, **19**, pp. 349–61.

LAWLER, E.F. and PORTER, L.W. (1967) 'The effect of performance on job satisfaction', *Industrial Relations*, **7**, 1, pp. 20–8.

PERROW, C. (1986) *Complex Organizations*, New York: Random House.

PITNER, N. (1988) 'The study of administrator effects and effectiveness', in BOYAN, N. (ed.) *Handbook of Research in Educational Administration*, New York: Longman.

SERGIVANNI, T.J. (1992) *Moral Leadership: Getting to the Heart of School Improvement*, San Francisco, CA: Jossey-Bass.

STOGDILL, R.M. (1948) 'Personal factors associated with leadership', *Journal of Psychology*, **25**, pp. 35–71.

STOGDILL, R.M. and COONS, A.E. (eds) (1957) *Leader Behavior: Its Description and Measurement*, Columbus, OH: College of Administrative Science, The Ohio State University.

YUKL, G. (1973) 'Toward a behavioral theory of leadership', in SCOTT, W.E. and CUMMINGS, L.L. (eds) *Readings in Organizational Behavior and Human Performance*, Homewood, IL: Richard D. Irwin.

4 Academic and Practitioner Perspectives on Values

Paul T. Begley

> Because a significant portion of the practice in educational administration requires rejecting some courses of action in favour of a preferred one, values are generally acknowledged to be central to the field. (Willower, 1992, p. 369)

Willower's observation notwithstanding, the achievement of consensus among academics on the nature and function of values in administration has been problematic. Academic debate on the subject has gone on for years; involving the likes of Greenfield and Ribbins (1993), Hodgkinson (1978, 1983, 1991, 1996); Willower (1994, in press); and certainly Evers and Lakomski (1991, 1996, in press). There is even a metaphor which captures the flavour of this debate in its earlier stages. It has been compared (see Begley, 1996a) to an endless medieval conflict; the champions of each side residing in craggy paradigmatic redoubts, emerging periodically for a skirmish or two on the battlefield of academic journalism. Moreover, of late a whole new generation of players has now appeared on the field. These relative newcomers include Beck (1990, 1993, and Chapter 13); Begley (1988, 1996a, in press); Campbell (1994); Campbell-Evans (1991); Lafleur (Chapter 10); Leithwood (in press), Leonard (1997, in press and Chapter 6); Roche (in press); Walker and Shakotko (in press) and others. It would appear that the debate has not abated, it has intensified!

This academic ferment may have seemed almost heroic at times to the academics engaged in it. However, many school practitioners would probably comment that very little has been achieved that has increased the clarity, coherence and relevance of values to their everyday administrative practice. It has been very much a conversation among academics, far removed from the day-to-day concerns of school administration. As a consequence, a significant relevancy gap has developed between academic and practitioners on matters relating to values and valuation processes in administration. Fortunately, there is recent evidence to suggest that this situation is changing. There has been a proliferation of books and research centres focused on the study of values and moral leadership. Furthermore, as the chapters comprising this book suggest, at least some of the traditional epistemological issues have come close to being resolved. A consensus is developing on at least some of the vocabulary and issues. Moreover, this is occurring just as practitioners are manifesting a renewed interest in values and valuation processes as responses to the realities of school leadership in our post modern societies.

This chapter is devoted to documenting these advances and examining practitioner and academic perspectives on school leadership and values. The intent is to further consolidate the case for adopting a values perspective on administration. The changing context of school leadership is explored, revealing it as the stimulus which is renewing interest in the study of values among school administrators. Particular theoretical perspectives on administrative values are discussed and the findings of recent values research are highlighted to illustrate the relevance of academic perspectives to everyday administrative practice. Finally, theories of cognition are considered as a promising conceptual lens for reviewing and classifying the theoretical and research literature on values in an effort to produce more clarity and coherence about the nature and function of values in educational administration.

Practitioner Perspectives on Values in Administration

A prevailing stereotype about administration holds that these professionals are highly pragmatic, unreflective and preoccupied with procedural matters. Although such notions may be largely outdated, they are still commonly articulated, especially in the university community. Such sentiments are sometimes perpetuated by those who have lost touch with the field or abetted by traditional organizational theories, e.g. (Simon, 1965) that emphasize the managerial functions of administration. However, in today's school leadership situations, competing value orientations manifest themselves within particular educational communities quite regularly. Administrators become aware of values issues without any particular need for prior training in philosophy, or exposure to the literature on administrative ethics. They have become increasingly sensitive to values issues simply because of the pluralistic societies in which they live and work.

As social and cultural diversity increases, as equity becomes a greater social priority, and as demands for fiscal restraint persist, the circumstances of decision-making in educational organizations have become more complex and challenging. As an outcome, there has been an increase in the frequency of value conflict situations to which administrators must respond. Such value conflicts have become particularly apparent as administrator perspectives increasingly run across the organizational boundaries that traditionally separated community from school, and school from district office, department or ministry. These are social thresholds that have become increasingly transparent organizational boundaries in a post-modern world.

Administrators now seem to recognize more readily that the values manifested by individuals, groups and organizations have an impact on what happens in schools, chiefly by influencing the screening of information or definition of alternatives. The more reflective among administrators are also conscious of how their own personal values may blind or illuminate the assessment of situations. These changing educational circumstances imply a number of conceptual as well as operational justifications for studying the nature and function of values in administration.

The Changing Context of School Administration

Education inevitably mirrors society, so these are not easy times for educators. Social unrest has become the norm, particularly in the industrialized nations of the world, and enormous challenges confront these societies; the outcome of repeating cycles of economic recession, global environmental problems, and the threatened collapse of our social security systems. In many sectors this general social malaise is compounded by concerns with equity issues, an increasing mistrust of bureaucracy and vested authority in all its forms, and a consequent trend towards decentralization and communitarian democracy. Educators experience this phenomena as an unprecedented press for wide-ranging educational reform. For many this constitutes a significant challenge because teachers and school administrators have traditionally preferred to work in isolation within relatively protected professional environments. Moreover, at the school level, adjusting to new social realities implies profound changes to established, career-long patterns of educational practice.

As challenging as the teaching profession has become, school administration may be even more demanding. This is because administrators inhabit an almost schizophrenic and much more public world where they are simultaneously autonomous individuals, agents of society accountable to an established system of educational governance, teaching professionals, and members of the community served by the education system. Like teachers, they feel strong social pressure to change their personal practices and orientations, however they are at the same time responsible for promoting, supporting and orchestrating these changes in educational practice within schools and communities.

As stated earlier, educational leaders, whether teachers or school administrators, increasingly find themselves working in environments where value conflicts are much more common. A heightened concern for the increasingly varied contexts of schooling has evolved. Some of these sources of value conflict have always been there. For example, students live in a world that reflects post-modern values and they regularly confront teachers and principals that represent, within educational organizations, a preceding modernist generation. However, racial, ethnic and religious groups also increasingly intermingle in our societies, and, as educational stakeholders, regularly disagree about what is desirable in school policies, procedures and outcomes. The outcome for school administrators is that the circumstances of educational decision making become ever more complex and challenging.

So, having barely adjusted to instructional leadership, a preceding wave of educational reform that occurred in response to another set of social trends and educational issues, school administrators are sensing once again the expectation that they must make yet more adjustments to their roles and functions. School improvement processes and even the more recent trend towards the promotion of teacher collaboration are no longer sufficient. The school leadership role is no longer the private preserve of principals, and new expectations even extend beyond the professional boundaries of teacher leadership to include parents, students and/ or members of the community. School administrators are not only expected to accept this devolution of their control over school affairs, they are also expected to orchestrate and promote this process of much expanded empowerment.

To summarize, changes in the contextual circumstances of schooling and the subsequent new expectations for school administrators imply the following changes in practice: Collaboration remains a key concept, but it is no longer limited to just teachers, the professional stakeholders. Parents and community members are to be increasingly engaged in significant decision-making about school affairs, often through school councils with much expanded responsibilities. While accountability is still a key watchword, there is a new emphasis on assessing accountability through the identification and measurement of learning outcomes. For administrators, this is the challenge presented by the changing context of school leadership. The nature of school administration continues to evolve rapidly and the implied changes in practice are profound.

Academic Perspectives on Values in Administration

Having considered the particular perspective that practitioners bring to the subject of values, attention shifts in this section to the place of values in administrative theory and recent research findings of relevance to practitioners. For the purposes of this chapter, a particular working definition of values proposed by Hodgkinson (1978) and drawn from Kluckhohn (1951) is tabled: Values are a conception, explicit or implicit, distinctive of an individual or characteristic of a group, of the desirable which influences the selection from available modes, means and ends of action.

This definition highlights the critical function of values in the making of choices. In administration, the making of choices is usually termed decision-making and/or problem solving, an activity familiar to most administrators. The Kluckhohn/Hodgkinson definition also usefully expands the scope of the term value to encompass several value constructs relevant to educational administration including: social ethics (Beck, 1993; Cohen, 1982; Frankena, 1973), transrational principles (Hodgkinson, 1978), the rational moral values of administration (Strike, 1990; Willower, 1994, 1999), as well as the baser value notions of personal preference (Evers and Lakomski, 1991; Hodgkinson, 1978). With this broadened definition of values, it becomes possible, and in fact necessary, to distinguish the values manifested by individuals from their professional values as well as the more collective social values of a group or organization. The interactive relationship between personal values and social values becomes highlighted, giving rise to important questions; such as, to what extent can the personal values held by individuals be considered antecedent to the formation of social values, or, to what extent are personal values the formatively developed outcomes of exposure to pre-existing social values.

Figure 4.1   Syntax of value terms

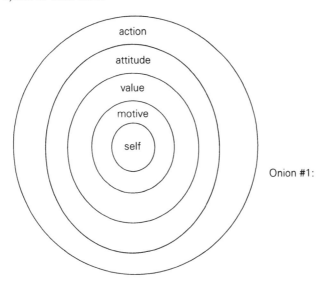

A Syntax of Values Terminology

A robust definition of values is not the only requirement for disciplined inquiry in this field. There are other matters of syntax. One of the simplest ways to illustrate a syntax of values terminology is through an adaptation of a graphic found in several of Hodgkinson's books (1978, 1991) (see Figure 4.1). When considering this first 'onion' it is important to keep in mind that it represents the perspective of one person, a single individual, not a collective or social context. The outer ring of the onion represents the observable actions and speech of the individual, the *only* way available for making empirical attributions of the value orientations of the individual. Most people intuitively know to rely on the clues provided by the actions and attitudes of people around them to obtain predictive insights into the nature of values held by these individuals. A sound general strategy perhaps, but there are some limits to its reliability. Observable actions may or may not be accurate indicators of underlying values, particularly when individuals articulate or posture certain values while actually being committed to quite different values. Political leaders are usually a rich source for examples of such behaviour.

The next layer into the onion represents attitudes. This is the thin permeable membrane situated between values and actions or speech. To illustrate the manifestation of attitude in the real world, consider how a father might inform a son that his attitude needs adjustment. The son's response might be to protest that he has not done anything, to which the parent can rejoinder, 'Yes, but I can tell you are about to.' Attitudes often foreshadow actions influenced by the specific values a person holds for whatever reasons. It is important to realize that any one value can be held in response to a wide range of motivations. For example, a person may subscribe to honesty as a value to avoid the pain of sanction for dishonesty, or because this is a shared community orientation, or because the consequence of widespread dishonesty is social chaos, or because it is the *right* thing to do. Furthermore, as suggested earlier, it is common for individuals to deliberately or unwittingly manifest or articulate one value while being actually committed to another, usually one associated with self-interest or preference, but also possibly with a transrational motivational base.

The key to understanding the nature and function of values is found in the next layer of the onion labelled motivational base. It represents the motivating force dimension behind the adoption of a particular value. Hodgkinson argues (1991) that motivational bases are at the core of the being of individuals, and that values held by an individual reflect these motivational bases. However, observers of human nature as well as researchers must exercise caution when attributing a motivational base to a particular manifested value. Once again, a given value may be held at any of several levels of motivation ranging from preferences, the rational values of consequence and consensus, to the level of transrational principles. The linkage is there, but it is difficult to know with any certainty the primary motivational base or bases. Finally at the centre of the onion we have the self, the essence of the individual – the biological self as well as the existential or transcendent self.

To summarize with another metaphor, the attitudes and actions manifested by individuals may be usefully construed as observable ripples and splashes on the surface of a body of water. It is important to keep in mind that the true intentions behind these observable actions may alternately be transparently obvious, superficial or running deep to the core. They can also remain fully obscured below the surface of the self, the organizational structure or the society. Hence the limited utility of conducting research that merely describes or lists the values manifested by individuals whether they be administrators, teachers, students, citizens, neighbours or members of the family. It may be interesting to know *what* they value, but what is often most crucial is *why* they do so.

The Arenas of Valuation; Sources of Values and Value Conflicts

A second onion figure can be used to illustrate the arenas where valuation processes occur and the dynamics among these distinct arenas (see Figure 4.2). With this second onion the individual is represented within the centre ring as *self.* Those who like to emphasize the existential nature of individuals appreciate the notion of this hard little central core. On the other hand, individuals more oriented towards the social formation of values might prefer the centre core to extend through each of the other rings in order to illustrate the formative influence of social forces on individual perceptions.

The second ring outwards from the centre of the figure is termed *group.* This arena includes family, peers, friends and professional colleagues. The third ring from the centre reflects the values arena traditionally of most concern to academics

Figure 4.2 Arenas of value action

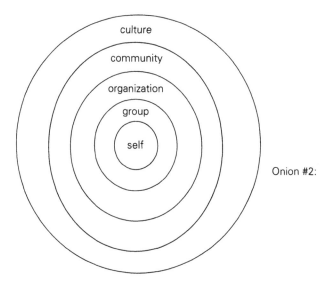

in the field of educational administration, the organization. Finally, one gets to the outer ring representing the greater community or society, and the culture. At this stage some readers may sense the need to add a sixth ring to the figure in order to accommodate the influence of another arena – the transcendental, God, or the Holy Spirit.

The onion of Figure 4.2 illustrates the various *sources* of values, however it also reveals the sources of value conflicts. For example, consider how personal values may conflict with those of community, or how professional values may conflict with organizational values. As a final thought and extension of the onion metaphor, consider what happens when an onion stays in the pantry too long and begins to sprout. When sliced in half it becomes apparent that germination starts at the centre and works out through the layers. It does not start in the middle layers. This imagery highlights the central importance of the individual as the catalyst for growth and development within groups, organizations, communities and culture – something easy to lose sight of when organizations and their processes are personified in the leadership literature. Of course, the flow could equally be construed as going from the outside rings inward if one wishes to emphasize how the values of individuals are shaped and acquired.

The Portrayal of Values in Theory and Research

Anyone who has spent any time trying to unravel or map out the values literature will appreciate how difficult it is to do this. Nevertheless, eventually one begins to notice some patterns. Some theories, particularly those grounded in philosophy,

Figure 4.3   Mapping theories and conceptions of values using a linguistic metaphor (Begley, 1996b)

| | | **Linguistic Metaphor** | |
Value Type (Hodgkinson, 1978)	Semantic (meaning)	Phonetic (descriptive)	Syntactic (application)
Sub/Transrational (Type 1 and 3)	Ashbaugh and Kasten (1984) Begley (1988) Hodgkinson (1978) Lang (1986) MacPhee (1983)	Beck (1993)	Ashbaugh and Kasten (1984) Begley (1988) Lang (1986)
Rational Values: Individual/Personal (Type 2)	Ashbaugh and Kasten (1984) Begley (1988) Campbell (1994) Hodgkinson (1978) MacPhee (1983) Simon (1965)	Beck (1993) Campbell-Evans (1991) Leithwood and Steinbach (1991)	Barth (1990) Begley (1988) Campbell-Evans (1991) Leithwood and Steinbach (1991) Sergiovanni (1992) Strike (1990) Willower (1994)
Rational Values: Collective/Objective (Type 2 Meta-values)	Evers and Lakomski (1991) Hodgkinson (1978)	Beck (1993) Leithwood and Steinbach (1991)	Hambrick and Brandon (1988) Leithwood and Steinbach (1991) Willower (1994)

tend to focus on motivations, basic intentions or the meaning of values. Other theories champion or promote particular moral orders, that is urging the adoption of the *right* values. When it comes to research, for example, on the values of administrators or teachers, the tendency is towards *describing* the values manifested by these individuals. Transformational leaders might be said to manifest values of collaboration, or of commitment to democratic processes. Although it may not be clear why they hold these values, their actions or speech demonstrate particular value orientations.

Begley's (1996b) efforts to map existing theory and research led to the adoption of a linguistic metaphor in three parts (semantics, phonetics, and syntactics).[1] A linguistic metaphor seems appropriate since anthropologists and sociolinguists regularly analyse language to derive insights into a culture's roles, norms, taboos, values and world views. On this naturalistic basis a metaphor based on language was used as a way of bringing additional coherence to the subject of values in educational administration. It allows the classification of various literature under three categories: theories and frameworks which are *defining* and metaphysical (semantic), those that are *descriptive* (phonetic), and those that are context specific or *applied* (syntactic). Figure 4.3 illustrates this classification scheme. A second dimension of the displayed matrix portrays three value categories; sub-rational and trans-rational values, the rational value types manifested by individuals; and thirdly, the rational values characteristic of groups, collectives and organizations.

To elaborate further on the categories, consider that the word *semantic* pertains to meaning. In the present context, the term is used to cluster together values theories and applications of values models which emphasize the motivational bases and philosophical or first principles aspects of values, literally the meanings associated with a particular value that may be manifested in multiple ways. An obvious example of a theory meriting placement in this category is Hodgkinson's value theory because of its focus on motivational bases and philosophical grounding.

A second cluster of theories and models is grouped around the word *phonetics*. This word is applied conventionally in reference to distinct symbols such as letters and other phonetic symbols used to represent the sounds of speech or to describe how a word is vocalized. In the context of mapping values theory, the term phonetic is used as an organizer for theories and models which are descriptive of particular values as they become manifest in the actions of individuals or collectives, as opposed to providing insights into their meaning or motivational bases. Beck's (1993) values model and several derivative models (e.g. Leithwood's in Leithwood, Begley, and Cousins, 1992) are examples of frameworks properly placed in this category.

The third and final category in the linguistic metaphor is *syntax*, a word generally used to denote espoused or appropriate patterns of language usage. In the context of theories and models of administrative values, the term is used to cluster the literature and research on values that describe values in particular applied settings or used to attain specific ends. Examples of this are Leithwood's administrative problem-solving model (Leithwood and Steinbach, 1995), and Sergiovanni's promotion of collaborative cultures (1992).

Although a number of theories and frameworks have been clustered within the dimensions of Figure 4.3 to illustrate this mapping strategy, it must be noted they are an illustrative sampling only, not an exhaustive listing of all the available literature on administrative values. Nevertheless, the patterns which emerge highlight the key differences among the frameworks and illustrate much of the preceding discussion about inquiry in the values field. It becomes apparent that the bulk of the available findings of applied research on the subject clusters in the domain of rational values; the administrative mainstream of consensus and consequential decision making. Relatively few research studies address the non-rational value types. The exceptions listed in Figure 4.3 are Ashbaugh and Kasten (1984), Begley (1988), and Lang (1986); all studies which relied on the Hodgkinson model to distinguish non-rational value types. It is also apparent that theorists and philosophers such as Hodgkinson , Evers and Lakomski restrict their intellectual activity to the semantics of value meanings, seldom venturing into the realms of application which are more comfortably the domain of practitioners. Conversely, those operating primarily in the syntax category of practical applied administration do not necessarily operate from established theory. Examples of such work, based on expert opinion rather than theory, include Barth (1990), and Sergiovanni (1992). The concept of values is an essential component of their argument, but the theoretical underpinnings are relatively unexamined. A few researchers, notably Ashbaugh and Kasten (1984), Begley (1988), and Campbell-Evans (1991), do appear in all three categories of the linguistic metaphor map. This perhaps illustrates the virtue of research that is grounded in theory, descriptive of the nature and function of values in administration, and situated in administrative contexts specific enough to have practitioner relevance.

The Values of Administration

Perhaps the best known, most influential, and specifically focused values theory applicable to educational administration is that proposed by Hodgkinson (1978, 1983, 1991, 1996). Others who have made theoretical contributions to the study of values in administration include Beck and Murphy (1994) and Evers and Lakomski (1991), plus a host of derivative models proposed by researchers including Ashbaugh and Kasten (1984); Begley (1988); Begley and Johansson (1998); Campbell (1994); Campbell-Evans (1991); Hambrick and Brandon (1988) and Leithwood and Steinbach (1991). Among existing values theories, only these relate well to the nature and function of values in educational administration. For example, the work of social psychologists such as Rokeach (1973) and philosophers such as Frankena (1973) is concerned with a generalized concept of human values and normative ethics, not the particular situations of administration. Beck (1990, 1993) concerns himself with values in adulthood and the pursuit of the good life in schools as well as in general society. Others, such as Cohen (1982) and Peters (1973) address pedagogical value systems: the goals of education, the modes of learning, critical deliberation.

Hodgkinson's (1978) analytical model of the value concept identifies four motivational bases that become the stimulus for adopting particular values and beliefs. These values and beliefs in turn shape particular attitudes and generate, or at least influence, the actions of the individual. Considered in a reverse order, the most basic motivational base is personal preferences (or self-interest), representing a conception of what is 'good'. They are grounded in the individual's affect, constitute the individual's preference structure, and are self-justifying and primitive or sub-rational. The remaining three motivational bases more accurately represent a *philosophical* hierarchy of valuation, differentiated on a continuum of 'rightness' or correctness of value. So, moving up from preference, the next step is *consensus*, expert opinion or the will of the majority in a given collectivity. Next up the hierarchy is *consequences*, a motivational base focused on a desirable future state of affairs or analysis of the consequences entailed by the value judgment.

Whereas the motivational bases of consensus and consequences may be arrived at rationally, the final motivational base in the Hodgkinson typology, situated at the highest level of the philosophical hierarchy, is *transrational*. Hodgkinson uses the term *principle* to denote this motivational base. Values adopted at this level are grounded in principle, the metaphysical (as in the study of first principles), and take the form of ethical codes, injunctions or commandments. They are not scientifically verifiable and cannot be justified by logical argument. They are based on will rather than on reason. According to Hodgkinson, the adoption of transrational values implies some act of faith, belief or commitment (1978, p. 112).

The findings of recent research on administrator values conducted in several countries highlight the value orientations of skilful principals, illustrating how values can influence practice and which value types predominate in principals problem solving processes. Personal values in general have been shown to be significant influences on decision-making. More specifically, the rational value types of consequence and consensus generally predominate in the valuation processes of administration. Personal preferences grounded in self-interest are also evident but infrequently articulated by administrators, and transrational principles tend to be employed under particular circumstances. However, the strongest finding by far across multiple studies conducted since 1988 is that rational values reflecting a concern for consequences and consensus appear to be the primary currency of the administrators from Canada, Sweden and Australia (Begley, 1988; Begley and Johansson, 1998; Campbell-Evans, 1991; Leithwood, Begley and Cousins, 1992; Leonard, 1997; Roche, in press). These findings are also consistent with three other studies that did not specifically focus on the practices of school administrators (Ashbaugh and Kasten, 1984; Lang, 1986; MacPhee, 1983).

As tempting as it might be to use these research findings as a basis for developing a prescriptive guide to value-added leadership – a catalogue of correct values which principals ought to adopt without question – the processes of valuation in school leadership situations are much too context bound to permit this quick fix. Furthermore, although we may know something about the problems currently confronting schools, none of us can predict with any degree of certainty the nature of future school leadership beyond the certainty that there will be more problems to solve and new dilemmas to confront. As a result, it is not enough for school leaders to merely emulate the values of other principals currently viewed as experts. Leaders of future schools must become reflective practitioners in the sense that Roland Barth (1990), Christopher Hodgkinson (1991), Donald Schon (1983), and Thomas Sergiovanni (1992) have advocated for some time. The first step towards achieving this state is, predictably enough, to engage in personal reflection – familiar advice to anyone who has kept up with the leadership literature. However, the adoption of a values perspective on school leadership can transform this perhaps vague advice into something specific enough for school administrators to act upon.

Applying Cognitive Perspectives to Values and Leadership

Having reviewed both the academic and practitioner perspectives on values in educational administration and the changing context of school leadership, and considered the contributions of theory and research to this field of inquiry, it is now appropriate to consider the potentially significant contribution of cognitive perspectives to the study of values and leadership. In this section notions of psychological cognition related to information processing are linked more directly to theories accommodating the function of values. The intent of this grafting exercise is to explore its potential impact on reducing the relevancy gap between values theory and administrative practice.[2]

Information Processing Theory

Information processing theory has for some time been considered an important theme in the literature of cognitive psychology. As well as being regularly identified as a key component in modern educational psychology texts (e.g. Ormrod, 1995), information processing theory is sometimes incorporated as a component of research methodologies aimed at studying leadership and school administration practices. For example, as part of a research project that led to the development of a detailed profile of principal practices aimed at promoting instructional leadership, Leithwood and Montgomery (1986) discovered that, among the alternative psychological explanations of individual human functioning, information processing theory was well suited to conceptualizing the actions of school administrators (see also Leithwood, Begley and Cousins, 1992).

Although a number of assumptions underlie information processing theory, two are particularly relevant to the purposes of this chapter. The first asserts that people can only handle a certain amount of information at a given time, and so are selective about the things they process and learn. This is reminiscent of Simon's (1965) very similar arguments in support of the *bounded rationality* of administration. A second assumption associated with information processing theory holds that people impose their own meanings on environmental events (Ormrod, 1995, p. 307). A related notion, *constructivism*, proposes that learners construct their own knowledge from their experiences (see Chan, Burtis, Scardamalia and Bereiter, 1992).

While information processing theorists do not necessarily agree about the exact nature of human cognitive processing, most support variations on a basic three component model of information processing (Ormrod, 1995, p. 315). With terminology varying from theorist to theorist, the basic dimensions of a three component model of information processing are: the *Executive, Short-term Memory*, and *Long-term Memory*. For a specific example consider the Leithwood and Montgomery (1986) research cited earlier. They adopted a three component model derived from the information processing theory of Calfee (1981), Robinson, Ross and White (1985), and Norman and Lindsay (1977).

Linking information processing theory to values theory raises a number of possibilities. For example, perhaps the value conflicts experienced by individuals in educational settings or in life generally are the consequence of a mismatch between executive knowledge schema developed over a lifetime and procedural schema imposed by external forces in organizations or society. Value conflicts may be generated when procedural schema implied by one node of knowledge schema conflict with other knowledge schema. Furthermore, as will be proposed, when values theory is integrated with information processing theory it becomes plausible to speculate that the increasingly sophisticated knowledge and procedural schema that produce superordinate executive schema may also over time contribute to the formation or generation of the goals, values and general aspirations of the Executive.

Figure 4.4 Integrating cognitive information processing theory and values theory (Begley, 1996b)

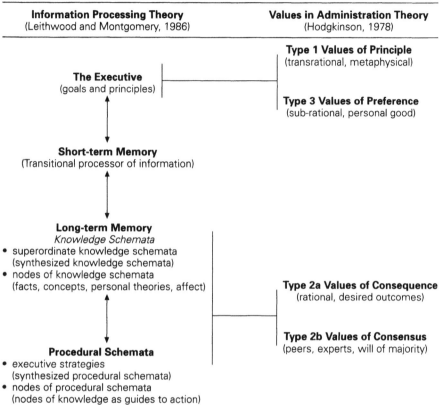

Information Processing Theory (Leithwood and Montgomery, 1986)	Values in Administration Theory (Hodgkinson, 1978)

Integrating Cognitive Theory with Values Theory

In this section a foundational theory, specifically information processing theory derived from social psychology (Bandura, 1977; Calfee, 1981; Chan et al., 1992; Norman and Lindsay, 1977; Ormond, 1995; Robinson et al., 1985) is employed as a reductive organizer for accommodating the notions of values theory in educational administration.

Figure 4.4 illustrates the hypothesized relationship between a representative and empirically verified (see Begley, 1988; Begley and Johansson, 1998; Campbell-Evans, 1991; Lang, 1986; Leithwood and Steinbach, 1991; MacPhee, 1983) theory of values in administration proposed by Hodgkinson (1978) and an adaptation of the information processing theory employed by Leithwood and Montgomery (1986) to explain the cognitive processes of school administrators.

According to this integrated framework, the Executive of information processing theory operates as a filter that can be matched with the sub-rational Values of

Personal Preference and trans-rational Values of Principle. This filter represents the short-term or long-term goals and principles of the individual as it screens for relevant inputs among those received by the brain. Aligning transrational values and subrational values together with the Executive usefully reconciles an epistemic difficulty Evers (1985) associates with the separation of these two value types in Hodgkinson's typology. Thus, inputs identified by the Executive as worthy of recognition by the mind can range from the relatively trivial perceptions of good, pleasure-seeking, or interest in personal gain, to the highest ethics of human enterprise including spiritual faith, justice and humanism. The common denominator for these two value types operating within the Executive is that neither requires rational processing in the way rational values do. They are the non-rational bases of thought and action. Consistent with the findings of Begley's (1988) and Leithwood and Steinbach's (1991) research on the function of values in problem-solving, transrational values are employed by individuals when domain specific knowledge is absent or unavailable, in situations of high ambiguity, and/or when urgency makes rational processes impossible or inappropriate.

Long-term Memory (see Figure 4.4) is where existing schema of knowledge and procedure reside, guide action, and augment themselves in response to new information. This is also where new schema develop as necessary. The processes of Long-term Memory are rational, although they may become relatively automatic as an outcome of frequent use. This theorized function of Long-term Memory correlates well with the rational functions of Hodgkinson's rational values based on consequence and consensus. Furthermore, the existence of superordinate, executive schema of knowledge and procedure, synthesized from the various existing and developing nodes, also begins to suggest how the goals and principles of the Executive might evolve or formulate. The obvious parallel implied for values theory would occur if rational values evolved or became synthesized into transrational Values of Principle. For example, this might explain how transrational religious dietary laws evolve from the hard consequences of experiences in the distant past, or how a transrational commitment to democratic forms of governance may derive from longstanding commitments to collective social action.

Value Conflicts in Administration

The notion of value conflicts is also nicely subsumed within this integrated model. Hodgkinson advises those interested in analyzing and resolving value conflicts to consider whether the conflict occurs between levels or at the same level of his values typology (1991, p. 145). Any parent who has debated, from a Value of Consequences level (i.e. cost), the purchase of expensive running shoes for an adolescent operating from the Value of Consensus level (peer pressure) will understand the significance of this advice. The knowledge schema, if not the procedural schema, of the two parties (parent and adolescent) are in high contrast and subsequently produce orientations implying quite different choices. Hodgkinson also indicates that the most profound of value conflicts occur when two or more Values of Principle are in conflict (1991, p. 150). Because they and Values of Preference are non-rational (either transrational or subrational), conflicts occurring at those levels are extremely difficult to resolve. In the case of Values of Preference, the conflict may resist resolution, but the consequences of this failure are likely relatively trivial, or at least non-lethal; as in the selection of new wallpaper for the dining room or choosing television channels in a family setting (1991, p. 49). On the other hand, transrational values involve deeply held beliefs, fundamental values, and/or spiritual matters of faith. Conversely, they may also address a darker side of the values continuum: for example, the negative kinds of blind faith associated with Nazi Germany decades ago, or the charismatic cults in Jonestown or Waco, Texas encountered more recently. Fortunately for educational administrators, value conflicts occurring at the level of personal ethics are relatively infrequent, and researchers have not often chosen to explore this class of values conflict. This is not to say that such profound conflicts do not occur. Social controversies over abortion, family life studies, AIDS prevention strategies, or even political correctness sometimes spill over into school settings. However, such conflicts may be essentially private battles, hotly contested, mercifully short in duration, fought by individuals within themselves, and sometimes not even formally acknowledged.

Research conducted on administrative problem solving by Leithwood (Leithwood, Begley and Cousins, 1992, p. 108) found that school administrators encounter two types of value-related conflicts. The first type of value conflict involves competition between two or more values vying for recognition in the formulation of a solution; for example, person A's value versus person B's, third party mediation of person-to-person conflict, or value A versus value B within one individual. When information processing theory is applied to these scenarios, it is apparent that this type of conflict is due to competing knowledge schema and perhaps also subsequently competing procedural schema – either within one individual or among several. Another variation on this type of conflict might occur when knowledge schema relevant to a situation implies a particular procedural response that is appropriate but in contravention of other knowledge schema held dear. For example, consider a situation where an elementary school principal must respond to a situation where a student performs so poorly academically that repeating a grade is called for, yet that violates a knowledge schema calling for the protection of student self-esteem.

The second type of value conflict that Leithwood identifies in administrative problem solving is that between a set of values and an implied action. An extreme illustration of this might be the police officer, trained to respond with lethal force under particular circumstances, who nevertheless hesitates to pull the trigger because of a fundamental respect for human life that interferes with the execution of that response. In this case, an executive knowledge schemata, or perhaps even a basic principle harboured in the Executive, interferes with the actualization of a practised procedural schemata response to a competing knowledge schema. Other issues related to the function of values in administration may be clarified, and in some cases reconciled, within this integrated theory of information processing and values. A few of these are explored further in a concluding section as implications for research and practice.

Conclusion

From the limited discussion presented in this chapter a number of implications can be identified. These are outlined here as a conclusion using two categories from the integrated theory of cognition and values as organizers.

Recent research findings (e.g. Begley and Johansson, 1998) appear to confirm the function of non-rational valuation processes within school administration processes. Within this realm of Subrational–Transrational Values and the Executive of information processing theory (see Figure 4.4), it becomes apparent that there can be a set of core values that individuals employ when knowledge schema is unavailable, ambiguity thrives or urgency requires. When they are extensively developed, or when situations of alienation, displacement or social chaos present a fertile environment for their manifestation, these core values of the Executive may be one source of charismatic leadership in its positive as well as it darker manifestations.

The same research findings confirm that the primary currency of valuation processes in school administrators are the rational value bases of consensus and consequences. Within the realm of these Rational Values (consequences and consensus) and Long-term Memory (see Figure 4.4), the motivational bases of individual and collective values are both encompassed. The sophisticated knowledge schema of expert problem solvers is accommodated, as is the procedural schemata of management, and, important insights are provided into the causes and nature of value conflicts.

It has been proposed in this chapter that the Executive component of the information processing model of the human mind may be formed from increasingly sophisticated knowledge and procedural schema. This is plausible and consistent with the original theory, but the extent to which personal values are antecedent to social values and/or formatively developed responses to pre-existing social values remains unresolved. Perhaps the correct answer is that the balance is culturally determined by the formative experiences of the individual and that such matters are individually determined through experiences in the same way that an administrator might rationally prefer to make a decision based on consensus or personally perceived consequences. What seems clear is that individuals follow different paths and sometimes arrive at the same locus of cognitive and valuation in radically different ways.

The matter of administrators articulating one value while being committed to other values is another issue clarified by an integration of values theory and information processing theory. Identifying the separate functions of knowledge and procedural schema, selected consciously or unconsciously, raises the possibility that one knowledge schema might reflect a commitment to one set of values while a selected procedural schema might articulate or respond to another set of values. When this occurs unconsciously it may reflect an absence of values coherence, administrative inconsistency, a source of values conflict or perhaps even a basic lack of administrative expertise. When it occurs consciously it is amoral or Machiavellian behaviour and likely the source of stressful value conflicts for the administrator within the role. Interesting territory requiring further inquiry.

Notes

1   The material presented in this section of the chapter relating to the linguistic metaphor was originally published in Begley, P., 1996b, Chapter 17: 'Cognitive perspectives on the nature and function of values in educational administration', in LEITHWOOD, K.A. (ed.) *International Handbook on Educational Leadership and Administration*, Boston, MA: Kluwer Academic.

2   A more detailed presentation of the material in this section was originally published in Begley, P.T. (1996a) 'Cognitive perspectives on values in administration: A quest for coherence and relevance', *Educational Administration Quarterly*, **32**, 3, pp. 403–26.

References

ASHBAUGH, C.R. and KASTEN, K.L. (1984) 'A typology of operant values in school administration', *Planning and Changing*, **15**, 4, pp. 195–208.

BANDURA, A. (1977) *Social Learning Theory*, Englewood Cliffs, NJ: Prentice Hall.

BARTH, R.S. (1990) *Improving Schools from Within*, San Francisco, CA: Jossey-Bass.

BECK, C. (1990) *Better Schools: A Values Perspective*, New York: Falmer Press.

BECK, C. (1993) *Learning to Live the Good Life*, Toronto: OISE Press.

BECK, L.G. and MURPHY, J. (1994) *Ethics in Educational Leadership Programs*, Thousand Oaks, CA: Corwin Press.

BEGLEY, P.T. (1988) *The Influence of Personal Beliefs and Values on Principals' Adoption and Use of Computers in Schools.* Unpublished doctoral dissertation. University of Toronto.

BEGLEY, P.T. (1996a) 'Cognitive perspectives on values in administration: A quest for coherence and relevance', *Educational Administration Quarterly*, **32**, 3, pp. 403–26.

BEGLEY, P.T. (1996b) 'Cognitive perspectives on the nature and function of values in educational administration', in LEITHWOOD, K.A. (ed.) *The International Handbook on Educational Leadership and Administration*, Boston, MA: Kluwer Academic.

BEGLEY, P.T. (ed.) (in press) *Values and Educational Leadership*, Albany, NY: SUNY Press.

BEGLEY, P.T. and JOHANSSON, O. (1998) 'The values of school administration: Preferences, ethics and conflicts', *The Journal of School Leadership*, **8**, 4, pp. 399–422.

CALFEE, R. (1981) 'Cognitive psychology and educational practice', *Review of Educational Research*, **9**, pp. 3–74.

CAMPBELL, E. (1994) 'Personal morals and organizational ethics: A synopsis', *The Canadian Administrator*, **34**, 2, pp. 1–10.

CAMPBELL-EVANS, G.H. (1991) 'Nature and influence of values in principal decision-making', *The Alberta Journal of Educational Research*, **37**, 2, pp. 167–78.

CHAN, C.K.K., BURTIS, P.J., SCARDAMALIA, M. and BEREITER, C. (1992) 'Constructive activity in learning from text', *American Educational Research Journal*, **29**, 1, pp. 97–118.

COHEN, B. (1982) *Means and Ends in Education*, London: George Allen and Unwin.

EVERS, C.W. (1985) 'Hodgkinson on ethics and the philosophy of administration', *Educational Administration Quarterly*, **21**, 1, pp. 27–50.

EVERS, C.W. and LAKOMSKI, G. (1991) *Knowing Educational Administration*, Toronto: Pergamon Press.

EVERS, C.W. and LAKOMSKI, G. (1996) *Exploring Educational Administration*, Toronto: Pergamon Press.

Paul T. Begley

FRANKENA, W.K. (1973) *Ethics*, Englewood Cliffs, NJ: Prentice Hall.
GREENFIELD, T.B. and RIBBINS, P. (1993) *Greenfield on Educational Administration*, New York: Routledge.
HAMBRICK, D.C. and BRANDON, G.L. (1988) 'Executive values', in HAMBRICK, D.C. (ed.) *The Executive Effect: Concepts and Methods for Studying Top Managers*, Greenwich, CT: JAI Press.
HODGKINSON, C. (1978) *Towards a Philosophy of Administration*, Oxford: Basil Blackwell.
HODGKINSON, C. (1983) *The Philosophy of Leadership*, Oxford: Basil Blackwell.
HODGKINSON, C. (1991) *Educational Leadership: The Moral Art*, Albany, NY: SUNY Press.
HODGKINSON, C. (1996) *Administrative Philosophy*, Oxford: Pergamon Press.
KLUCKHOHN, C. (1951) 'Values and value-orientations in the theory of action: An exploration in definition and classification', in PARSONS, T. and SHILS, E. (eds) *Toward a General Theory of Action*, New York: Harper and Row.
LANG, D. (1986) *Values and Commitment: An Empirical Verification of Hodgkinson's Value Paradigm as Applied to the Commitment of Individuals to Organizations*. Unpublished doctoral thesis, University of Victoria. Victoria, BC.
LEITHWOOD, K.A. (in press) 'An organizational perspective on values for leaders of future schools', in BEGLEY, P. (ed.) *Values and Educational Leadership*, Albany, NY: SUNY Press.
LEITHWOOD, K.A., BEGLEY, P.T. and COUSINS, J.B. (1992) *Developing Expert Leadership for Future Schools*, London: Falmer Press.
LEITHWOOD, K.A. and MONTGOMERY, D.G. (1986) *Improving Principal Effectiveness: The Principal Profile*, Toronto: OISE Press.
LEITHWOOD, K.A. and STEINBACH, R. (1991) 'Components of chief education officers' problem solving strategies', in LEITHWOOD, K.A. and MUSELLA, D. (eds) *Understanding School System Administration: Studies of the Contemporary Chief Education Officer*, New York: Falmer Press.
LEITHWOOD, K.A. and STEINBACH, R. (1995) *Expert Problem Solving*. Albany: SUNY Press.
LEONARD, P. (1998) *Understanding the Dimensions of School Culture*. Unpublished doctoral dissertation. University of Toronto.
LEONARD, P. (in press) 'Examining educational purposes and underlying value orientations in schools', in BEGLEY, P. (ed.) *Values and Educational Leadership*, Albany, NY: SUNY Press.
MACPHEE, P. (1983) *Administrators and Human Comprehension: The Intrusion of Values*. Unpublished MA Thesis. University of Toronto.
NORMAN, D.A. and LINDSAY, P.H. (1977) *Human Information Processing: An Introduction to Psychology*, New York: Academic Press.
ORMROD, J.E. (1995) *Educational Psychology: Principles and Applications*, Englewood Cliffs, NJ: Merrill.
PETERS, R.S. (1973) *The Philosophy of Education*, London: Oxford University Press.
ROBINSON, F.G., ROSS, J. and WHITE, F. (1985) 'Psychological models of instruction', *Curriculum Development for Effective Instruction*, Toronto: OISE Press.
ROCHE, K. (in press) 'Moral and ethical dilemmas in Catholic school settings', in BEGLEY, P. (ed.) *Values and Educational Leadership*, Albany, NY: SUNY Press.
ROKEACH, M. (1973) *The Nature of Human Values*, New York: Free Press.
SCHON, D.A. (1983) *The Reflective Practitioner: How Professionals Think in Action*, New York: Basic Books.
SERGIOVANNI, T.J. (1992) *Moral Leadership: Getting to the Heart of School Improvement*, San Francisco, CA: Jossey-Bass.

SIMON, H. (1965) *Administrative Behaviour*, 2nd edn, New York: Free Press.

STRIKE, K.A. (1990) 'The ethics of educational evaluation', in MILLMAN, J. DARLING-HAMMOND, L. (eds) *Teacher Evaluation: Assessing Elementary and Secondary School Teachers*, Newbury Park, CA: Sage Publications, pp. 356–73.

WALKER, K. and SHAKOTKO, D. (in press) 'The Canadian superintendency: Value-based challenges and pressures', in BEGLEY, P. (ed.) *Values and Educational Leadership*, Albany, NY: SUNY Press.

WILLOWER, D. (1992) 'Educational administration: Intellectual trends', *Encyclopedia of Educational Research, 6th edition*, Toronto: Macmillan Publishing, pp. 364–75.

WILLOWER, D. (1994) *Educational Administration: Inquiry, Values, Practice*, Lancaster, PA: Technomic Publishing.

WILLOWER, D.J. (in press) 'Values and valuation: A naturalistic approach', in BEGLEY, P.T. (ed.) *Values and Educational Leadership*, Albany, NY: SUNY Press.

5 Complexity, Context and Ethical Leadership

Colin W. Evers

How is ethical leadership in educational contexts possible? On the one hand, some well known approaches to leadership emphasize the importance of moral guidance as part of what is required in being an inspirational leader, one able to transform followers and initiate significant organizational change (Leithwood, Tomlinson and Genge, 1996, p. 786). On the other hand, the ubiquity of uncertainty and the sheer complexity of modern organizational life conspire to compromise the value of knowledge behind any proposals for moral guidance. This chapter offers a scheme for integrating the demands of leadership with the constraints that make moral knowledge so difficult to achieve. The main strategy will be first to outline an approach to moral knowledge and then, supposing that a theory of leadership is required to cohere with it, use the coherence constraint to develop the main features of that theory of leadership as it pertains to ethical matters.

Requiring coherence between these two bodies of theory is not unreasonable, especially where large scale theorizing is being attempted. For example, Hodgkinson's (1991) model of leadership in terms of position within a stratified hierarchical organizational structure is based directly on his model of ethics as a stratified hierarchy of differently justified claims. Adequate leadership at the top of the organizational hierarchy requires cognitive access to a special class of values (those that are 'transrationally' justified) at the top of the values hierarchy (Hodgkinson, 1991, pp. 143–65), and critical theory accounts of ethics based on the alleged moral presuppositions of maintaining what is known as an 'ideal speech situation' emphasize the kind of moral principles used to defend democratic and participatory styles of leadership, principles to do with tolerance, equity, fairness and justice (Foster, 1985). Even the implicit theorizing embedded in cultural practices appears to press for coherent resolutions in these matters. For example, Wong (1996) draws attention to some significant differences between Eastern and Western moral cultures noting, in Confucian thought, the ethical importance of learning in both character development and in the goal of serving the people. But he also observes that these values are consonant with leadership practices that emphasize consensus, group processes and communitarianism.

Linguistic Representations of Moral Knowledge

Codes of Practice

One way of demonstrating moral leadership is through the development of a code of practice, to prescribe appropriate conduct by articulating a set of written guidelines or rules. The Ten Commandments is an example of one such set of rules. Many organizations and professional associations with less lofty purposes develop their own distinctive codes. The Statement of Ethics approved in the US by the National Association of Secondary School Principals prescribes that the educational administrator, for example: 'Makes the well-being of students the fundamental value in all decision-making and actions', and 'fulfils professional responsibilities with honesty and integrity'. Actually, these two principles highlight one of the difficulties to be found with ethical codes. Because a code is meant to be applicable in general and across differing circumstances, its statements will be fairly abstract. Perhaps the most general and abstract prescription is the injunction to 'do good and avoid evil'. The problem is that what counts as doing good and avoiding evil is left entirely open. As a result, the statement provides no guidance. Similarly, there will be little controversy over making the well being of students the fundamental value in schools administration, but much debate over what counts as student well being, or whether certain particular proposals will effectively promote it.

To increase the use of value of codes as moral guides providing a source of moral leadership in the light of the generality problem, it might be thought that some specifics should be included, or that moral principles be made more explicit. An example of explicitness would be, 'Always tell the truth'. Unfortunately, without any qualifiers, this statement looks to be mistaken, as it assumes that all people in all circumstances have a right to be told the truth. But the misuse of knowledge can sometimes be a reasonable ground for withholding truth, or even for lying. A person robbing a bank is not automatically entitled to be truthfully informed of the combination to the safe. Explicitness also renders more likely a clash with other moral principles. Concern over hurting the feelings of another may prompt lying about relatively trivial matters: e.g. responding to a question about the appropriateness of a choice of footwear with the words 'That's a nice pair of shoes you're wearing.' Two or more explicit, independent, non-trivial moral rules can always be shown to conflict in some situation. Under these circumstances, most of the effort required for moral leadership comes from outside the code of conduct.

The same point can be made when a code's principles are hedged in with written qualifiers, as in 'Always tell the truth except when conditions C1, C2, C3 . . . Cn obtain'. Either the qualifiers (C1, C2, etc.) are quite general, in which case a version of the generality problem will break out again, or they are specific. But the trouble with specifics is that there is no obvious end to them. The hedged statement is what is called 'infinitely defeasible', admitting an open class of legitimate exceptions.

These difficulties in using codified maxims for moral guidance can be characterized more broadly as follows. Inasmuch as the maxims are expressed in general terms, they will derive their force as moral guides through the process of interpretation, a process that lies outside the code, and inasmuch as the maxims are written to try to capture specifics, the particularities of contexts will always outrun the particularities able to be captured in linguistic formulations, thus requiring an external source of guidance to waive some maxims and augment others with missing detail. (For some of these points made in relation to the evaluation of codes of ethics in educational research, see Small, 1998.)

Moral reasoning

Because models of leadership that articulate with the provision of ethical leadership through the development of codes of conduct are relatively open, pending some specification of the code-maker's moral authority, we look naturally to moral theory as a potential antecedent source of guidance. The two most influential models of moral reasoning to be found in the literature are best seen as articulating with the broad decision-making tradition of leadership. This tradition places a heavy premium on representing knowledge as symbolic, linguistic structures. Developed most comprehensively in administrative studies by Herbert Simon (1976) it is associated with a highly influential view of cognition, according to which intelligent thought is a matter of transforming symbolic strings into other symbolic strings via the operation of subject-appropriate rules for symbol manipulation. That is, thought consists in the valid mapping of classes of language-like representations onto themselves. Known formally as the physical-symbol system hypothesis (Newell and Simon, 1976) its applications to administrative practice have mainly been around the themes of problem solving and decision making, which is not surprising since these themes are most easily formulated within the symbol representationalist tradition.

In applying symbolic representationalist accounts of knowledge to ethics consider, for example, classical (or hedonistic) utilitarianism, which may be formulated roughly as the moral principle that one ought to do that which maximizes the total amount of human happiness (or minimizes the total amount of human misery). Typically, rational moral evaluation under this rule is assumed to require a close specification of the circumstances of each action sufficient to yield an empirical estimate of the quantity of happiness that would result. Although the principle can be simply stated, hedonistic utilitarianism places formidable demands on the cognitive powers of anyone using the theory as a source of moral guidance. First, because it requires an estimate of outcomes of unrealized alternatives – it needs to take into account hypothetical courses of action – moral agents would need to possess quite detailed theories of the causal operation of complex social systems such as schools or education bureaucracies. But these theories are simply not available, except in very abstract functionalist versions ill suited for fine-grained causal prediction and analysis. Second, there is a puzzle over whether the only morally relevant outcome is quantity of happiness, or whether quality is also important. John Stuart Mill thought that quality was important. But if so, how are the two to be traded off in a decision-making context? Indeed, with the resources of language, how are we to describe, in measurement-theoretically useful ways, the relevant levels or amounts of both quality and quantity of happiness? Finally, there is the problem of how happiness could be measured at all: how could one ever know what lies behind the often inscrutable behaviour of others.

Preference utilitarianism, the form that has been most influential in administrative science, has attempted to bypass all these difficulties. If the good for an individual decision-maker is judged to maximize expected utility, then there is no strong demand for getting the causal story correct about how much utility will be produced. It is merely a question of what the agent expects to occur. Also, if all the evidence for an agent's evaluation is an expressed preference, then the distinction between quantity and quality drops out along with the demand to measure the subjective happiness states of others. Reducing cognitive load down to this level, however, raises the question of why preference utilitarianism should count as a moral theory at all. Why is it not merely a description of an agent's expectations and preferences? The answer, briefly, is that the descriptive task of explaining an agent's moral choice making in terms of maximizing expected utility does double duty as a theory of rationality, with the suppressed normative premise being that one ought to act rationally.

There are at least two significant issues raised by this version of preference utilitarianism. The first is that equating normativeness with the demand to be rational is regarded by some as committing the naturalistic fallacy, the supposition that it is a fallacy to equate a moral property (e.g. goodness, rightness, justice) with a natural property (e.g. happiness, growth of knowledge, rationality). I am not much impressed by this concern and will deal with it only briefly later. (For more discussion, see Evers and Lakomski, 1991, pp. 169–72.) The second I regard as rather more serious. Once rationality is thought to have normative force, it needs to be more than a matter of just having a consistent preference structure. The expectations that feed into the construction of utility functions as assigned probabilities – our estimates of the likelihood of expected events occurring – need to be warranted. Without warrant, ignorance compromises the assumption of rationality. However, meeting this demand now reintroduces the same cognitive load problem about computing causal consequences of actions performed in complex social contexts as that which attended classical utilitarianism.

Not surprisingly, the demands of moral leadership require a certain amount of cognitive elitism, drawing on skills of situation analysis, a grasp of the causal workings of complex social scenes, a well structured set of preferences, and a knack for calculation. Given that a technical result due to Kenneth Arrow means that there is no rational way for aggregating individual judgments of utility into a function that maximizes collective well being, elitism, on this view, is essential since someone's preferences must prevail in the collective (see Arrow, 1963; Evers and Lakomski, 1996, pp. 154–64).

The other major tradition in moral reasoning, after varieties of utilitarianism, is Kantianism. Broadly speaking, on this approach particular moral precepts are evaluated is the light of some general canon, or canons, of rationality. Perhaps the best known modern example is John Rawls's (1971) attempt to demonstrate what principles of justice would be chosen by persons acting rationally under conditions of impartiality. The argument is based around a thought experiment where people, unaware of what position they would occupy in a society, reason about what principles of justice should regulate their social life. I do not want to go into any detail about the theory, but I do want to indicate a consequence for practical application when it comes to moral guidance. Once impartiality is construed as requiring ignorance of organizational or social detail, the deduction of principles becomes a very abstract and intellectually demanding task. Moreover, we end up with linguistically expressed principles of a fairly high level of generality, sufficiently so to cause a version of the generality problem afflicting moral codes to break out. But once we attempt to ease the cognitive burden by plugging in familiar social detail, the impartiality that is a presumed condition of valid reasoning about circumstances that includes oneself is compromised. The resulting Kantian moral leader is stereotypically familiar: highly rational in defence of principles, and affecting a detachment irrespective of the pattern of disbursement of their material consequences.

In dealing with ethical guidance from theories of moral reasoning, the worry is not primarily about a lapse in coherence between the ethical component and the theory of leadership required to implement it. The worry is that the demands of implementation expose weaknesses in the psychological plausibility of both bodies of theory. For unfortunately, several serious problems attend the predominantly linguistic-computational view of cognition that underwrites much thinking about moral knowledge. First, the organ that does the computation, for example, adjudicating the relative probabilities of alternative expectations, attaching weighted preferences to each and multiplying out the matrix of results, is not a computer but a brain whose processes of decision-making are known to be quite different in operation (see Evers, 1998, for an overview). Second, in most cases of decision-making, or what might be classified as intelligent action, there are no symbolic structures on which to operate. For the countless acts of judgment that are performed every day, people classify, sort, prioritize, adjudicate and recommend without the benefit of any language-like theory formulation of the issues at hand. Much of this cognitive activity is better seen as a species of pattern processing; for example, of processing visual representations of complex scenes associated with work or interpersonal matters. Indeed, most knowledge to do with skilled practice does not exist in the form of language-like representations. Third, although computational models of cognition devote attention to the sequential ordering of processes, they give no detailed consideration to real time processing and its consequences for decision. The psychology of deliberation is replaced with the logic of calculation. Unfortunately, the replacement is not without loss. For example, we know that deliberation time affects decision outcomes. We also know that non-equivalent descriptions of the same outcomes can affect rankings of values. Fourth, computationalism's focus on logical and quasi-logical relations among symbolic representations fails to mesh with the most developed accounts of cognition in terms of the causal machinery of human learning and information processing. But for computationalism to be an account of human cognition some rapprochement is called for. Finally, computational models lack links with epistemology, with accounts of how knowledge is built up. Yet without these links, their capacity to offer justifications of posited expectations is compromised.

Meeting these difficulties, especially for practical knowledge in general, and ethical knowledge in particular requires, in my view, an account of knowledge representation that coheres with a naturalistic view of cognition as neural information processing. This will be an account for which the primary elements of cognition will be non-symbolic. I shall sketch such an approach in the context of the sort of practical knowledge assumed for leadership.

Non-Linguistic Representations of Knowledge

How is knowledge built up through experience to the point where it results in skilled performance across a wide range of circumstances? Take the case of a school principal who has to make regular judgments about admitting children with special needs into a mainstream school environment. In common with most practical problems, it is not possible to formulate a decision rule of the form: 'admit student X when conditions C obtain'. The issue is really a cluster of ethical, social, interpersonal, resource and policy considerations with a smooth continuum of relevant factors falling between a decision to admit or to refuse. No symbolic theory formulation is ever likely to be helpful in deriving a conclusion and none is ever used in real time practice. Yet after what are agreed to have been a series of decisions of mixed success, learning has occurred, with subsequent admission decisions being regarded as mostly right, or appropriate. How has learning from experience occurred?

One general schema that draws on recent developments in cognitive science runs as follows. A person brings to experience some prior set of dispositions that provide an initial set of classifications, or similarities, and saliences. These serve to group the passing show into kinds that elicit responses in turn subject to interpreted feedback that leads to a change in our initial stock of knowledge. We learn to recognize socially important kinds, for example, people that are helpful, or competent, or even good. In organizational settings we might classify staff into those easy to work with, innovative, task oriented or difficult. We would include in the way we extract patterns from experience, observable clues to the existence of these social kinds, so that we might more efficiently recognize them in the future. Learning occurs over time when the accumulating knowledge, or map by which we steer or navigate our way around the world, results in an increasing, non-random, chance of success relative to particular tasks.

Over the last 10 years it has become possible to use mathematical models of brain functioning – called artificial neural networks – to give a more precise causal model of non-symbolic learning from experience and how that knowledge might be represented in the brain. Figure 5.1 is an example of a simple neural network and an account of how it learns and represents knowledge:

Figure 5.1   A three-layer net with some connections shown. Each connection has an associated weight for changing the signal transmitted from one layer to the next.

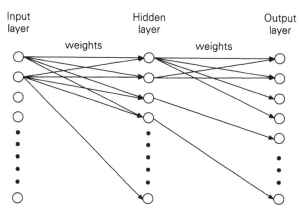

This network consists of three layers of nodes, or artificial neurons. The first is an input layer, the last an output layer, and the one in the middle is called a hidden layer. Each node in earlier layers is connected to every node in the next layer. As a signal from an input node is transmitted to the next layer, it is multiplied by a weight, usually a number between +1 and −1. At first these weights, which represent the synaptic junctions between neurons, are set at random, but they are gradually adjusted as the network learns some task. In a feedforward backpropagation network, the input signal moves in one direction through the network to the output layer. Learning occurs when the net's output converges on some target output. A mismatch indicates an error that has been caused by the numerical value of the weights. An adjustment to weights, in proportion to their contribution to the error, is then transmitted back through the net in a process known as error correction by backpropagation. As input and target output pairs of patterns, or vectors, are presented over and over again, in an appropriately designed network the output vector will almost always converge on the target output. The net has then learned all the pairs in the data set. The knowledge that has been acquired is distributed across the whole network, residing in the configuration and value of all the weights (Evers, 1997, p. 175).

Applying this model to the earlier decision task of admissions procedures would result in the following portrayal of learning. An initial typology of relevant features, for example, type of impairment, level of support required, available resources, distance from school, availability of alternatives, etc. would function as the input nodes, with some judgment of degree of presence serving as the values making up the input vector. The target output could be just a two-value vector indicating either a satisfactory or unsatisfactory outcome. Multiple experiences, where the principal learns what degree of features are associated with successful and unsuccessful outcomes produces an appropriate set of weights for classifying input vectors into two prototypes for admission – those features of admitted students that make for successful integration and those that do not.

There is no expectation that the graded nature of classification by similarity to learned prototype, easily represented by the non-linear mathematics of the net and its operation, can be captured by a linguistically expressed formulation. The principal's competence is not to be found in any linguistically formulated decision rule that the principal is able to express. From this portrayal of learning from experience there is no such rule. Rather, competence is a matter of efficient learning and resulting good judgment in the contexts at hand. There is no essence, or even a law-like generalization about success in admissions practice and this is true for the vast bulk of practical judgments and decision tasks that are made every day. Generalizing a bit, we can make the same point about the constellation of dispositions that make up a practical skill like leadership. Exhibited under many circumstances, with many outcomes, and subject to the interpretations and behaviours of many participants, the conditions under which we would learn to identify and classify acts as instances of leadership are most likely to reflect all the features associated with learning from experience. Through a process of mutual adjustment of expectation and performance perhaps funded initially from everyday commonsense conceptions embedded in the learning of language, we build up a leadership prototype, though one located within the circumstances of experience. Under these conditions, the quest for even a set of common characteristics, is most likely a forlorn quest, as reasonable as supposing in advance of inquiry that Gandhi, Thatcher, Stalin, or Boutros Ghali must have some special feature in common. It is simply an open question whether the prototypes developed through experience in one context are useful in other contexts – a matter for further experience.

As an interesting corollary to the above reflections, note that on this view of practical knowledge, many of the generic functional concepts of administrative theory outrun the available cognitive evidence for their successful implementation. So leadership that is expected to produce large scale social change contrary to the normal operation of major institutions will probably require a prototype of power instantiated in the minds of a followership that lies well and truly beyond the local and particular orbit of experience of successful piecemeal change. Experience is more able to fund a practical notion of effective action than a generic notion of power (Robinson, 1994). Of course, generic theories of power do exist in symbolic form, but these are often accessible only to elites, with the usual political risks of vanguardism and the social production of new hierarchies.

Representing Ethical Knowledge

When it comes to ethical knowledge, the chief point I want to make is that it is acquired in the same way as other practical knowledge – mainly through learning from experience in complex, shifting context-bound circumstances. That is, categories of moral appraisal are prototypical patterns extracted from experience through the epistemic practice of learning. To develop an account of ethical knowledge that coheres with a naturalistic view of moral agents, and which counts ethics on a par with any other knowledge that is acquired and validated through the usual processes of learning, one needs to address the still lingering influence of the so-called 'naturalistic fallacy'.

Naturalism in ethics involves two main components (Flanagan, 1996, pp. 193–94). The first is a descriptive-genealogical component, concerned with describing our moral dispositions, their origins, and their operation in deliberation. Moral psychology is part of this domain, as are sociology and history. There is little controversial about the project of a naturalized ethics in this first sense. There is, however, deep controversy about naturalizing ethics in a normative sense. For here additional claims need to be made and defended, not about further information on how we arrived at the moral judgments we make, but whether these moral judgments are good or bad – whether they are normatively appropriate. That is, when all the facts are in concerning the totality of our moral behaviours, when the descriptive-genealogical story has been completely told, there still remains the question of whether these behaviours are ethical, and giving a naturalistic account of this normative component is claimed by some to be in principle impossible because any naturalistic reduction of ethics looks like it will commit the naturalistic fallacy.

First formulated by the Cambridge philosopher G.E. Moore in 1903, the assertion of a fallacy turns on an argument that no adequate naturalistic definition of 'good' can be given. For to any purported definition, such as 'good is that which promotes the greatest happiness for the greatest number', Moore thought that one could always meaningfully ask the question, 'But is that a sound definition?' His point was that a definition which accurately captured the essence of a thing was a necessary truth and could not meaningfully be questioned. Other examples of the open question argument would be the alleged meaninglessness of the question, 'Do the angles of a triangle really add to 180 degrees?' – a question that is, incidentally, entirely reasonable in non-Euclidean geometry – or perhaps the question, 'But are humans really rational animals?' The second example shows just how sensitive the open question argument is to background assumptions about what is supposed to be meaningless. Nowadays, having feathers would function as a more serious ground for one's disqualification from humanity than being irrational. My point is that unless some independent reason can be given for defending intuitions about what is a meaningful definition of some ethical term, the assertion of a naturalistic fallacy just begs the question against naturalistic candidates.

The candidate I favour links the development of ethical knowledge to what I take to be a set of defensible epistemic practices – practices that over the medium-to-long run do better than chance in leading to reliable knowledge. The naturalistic philosopher, Paul Churchland, deals with this issue in a particularly insightful way:

> When such powerful learning networks as humans are confronted with the problem of how best to perceive the social world, and how best to conduct one's affairs within it, we have equally good reason to expect that the learning process will show an integrity comparable to that shown on other learning tasks, and will produce cognitive achievements as robust as those produced anywhere else. This expectation will be especially apt if, as in the case of 'scientific' knowledge, the learning process is collective and the results are transmitted from generation to

generation. In that case we have a continuing society under constant pressure to refine its categories of social and moral perception, and to modify its typical responses and expectations. (1989, pp. 301–2)

What Churchland has in mind as an account of social and moral learning is the neural network story, with children building up their social and moral categories from infancy onwards, through a naturalistic process of coherently matching feed-forward expectations against feedback from outcomes to produce a socially useful fit. The reason this process can be regarded as normative rather than merely descriptive is because it involves a critical dimension that makes it more than mere socialization (see also Churchland, 1995, pp. 123–50).

In Owen Flanagan's terms . . .

> Social experience provides feedback about how we are doing, and rational mechanisms come into play in evaluating and assessing this feedback. So there is an aim, activity to achieve this aim, feedback about success in achieving the aim, and rational mechanisms designed to assess the meaning of the feedback and to make modifications accordingly. (1996, pp. 206–7)

This puts the case for ethical naturalism squarely where it belongs: in the company of a naturalistic tradition that links the growth of ethical knowledge with a defence of the possibility of good epistemic practice for all knowledge. On the view of natural knowledge representation as a geometric configuration of distributed weights, the quest for universal moral rules or context-free moral generalizations, is misguided, more an artifact of linguistic representations than a reflection of the myriad of details that go into the critical development of a learned moral prototype.

Ethical Leadership

From the vantage point of the new cognitive science, the link between leadership and ethics in administrative contexts can be characterized roughly as follows. It is doubtful if the successful solution of diverse human problems can be explained by their possessing some essence, or even some feature that they all have in common. 'Advancing human flourishing' is the usual formulation, but it is as normatively useful as a guide to practice as 'doing good and avoiding evil' is. These are linguistic formulations which take their place in the construction of rules where in fact little or no rule following occurs. People merely behave, most of the time, *as if* they are following rules. The conditions circumscribing the development of ethical prototypes are diffuse and fragmented. However, a condition of their acceptability is that they are the product of progressive epistemic practices – practices that reduce the randomness of our response to the passing show of experience and increase the amount of information in the coherent global map by which we navigate our way through the option spaces of social life. Moral leadership in the contexts of organizational life is therefore a matter of securing the social conditions of effective learning in these contexts. As Dewey and others have seen, the conditions for the growth of knowledge involve an ethical infrastructure. That is, knowledge, including moral knowledge, develops more efficiently under some ethical arrangements than others. Nor are these arrangements surprising or novel. The progressive application of feedback against bias and error requires freedom of speech, tolerance of opinion and respect for persons and their right to participate in the growth of knowledge. There is also a host of more derivative imperatives, expressible in the broad-brush strokes of language.

This point at which the theory of leadership and the theory of ethics converge, namely over the question ·of how to solve the epistemic problem, or how best to arrange matters so as to successfully navigate the complexities and uncertainties of social and organizational life, suggests useful possibilities for the theoretical development of each. Earlier, I claimed that people may build up prototypes of leadership through the sifting of examples in shifting contexts. However, where leadership involves an ethical dimension, an unrealistic cognitive load can accrue to the leader under some of these prototypes. Ironically, the usual way in which cognitive load is diminished for individual cognizers is by the adoption of organizational structures that enhance learning through the processes of distributed cognition (Lakomski and Evers, in press). In keeping with this strategy, the acquisition of moral knowledge as well as much other knowledge relevant to decision-making within the complex uncertainties of organizations, will benefit from the adoption of a more distributed model of leadership committed to organizational learning. The ethics thus acquired can be applied recursively to the problem of what ethical arrangements among people in social life can best provide for more ethical and other learning. In this way, a view of ethical leadership can also have moral value.

References

ARROW, K. (1963) *Social Choice and Individual Values*, New York: Wiley.
CHURCHLAND, P.M. (1989) *A Neurocomputational Perspective*, Cambridge, MA: MIT Press.
CHURCHLAND, P.M. (1995) *The Engine of Reason, the Seat of the Soul*, Cambridge, MA: MIT Press.
EVERS, C.W. (1997) 'Philosophy of education: A naturalistic perspective', in ASPIN, D.N. (ed.) *Logical Empiricism and Post-empiricism in Educational Discourse*, Johannesburg: Heinemann, pp. 167–81.
EVERS, C.W. (1998) 'Decision-making, models of mind, and the new cognitive science', *Journal of School Leadership*, **8**, 2, pp. 94–108.
EVERS, C.W. and LAKOMSKI, G. (1991) *Knowing Educational Administration*, Oxford: Pergamon Press.
EVERS, C.W. and LAKOMSKI, G. (1996) *Exploring Educational Administration*, Oxford: Pergamon Press.
FLANAGAN, O. (1996) 'The moral network', in MCCAULEY, R.N. (ed.) *The Churchlands and their Critics*, Oxford: Blackwell.
FOSTER, W. (1985) *Paradigms and Promises*, New York: Prometheus Books.
HODGKINSON, C. (1991) *Educational Leadership: The Moral Art*, Albany, NY: SUNY Press.

LAKOMSKI, G. and EVERS, C.W. (in press) 'Values, socially distributed cognition, and organizational practice', in BEGLEY, P. (ed.) *Values and Educational Leadership*, Albany, NY: SUNY Press.

LEITHWOOD, K., TOMLINSON, D. and GENGE, M. (1996) 'Transformational school leadership', in LEITHWOOD, K., CHAPMAN, J., CORSON, D., HALLINGER, P. and HART, A. (eds) *International Handbook of Educational Leadership and Administration*, Dordrecht: Kluwer.

NEWELL, A. and SIMON, H.A. (1976) 'Computer science as empirical enquiry: Symbols and search.' Cited as reprinted in BODEN, M.A. (ed.) *The Philosophy of Artificial Intelligence*, Oxford: Oxford University Press.

RAWLS, J. (1971) *A Theory of Justice*, Cambridge, MA: Harvard University Press.

ROBINSON, V.M.J. (1994) 'The practical promise of critical research in educational administration', *Educational Administration Quarterly*, **30**, 1, pp. 56–76.

SIMON, H.A. (1976) *Administrative Behavior*, 3rd edn, New York: Free Press.

SMALL, R. (1998) 'Towards an unprincipled ethics of educational research', *Australian Journal of Education*, **42**, 1, pp. 103–15.

WONG, K.C. (1996) 'Preparing educational leaders in moral education: A reflection on traditional Chinese leadership thinking.' Paper presented to APEC Educational Leadership Centres, Chiang Mai, Thailand.

Part II

Research on Values and Valuation Processes

6   Inhibitors to Collaboration

Pauline E. Leonard

Belief in the power and wisdom of school collaboration over working in isolation is widespread (da Costa and Riordan, 1996; DiPardo, 1996; Fullan and Hargreaves, 1991; Rottier, 1996). Collaboration is the cornerstone of many educational reforms including school restructuring, site-based management, school councils, shared decision-making, and team teaching (da Costa and Riordan, 1996). Collaborative practice in schools is said to occur when teachers and administrators work together, share their knowledge, contribute ideas and develop plans for the purpose of achieving educational and organizational goals (Cavanagh and Dellar, 1996). Increasingly, however, there is recognition that the mere presence of collaborative structures, while important, does not guarantee that a *culture* of collaboration exists (Fullan and Hargreaves, 1991, p. 52). If collaboration does not rest solely on a school's infrastructure being designed for team interaction and participative decision-making, then what else might facilitate collaborative practice? A difficult question to answer, for while much is written about the problems of teacher isolation (DiPardo, 1996), little is known about 'what happens when teachers work closely together' (p. 110).

Perhaps good advice for administrators who wish to facilitate the collaborative process is to 'look for the candidate's ability to function on a team' (Rottier, 1996, p. 31). However, if little is known about what makes for successful collaboration, then it may be a challenge to recognize good collaborators. What *is* known is that teachers need to 'actively create themselves in ways that connect to and communicate with their colleagues' (Hargreaves, 1994, p. 18) in the interest of 'build[ing] equally and mutually beneficial relationships' (Knop, LeMaster, Norris, Raudensky and Tannehill, 1997). Further, it is believed that leaders interested in creating learning organizations (Leithwood, 1996) should promote 'a professional culture which encourages considerable collaboration among staffs' (p. 20). The contention is that, while it may be worthwhile to recruit teachers who subscribe to collaborative values, it is also imperative to understand the collaborative process in order to recognize conditions that may either contribute to, or inhibit, the manifestation of these values. The optimistic implication is that, with increased understanding of the collaborative process, teachers and administrators can *learn* to be good collaborators.

In pursuit of this goal – to better understand the collaborative process – the purpose of this work is to report one urban multicultural elementary school's experience with the adoption and implementation of collaborative structures in the form of team teaching and committees. The report consists of an examination of the interactions of teachers and administrators working within these collaborative structures, and an analysis of the values and conflicts that emerged as significant for understanding the collaborative process. Also included is a discussion of the conditions that appeared to inhibit the manifestation of collaborative value practice. In alliance with the purpose of this chapter, the study adds insight into the collaborative process; its conclusions may have significant implications for educational administrators who wish to promote an authentic collaborative school culture.

Values as a Way to Explore Collaboration

Values figure highly in the life and interactions of educational stakeholders (Beck, 1996; Begley, 1996; Campbell-Evans, 1993; Greenfield, 1986; Hodgkinson, 1996; Roche, 1997) and they are manifested in both tangible and intangible ways (Caldwell and Spinks, 1992; Schein, 1990). In order to etch a clearer picture of how to arrive at a *culture* of collaboration, we need to look beyond the more readily observable organizational structures of committees and teams and past the observable artifacts manifested in policies, espoused philosophies and rituals. A better understanding of collaborative cultures requires a search for and examination of the intangible, underlying values that come into play when individuals work together.

Within a given culture, values may be shared (Schein, 1984; 1990) or contested (Erickson, 1987; Hargreaves, Earl and Ryan, 1996), creating a multitude of choices and impacting greatly on decision making. Consequently, in the process of collaboration, negotiating, compromising and mediating between competing values become 'essential skills' (Campbell-Evans, 1993, p. 98) for administrators who do not wish to impose values. Exploring significant values and value conflicts as they emerge when a group of people are engaged in teaming relationships and interactions on committees can contribute to our understanding of the collaborative process. Understanding how to facilitate the *process* of collaboration means understanding the role of values in school organizations and understanding how to promote a culture where values may be negotiated.

A Multi-perspective Research Design

This research was a qualitative, instrumental (Stake, 1994) case study in the sense that a particular case (i.e., the multicultural school) was examined to provide insight into an issue (i.e., collaboration). Pseudonyms are used for the school and all participants.

Sample

A purposive sampling procedure was used to select one multicultural urban elementary school as the focus of this study. A muticultural school setting was chosen in anticipation that it would be a rich source of data related to gaining insight into patterns and variations in value orientations. Hillside Elementary School was one of approximately 130 other schools in a large Canadian metropolitan school district. It had an enrolment of approximately 600 students in grades JK–6 and there were approximately 40 teaching staff including 25 classroom teachers, the principal and vice principal, and various specialists positions (i.e., computer, French, resource, reading recovery, music). Of the 40, there were 32 females and 8 males. Overall, 90 per cent of the staff had been born in Canada. By contrast, the student population was highly diverse in that approximately 87 per cent of either, or both of, the students and their parents had immigrated to Canada. There were 48 countries and 33 languages represented in the school's student population.

The research focused on eight individuals working as members of three teams: Primary Division Team, Junior Division Team, and Administrative Team. The Primary Division Team consisted of three female teachers, Bernie, Gail and Mavis, and one male teacher, Ted. These teachers had from seven to twenty years of teaching experience, with most or all of it having been in their current school district. However, each of these four teachers was new to Hillside Elementary School. The Junior Division Team was comprised of two female teachers, Ester and Louise. Ester had spent approximately seven years teaching, all at Hillside. However, she had held several different assignments during this time. Louise had spent three years at Hillside and four years elsewhere in the District. Both teachers had elected to work together as a team. The Administration Team included one male principal and one female vice principal. Mark Butler was into his second year as principal at Hillside Elementary School. He had over 20 years experience both as a teacher and as an administrator and teacher in other multicultural schools with the board. The vice principal, Karen Brown, was also new to the school, having been in her current position only four months at the start of this research. She had experience teaching in other schools in the district and also had experience as a District program consultant.

Procedures for Collecting Data

During a five-week study at the school, I spent two full weeks with each of the two teacher teams. During the process of participatory observation, the interactions of Hillside's teachers, students, visiting and volunteer parents, and administrators in the school were observed. As the investigation unfolded, I interviewed five additional teachers, two parents, four specialists and the two administrators. Guiding and emergent questions characterized the semi-structured interviews. Furthermore, unscheduled and informal discussions with various members of the organization occurred throughout the research. Informal and formal documents, school rituals and ceremonies were also observed, recorded and analyzed.

Findings

This section of the findings presents a summary of the overall perceptions of the two collaborative initiatives (i.e. team teaching and committee work) at Hillside

Elementary. The following section addresses the values that emerged as significant to the collaborative process.

Overall Perceptions of Team Teaching

Principal Butler was a firm believer in team teaching for many reasons, one of which was because he saw it as a means to enrich the educational program through teachers sharing their ideas and pooling their strengths. As he put it, 'If you're good at mathematics and I'm good at music, I don't think I should necessarily do your music, but I should certainly help you.' The staff handbook provided a clear outline of why teaming was important:

- often a sense of loneliness prevails in a self-contained classroom when a teacher lacks stimulating contact with another teacher;
- team teaching breaks down the walls of instructional isolation and invites the capabilities and efforts of several teachers to focus on common instructional concerns;
- teaming is not a curriculum but a process to present curriculum which demands co-operation.

Team teaching was not something that just happened when teachers were put together but required commitment and planning:

- teams are expected to hold weekly planning meetings and share a common budget;
- an effective team member: puts forth vigorous effort and encourages others to join in; gets the group back on track when they wander; clarifies problems or issues when members are unclear; confronts ideas and individuals (e.g. 'I don't agree with you – here's why'); summarizes from time to time 'Here is where we are now'.

Principal Butler felt that the teaching teams varied in terms of how well they were collaborating:

> I see very few [teachers] who don't have the best interests of the children at heart [but] right now I don't see a lot of teams functioning too well. Probably the grade —s have the strongest team situation. Grade —s do some of it but not a lot. They had come in gung-ho this year. They did so much planning ahead of time before they had the children, and when the children came they said, 'This isn't going to work.' And that is a struggle that they are trying to skirt around rather than deal with.

The principal was quite right in his estimation that team teaching was not functioning uniformly throughout the school. In my discussions with various teachers in the school there were varied opinions as to the benefits of teaming. One teacher who was a member of a four-teacher Junior Division team demonstrated mixed feelings about it: 'Oh, don't talk to me about team teaching. Decision-making gets centralized. You lose your autonomy to a certain extent. However, you also get to share your ideas, so the program becomes enriched.'

Another teacher who was also a member of a Junior Division team explained why some teachers had difficulty with the collaboration required in team teaching:

> For them, some have to sit, explain and listen. It can be boring and time consuming. The decision-making process is complex. You have to be sure that people are happy with the decision. As long as people buy into the system they are willing to make the time commitment and concessions. I wanted to be a part of a team. However, some people were already here and were forced to be on a team. Therefore, they may not be happy with giving the amount of time and effort that team teaching requires – having to check with other people, the ramifications of their decisions for other people, and so on.

There were three discernible responses by individuals in the school to team teaching: a) One response was enthusiasm, nourished by a firm belief that this was the best instructional process, a belief which was also borne out in terms of the overall personal and professional benefits; b) Another response was a belief that there are advantages and disadvantages to team teaching, and an appreciation that it places added demands on teachers; and c) Finally, some individuals manifested ambivalence toward the benefits of team teaching for students and teachers.

Whereas the Primary Division Team teachers felt that team teaching had benefits for teachers and students, they felt that the amount of collaboration required put considerable demands on teachers, particularly when the team was comprised of more than two teachers. As Gail stated, 'I think it's the absolutely best way to teach but we've all agreed that three is too many and four is not workable. The only way you could do it is if there were two and two and then you brought together the two pairs into a foursome.'

Mavis expressed a similar position when she stated that team teaching was 'great in a lot of ways but when there are four teachers there are just too many'. She added that when she had team taught before she and the teacher had been 'in sync', whereas now there were so many of them that the 'co-ordination takes over your life'.

Bernie added further insight into how the planning and coordinating that went into team teaching could become a lengthy process. 'Down side, you have to spend too much time planning and someone like me who talks and thinks everything so much, I drive them crazy, you know, meetings have to go too long. And for me, the opposite drives me crazy. I find it really hard to make a flip decision.'

One member of the Junior Division team, Ester, felt very comfortable with the way she and Louise collaborated. She suggested that one of the reasons they worked so well together was because there were only two of them. Technically, there were four teachers on the team, however the other two members were not in close proximity to Ester and Louise. Therefore, they did not collaborate as a foursome on a daily basis. She explained why she felt it would have been more difficult had they been functioning as a team of four:

> I've been in a group of four on a daily basis and it's just tough getting all, I mean, you spend 90 per cent of the time just making sure everybody knows what's going on and at times somebody forgets to tell somebody something and it gets confusing. I think a team of two or three works better.

Ester went on to say that when you get a couple of people who work really well together 'they can almost read each other's thoughts'.

Louise concurred with Ester's views on why they collaborated so well as a team:

> I think because Ester and I are basically in here and the two others are out in the portables, if it's a matter of classroom expectations or behaviour, we're not directly affected [in terms of the four teachers]. Ester and I do have to agree on things and we really do ... Sometimes we over react and sometimes we under react. But I think on the whole we're pretty good about keeping on an even keel with one another, and I think it's working pretty well.

Overall, Ester felt that teaming was worthwhile but she was not blind to the amount of collaboration that it required to work well, even with just two teachers on a team:

> When you're working with 50 kids as opposed to 25 that's 50 parents that you need to communicate with so we both have to sit in on the interviews and be there at report card and interview time. Sometimes there's a lot more organization and it's a little more difficult to coordinate it all, so that can be another area of frustration. But I find that for the most part that it's very rewarding.

Overall Perceptions of Committee Structure

The second form of collaboration manifested itself through the committee structure. According to the school handbook, the following committees were in place: Literacy, Math, Technology, Arts, Sports, Life Skills, Environmental Studies, Social and School. Vice-principal Brown explained how the committee structure allowed teachers to collaboratively manage, plan and share the workload for a more efficient school:

> The committees are a structure for the teacher and they sort of run the full range from academic to social. What it does is it's really helpful to manage all the stuff that comes in the school that needs to be managed or planned for, and so professional development for teachers can be planned out of that. And it really distributes the workload. And actually it's wonderful to have a school where you have enough people to do that kind of thing because all of that comes into a smaller school but you don't have the opportunities to manage it as efficiently.

One teacher stated that the previous year a few teachers were doing 'all the work' and so the conveners approached the principal and vice principal to suggest setting up committees. The teacher added, 'Now, everyone has to be on two committees.' Teachers were permitted to choose the two committees on which they wanted to serve.

Many teachers had mixed feelings about the effectiveness of the committee structure. Several teachers expressed dismay about the workload and others were frustrated with the rigidity of the committee structure. There was no room for the kind of spontaneity and creativity that usually comes out of teachers doing things purely out of interest throughout the year.

As a member of the Primary Division Team, Gail had strong misgivings about the effectiveness of the committees in terms of helping teachers become more collaborative as a staff:

> I don't like it at all. I don't think what Mark [the principal] wanted to address, he's not addressing, which is people that never do anything. And so he's trying to force everybody, trying to mandate committee work and I just find that you end up, the end result is exactly the same as every school everyone's worked in. Even though they're on a committee, that doesn't mean that when a job comes up they're going to be the ones to do it. And I find that the committees are so big – I mean there are 43 people on staff so every committee has about 8 or 9 people. So it's still pretty big. You can still be anonymous and still shirk all your responsibility and I find that there's always a small group of people that are go-getters that do everything and I don't find that any different here.

Gail felt that instead of having organized committees whereby the same few people did all the work, the principal should step in and say, 'You know, I want to see different people running this project'. However, she also suggested that this was unlikely to happen given the principal's view that teachers, via committees, should fully participate in the decision making process.

A Junior Division Team member, Louise was aware that there were variations in attitudes towards the committee structure and that some teachers were 'grumbling' because they were busier this year with running meetings. However, she explained that it was the first year for trying it, and she felt that as they worked through it they would come to realize that it was only certain times of the year that certain committees would be busy. She explained it this way:

> For example, the school committee, its busy time is in June when they have to make all the decisions for the following year, when all the dates will be and how many kids will be in each classroom and which teachers will teach those classes. But I'm on the Arts committee right now and it's kept me very busy, especially right now with this upcoming concert. I'm trying to change artwork and all the rest of it, and again, I'm doing auditions for next year's performance. But, you know, it'll quiet down after the performance is over and then we'll get back into it and when it's time for the spring concert again, it'll be busy.

Louise felt that it was a very equitable way of getting teachers to work collaboratively. Just going through the experience, she stated, would help them learn and perhaps next year there might be some changes made. 'I think what we need to look at is what committees are the very busy committees and what committees are not and try and get everybody on one committee that's not as hectic and one committee that does have a lot of work to sort of even it out.'

Collaborative Values

The previous section demonstrates that, although there were tangible manifestations of a collaborative culture in the form of teaming, committees and in policy handbooks, there was considerable variation in commitment to the collaborative process. Moreover, there were many reports of conflict in the values that emerged as significant in the implementation of team teaching and the committees. The following includes an examination of these values.

Collegiality.   Collegiality has been described as interaction between individuals where the interrelationships are characterized by honesty, trust, rapport and respect, a willingness to participate in group activities and a collegial bonding (Cavanagh and Dellar, 1996; Hargreaves, 1994; Lieberman, 1988). Inasmuch as collegiality involves teachers interacting with one another in a relationship built on respect, it may be said that Hillside Elementary School had a collegial staff. However, there were reports of strained relationships among some members of some of the teams and committees.

Principal Butler felt that a collaborative environment required positive interpersonal relationships among those involved. There were plenty of opportunities for informal interaction and bonding within teams; however, this was not necessarily the case for the staff as a whole. There were far fewer occasions whereby the *staff* met informally as a group. Whereas teachers and students used the staff room frequently during the day for educational activities, it was under-utilized as an informal gathering spot. To encourage socialization and group cohesion, the social committee had initiated a 'Friday Treat-day' whereby each week a different group of selected teachers would bring food to share with the entire staff at recess time. An announcement would be made each Friday inviting teachers to gather in the staff room. This was considered to be an opportunity that would foster the interpersonal relationships of teachers at Hillside.

Ester, a Junior Division Team teacher, spoke about the importance of staff-wide collegiality and believed that the committee structure contributed to it in that it provided a way to penetrate strong, self-sufficient teams. In other words, teachers were not stuck in their own little group because 'you had to go out and interact with other segments and everybody has to be on two committees and you're responsible for reporting back'.

There were indications that the Primary Division Team teachers interacted in terms of sharing resources and working together each day to prepare for class.

Nevertheless, by their own admission, things did not always run smoothly. They were not 'in sync'. Bernie, Mavis and Gail, in particular, expressed concern over the difficulty of working with four teachers and planning for four large groups of students. There were also expressions of concern over the underlying dynamics that characterized this kind of social relationship. These teachers described how they felt they had to be careful not to offend others on the team by inadvertently excluding someone from the conversation. One teacher reported feelings of self-reproach for forgetting to share a teaching idea with another after the teacher observed the idea being carried out.

Compatibility.   Vice-principal Brown stated that teacher compatibility facilitated the collaboration process, particularly in teaming situations. She felt that it was important for members of a team to share a 'philosophy about children and how [they] teach children and how [they] discipline'. There needed to be 'compatibility because they can be very destructive if somebody is really heavy-handed and somebody else wants to know what caused that, [and wants] to look at it in the larger scheme of what to do with something like that'. As Vice-principal Brown put it, 'There's nothing worse than a dysfunctional team relationship where everybody's at odds all the time.' She felt that collegiality was fostered by shared beliefs about teaching, and therefore it was important to match team members in terms of these shared beliefs. The matching, according to the vice-principal, allowed the team to be stronger because 'when you've matched and you've chosen and you're solid then it's another level of team, like, it's really a meshed team in terms of thinking and beliefs and how you operate'.

   Louise, a member of the Junior Division Team, concurred with the vice-principal stating, 'You need to find someone you can click with.' She described an earlier teaming experience whereby she worked with individuals with whom she had not been happy to be working. Not that they were 'bad' teachers she claimed, but because their expectations and views were very different from her own they did not function successfully as a team.

Honesty and trust.   Principal Butler felt that 'honesty and trust' were important for collaboration to occur. One Primary Division Team member, Ted, also spoke about the value of honesty and trust for building a good teaming relationship. As he explained it:

> You have to have people that are comfortable coming up and saying, 'You know what, you made a heck of a lot of noise today. Is there any way we can work that out?' and realize that they're not knocking you for making noise because that's what you had to do – but work it out. That's part of the comfort level.

However, as already addressed, the Primary Division Team teachers experienced difficulty being open and honest. By one teacher's admission, the problem was exacerbated by the fact that these four teachers were new to the school and to their team. Also, at the beginning of the year there had been little contact with other teachers in the school and they felt pressure to 'make the team work'. During that time they had been inundated with concerns such as how to manage their many students, how to deal with behaviour problems, how to communicate with parents who could not speak English, and how to make the team work. The pressure of all of these concerns created a stressful situation that may have contributed to the challenge of building a trusting and honest team relationship.

On the other hand, the Junior Division Team teachers were very comfortable in their team relationship. Ester spoke about the importance of trust, explaining, 'There's a lot of communication that has to happen and trust that the person is communicating what they say they're communicating.' Both Ester and Louise felt that they could be honest with each other. However they also felt that since they had similar expectations for their students in terms of behaviour and academic outcomes, then this made it easier for them to be trustworthy and honest with each other.

Shared decision-making.   One teacher's perception of decision making at Hillside Elementary was that it was a democratic process:

> Well, I think we arrive at a consensus the way any group of 30 would, with a lot of difficulty and a lot of discussion. There will always be some people who go away disappointed at the outcome but we have to go on a democratic system. We like to . . . get all the ideas out, sort of an open forum, just to say what you feel and we tend to tabulate those and then they're brought to maybe a smaller committee to make the final decision. Those decisions are made, implemented, the school committee makes a decision, then they bring it back to staff for confirmation and if there's any concerns that are brought up at that point then we can modify the staff decision as a whole.

Several teachers in the school acknowledged that they were part of the decision-making process. They expressed satisfaction in that they had participated in the decisions about the composition of their teaching teams.

When asked how much input the staff had in decision making, Ester replied:

> Well, in some respects too much and in some too little. I feel there are too many meetings and too many discussions about the same thing. It's getting better this year, but last year the first seven staff and division meetings, one topic was repeated seven times. It was repeated because it hadn't been resolved or something changed or this group had said this and this group had said that.

Louise suggested that it was not necessary or efficient to spend so much time on matters that might remotely affect the teaching and learning process. However, there were issues in which she did want to have input so that she would have some sense of control over how things were done:

> Staffing for sure, where I'll be teaching, anything that has to do with the daily running of my classroom. But things to do with the buses or, who covers for

caretaking, or how much photocopy paper needs to be ordered, the mundane things, I don't want to be involved with. Anything that has to do with my teaching the kids, the kids themselves, or the organization of the school then I do think I want to be involved in that.

However, according to Louise, sharing in the decision-making presented 'the opportunity for people . . . to voice their opinions and their thoughts'. This process was an empowering one whereby teachers were able to take part in what went on at Hillside Elementary School.

Facilitative leadership. Many teachers at Hillside felt that the principal had the best interests of all at heart; however, *some* felt that he should be more direct. The Primary Division Team teachers felt that Mark should have been a little more direct in encouraging all teachers to collaborate and share the workload. Others suggested that, in matters where staff could not come to a consensus, the *principal* should make the decision. Otherwise, too much valuable time was wasted on meetings where some issues were repeated unnecessarily. This sometimes worked to the advantage of 'strong' teams or 'strong' individuals because individuals or groups would impose their values on others. One teacher gave the following example:

They [school committee] put up this big chart paper and 40 teachers went in with stickies and put up what they wanted or whatever and if you had a really strong team – not even team, team member – individuals who wouldn't budge and they wouldn't listen to you . . . It was very difficult and it was the end of last year and people were shutting down mentally and then this came up. It was really tooth and nail and it was difficult. We didn't get what we wanted [preparation periods] in the first place so we made some changes within ourselves.

Regarding this incident, still another teacher seemed to realize the grey area of shared decision-making stating, 'I would have liked it if the administration got more involved [but] they were trying to let us do the decision making which is excellent, but the frustration level was high on the staff'. However, there was little ambiguity surrounding this kind of situation for some:

I think there has to be a certain amount of very specific direction because many people want it and there's a few that need it . . . I think a lot of it should be structured. There should be specific directions. I fully expect them [administrators] to take some initiative and some direction or force direction. Those people are making $100,000. They are responsible for us. They are responsible for students.

These beliefs contrasted with Principal Butler's conception of his role as facilitator and not as one who is vested with power and control by virtue of his position. The principal believed that his primary role was to facilitate growth in teachers, and by extension, growth in students. He felt that it was a challenge to be a facilitative leader because staff members had different expectations about the role of principal:

And that's the struggle that I have with administration in that you have power simply by the position that you are in. And this staff still, I find it usually takes about three or four years before the staff learns to trust you enough so they can come and say, 'This is stupid. Why are we doing this?' Some of them are at that stage and some have worked with me before so they have no problems coming to me. But others think they've got to do it [serve on committees] because, and yet it [committee structure] wasn't a decision I made, it was a decision staff made. But that's the struggle that we go through.

Not all of the teachers at Hillside Elementary disagreed with Principal Butler's facilitative role:

Now with Mark, his approach is much more team based, much more team building going on. When I started I suggested we have a [particular] committee and no one had even thought of a committee. They never had committees before. Now we have committees for just about everything. So hopefully that sort of spreads the decision making amongst everybody and it also makes sure that everybody has an opportunity to be part of the decision making in some capacity.

Louise and Ester felt that Hillside Elementary's principal sought staff input and valued shared decision making. Louise described it this way:

I think for the most part Mark goes to the staff, asks their opinion, listens to the feedback from the conveners who are often sent out to find out how the staff feels. The conveners bring it back to him and then he sort of will make a decision. If we haven't been able to come to a decision ourselves often he has to make the decision. I think he very much wants it to be staff decisions, things that we have agreed to and, again, it's difficult to get 100 per cent agreement on anything.

Whereas Ester agreed with Louise that the principal believed in cultivating a collaborative relationship with staff and was committed to shared decision making, she felt that he should be more direct in the decision-making process. Ester felt the lengthy process that was involved in getting staff input on all decision making was time-consuming and nonproductive and, therefore, should be the responsibility of the principal:

Some of those little things, that's why Mark's here, make those decisions, inform me, that's fine. Other things, yes, maybe then I do want to have input. But that's a tough call. What I think I want input on, maybe somebody else doesn't care about. But there has to be, you have to draw that line and say, 'I'm the principal. I'll make a decision on this one' because otherwise you end up with way, way too much input. You can't get forty people to agree.

As Ester put it, 'They've been given the training and the job, so make the decision personally.' The principal should be guided by the question, 'Is this something you [I] need staff input on or is this something that I'll make the decision and inform them?'

Empowerment and accountability. Principal Butler suggested with shared decision making comes teacher empowerment. And with empowerment came accountability. Team teaching was one way in which teachers could be held accountable:

> Some of them [teachers] have never had to be accountable to anybody else for what they do. I think that they should be accountable because I'm not going to be in there all the time. Parents are not going to be in there all the time . . . A plus that comes out of teaming is that those who tend to sit back aren't allowed to do that.

It seemed that the principal's belief was that the more involved teachers became involved with each other, the more collaboration that went on, and the more teachers shared in the decision-making process, whether on a classroom team, or on a school committee, then the more likely teacher accountability for students' learning would be to each other and not to administration or some other external source.

One teacher held a similar view regarding the accountability aspect that was inherent in the structure of the committees at Hillside. That is, by its very nature, committees imposed accountability on teachers. This was considered to be important for those teachers who did not voluntarily accept the full responsibility that went with being a teacher:

> It's more structured here each year that I've been here. I'm a firm believer in that, because there's a great variation of commitment from next to zero to what do you want me to do next? Some people say they love their job and other people, it is a job and that's it. We have people on staff that are not here after the kids are allowed to leave and a couple of those do not even come in early in the morning but that's all, only a few. I think they need the recognition and I do think they need the structure.

Mentoring. Principal Butler saw teaming and collaboration as a means to fostering professional development through mentoring. The vice principal also suggested that teaming provided a built-in support system whereby teachers would have someone they could 'run things by' and get immediate 'feedback and input from somebody else [when dealing] with difficult students'. Interestingly, the team that the principal saw as being the one that was functioning 'best' in the school had described how they had learned from each other through their team teaching. One them stated:

> I found a real benefit in that this is my first year in a classroom and I felt like a first-year teacher coming into the classroom. I was really not sure exactly how grade Xs learn. I've never been full-time in the classroom and I found I learned so much and I don't think I could do that going into a classroom and being in a closed room. I don't think I would learn nearly as much.

A beginning teacher had similar views on the value of peer coaching in a teaming situation. She felt, 'seeing experienced teachers in action helps you know that you are on track'.

Both Ester and Louise saw the value of team teaching for learning from their peers. Ester's first teaching experience was in a team arrangement and she described the 'big, open area' where there were 'four or five of them, and I could see the different styles that they used and the different things that they tried'. Ester stated that she had done a lot of observation and remembered how she learned how to deal with various classroom situations:

> I wasn't overwhelmed with having my own class at the time which I think is tough for a new teacher to come in and get thrown into a new class and I had that whole year to see how teachers deal with certain types of kids, certain situations, the whole gambit, and I sort of felt confident that I could do it myself using some of the techniques that they did.

Louise described how teaming with Ester provided them with opportunities to learn from each other:

> Well, with my teaching partner and I, she has strengths in areas, for example, in the science area, that I don't have. That's not the stronger point of my program. My strength is in the arts and the drama, that side of it. It's almost like a professional development, I see the things that she's doing, she sees the things that I'm doing and then, if we're not teaching together next year, I'll remember when she did that. And so that's very nice.

Discussion: Inhibitors to Collaborative Value Practice

In examining the values that emerged as significant to the collaborative process in the implementation of team teaching and committees at Hillside Elementary School, certain conditions that appeared to inhibit commitment to these values emerged. The following is a discussion of these inhibitors.

Uncertain Sense of Teacher Efficacy: Inhibited the Development of Trustful and Honest Professional Relationships

Teacher efficacy is 'belief in the application of pedagogical principles and practices to effect changes in the development of children' (Cavanagh and Dellar, 1996, p. 19). Research shows (da Costa and Riordan, 1996) that teachers who have a strong sense of teaching efficacy are more likely to enter into trusting relationships with their colleagues. As earlier addressed, Ted (and others) suggested that a workable team teaching relationship was possible only if the teaming arrangement was built on honesty and trust. However, for some teachers exposing themselves on a daily basis was stressful. Bernie described one situation where, becoming frustrated with an inattentive student, she shouted at him. Whereas she did not think that made her a 'poor' teacher, she did suggest that if her colleagues saw this vulnerable side of her, they might judge her as such. Bernie wanted control over the image she projected to others, particularly to the administrators:

For me I want control over that image [of herself as a teacher]. It's not that I don't want anyone to know [that she lost her patience], but I want control over it in the sense that I want Mark [the principal] to know that I lose control. I want him to know that I do it and that it's not okay and I want to laugh about it with him because I want him to know me as a person and I want to build my trust with him and I know that you have to disclose these things. But I don't want him to catch me. Do you know what I mean? I want me to decide when I'm going to tell him. I want to know when I tell it I control that it's funny. I control who heard it.

Not only was Bernie reticent about displaying her self-perceived imperfections as a teacher to the principal, she had misgivings about presenting them to her team members as well:

I don't want Mavis [a team member] to know those things about me. I don't want her to know I yelled at Leon. I probably wouldn't tell those stories very often in front of her. And if I did I would probably be even more hilarious about it. Or stressing more how I know how bad it is – that's my *little* flaw.

Considering that Bernie worked on a daily basis in a teaming relationship with three other teachers, this type of stress would have been fairly constant in light of her admission that she wanted to *control* her image. Moreover, considering the principal's view that one of the benefits of teaming was that it placed accountability for each other in the hands of the teachers themselves, one's image could become very important, making it difficult for those with low self-confidence to be trusting and honest in their professional relationship with their colleagues.

Time Constraints: Inhibited Shared Decision Making and Collegiality

Ester believed that staff collegiality had deteriorated since she had first come to the school. There was a time when at '8:30 every morning you'd go down to the staff room and have coffee around the table'. And at recess time 'you would not miss going in there because there were so many jokesters'. She was quick to point out that this was not a negative reflection on the group of people that was there presently, because many of them still liked to joke around and were professional in their interactions with each other. But teachers did not voluntarily go to the staff room anymore. Ester was not sure why this was so, but believed that it might have been due to the increase in teachers on staff. She felt that with the larger group there were fewer opportunities for contact. In addition to the increased number of teachers, the workload had increased:

Even recess time, I mean, most of the teachers that I have been with are doing things at recess time. Like it's not the teaching part that's got any harder but it's all the documentation, the paper work, the requirements of things that have to be done and the things that the principal wants us to do, it's just growing and growing and growing so what do you cut, you cut your recess. You don't get a break in the day.

For three months Louise [her teaching partner] and I had one day where we've been able to sit down and have coffee together so we could sit and plan. Well we don't do that, we plan on the fly and it's a good thing that we think alike and have sort of the same ideas because you'd never get it to work.

There were indications from other teaching teams as well that there was never enough time to meet in the way that would allow them to plan and prepare in the manner necessary to achieve their goals.

Fragmented Vision: Inhibited the Development of Conceptions of Facilitative Leadership and Feelings of Empowerment

School principals who encourage the professional growth of colleagues, support the ideas of shared planning and decision making, and attempt to share power by encouraging teachers to exercise their professional judgment and accept responsibility for the educational and organizational goals of the school, are considered to be facilitators in the educational process (Cavanagh and Dellar, 1996). Principal Butler's goal as a principal was to be a facilitative leader so that teachers would collaborate in the pursuit of Hillside Elementary's goals. He felt that his role as facilitator would serve to empower teachers in the decision-making process. According to Cavanagh and Dellar (1996), teacher empowerment occurs when teachers *willingly* accept invitations to share in the planning, organizing and implementing processes that go into achieving educational and organizational goals. Teachers who feel empowered have some sense of sharing control over what takes place in the classroom and school.

However, it seemed that the teachers and administration did not all share this vision of collaboration. A clearly articulated vision is important for it 'guides decision making and problem solving so that situations are resolved in a way that is consistent with goals, priorities and direction of the school' (Campbell-Evans, 1993, p. 102). That the problem solving and decision making at Hillside was not consistent with the principal's vision of collaboration and teacher empowerment is clear. For example, not all of the teachers conveyed a sense of empowerment. Many did not agree on that they had input into the committee arrangement. Actually, it seems that many have been getting mixed messages with regards to serving on committees. The principal stated that teachers were not compelled to serve on two committees. However, as the following excerpt from the staff handbook shows, the expectation was clear:

- It is expected that all staff will share in extra curricular clubs, groups and curriculum responsibilities. Ideally each staff should be on two committees with a major (chair) and minor (committee member) responsibility.

The committee structure was a source of conflict for many teachers. Some teachers believed that the rigid structure imposed by committee obligations stifled their creativity and curbed their flexibility. One teacher had indicated that it limited her options because she liked to be involved in everything. Several teachers felt that teachers who were not 'pulling their weight' previous to the implementation of the committees, had continued to reject responsibility for duties outside of their regular classroom duties. Another teacher, however, in response to a question about where the treats came from during recess one Friday, quipped: 'They come from us. There's a list. It's very structured. Everything's structured around here.' The nature and tone of the response suggested that this teacher felt that there was no choice about participating in this activity. It would seem that, at the time of this research at least, this school's vision was fragmented at best. If collaboration was part of that vision, then there was work needed on helping all members of Hillside share that vision.

Disabling Competition: Inhibited the Development of Trust, Honesty, Mentoring, and Collegiality

There were two types of competition that served to have a disabling affect on the collaboration at Hillside Elementary: a) within teams, and b) among teams. Bernie spoke of former in this remark: 'And Mavis and I are more competitive with each other than either of us is with Gail, because both of us are similar in the sense that we have very high expectations of ourselves.' This competitive spirit seemed to have had a negative influence on the team. As another member of that team suggested:

> And now where there's four of us it also means that social relationships happen. So if one teacher and I talk about something, another one feels left out. If two others do something, I feel left out. One teacher and I often get into conflicts and the others are in the middle and that's awful. So that's also hard, when you have a team, you have social relationships, and that can be really difficult to mix personalities.

The second type of competitiveness, among teams, also did not work in the favour of authentic collaboration. Another member of the Primary Division Team laid blame on the teaming structure for the lack of collegiality at the school. She felt that Principal Butler, in promoting the teams, contributed to the 'downfall of the rest of the school'. Though the staff overall was a good one, the emphasis on the teaming aspect created 'pockets'. She described the isolating effect that that had on their team at the beginning of the school year.

> The first month and a half we didn't talk to anyone else except the four of us. Like we never went out of the room and we ate lunch at our desks and we'd do everything in here. And even the principal and vice principal, I've never had so little contact with them and again, with it being such a big school. The teams seem to be so self-sufficient that it doesn't lend itself to the bigger picture. If there's a problem on your team you need to go somewhere else for support. If you haven't built any relationships with anybody else, it's very difficult.

What this teacher described as pockets, Fullan and Hargreaves (1991) call a balkanized culture which consists of 'separate and sometimes competing groups, jockeying for position and supremacy like loosely connected, independent city states' (p. 52).

Ester, on the Junior Division Team, agreed that the teams might have contributed to the apparent weakening of a strong school culture because some teams were 'self-sufficient'. Louise, her partner, provided insight into the nature of these pockets of culture.

> I think that there are some teams that have become very close and have sort of included a few members of the staff so that there's almost like a little clique and it's almost a little group of students, teachers that have become like their own little clique. And when you teach on a staff this large people are going to form different friendships with different groups so you're going to see those differences. I think we have a long way to go on this staff to become a staff that, not only do we work in teams, but that you [belong to a larger] group.

Competition may both generate excitement and promote excellence. Too much competition, or misplaced competitiveness like the type that these teachers described, does not appear to have a positive influence on the collaborative relationship, either in relationships within a team or among teams.

Conflict Avoidance: Inhibited Compatibility, Shared Decision Making, and Honesty and Trust

The research literature supports the vice principal's belief that teachers who participate in their own team selection are more likely to be compatible and therefore to be more collaborative (da Costa and Riordan, 1996, p. 15). However, a compatible team should not be confused with a team that is never in conflict. Too often teachers in collaboration will acquiesce to others who are more dominant because they are not willing to risk alienation from the team or staff. They wish to avoid conflict and the uncertainty that comes with it. Conflict avoidance may be synonymous with uncertainty avoidance. When decision making is riddled with conflict, teachers are uncomfortable bringing about resolution themselves. This seems to have been at least partially the reason many teachers wanted Principal Butler to make the final decision on highly contentious issues such as timetabling. As one teacher stated, emotions were running high during that time and the staff did not function well when it came to arriving at consensus in such situations.

Implications

There are three main areas which need to be discussed in terms of implications related to fostering the development of authentic collaboration: a) Negotiation; b) Teacher Efficacy; and c) Leadership.

Negotiation

If educators are to value collaboration and not engage in conflict avoidance practices, then it is necessary for participants to recognize, understand and embrace
negotiation as part and parcel of the collaborative process. Whereas collaborative
structures such as a highly sophisticated committee arrangement or implementation
of team teaching are helpful, they are insufficient for reaching the goal of authentic
collaboration. The goal of shared decision making is a challenge inasmuch as
organizations are generally made up of individuals who together reflect a wide
array of values (Beck, 1996; Begley, 1996; Campbell-Evans, 1993; Hargreaves, 1994;
Hodgkinson, 1996; Willower, 1996). Consequently, a culture of collaboration where
all participate in making decisions is a process that does not necessarily emerge
smoothly, orderly or without conflict. Rather a collaborative culture is 'actively
created and contested against competing visions and values of what people in the
organization should do' (Hargreaves, Earl, and Ryan, 1996, p. 8). A true appreciation of the dynamics of the collaboration process, which acknowledges that it is
characterized by value consensus, negotiation and compromise, should help facilitate
the development of authentic collaboration. Teachers need to be prepared to deal
with conflict (Hargreaves, 1994) and they need to understand that the 'grey areas'
(Willower, 1996, p. 17) of valuation in education are ongoing but not despairingly
unmanageable.

Understanding that the process of decision making and collaboration is characterized by conflict and ambiguity is important when developing vision statements
as well. The fragmented vision of collaboration at Hillside Elementary suggests that
the principal's vision of teacher empowerment and participative decision making
was not shared by all. This is not to suggest that there is no room for *different* ideas.
On the contrary, tolerance for divergent points of view is important in a learning
organization (Leithwood, 1996). The important thing is that conflicting visions
should be examined with an emphasis on vision building as a *shared* development.
The process of developing a shared vision should include value inquiry and the
resolution of value conflict should be a democratic process (Beck, 1996, p. 5). Staff
involvement in this type of vision building works toward the development of ownership (Campbell-Evans, 1993).

Teacher Efficacy

It was argued that too much competitiveness combined with a weak sense of
teacher efficacy will not likely breed honest, open and trusting relationships in the
collaborative process. Teachers need to feel confident in their teaching abilities in
order to allow them to expose their 'little flaws' without developing strong competitive feelings within teams. Moreover, to counteract team competitiveness, Rottier
(1996) suggests that team leaders meet weekly to keep the lines of communication
open. While this is good advice, without a sense of *shared* ownership for school
goals as opposed to an emphasis on team accountability, the lines of communication

may merely serve to fuel team competitiveness, especially if the communication is not imbued with trust and honesty.

This was especially the case with the Primary Division Team. Initially the team had come together with enthusiasm and energy. However, considering that the four of them were new to the school, they were undoubtedly in a state of disequilibrium from the start. Furthermore, these teachers had got the impression that everyone at Hillside team-taught to full capacity and, consequently, they felt pressure to *make* the team work. When they realized that things were not working out as planned, they withdrew from the teaming relationship to the point where they would collaborate on some aspects of curriculum planning and teaching. However, they seemed to have become somewhat disillusioned with the highly collaborative process that a total commitment to team teaching required and feelings of insecurity grew.

Indeed, strong sense of teacher efficacy fosters an environment of trust, honesty and can engender a sense of shared ownership. How then is this done? There is already much in the literature on teacher efficacy and how to improve teachers' beliefs in their ability to teach ranging from periodic workshops and feedback on teaching techniques (da Costa and Riordan, 1996) to mentoring and reflective journals (Hargreaves, 1994). The implication is that further research should address 'other techniques . . . [for] . . . increasing teachers' confidence in their teaching abilities (da Costa and Riordan, 1996, p. 16).

Leadership

Transformational leadership is 'a function of self-knowledge and of values' (Hodgkinson, 1991, p. 16) where leaders can both 'harness the collective genius' (Senge, 1990, p. 257) and help 'develop a set of shared values and commitments' (Sergiovanni, 1990, p. 23). In facilitating the development of a collaborative culture, the school administrator is pivotal, inasmuch as this development stage is generally characterized by a high degree of ambiguity and conflict. As Duke (1996) suggests, where 'drift and detachment exist . . . the need for leadership is likely to be great' (p. 32). Transformational leaders can facilitate the development of the underlying values of collaboration: ownership (not accountability), teacher efficacy, collegial relations built on honesty and trust, compatibility and mentoring.

Conclusion

This analysis of the research into school collaboration provides no simple solutions. This is particularly the case when trying to address the issue of time constraints on the collaborative process. With the exception of strongly recommending that school administrators provide the necessary time for teachers to collaborate, there is not much other concrete advice. Perhaps, however, if other issues are addressed – issues related to exploring how to create a culture of collegiality where individuals

Pauline E. Leonard

interact in open, honest and trusting relationships, where there is a shared vision and a sense of ownership for achieving the goals embedded in that vision, where teams and individuals are not competitive in a one-upmanship sense, and where teachers and administrators recognize conflict as a potential for change and growth – then constraints on time might be a manageable issue inasmuch as time will take care of itself when priorities are clear.

References

BECK, C. (1996) 'Values, school renewal and educational leadership.' Paper presented at the 1996 Toronto Conference on Values and Educational Leadership, Toronto.

BEGLEY, P.T. (1996) 'Cognitive perspectives on values in administration: A quest for coherence and relevance', *Educational Administration Quarterly*, **32**, 3, pp. 403–26.

CALDWELL, B.J. and SPINKS, J.M. (1992) *Leading the Self-Managing School*, London: Falmer Press.

CAMPBELL-EVANS, G. (1993) 'A values perspective on school-based management', in DIMMOCK, C. (ed.), *School-based Management and School Effectiveness*, London: Routledge, pp. 92–113.

CAVANAGH, R.F. and DELLAR, G.B. (1996) 'The development of an instrument for investigating school culture.' Paper presented at the 1996 Annual Conference of the American Educational Research Association, New York.

DA COSTA, J.L. and RIORDAN, G. (1996) 'Teacher collaboration: Developing trusting relationships.' Paper prepared for presentation at the XXIV CSSE Annual Meeting, St. Catherines, Ontario.

DIPARDO, A. (1996) 'Seeking alternatives: The wisdom of collaborative teaching', *English Education*, **28**, 2, pp. 109–26.

DUKE, D.L. (1996) 'A normative perspective on organizational leadership.' Paper presented at the 1996 Toronto Conference on Values and Educational Leadership, Toronto.

ERICKSON, F. (1987) 'Conceptions of school culture: An overview', *Educational Administration Quarterly*, **23**, 4, pp. 11–24.

FULLAN, M. and HARGREAVES, A. (1991) *What's Worth Fighting For? Working Together for Your School*, Toronto: Ontario Public School Teachers Federation.

GREENFIELD, T.B. (1986) 'The decline and fall of science in educational administration', *Interchange*, **2**, 2, pp. 57–80.

HARGREAVES, A. (1994) 'Development and desire: A postmodern perspective.' Paper presented at the Annual meeting of the American Educational Research Association, New Orleans, April 1994.

HARGREAVES, A., EARL, L. and RYAN, J. (1996) *Early Adolescents*, London: Falmer Press.

HODGKINSON, C. (1991) *Educational Leadership: The Moral Art*, Albany, NY: SUNY Press.

HODGKINSON, C. (1996) *Administrative Philosophy: Values and Motivations in Administrative Life*, London: Elsevier Science Ltd.

KNOP, N., LEMASTER, K., NORRIS, M., RAUDENSKY, J., TANNEHILL, D. (1997) 'What we have learned through collaboration: A summary report from a National Teacher Education Conference', *The Physical Educator*, **54**, 4, pp. 170–9.

LEITHWOOD, K. (1996) 'An organizational perspective on values for leaders of future schools.' Paper presented at the 1996 Toronto Conference on Values and Educational Leadership, Toronto.

LIEBERMAN, A. (1988) *Building a Professional Culture in Schools*, New York: Teachers College Press.

ROCHE, K.W. (1997) 'Principals' responses to moral and ethical dilemmas in Catholic school settings.' Unpublished doctoral dissertation, University of Toronto, Toronto.

ROTTIER, J. (1996) 'The principal and teaming: Unleashing the power of collaboration', *Schools in the Middle: Theory Into Practice*, **5**, 4, pp. 31–6.

SENGE, P.M. (1990) 'The leader's new work: Building learning organizations', *Management Review*, **Fall**, pp. 7–23.

SCHEIN, E.H. (1984) 'Coming to a new awareness of organizational culture', *Sloan Management Review*, **Winter**, pp. 1–15.

SCHEIN, E.H. (1990) 'Organizational culture', *Sloan Management Review*, **February**, pp. 109–19.

SERGIOVANNI, T.J. (1990) 'Adding value to leadership gets extraordinary results', *Educational Leadership*, **47**, 8, pp. 23–7.

STAKE, R.E. (1994) 'Case studies', in DENZIN, N.K. and LINCOLN, Y.S. (eds) *Handbook of Qualitative Research*. New York: Oxford University Press.

WILLOWER, D.J. (1996) 'Values and valuation: A naturalistic inquiry.' Paper presented at the 1996 Toronto Conference on Values and Educational Leadership, Toronto.

7 The Value of Language and the Language of Value in a Multi-ethnic School

James Ryan

In all schools language plays a central role in learning. Corson (1993) contends that language takes on such a crucial function in schools because learning is driven by interpersonal communication. He says that we learn how to perform even the most basic acts by observing how others do it, by using and listening to those others as models, by noticing others' reactions to our performances, and changing them accordingly. More than this though, Corson (1998) notes that language is the primary medium through which students make new concepts their own. Students learn as they listen, talk, read and write about new concepts and ideas and relate them to what they already know. But language is much more than just an instrument of communication, or a tool that facilitates through its communicative capacities the intellectual development of students. Language is also a symbol that communicates value to those who are associated with its various networks. Those who participate in language conventions assign worth to language users on the basis of the ways in which they employ these conventions both in the classroom and out. This attribution of worth, however, does not occur through natural or preordained processes. Rather it is the result of struggles between and among groups who vie to have their various conventions, styles and meanings accepted as legitimate and accorded corresponding value. The results of these struggles are particularly evident in schools where more than one language is used. In these situations certain languages and language varieties are inevitably favoured over others. The value attached to favoured language practices is regularly displayed in those linguistic conventions which are generally employed in the classroom and out, and in the attitudes of students and educators towards the various conventions.

While language generally takes on a valued role in learning, not all varieties of language have equal value in this and other related roles. In most schools in North America, for example, the standard versions of the English language are accorded a higher value than other languages and language varieties. Those who are able to demonstrate a certain degree of skill in speaking and writing standard English will find themselves with more opportunities than those who are either unwilling or incapable of using these forms of English in the required situations. This is evident in the case I describe below. Here the differential worth assigned groups and their language conventions has led many to see language both as a 'problem' and as a 'resource'. Most take for granted the value of the dominant language in the school – English. In an important way, many parents, educators and students see English as a resource, something that when learned will assist students to master the curriculum and improve their life chances. On the other hand, many – but not all – see non-English languages and non-standard English language varieties as a problem. Parents, students and educators alike see students' home languages, non-standard varieties and various accents as impediments to learning English and subject matter content, as well as being barriers to the opportunities that the market has to offer them. Not all students, however, view non-English languages and varieties in this way. Some see them as resources. They perceive, sometimes implicitly, that home languages and varieties can help them not only rescue a measure of social worth, but also assist them to master an English-based curriculum.

This chapter describes the effects of the process of valuing associated with linguistic practice at Suburbia Secondary School (a pseudonym). Towards this end, I first outline the dimensions of language variety at Suburbia. Next I describe how linguistic expressions are valued and the effects that this has on various groups of students. An account of teacher attitudes towards the speaking of non-English languages and non-standard varieties is then followed by a number of suggestions for the ways in which educators can value all languages and their speakers. Before moving on, however, I will first describe the school and methods.

Methods

This study is based on research conducted in one suburban school, which I will call Suburbia Secondary School.[1] The school itself is very diverse and is located in an equally diverse large urban centre (for a similar account of these methods see Ryan, 1997, in press). The school community itself is also diverse, both in terms of the financial well being of the residents and of their heritage. Many of the students who attend this school come from families that are well off financially. Many families, however, are also struggling to make ends meet. The larger metropolitan area in which Suburbia is located has over the past 20 years become much more visibly diverse with the change in immigration patterns. Most of these immigrants no longer emigrate from western Europe as they once did. Instead many new residents come from such places as Hong Kong, Poland, China, India, the Philippines, Lebanon, El Salvador, Sri Lanka, Vietnam and Guyana to take up residence in Canada (Statistics Canada, 1993). Many immigrants find this urban area a particularly attractive place to settle. As late as 1991 they constituted 38 per cent of its population (Statistics Canada, 1993).

Suburbia Secondary School reflects this growing diversity. A recent school-administered survey confirmed this fact. It indicated that students identified with over 60 different heritages. The largest groups of students included students of Italian (18 per cent), Filipino (14.7 per cent), Portuguese (9.5 per cent), Chinese (8 per cent), and Polish (6.3 per cent) heritage. At the time of this study, the school was barely four years old, and its student population topped 1700. Student numbers had grown considerably since its first year, and as a consequence, the school has had to add a number of portable classrooms. The teaching staff is also young, and many were hand-picked by the principal. Almost all of these people, however, are of European heritage.

The study was initially conceived to explore the ways in which administrators, teachers, students and parents were responding to student diversity in this particular school. During the course of this study I worked with three other people – a research officer and two graduate students. We divided the data collection tasks among us and met regularly to talk about such things as emerging themes and future strategies. The first thing we did was to observe the teaching practices of four teachers. We selected them on the basis of their variation in teaching experience, subject expertise and gender, and spent two days observing in their respective classrooms. In addition to observing these teachers, we also talked to them about their teaching practices and selected incidents that occurred during the course of the observations. We also interviewed a number of other teachers, guidance councillors and administrators, and shadowed an administrator for two weeks. In all we talked to 25 staff members. We also talked to the only two teachers who were not of Caucasian background, but we did not observe their teaching practices.

We also observed and talked to students. Like the teachers, these students were selected to represent as much variation as possible. Initially we looked for student candidates in the classes we observed, and eventually made decisions about their suitability after comparing notes on them. The first thing we did was to shadow them for two entire days. We also talked to them about their school experiences. These students were not the only ones who participated in the study, however. We conducted student focus groups and talked individually to students who we felt might provide us with unique insights. In one instance we sought out and interviewed a student who we believed reacted in a particularly constructive way to an ugly racist incident. In all 40 students participated in the study. The last group of people we talked to were parents. Initially we tried to talk to the parents of the six students who we shadowed. When this was not possible in all of the cases, we chose replacements who were of similar backgrounds.

In the initial stages of the study we met regularly in order to compare notes and, among other things, to pick out promising themes to pursue. One of the most prevalent of these proved to be language. It emerged early in the study as we had our initial conversations with students and teachers. They drew our attention to the challenges associated with language. We decided at this early stage to pursue this phenomenon and we subsequently looked for it in our observations in classrooms, hallways and the cafeteria, and we asked pointed questions about it when we talked to teachers, students and parents. Eventually after all the data were collected, I isolated all descriptions and/or opinions regarding language, and organized them for presentation in a systematic way. What follows is a summary of this.

Language as an Issue at Suburbia

Suburbia's students speak many languages. The extent of this linguistic diversity was made plain by a recent survey which indicated that the student body speaks over 60 different languages. Language becomes an issue here because the over-whelming majority of teaching/learning interactions occur in one language – English. School officials expect all students who enroll at Suburbia to be prepared to learn from English-based curriculum materials and to listen to classroom inter-changes in the English language. If students are to have any hope of mastering the curriculum they have little choice but to learn the English language. Some, how-ever, experience more difficulties than others as they attempt to learn English.

Most teachers are on the lookout for students who have difficulty with English, and many are adept at diagnosing problems. Ginger, however, never ceases to be surprised at how little English some of her newer students actually know. She recalls her most recent new arrival.

> One boy, Johnny, he came from Hong Kong a few weeks ago, so he told me. He came into my class and he couldn't understand what I was saying. I was kind of shocked. He couldn't understand what I was saying. I said, 'When did you get here, when did you come here?' He said, 'Friday'. So I'm thinking he meant that he arrived here the Friday before.

While Johnny has managed to overcome some of his problems, at least to the point of being able to deal with course work, other students in this class have not been as successful. Bill continues to experience difficulties, although he has told Ginger that he understands everything. Ginger however, maintains that he 'doesn't understand anything that's difficult'. She has another student from Sri Lanka who is also having problems. Ginger says that 'she's having troubles, but I think it's just the language. She's kind of frustrated because she's working hard and getting 50s and I told her just make this your "getting used to culture year" . . . She asks questions and she nods and says she understand, but there's always a word in there [that she doesn't understand]'.

Fred, another teacher, is getting better at recognizing students with language problems. He says that he recognized the difficulties that one of his newest student was experiencing.

> Right off the bat. Just as the first time I talked to him, I noticed he was very . . . not slow with his English, but you could see that he was always thinking before he was speaking almost to make sure he has the words correctly and he has chosen it in the right form before he starts talking to me. And then I got a memo that he is at ESL and that the first test . . . when he did the first test, he came up and asked if he could write it with the ESL class. So I said, 'fine'. But I think his speech is the hardest point right now. The written stuff that he does is fine. Just as I said, he does very well on the test. So I think he can read and write fine. It's just when he tries to speak that he has a little bit of difficulty.

Fred also notes that this particular student, like many of the newer students who come into his classes, exhibits a certain kind of behaviour. He appears shy, but will approach him when he experiences difficulties. Fred says that:

He does have a little difficulty with the English language so I think that makes him a little bit even shyer in the group. I don't think he's that outgoing type of person. At least he hasn't struck me as [that type]. When he needs help, he'll ask for it. But he doesn't ask for it in front of the group. He will come up to me after class. He'll wait patiently till everyone leaves after class. 'Sir, can I borrow a textbook to take home?' Or, he'll catch me in the hall or he'll knock on the office door. 'Sir, can I borrow a textbook to take home?'

Ragini is perhaps typical of many students who travel from distant lands and end up at Suburbia. She is a recent immigrant to the country and regularly experiences language difficulties. Among other things, she often has trouble understanding fellow students and teachers. Ragini believes that 'Canadians, they speak too fast'. She often has to ask them to repeat themselves, something that she feels uncomfortable doing. She also believes that she has trouble making herself understood. As a result she is sometimes unwilling to speak up or let teachers or other students know that she has not understood what they have said to her.

Mary is also a recent immigrant, but knows even less English than Ragini. This was particularly evident when we talked to her. She had trouble understanding what we were saying and had even more difficulty making herself understood. Unlike Ragini, however, she rarely speaks English, preferring to stay within her own ethnic group and speak to her friends in her native tongue. For her 'English is the main problem'. She admits that she becomes 'nervous' with the prospect of having to talk to someone in English. Although she is a good student in sciences and maths, she worries that teachers will think that because of her language problems that she does not have a grasp of the subject matter. Mary believes that the language barrier gets in the way of establishing better relationships with her teachers. She wants to be in a position to talk with teachers more than she is now able. In the country she emigrated from she 'could talk [about] a lot of things [with] the teachers. But here if I don't know how to [talk] to you [in] English, I don't know how to explain to you what [I think]. And I think they [teachers] haven't got a lot of time for you to explain your feelings'. She wishes that she had a teacher who could speak her language. If this were the case then she feels that she would be able to establish a better relationship with the teacher, who in turn would be able to provide clear explanations of some of the things with which she experiences difficulties.

Language, Power and Value

The fact that English is the language of instruction at Suburbia is not the result of a coincidence or of a naturally occurring process. It is entrenched in its current, obviously secure position, as a consequence of an ongoing struggle. In other words, English assumes such a dominant position in this and in many other schools in the western world, because power relationships over the years have favoured it over other languages. Teachers and students conduct their interactions in this language not because it is an inherently better language for instruction, but because the various arrangements that are part of the wider social structure have dictated that English be used in this context.

The English language and the various discourses associated with it in this case, play a unique role in mediating and shaping the power relationships that are responsible for its current dominant position. One of the ways that it does this is through the attribution of value. The language employed in the classroom, for example, works in important ways to establish the worth of various social practices and of the individuals and groups associated with them. It does this in at least two ways. First language can act as a determiner of worth. In this regard, certain arrangements of words have the power to allocate value. On the other hand, language itself is also a reflection of worth. Educators commonly evaluate students on the basis of how they use language in the classroom. Particular English language discourses then can predispose men, women and children to believe in their particular worth, as a consequence, to look upon them as important resources. At the same time, however, they also depend on a supportive social context to generate conditions that allow for this attribution of worth. Walsh makes this point, emphasizing as she does so, the reality that language is much more than simply a mode of communication.

> Language is more than a mode of communication or a system composed of rules, vocabulary, and meanings; it is an active medium of social practices through which people construct, define, and struggle over meaning in dialogue with and in relation to others. And because language exists within a larger structural context, this practice is, in part, positioned and shaped by the ongoing relations of power that exist between and among individuals. As such language affects as well as reflects the individual reality of its speakers, and the socio-historical and ideological environment in which these speakers reside. (1991, p. 32)

How can particular arrangements of words or styles of language have the power to assign worth? Of the various historical beliefs about the power of language that Corson (1993) traces, two are relevant here. The first concerns the relationship of language and thought. In the tradition of the 'strong' version of the Sapir-Whorf hypothesis and various Orwellian-like schemes about language (Corson, 1993), this theory posits that language determines thought. Over the years, however, scholars have successfully refuted the more extreme versions of this theory (Lucy, 1992). Nevertheless most agree that language, and the previous dialogues that people have taken part in, although not the ultimate determiner, are in important ways associated with the way they think about things, including their world views and the values to which they subscribe (Corson, 1998). In this regard, language is also an important vehicle for voice. Walsh (1991), for example, maintains that language enables people to fashion a voice, a 'speaking consciousness', that is rooted in their collective histories and lived experiences. Not all languages or discourses are able to do this equally for all people, however. Some will enable, confirm and validate the collective interests and experiences of certain groups, while others will do just the opposite.

James Ryan

Corson (1993, 1995) also refers to the idea that particular patterns of words can carry with them certain powers. He acknowledges the power that great orators of the past and present seem to possess and the ways in which some individuals, including academics, can mystify others with the language that they use. Corson (1993, 1995) goes on to point out that the syntax of a language can offer a ready vehicle for capitalizing on power relationships and conveying a highly partisan reality. In this capacity, he maintains that the role of syntax in drawing causal relationships between participants and processes facilitates the designation of relative status of social actors. It can do this by placing them in different roles in sentences. A writer, for example, can designate individuals as agents, experiencers or objects, or as Corson maintains, delete them entirely by using a passive voice, a transformation or a substitution. In this regard, professional educators can deploy power and worth in the terms they use to describe their students. By assigning labels to students like 'gifted', 'underachiever', 'delinquent', 'disabled', educators are also, in a fairly obvious manner, employing language to differentially allocate worth.

As emphasized above, language is inextricably entangled in a wider social context, and as such, depends on this social context for its power to assign worth. This means that this power does not reside in words alone. Rather all who use language avail themselves of a form of power that is part of a social institution. Individuals and their linguistic practices will always bear the trace of these various institutions. As a consequence, the power, value and sense of particular linguistic expressions are as much a product of the (often unequal) relationships between and among groups and individuals as are the various arrangements of symbols and sounds. The power of language to assign or reflect worth then will always depend upon who is speaking, when, where, why and with whom. In this regard institutional frameworks routinely endow particular individuals (and not others) with the power to assign value. Teachers, for example, as illustrated above, are empowered by virtue of their positions in educational settings to assign value to student actions through their linguistic practices. On the other hand, their power to assign value in other institutional settings, such as factories, dentist's offices and courtrooms, will be decidedly less, even when they employ the same language or phrases.

Bourdieu (1991) employs an economic metaphor to capture the role of institutions in the attribution of linguistic worth. He prefers to see the institutional context in terms of markets. Bourdieu believes that linguistic expressions are always produced in particular markets. These markets, in turn, endow certain linguistic products with value. Some products, of course, are valued more highly than others. Those who are able to produce the right expressions will inherit this value and the power that accompanies it. Doing this, however, requires the possession of what Bourdieu refers to as capital. Those endowed with appropriate linguistic capital then will have an ability not only to create the right language forms, but also to understand the norms of language enough to produce the right expression at the right time for that particular linguistic market. Those who are able to do so are best placed to exploit this system of differences to their advantage and to profit from it. While some may enjoy persistent advantages over others in particular markets, the institutional rules that govern these markets, however, are not fixed. All those who participate in them continually contest each others' forms of capital, working as they do so, either to maintain the current, largely unstated rules or to change them.

Valuing English

Many linguistic markets in western countries value the English language over many other languages. These markets extend to most institutions, including schools. This value may be demonstrated in a number of ways. The mere fact that the language of instruction is English, as it is in Suburbia, will send a message to all about the value of the respective languages. The awareness of this reality inevitably engenders particular attitudes towards the various languages. Teachers can and do make incorrect assessments of students' abilities because they do not or will not always acknowledge that culturally different students often approach literary activities in ways inconsistent with school norms (Corson, 1998). Philips (1983), for example, notes that teachers saw the Native students in her study as disrespectful, misbehaving and uninvolved rather than as users of different language norms. It is not surprising then that minority language users may learn to devalue their heritage language, while the majority English users may come to believe in the inferiority of various minority languages and the superiority of their own (Walsh, 1991). Those whose first language is not English may see their own language as a problem, while seeing English as a resource. Majority language users may also adopt this same attitude, as is commonly the case at Suburbia.

Teachers at Suburbia acknowledge the value of the English language. Many take for granted their belief that a facility in the English language will assist students in their studies, and later on in life, when they move into the world of work. As a consequence, some object to students speaking their first language if it is not English not only in the classroom, but also in the halls. Tish's attitude typifies the approach of many teachers at Suburbia. She believes that English should be the language of the classroom, and that all students should speak it when they are in her room. She says, with reference to one group of Chinese students who tend to speak their native language much of the time, 'in the class we speak English and I feel that they should communicate to each other in English'. She has a number reasons for wanting all students to speak English in class. The first is her concern for order in the classroom. She believes that whispering or talking in students' native tongues can create noise levels that are unacceptable. She says:

> The last week in December I left the class to go and get a review sheet for them and came back, and I didn't know anything was going on. And then at the end of the class some girls came over and said, 'As soon as you left it was like Hong Kong in here. They were just speaking so loud and we couldn't hear anything and they were all speaking in their language.' And I think it's frustrating for them. Maybe that's wrong of them but I don't think it is. I think you should speak the language which is the norm for that area so that everyone can understand. Because at the very first week of school I was thinking: 'I've never had a problem with

> noise in my class before.' And here there was a little whispering going on and I was thinking: 'Why is this bothering me so much? I've never noticed it.' And I mentioned it to my department head, and he said it's because they're whispering in Cantonese or whatever language, and it's such a high tone that it's distracting.

Another reason Tish has for insisting on spoken English in the classroom is to help the non-speakers, she believes, to learn English. Practicing and interacting in English is one of the ways to learn and improve students' use of the language. She rationalizes that 'the languages in Canada are English and French, and if you get hired [for a job after graduation] you're going to have to speak English or French'. Tish also feels that if students are to learn from other students then anything students say should be understood by everyone else in the class. She maintains that 'if they're going to say something, it should be for the benefit of everyone to understand, especially if they're bright'. Finally, Tish believes that certain groups isolate themselves from the rest of the students when they speak their native tongue in the classroom. She feels that using English and separating such groups will help these students integrate with the other students.

The belief of many teachers at Suburbia that speaking English at the expense of their first language in classrooms and in the halls of the school will speed up their learning of English is not something that is supported by research, however. Corson and Lemay (1996), Cummins (1995), Cummins and Swain (1986), and McLaughlin (1986), for example, maintain that such a practice, particularly with respect to so-called minority groups, will neither enhance English language learning nor will it help students master the curriculum. Intensive exposure in school to the majority language, particularly in early stages, accompanied by school neglect of the first language may not only produce low achievement in the majority language, but also mark a decline in mother tongue proficiency. On the other hand, developing proficiency in the first language, which may include conceptual information and discourse strategies, enhances second language development. What is also important, however, is that the school value the respective mother tongues. In this regard Cummins (1986) maintains that educational success for minority language speakers depends on the extent to which the language and culture of these students is incorporated into the curriculum.

While many students may see the English language as a resource, some may also see their mother tongue in the same light. Not only may mother tongues be important in a social sense, they may also assume a crucial role in students' intellectual development. This may explain, at least in part, the Chinese students' tendency as described above to speak frequently in their native tongue. Goldstein (1997) sheds light on this issue in her study of a group of Cantonese-speaking students in an English-speaking school. She maintains that Cantonese is important to these students in both a social and academic sense. Students use Cantonese to gain access to friendship groups. Not only are friendship groups important to these students for the usual reasons such as camaraderie, security and so on, but they are also important for academic reasons in two ways. First, friends are helpful in explaining math concepts to those who, partly because of language difficulties, cannot understand them. Second, friends are also important in the role they can play in helping students advocate for marks in cases where students feel the marks they receive are not appropriate. Ironically students see the use of English in certain contexts as a liability. These Cantonese-speaking students consider their fellow students 'rude' if they speak to them in English, a practice that will in turn jeopardize friendship opportunities.

Differentiating Forms of English

The structure of North American society provides the conditions for the English language to flourish. It does so through markets that value English over other languages. These markets make their presence felt in many schools, including Suburbia. Here parents, educators and students alike acknowledge the value of learning the English language and adopt strategies to facilitate it. But these markets generally favour more than just the English language *per se*. They also adjudicate the *way* in which it is spoken. Variations in syntax and accent are socially marked to the point that even a basic exchange between individuals may reveal these differences, and as such, give evidence of their respective positions (Corson, 1993; Corson and Lemay, 1996). The result is that not only people trying to learn English who display an accent, but also those who employ various English language varieties, may find themselves at a disadvantage in schools and elsewhere.

This concern with accent is part of a process in schools that Corson (1993) refers to as the 'ideology of correctness'. Corson points out that schools routinely hold up a standard language as a model of excellence against which all linguistic practices are measured. Speicher and McMahon (1992), on the other hand, trace this preoccupation to the centuries-old affiliation between good grammar and good morals that permeates our attitudes. They maintain that the propagation of such views has been so successful over the years that it persists even among those who routinely depart from this ideal. While morality may not always enter the equation, those who employ deviant practices will inevitably be marked in unfavourable ways. A number of these individuals may come to accept this inferior status. The consequence is that many who do not speak English perfectly may be troubled by it and take steps to get rid of these imperfections. Such is the case at Suburbia.

At Suburbia there are those who find themselves in the position of trying to eliminate any trace of 'accent' and others who resent the attitudes some have towards their form of English language variety. Juanita is one student who is very conscious of her accent. She came to Canada in grade three and over time has acquired enough English language skills to get by in school and out. Nevertheless her speech still bears the traces of what she believes to be an accent, and she wishes she could eliminate it. Juanita says, 'sometimes it (her accent) bothers me because I want to do better and improve myself in English'. To do so, she wants to acquire what she refers to as a 'normal' accent.

Shemina and her parents display a similar attitude. Their arrival in Canada, however, was more recent. They have been in the country only six months. Shemina's parents believe that learning English is 'very important' both for their daughter and themselves. They want their daughter to be 'just like other children' and believe that in order to do so they will have to learn how to pronounce words properly and eliminate any traces of accent. Indeed they themselves work very hard on such pronunciation. Shemina's father says 'we used to pronounce every word. "Tee" and "dee" is "duth" here. We would pronounce that word'. Shemina's mother is particularly concerned with speaking correctly. She has a job as receptionist and as such she feels it is vital for her to learn the language. She wants to eliminate feelings of inferiority that arise in situations where people refuse to talk to her. She maintains, 'I feel inferior because when I talk over the phone some say, "I can't understand you. I don't want to talk to you. I want to talk to your supervisor"'. Shemina's parents are also worried that she 'won't be able to express herself' well enough to master the technical terms in science. They are concerned because they want their daughter to be able to master the language of science so that she can someday become a doctor. They have considered paying for English language classes for themselves and their daughter, but hope that Shemina can learn the English that she needs at school.

Accents are routinely diminished by the school's language correctness phobia. On the other hand, though, they can act as a positive source of capital. In a French language high school not too far from Suburbia, Ibrahim (1997) documents the importance that the French language teachers place on accent. He describes the surprise of these teachers when they first hear the Parisian accents of some of the students who have emigrated from East Africa. These teachers are surprised because they do not expect students from this part of the world to be able to speak in an accent that has a higher capital than their own Canadian accent. They also, as a matter of course, make a connection between this highly valued accent and what they believe to be students' academic abilities. Teachers have questioned, after hearing students speak, whether the general stream is the appropriate one for them.

Accents, however, are not the only aspect of linguistic practice that draw attention. Other variations from the standard ideal that revolve around vocabulary and syntax are also frequently diminished in schools. Those who deviate in their language practices from the standard or ideal variety are routinely marked. According to Toohey (1987) a standard variety is usually defined as that variety of language which is considered appropriate for communication over a wide area. It is commonly used in institutions, radio, television and newspaper, is usually taught in schools and has its norms of accuracy written down. Standard varieties, not by any coincidence, are almost always the mother tongue of the generally powerful educated middle class, who according to Corson (1998), attempt to cement their status in society by using their relatively powerful position to uphold these ideals. Because they have generally been successful in propagating the idea that the status of these ideals is due not to inequalities in power, but to their inherent goodness, many of those who do not or cannot meet these standards are more or less willing to accept the limited opportunities that await them.

The maintenance of the status of the standard language variety generally includes a simultaneous devaluation of non-standard varieties. As part of this process language, practices which deviate from the ideal are sometimes wrongly described as poor or sloppy, arising from speaker's laziness, lack of education or even perversity (Corson, 1993). The problem for students who do not speak the standard variety is that these negative attitudes affect teacher expectations (Edwards, 1989), and in turn, student performance. Citing research by Giles et al., Corson (1993) contends that teachers' perceptions of children's non-standard speech produces negative expectations about children's personalities, social backgrounds and academic abilities. He also refers to studies in Great Britain that reveal that the standard variety is rated much more favourably than the non-standard varieties. These and other findings emphasize that it is the attitudes toward the non-standard varieties rather than the actual differences that are more critical in these negative judgments, something that I address later.

Negative evaluations of non-standard varieties occur routinely at Suburbia. For example, teachers take a negative view of a non-standard form of English spoken by a number of students from the West Indies, which they refer to as *patois*. Most teachers to whom we talked were aware of *patois*, but some did not consider it a legitimate language. One teacher referred to it as a type of 'slang'. He says 'the Black people [from Trinidad] speak their own language. Is it *patois* or something? It's a kind of a slang that they use . . . It's almost like it's kind of not recognized in the same class as the English you know.' Another teacher maintains that *patois* is 'backward' sounding.

Others disapprove of *patois* for reasons other than its sub-standard status. Some teachers do not like it when students speak *patois* because they believe that it has the potential to undermine their control. Ashley, a teacher, maintains that the speaking of a language (which turns out to be *patois*), with which she is not familiar, disrupts the classroom. She says, with reference to one of her Caribbean students, 'He's sort of loud and I guess it's just the language. And he is actually speaking a different language than some. I don't know whether he's speaking some Pakistan language.' Caribbean students may resort to *patois* in confrontational situations and say things that teachers may not understand. Students may also use it, some claim, to talk about other students 'behind their backs'. One staff member clearly recognizes the loss of control which some teachers may feel in such situations. She says,

> When students are speaking *patois* to someone who does not understand it, it's totally foreign. For instance, if I'm speaking it to you, you may interpret it as losing control. You don't know what's going on, you don't want them to speak it, 'cos you don't have that control. So I see it as that, from a teacher's perspective, 'If they're speaking that language I don't know what they're saying, they could be saying, swearing at me, whatever.' So it's a loss of control, power, that kind of stuff. And that's when their [teachers] back gets up.

Speakers of *patois*, on the other hand, who are virtually all students, are generally upset with others' attitudes toward their language. They don't like the negative depiction of it, and they resent instances where they are told not to speak it. John, for example, says, 'It is a proper language, but I think that the whole system throws a negative connotation on *patois*.' Joan, on the other hand, generally accepts not being able to speak it in the classroom, but becomes very upset when told not to speak *patois* when she is not in the classroom. She says:

> I was speaking *patois*, myself and a friend. We were speaking *patois* in the hall and [a teacher] came and told us we shouldn't be speaking. Who is she to tell me when and where I can't speak my language? I'm not in the classroom. When I'm in the classroom I know that I don't speak *patois*.

At Suburbia, as elsewhere (see for example, Solomon, 1992) the academic market does not value *patois*. As a consequence, those who value standard English, as many teachers do, look upon *patois* not as a resource but a liability, and commonly discourage speakers from using it. While there is no data that points to a relationship between these negative attributions, school success and identity, it is reasonable to assume here as in other similar settings, that students do not benefit from this attitude. For example, students who speak non-standard varieties of English, including *patois*, are routinely placed, often inappropriately, in language development or lower streamed classes (Anthony, 1998; Corson and Lemay, 1986). There is, however, a market where *patois* is valued. It is obvious that it is a favoured form of currency in those peer groups that speak *patois* here at Suburbia and elsewhere in the region. Both Solomon (1992) and Ibrahim (1997) maintain that various forms of 'black English' and *patois* constitute an important part of the identities of members of groups, and as a consequence, become important resources for the speakers in contexts that involve group members.

One of the principal reasons why teachers at Suburbia and elsewhere consistently devalue non-standard varieties, including *patois*, is that they accept the idea that these varieties are inherently inferior to the standard variety. This may be the case in a number of reasons. One of them has to do with the fact that people who live in monolingual societies do not always realize the presence of wide variations in language use, attitudes and behaviour. They are also probably not aware that everyone makes 'errors' in language use at some time. But as Corson (1993) maintains, many of these errors are not errors at all, but rather varieties of language that preserve their features as regularly as any language. Furthermore, there is no evidence to suggest that any one variety is inherently superior to the next. All languages and varieties are equally adept at communicating necessary information between speakers (Speicher and McMahon, 1992). Most linguists agree that standard varieties are no more linguistically pleasing, accurate, true to tradition or in any sense structurally superior to any other variety. All are as rule-governed, creative, logical and capable of elegance as the next (Toohey, 1987). All language users develop various forms, styles and language functions that are necessary for them to live their lives in the circumstances in which they find themselves: those linguistic forms that cease to be useful are simply discarded. Thus, whatever disadvantage children experience in schools because of their use of one variety or another, it is not due to the disfunctionality of the language variety, but to the attitudes towards the use of that style or form of language use.

This functional view of language finds support in a number of areas in society, including the courts. Indeed the legal system in the United States has ruled in favour of this view of languages. In Ann Arbor, Michigan, parents of African American children brought an action against a school for failing their children (Labov, 1982). The lawsuit alleged that the school failed the children because it misidentified them as 'educationally disabled'. The school based this decision, the parents claimed, on the basis of the children's use of an African American non-standard variety of language. After hearing arguments, the court ruled in favour of the parents, maintaining that the children's use of this variety in itself was not an obstacle to their success. It further ruled that teachers' mistaken stereo-typical beliefs about this form of language influenced their expectations of stu-dents' academic abilities and led them to misjudge the students' potential. These lowered expectations eventually caused these students to fail. In the end the children were deemed deficient in their academic pursuits because their language variety was mistakenly judged to be deficient (Corson, 1993). The courts did not stop with these observations, however. In an attempt to rectify this injustice it also ordered teachers of culturally different children to take some in-service training in socio-linguistics.

Valuing Language

As illustrated above, school practices, including those at Suburbia, generally assign differential worth to different forms of linguistic expression. Suburbia's educational community exists as part of a market that values non-English languages and lan-guage varieties that depart from standard English less than standard English prac-tices. This attribution of worth generates effects that are both social and academic in nature. Speakers of the various languages and language varieties are socially marked by virtue of the language or version of the language which they employ. Those who make use of language practices that differ from standard English prac-tices will find that not only are their language practices devalued, but they will also discover that they themselves, their respective cultures and communities are held in lower esteem than those who employ standard English.

These social consequences are closely related to the academic effects of using language in what amounts to a linguistic market place. Those who employ practices that the market favours tend to do better in school than those whose practices the market does not value. Cummins (1986) provides convincing evidence of this. He maintains that the extent to which school practices reflect a valuing of certain languages and language varieties will dictate how well students perform. Those students whose language and culture is incorporated into the curriculum, and thereby valued, tend to do better than those whose language and culture is either ignored or devalued in school practices. On the other hand, Toohey (1987) maintains that when the form and content of students' oral expression is stigmatized or ignored, reading and writing pose formidable challenges. If what students are given to read in no way touches their experience or expression, if the background knowledge it assumes of the world and language is not theirs, they will have difficulty making sense of print. Furthermore, if what students write about is foreign in content and form to their teachers' then they cannot have a conversation about their work.

The lesson to be learned here is that the mode of expression employed by students is important to their success in school and in life generally. This is so not only because of the technical role linguistic practices play in communication functions, but also because of the status and power it confers on speakers. Thus those interested in helping students (particularly those who do not speak standard English) to succeed in school and life must find ways to value all students' linguistic expressions and the cultural practices that accompany them. The most obvious way to do this is to recognize the respective languages and dialects to the point that they are institutionalized in school practice. Instruction in students' first language or variety is one ideal option, for both social and academic reasons. It signals to all students the importance of the respective form of expression and provides the best means to master a curriculum in a second or third language. Research indicates that this holds for varieties of languages (Rickford, 1997) and for languages (Cummins and Swain, 1986).

The latter option, however, is not always possible. One of the reasons for this revolves around numbers. As is the case at Suburbia, there are often too many students who employ many different linguistic forms and too few teachers who either understand or are capable of instruction in the various languages or varieties. For example, only a couple of teachers at Suburbia speak any of 60-plus languages other than English spoken by the student body. This pretty much precludes any instruction in languages other than English. Even so there are ways in which educators and educational institutions can show respect to languages and language varieties. With respect to the latter, various ways of attending to *patois* may generate positive results. Corson and Lemay (1986) for example cite a number of studies that explore ways of promoting Caribbean varieties of English. Ladson-Billings and Henry (1990) describe a number of ways in which successful teachers of black students use Caribbean varieties of English to help reinforce the children's identity and provide a bridge between the language of the home and the language of the dominant culture. Morrison, Luther and McCullough (1991), on the other hand, introduced a special program to Caribbean speakers. In doing so they sought to find ways to encourage free expression in a setting where students were learning standard English, while at the same time respecting and reinforcing children's pride in their own variety. This program featured an emphasis on reading activities, narratives, storytelling, and the development of language skills. Corson and Lemay (1996) observe that the results of this study suggest that assisting teachers to help students who regularly employ non-standard English varieties focus on rich language acquisition activities can produce meaningful changes in the children's speaking, thinking and writing in both varieties.

While many scholars and practitioners recognize the academic value of instruction in home languages or varieties, not everyone supports efforts of this nature. With respect to instruction in varieties, for example, some who look to enhance the opportunities of minority variety or language speakers may not favour the use of *patois* in the classroom. In Britain, for example, parents and sociologists believe that such efforts are tokenistic and doomed to failure. Citing Stone and Carby, Edwards (1986) makes the point that the introduction of *patois* is simply an attempt to defend the legitimate culture of the school against the 'heretical' culture of black people, and that it will do little to remove the racist attitudes in school and society which are the most serious obstacles to social equality for black people.

This does not mean, however, that there is nothing that the school as a whole or teachers individually can do to acknowledge, and thereby value, student languages and dialects. One place to start is with both student and teacher knowledge. Educational programs need to begin to encourage minority dialect and language students to believe in themselves. Educators need, as Walsh (1991) contends, to invite them to believe that they have knowledge. Students need to understand, furthermore, that their knowledge, just like any other forms of knowledge, is valuable. It means, Toohey (1987) maintains, not necessarily understanding or knowing the right words, but in knowing that they have a right to words. She contends that reading and writing programs for speakers of non-English or non-standard varieties of English must aim at increasing the confidence of learners to find their own forms of comprehension and at increasing their belief in the importance of the expression of their particular experiences and perceptions. Finally, Corson (1993) maintains that for this type of valuing to count it must be carried on in a genuinely critical context. This requires that children need to become aware of the social and historical factors that have combined to make one variety of language or dialect more appropriate in contexts of prestige, while relegating other varieties as appropriate for marginalized settings.

In order to be in position to help students in this regard, teachers need themselves to understand linguistic matters. They must become aware of the conditions of language development and use preferred in their classrooms. Educators need to become aware of both the technical and symbolic aspects of students' linguistic practices. With regard to the former, Rickford (1997) and Corson (1993) recommend that teachers acquire an understanding of the variation of language practices, even in what may be superficially monolinguistic settings and the relationships between these variants and standard English. It is important for them to know, in the case of non-standard English variations, that there are enduring patterns that underlie these forms of speech. At Suburbia, for example, it would be important for teachers to understand that *patois* has a legitimate structure to it that has evolved over a period of many years.

It is also important for teachers to understand the symbolic functions that language plays in the lives of students. They need to be aware of the rewards and penalties that await students when they (attempt to) speak in standard English or in their mother tongues. It would be helpful at Suburbia, for example, if teachers could understand what Chinese and other non-English speaking students can gain from speaking their mother tongue in the classroom and hallways, and the penalties they are likely to pay from trying to speak English to teachers or to their friends (Goldstein, 1997). These teachers might also benefit from a knowledge that *patois* and other non-standard variety speakers may regard their speech as an act of defiance, and its features as signs of friendship and solidarity among fellow speakers (Edwards, 1986). They may also have an ambivalent attitude toward language. As a consequence, these speakers may be reluctant in some circumstances to admit using a stigmatized variety of language.

Toohey (1987) maintains that in order to impart to students the importance of their language and the culture and knowledge associated with it, teachers need to do much more than to document how students' dialects and/or language differs in a structural sense from standard or dominant varieties. She contends that it is essential for teachers to know something of what their students know, and of how students form this knowledge. Toohey recommends Heath's (1983) example of teachers helping students take community knowledge and reformulate it into the language of schooling as one method of acquiring this kind of knowledge (see also Ryan, 1994). In this setting teachers were convinced that learners brought valuable knowledge to the educational process, and as a consequence, were actively engaged with students in validating and building on this knowledge. Their conviction that these students knew something was not based on abstract liberal sentiments or a detailed knowledge of the grammatical features of the students' variety, however. Rather their belief can be traced to the fact that teachers had learned something of what the students knew and they had become more familiar with the ways in which their students communicated.

Corson (1998) recommends a wide range of policies and practices designed to promote the value of non-English languages and language varieties and the speakers of these varieties. These policies and practices target staff and visitors, curriculum and teaching, parents and communities, professional development and school organization. Among other things, Corson (1998) recommends that schools: recruit people who can tutor fluently those students whose first language is not standard English; appoint as many staff as possible who share students' language and culture; invite guests who represent various student cultures and language groups; employ professionals who understand the influence of home language and culture on students' development; provide leaders, mentors and models of culturally sensitive practices; make wide use of the language and skills of community members in the school; involve children and parents together in family literacy programs; arrange for professional development that explores the languages and language varieties used by students; base management on clear principles that promote culturally sensitive practices; provide bilingual or multilingual signs that welcome people to the school; use a variety of languages in school newsletters; involve various language communities in the school's management; and ask teachers to allow the minority languages to be used freely whenever possible.

Conclusion

Everyone has much to gain from efforts to value the wide varieties of languages that show up in schools. Perhaps those who will profit the most, however, are those students who use languages and language varieties that are generally shown little esteem. Among the many potential benefits, two stand out. The first is primarily social. When respect is shown their languages and cultures through various means, some of which are described above, students tend to experience more pride in their cultures and in themselves. This in itself should be reason enough to show respect for varieties of language. The second effect is academic, and it relates to student success in school and the scope of their opportunities when they leave school. Students whose language is respected and thus included in a meaningful way in school activities, not only tend to master the dominant language, in this case English, in more complete ways, but they also are inclined to do better in their studies generally, which in turn eventually translates to more opportunities in the world of work and in the life generally. Thus, educators can ill afford to ignore or marginalize the wide range of language varieties that are currently showing up in schools. If they are genuinely concerned with the well-being of all students then they must go out of their ways to value as many languages in their activities as they can.

Note

1   I acknowledge the financial support of the Ontario Ministry of Education and Training and the Social Sciences and Humanities Research Council of Canada in the study.

References

ANTHONY, S. (1998) 'Black-eyed Susan: "Blue-eyed" schools: Academically-oriented black girls in school.' Unpublished PhD Thesis, The University of Toronto.

BOURDIEU, P. (1991) *Language and Symbolic Power*, Raymond, G. and Adamson, M. (trans.), Cambridge, MA: Harvard University Press.

CORSON, D. (1993) *Language, Minority Education and Gender: Linking Social Justice and Power*, Clevedon: Multilingual Matters.

CORSON, D. (1995) 'Discursive power in educational organizations: An introduction', in CORSON, D. (ed.) *Discourse and Power in Educational Organizations*, Toronto: OISE Press, pp. 3–15.

CORSON, D. (1998) *Changing Education for Diversity*, Buckingham: The Open University Press.

CORSON, D. and LEMAY, S. (1996) *Social Justice and Language Policy in Education: The Canadian Research*, Toronto: OISE Press.

CUMMINS, J. (1986) 'Empowering minority students: A framework for intervention', *Harvard Educational Review*, **56**, pp. 18–36.

CUMMINS, J. (1995) 'Discursive power in educational policy and practice for culturally diverse students', in CORSON, D. (ed.) *Discourse and Power in Educational Organizations*, Toronto: OISE Press, pp. 191–210.

CUMMINS, J. and SWAIN, M. (1986) *Bilingualism in Education: Aspects of Theory, Research and Practice*, London: Longman.

EDWARDS, J. (1989) *Language and Disadvantage*, London: Cole and Whurr.

EDWARDS, V. (1986) *Language in a Black Community*, Clevedon: Multilingual Matters.

GOLDSTEIN, T. (1997) 'Bilingual life in multilingual high school classroom: Teaching and learning in Cantonese and English', *The Canadian Modern Language Review*, **53**, 2, pp. 356–72.

HEATH, S. (1983) *Ways with Words: Ethnography of Communication in Communities and Schools*, Cambridge: Cambridge University Press.

IBRAHIM, A. (1997) Becoming black: Race, language, culture and the politics of identity: African students in a Franco–Ontarian high school. Unpublished PhD Thesis, University of Toronto.

LABOV, W. (1982) 'Objectivity and commitment in linguistic science: The case of the black English trial in Ann Arbor', *Language in Society*, **11**, pp. 165–201.

LADSON-BILLINGS, G. and HENRY, A. (1990) 'Blurring the borders: Voices of African liberatory pedagogy in the United States and Canada', *Journal of Education*, **172**, 2, pp. 72–88.

LUCY, J. (1992) *Language, Diversity and Thought: A Reformulation of the Linguistic Relativity Hypothesis*, Cambridge: Cambridge University Press.

McLAUGHLIN, B. (1986) 'Multilingual education: Theory east and west', in SPOLSKY, B. (ed.), *Language and Education in Multilingual Settings*, Clevedon: Multilingual Matters, pp. 32–52.

MORRISON, D., LUTHER, M. and McCULLOUGH, J. (1991) 'Language programming with dialect students', *Orbit*, **22**, 3, pp. 8–9.

PHILIPS, S. (1983) *The Invisible Culture: Communication in Classroom and Community on the Warm Springs Indian Reservation*, New York: Longman.

RICKFORD, J. (1997) 'Unequal partnership: Sociolinguistics and the African American speech community', *Language in Society*, **26**, pp. 161–97.

RYAN, J. (1994) 'Organizing the facts: Aboriginal education and cultural differences in school discourse and knowledge', *Language and Education*, **8**, 4, pp. 251–71.

RYAN, J. (1997) 'Student communities in a culturally diverse school setting: Identity, representation and association', *Discourse*, **18**, 1, pp. 37–53.

RYAN, J. (in press) 'Stereotyping in a multiethnic school: From image to discourse', *The Alberta Journal of Educational Research*.

SOLOMON, P. (1992) *Black Resistance in High School: Forging a Separatist Culture*, Albany, NY: SUNY Press.

SPEICHER, B. and McMAHON, S. (1992) 'Some African-American perspectives on Black English vernacular', *Language in Society*, **21**, pp. 383–407.

STATISTICS CANADA (1993) *Ethnic Origin*, Ottawa: Ministry of Industry, Science and Technology.

TOOHEY, K. (1987) 'Minority educational failure: Is dialect a factor?', *Curriculum Inquiry*, **16**, 2, pp. 127–45.

WALSH, C. (1991) *Pedagogy and the Struggle for Voice: Issues of Language, Power and Schooling for Puerto Ricans*, Toronto: OISE Press.

8   Context and Praxis in the Study of School Leadership: A Case of Three?

Peter Ribbins

First Thoughts

At a key point in *Educational Leadership: The Moral Art*, Hodgkinson 'having considered at length the general theory of value' and the relationship of theory to practice concludes 'we can proceed to examine their workings in the practice, or, more correctly, *praxis* of educational administration and leadership' (1991, p. 110). His analysis of 'value praxis' and account of 'prescriptions and practicalities', offers much leaders will find thought provoking. However, as he is the first to acknowledge, his approach is essentially abstract. I am aware that there is nothing so practical as a good theory, but my interests have been rather more concrete. As such, my research over the last 25 years has focused mainly on trying to understand how a number of educational leaders at a variety of levels within the educational systems of the United Kingdom and elsewhere describe, justify and enact their leadership. Much of this has been, and continues to be, ethnographic in character, but I have come to supplement this with life and career history based approaches. In doing so with Ron Best, Peter Gronn, Christine Pascal, Steve Rayner and Brian Sherratt, I have tried to work out the theoretical implications of doing so. In what follows I will say something about this approach and its implications for context and value in the study of administrative praxis. I will seek to illustrate the possibilities of the approach drawing on a case study of three successive regimes of headship enacted at a comprehensive school in England.

Appreciating Context

I believe that studies of leaders, leading and leadership need to be contextualized. What does this mean? I begin from the idea that the world of the institution is a complex one in which, in an important sense, there are as many 'realities' as individuals. To accept this is to be committed to an approach which makes the study of the person and his or her subjective interpretation of reality a 'foundations block' of any satisfactory account of social life (Ribbins, 1986). In taking this view, I have been influenced by Greenfield's subjectivist critique of educational administration (Greenfield and Ribbins, 1993). Greenfield acknowledges the influence of Weber on his thinking but, unlike his mentor, concentrates on human agency to the virtual neglect of social structure. I take Weber's view (Best, Ribbins, Jarvis and Oddy, 1983). Accordingly, Gronn and I, following Seddon (1994) and others, propose a 'contextualized perspective' for the study of leaders (Gronn and Ribbins, 1996). In doing so, we advocate the need for approaches which have a concern for both *agency* and *structure* viewed within a context seen to be shaped by the interaction of one or more of macro (the societal), meso (the institutional) and micro (the individual) levels of relationship. Reconceptualized as the sum of the situational, cultural and historical circumstances that constrain leadership and give it meaning, context can be regarded as a vehicle through which the agency of particular leaders in specific situations may be empirically understood. Amongst other things, this would have the advantage of refocusing attention away from an overconcentration on *leadership*, characteristic of traditional approaches, and towards *leaders* and *leading*. Applied to education what might such an approach look like?

Regarding Context: A Three-level Approach

I have developed a framework with five propositions which taken together comprise a *prolegomenon* (a preliminary and tentative sketch for a yet to be produced fully worked out theory) for the study of leadership during periods of radical reform (relevant to steady-state conditions) which has yet to be produced. Applied to the case of the headteacher, such an approach would need data on:

1   the reforms in their specific historical, social, economic, cultural and values framework;
2   the contemporary scope, dimensions and character of the reforms;
3   the interpretations of, and responses to, the reforms of key national/local stakeholders;
4   the interpretations of, and responses to, the reforms by key institutional stakeholders as seen from the perspective of particular schools;
5   the interpretations of, and responses to, the reforms by individual headteachers within the schools identified in 4 above.

Propositions 1 and 2 constitute macro-level, longitudinal and comparative elements of the relational context; 3, 4 and 5 cover actors operating in a variety of interpretive contexts and at a variety of levels. In what follows, I focus on propositions 4 and 5 and will argue for meso- and micro-level ethnographies of educational leaders. Three main elements of interpretive contexts are implicit: I have termed these situated, individual portrayals; multi-actor perspectives; and multi-actor perspectives in action.

A Situated Portrayal

Such an approach would present the reader with sets of portraits of individual heads, and of their views across a representative range of issues, each reported in some depth (Mortimer and Mortimer 1991a, 1991b; Ribbins and Marland, 1994). It can take various forms. I know of no study which replicates for headteachers the kind of approach Gardner (1995) has used. His portraits of leaders are his, and presented in his words, rather than theirs and in their words. In contrast, the studies listed above are largely in the words of the heads involved. Even so, they differ in important ways.

The Mortimers, for example, invited seven primary and eight secondary heads, to respond *in writing* to issues specified by the researchers. My work on headship has emphasized the need for greater spontaneity and a more open process of agenda negotiation. As such I have derived my various accounts from *face-to-face* interviews and have used the same broad format. A group of heads/other educational leaders are invited to take part. Those who agree are sent a list of topics and asked to indicate any they would not wish to discuss and/or to add any they felt might be helpful. In an interview it is usually possible to renegotiate the agenda as the conversation progresses. Interview schedules have varied between projects in terms of agenda and the level of detail set out for individual themes. All were interviewed once, some twice, for about two hours. They knew the discussion was 'on the record'. The interviews were recorded, transcribed and edited. The editing sought to create a text which was authentic and readable. Censorship was restricted to the deletion of likely libels. Each respondent was sent a full transcript of the edited interview and invited to propose such additions and amendments as he or she wished to see included. The original letter of contact usually made clear they could pull out at any time and that should their interview be published there would be regard to their wishes for revision. Some have made considerable use of the right to propose revisions, others very little. It is possible that the advantage of allowing respondents to have sight of the interview schedule and enabling them to propose revisions to the draft text might entail some loss of spontaneity or authenticity. This was a risk worth taking and in any case was the price of an on-the-record interview. I do not believe the published texts lack colour or authenticity.

Multi-perspective

Traditional reports of headship *decontextualize* in the way described above but also insofar as they do not attempt to locate what headteachers *say* within a context of the views of *significant others* (staff, pupils, parents, governors) in the *community of the school*. A multi-perspective gives the reader some access to such information.

Multi-perspective in Action

Relatively few studies explore what heads say in the context of what they do. To achieve this the researcher must do five things: collect relevant documentary evidence which touches upon the role of a specific headteacher in a particular school; observe such a head as he or she enacts his or her role in practice in relevant situations; discuss with the head what he or she is trying to do and why; set this account against the views of significant others; and, compare and contrast the available evidence. Ethnographic research of this kind can offer an enhanced understanding of the headteacher and headship in a variety of settings. The following examples are classified into three categories according to the extent to which the headteacher is the principal focus and his or her status in undertaking the research.

Category 1 research treats the head as one among a number of actors at the school to be studied. Since the case study reported in the latter part of this paper is just such a case in point, I will not discuss the issues which this category raises until then.

Category 2 studies are characterized by their concentration on the perceptions and actions of particular headteachers. Insofar as Elizabeth Richardson's on-the-record study of Nailsea Secondary School focuses on the views and actions of Denys John, its headteacher, it is an exemplary case (Richardson, 1973).

Southworth has recently published an interesting ethnography of a primary school. In it he studies 'a headteacher by observing him at work inside the school . . . I investigated the idea of producing a portrait of the subject and saw parallels with biography' (1995, p. 1). The book is a 'case study of Ron Lacey, head of Orchard Community Junior School' (p. 2). He is described as 'the informant' and Southworth emphasizes that 'Ron was the *native* I was studying and the research was aimed to elicit his vision of his world' (p. 38). Lacey is the subject of the research, not a partner in it. As such it is a Category 2 study of headship, albeit a full and interesting one.

Category 3 studies identify the headteacher as co-researcher. Since 1989 I have been involved in third level research at Great Barr GM School in Birmingham. At first, this study was informed by ideas developed at Rivendell and refined elsewhere. It was planned to investigate how a large urban comprehensive school was responding to the reform agenda initiated by the 1988 Education Act and, in this form, was Category 1 research. As the work progressed I became increasingly interested in the role of the head as an interpreter and enactor of change. As a portrait of Brian Sherratt at Great Barr, during this phase, it had much in common with Southworth's study of Ron Lacey at Orchard and could be classified as Category 2 research.

Since 1992, however, with Sherratt's active involvement, I have been trying to develop a novel third level approach to the study of headship. In this version the head is *both* the principal subject of the research and a full partner within it. As such the research in which we are jointly engaged is autobiographical, insofar as it enables the head, as internal researcher, to reflect systematically and critically on his praxis during a period of intense reform. The study is also biographical insofar as I, as external researcher, have talked to him and many others at Great Barr and have observed a wide variety of events related to the exercise of his leadership in practice. We have recently called a halt to the field research and have begun to think about writing it up. This is not proving straightforward; we know of no close precedents upon which to draw in resolving some of the difficult theoretical and methodological problems entailed.

What has been fully written up is the kind of Level 3, Category 1 research which has been discussed above. To an example of this, I will now turn. In doing so, I will focus in particular upon the issue of leadership praxis in action.

A Case of Level 3, Category 1 Research: Three Heads for Rivendell

Values, Power and the Administrator

In a conversation I once had with Thomas Greenfield, he talked movingly about Boethius:

> a Christian who stood at the hinge between the Roman World and the Middle Ages. He is an administrator, one caught between the Emperor and the Pope, or as it turned out, the wrong Pope. He is condemned, and as he awaits his death he thinks back on his career and writes, thus bringing us new insights into the administrative task. Few of us will face the horror that Boethius did, but I am convinced that potentially there is that same dimension in all administrative rule, a kind of horror. The wielding of power is terrible, and the more power, the more terrible it becomes. If there is to be a kind of humanizing of that power a contemplative, philosophical dimension must and should be brought to it. (Greenfield and Ribbins, 1993, p. 262)

Acton has said 'all power corrupts, absolute power corrupts absolutely'. Less famously, and in less politically correct times, he went on to claim that 'almost all great men are bad men'. I have met many fine educational leaders who I could not describe as bad. Even so, I have long been interested in the potential which leadership can have for corrupting those who seek to exercise it and of the ways in which its horrors can be humanized.

Applied to the study of leaders, leading and leadership in education this can entail many different things. In this chapter, I will restrict myself, among other things, to a comparative examination of the more or less coherent and consistent framework of educational and managerial values of each of three successive head-teachers at one school, 'Rivendell', and of the ways in which this shaped their actions in terms of the strategies and tactics of management they sought to apply.

Contextualizing the Case

Rivendell, at the time of our research, was a fairly large, coeducational, comprehensive located within the south-east of England. Our intention had been to engage in an ethnographic study of pastoral care at the school (reported fully in *Education and Care* – see Best et al., 1983). We soon found it was necessary to engage in a wide ranging examination of education, order and welfare at the school if we were to hope to understand pastoral care in context. Thus our 'three year study' took almost six years from start to finish, but that is another story. However, we were fortunate enough to encounter three headteachers at Rivendell and this encouraged us to attempt an account of the characteristics of three successive regimes of head-ship over a 25-year period at the school. In undertaking our research we drew upon a model which postulated that individuals within social settings of all kinds can be located along a continua of power and authority and in terms of their policies by the degree of their attachment to, or rejection of, the status quo. This means that the extent to which headteachers can manage either continuity or change along lines which they prefer, is to an important extent dependent upon the accuracy of their appreciation of these configurations and on their ability to mobilize support and minimize opposition. In analyzing these three regimes of headteacher we wished to explore the educational and managerial values espoused by 'Mr Barber', 'Mrs Sewell' and 'Mr Lucas'; the extent to which and how they sought to enact these in practice and with what outcome; and, the responses which this engendered in other members of the school community.

Mr Barber

At the time of Barber's appointment, Rivendell did not exist. What was to become its site was occupied by two schools, one for boys and the other for girls. His first task was to put them together into a secondary modern. Ten years later he presided over its comprehensivization. At the time of his retirement, ten years later still, Barber's period of tenure tended to be described by himself and staff as character-ized by its commitment to egalitarian, democratic and curriculum-centred reform. In fact these policies were associated with his second, and not his first, decade in office. Shortly after comprehensivization, Barber's philosophy of education under-went a major transformation. Why this happened need not trouble us here, but a consequence was that under his driving influence Rivendell came to have a coherent policy which underlay a set of largely consistent policies on key features of its provision.

Teachers' accounts demonstrated the depth and breadth of this philosophy and of its effective implementation in practice. As a deputy head put it, 'It is unusual to find a school with a cohesive philosophy across the whole spectrum of its work. Barber's philosophy underlay everything that went on in the school. The philosophy went back to the 60s and the provision of a well-rounded person.' The policies which flowed from his conversion represented a radical reform agenda which was generally believed by staff and others to have fundamentally altered the whole ethos and practice of the school. At the time, other schools were also attempting to introduce similar reforms. Usually with much less success. Why was Barber successful?

There were several factors which worked in his favour. First, since his policies were broadly in tune with the drift of educational thinking towards more informal-progressive, open, egalitarian and child-centred methods, some staff would have been receptive. Second, his initial attempts to achieve change coincided with comprehensive reorganization and the increase in resources which this made available to the school. This made staffing and resourcing his innovations practicable. Third, the very fact that in his early years he had been seen as an effective and successful conservative helped when he wanted to implement change. Fourth, some teachers who did not favour aspects of his reform agenda nevertheless felt, as they told us, it would have been unprofessional to have opposed him. Even so not all staff, initially at least, were willing accomplices. What strategies did he use to secure at least their acquiescence? Some he seems to have won over by securing their commitment to his educational values. How he did this was not always clear, but several commented on his ability to articulate and justify his policies in terms of a coherent and watertight philosophy. Attempts to better him in debate rarely succeeded. He came to be seen by staff as far-sighted, even visionary. Many attested to the power of his argument. By good and determined argument and appeals to certain normative values, Barber, it seems, re-educated his staff to see their work in a new light and in doing so to accept the policies entailed in such a redefinition. By fostering the same kind of enthusiasm he felt himself, he gradually gained the support of more and more staff. For some this 'was very exciting. It was just like being back at college. The atmosphere was one of continual debate and discussion'. For others, 'You could almost describe some (teachers) as brainwashed.'

This last comment hints that there was a darker side to Barber's strategies of reform and to his values as a manager. There is evidence that there was some more-or-less blatant coercion of staff who did not easily accept his policies. According to one 'If you did not toe the line, Barber would come round and thump the table and boot you in the pants', although another suggested 'he tended to ask opponents to go elsewhere'.

Conversely, he was good at assembling allies through appointment. He was also skilful in giving potential allies a stake in the innovations as they progressed and in doing so promoting them to positions of greater authority within the school. How he did this can be seen from the way in which he implemented mixed ability and integrated humanities throughout the school. A member of the humanities team described it as follows

> Barber set up the system year by year. He, the deputy and head of humanities began with the first year, when they had worked through the year left 'Jane Rayner' in charge and moved to the second year. When they had devised the 2nd year work and worked through that they left 'Roslyn Parker' in charge and moved on to the 3rd year . . .

By such a process converts were systematically and gradually located in key positions.

This seems to have been a feature of his approach generally to the system of meetings and teams he established to make key decisions within the school. Here he used powerful allies to instigate and defend the changes dictated by his broad philosophy, and through his personal membership of almost all these groups, he was able to monitor progress and if necessary to veto proposals which ran counter to his policies and values. Many staff considered the deliberations of these groups and committees to have been systematically rigged. It would have been possible to offer numerous examples of this view but I must be content with two or three:

> In Barber's day he had a 'Cabinet' meeting . . . of between 15 and 20 people . . . It did not work formally through agendas, resolutions and minutes, rather through the discussion of issues brought to it, an informal agenda under the control of the head and deputy.

> The School Council met monthly, chaired by the head . . . it was meant as a vehicle for children to influence democratically the working of the school, but he was an authoritarian not a democrat so it didn't work in practice. There was a lot of verbiage from him which meant that he restricted the questions . . .

> Barber was good at manipulating people to get them to do what he wanted.

Not surprisingly, Barber was widely described as a 'totalitarian', an 'autocrat' and a 'ruthless manipulator'. Yet, overwhelmingly, staff also spoke highly, if grudgingly, of his qualities. They commented on his 'visionary powers', his impressive ability to articulate and defend his values and philosophy, and his powers of leadership. Even those who did not prosper under his regime acknowledged his immense ability to work and his dedication and involvement in the work of the school. As one put it 'he was always around the school, he attended pretty well every team meeting and there were a lot of team meetings'. Barber was seen as devoting his working hours to the real work of the school, only beginning his administration after school and always working late. We met no teacher who believed that he or she or any other member of staff worked as hard as Barber. Moreover, several acknowledged that 'With Barber, if you agreed with his philosophy, or at least attempted to apply it, he would back you to the end.' Finally, as time went on, the visible success of his policies in the public arena, expressed in growing numbers of visitors to the school and increasing and often flattering media attention, made it more and more difficult to stand against him. However, all good things come to an end and after 20 years in office Barber finally, and reluctantly, reached an age when he was required to retire.

Mrs Sewell

By the time of his retirement in the late 1970s, the circumstances of the school had changed substantially. Public expressions of a conservative backlash on many of the developments he had fostered such as mixed-ability teaching, 'soft-option' integrated studies course, liberal exam methods were becoming more frequent and trenchant. In addition, there were those within the school for whom discretion had been the better part of valour during the Barber years, who began to express disenchantment with aspects of the existing regime. The new head therefore took up her appointment in a situation which had a strong and established pattern of policy and practice, but which was also moving out of a period potentially ripe for change. As it turned out, her values, policies and strategies differed in a number of important ways from her illustrious predecessor.

We, and many staff, found it difficult to decide if her overall policy either in general or in terms of Rivendell was conservative or radical. Sewell seemed to approve of the overall philosophy of education which Barber had tried to implement, and she seemed to have wanted to conserve much of the best of his era. Yet she also seemed to believe that some structural change was necessary to make their implementation more effective. One thing was clear. She recognized the potential difficulties of succession. As she put it:

> I knew it was going to be a hard act to follow . . . the very fact that he had made such an outstanding and such a morale-boosting success of the school's reoganization to comprehensive education by his avowed policy – which I thought was absolutely the right one of not imitating the grammar school but of becoming a different kind of school – this seemed to be absolutely the right thing to have done.

However, on specific issues, notably attempting to raise the profile of science and technology and diminishing the overwhelmingly privileged position of the humanities, she clearly wished to encourage some change. In attempting these and other innovations she seems to have tried to employ a strategy of assembling allies in a way substantially similar to that used with such success by her predecessor. As she told us, 'It was very much with the sort of object I had in mind that one of the deputy head appointments was made.' Again, she used a similar approach in appointing staff to new positions in the revised pastoral structure of the school. For whatever reason, these strategies were not effective in strengthening her position within the school. Those she chose as allies and sought to promote by no means always reciprocated. This was recognized by a senior member of staff who quickly became an important opponent. As he put it, 'It is worth remembering that some staff gained from her coming. Some of them reneged on her afterwards. *They* had no right to do so.'

This is an interesting comment in various ways, not least because it demonstrates that this member of staff recognized the 'rules of the game' of these appointments and promotions for what they were: a strategy for gaining loyalty and support. If this is what they were, too many were unsuccessful. This was notably the case with the appointment of two relatively young teachers to deputy headships within the school. Both found the struggle to make their own position within the school too demanding to have much time for lending support to the person who had appointed them. In addition, some members of the old guard felt they had been passed over for unacceptable reasons for inexperienced people which the new head had known and brought in from outside the school. However, as she recognized, some, at least, of the resistance which she encountered owed something to rather less rational reasons: 'I think there was bound to be . . . an element of suspicion and a little bit of antagonism in that a relatively inexperienced teacher was appointed to what was obviously a very coveted headship . . .' How, then, did she try to exercise this coveted headship?

Reflecting in retrospect, she described her values and management style in the following terms:

> I tended to be a consultative head . . . and probably in the upshot found that there were certain decisions which everybody expected a head to take and that if you spend too much time consulting about them you just end up offending everybody . . . If you didn't make the consensus of opinion type decisions . . .

Certainly, she fostered discussion on a number of highly contentious issues and established working parties of various aspects of organization and management of the school. In doing so she sought to involve as many staff as possible on these groups and committed herself to having their reports being presented to the governors. In the early days of her regime, quite unlike her predecessor, she even tried to make full staff meetings opportunities for full, free and open discussion. As far as we could tell from our conversations with her and our observations, her policies on decision making, the committee structure, and her role as a consultative head did not seem to have been conceived or employed as a means of manipulation and control. However that may be, they were not well received.

Within a few months of her appointment, a growing number of staff became highly critical. Some argued that her management was undirected by any clear philosophy of her own. As one senior teacher put it to us, 'She had no real philosophy of the comprehensive school and saw her job as dealing with day-to-day things.' Others shared this view and concluded that as a result, the school lacked leadership: 'the school is falling into the trap of too many people doing what they want without any real direction . . .' Yet others criticized her policy and practice on all aspects of staffing, including establishment, appointment and promotion, suggesting that decisions were made on inappropriate grounds and this had led to the institutional-ization of unhelpful bureaucracies. There were certainly some grounds for the latter claim. During her term of office Rivendell developed a pastoral structure of such impenetrable complexity that it was commonly described by staff as a 'bureaucratic nightmare'. Finally, there was also much censuring of her alleged failure to support the teachers she had appointed and her use of these appointments as a means of evading her responsibilities. I can only illustrate the vigour with which these and other criticisms were made:

> She made an absolute mess-up of things. She had a thoroughly bad effect on the school. Despite all you hear about how good she was, she didn't back her teachers . . . She gave rapid promotion to people she knew outside the school. All this had a very bad effect on the school.

> Mrs Sewell has introduced a series of faculty, year and house meetings partly in order that she can farm out responsibility to the people involved. If a criticism came she could say, for example, I am sorry, I have to consult my head of faculty, house, etc. She would not let the 'can' come back to her.

There was also a good deal of resentment over the distinction which she was purported to make between administrative and other posts, and, especially worrying for those of us who teach the subject, her enthusiasm for the jargon of educational management:

> Under Barber there was no talk of administration, you did your administration in an odd minute here and there. Barber didn't start his administration until after 5 o'clock. During the day he was always around the school. So when 'Madam' came, she was talking 'a language that nobody understood' . . . Of course, now I have been on courses and heard people talking about 'top management' and 'middle management' and realize that I have been in a backwater.

A few staff did speak with approval about what she was trying to do and compared her favourably with her predecessor but they were very much in the minority. Most saw her brief term of office as a bad thing for the school. Yet, as I have tried to show, she claimed to have approved of much of her predecessor's values and philosophy, she sought to conserve the best features of the school as she had found it and, in particular, she encouraged consultation and attempted to replace manipulation and coercion with more open and democratic methods. But she failed to carry staff with her. She came to be seen as a head who lacked clear values and a discernible philosophy, who gave little leadership and shuffled off responsibility whenever she could and, and who had presided over a sharp decline in the quality of life and schooling at Rivendell. Where did she go wrong?

Several possible explanations are possible. We did consider if gender was a significant issue and did find some limited evidence in support of this. But Sewell herself did not seem to regard this as important. Rather it was her youth and relative lack of experience and, therefore, of understanding of how to proceed which seems to have been much more critical. That both she and others understood this is evident in some of the quotations presented earlier. In conversation with us she talked about the kind of head that she would like to have become in time, rather than the kind of head she actually was. This led to a lack of certainty on how to handle difficult matters. As she says, 'It's very difficult, I think, to know just how properly to manage such things . . . I hope I would have had the wisdom and insight to have done (what her predecessor did) had I been, you know, that much older . . .'

In the face of such inexperience and uncertainty, a policy of consultative and democratic decision making might seem a logical response, but in practice it led to a mixture of ad hoc management on the one hand, and a large measure of *laissez faire* on the other. In retrospect she believed she did have significant polices on a number of matters, but these were not given coherence by the kind of over-all philosophy which Rivendell had enjoyed under the previous regime, or if they were, this was not clear to the staff. In seeing her predecessor as a hard act to follow, she was more correct than she knew. First, because at a macro-level the climate of opinion which had supported Barber's core innovations was becoming more hostile. Insofar as she sought to preserve key aspects of his legacy she did so in markedly less favourable circumstances. Second, not only did she seem to lack a philosophy as coherent as her predecessor, she also lacked his capacity to win and strengthen allies and to lose and neutralize enemies. Third, she was unwilling or unable to press home the kind of strategies of manipulation and control which Barber had used so ruthlessly and effectively. She soon came to see herself as a failure and this view was shared at Rivendell. In little more than two years she left headship and moved to another post.

Mr Lucas

Perceived failures of the previous administration meant staff morale was generally thought to be low, with many hoping that the new head would give some sort of lead to fill the vacuum left by Barber's retirement. But there were also misgivings. Some were concerned that the new head might 'initiate even more changes from the Barber philosophy'. Others feared the prospect of some dismantling of the structures of posts which had mushroomed during Sewell's brief period in office and from which they had benefited. One even threatened to resign if this took place. In the event some restructuring did take place but he proved to be a major beneficiary. No more was heard of this threat.

Sewell had been 34 when she took up the headship at Rivendell. She had been a teacher for some 10 years. Her first and only prior post had been as a Deputy Head to which she had been appointed directly from a managerial post in publishing. On appointment Lucas was in his early fifties, had spent his working life as a school teacher and, before he came to Rivendell, had been for many years the head of another, if smaller, comprehensive school within the same local authority. He had some knowledge of what had happened at Rivendell under his predecessor and came determined to achieve rapid change. He saw the innovations he wished to make as a rational response to change in the light of perceived constraints. He was also clear about the potential advantages of the new systems that he wished to put in place; we at the time, as researchers, saw these as being primarily to do with achieving a smoother and more streamlined administration in which better use might be made of the resources invested in various positions of responsibility.

The changes were driven through very rapidly and with little general consultation. Lucas once told us he believed that 'any meeting for more than 20 minutes is useless'. He tended to be as good as his word on this. Staff meetings became 10-minute weekly meetings 'for the dissemination of information', mainly in a top down format. When major meetings took place they were usually carefully stage managed. At the key meeting at which staff had the 'opportunity to discuss' the structural changes he was intending to implement, they found themselves filing in faced by a semicircle of people seated at the front of the room who represented the new order and who had most to benefit from the reforms. Lucas opened his remarks by making it clear that he did not welcome debate on the broader principles and concluded that, 'I will be happy to end this meeting at 10:20 but would definitely want to finish by 12:00; I don't want to dwell on the reasons for these changes'. He used much the same approach when introducing the proposed changes to a meeting of the Parent–Teacher Association.

Although there was a good deal of support, along with some opposition, to the structural and other reforms Lucas proposed, there was strong objection to the way in which these changes were being introduced. There were numerous references to the *fait accompli*, to inadequate or non-existent consultation, and to the various discussion documents which were being produced at the times as the pronouncements or the edicts. Perhaps because of all this, a number of staff quickly concluded that, like his predecessor and unlike Barber, Lucas had no educational policy and was not much interested in trying to develop one. Yet for us it seemed that there was a clear, if implicit, philosophy behind the quite radical educational changes he sought to implement at Rivendell. Conversely, there was a widely shared understanding that a major change in the rules of the game had taken place in terms of the values which underpinned management and decision making at the school. Everyone was clear, including Lucas, that the authority resides in the head and, by their inclusion in policy formulation, in his deputies. The new system was at best hierarchical and at worst overtly autocratic.

However one evaluates the changes Lucas introduced, or the methods he used to achieve them, there can be no doubt that within his first year at the school sweeping educational and managerial changes were made and more were on their way. It is also beyond doubt that these changes were by no means welcomed by all. Yet the actual level of resistance, despite the heated rhetoric sometimes heard within the school's staff rooms and elsewhere, was relatively small. Why was this?

In part, this was because Lucas was skilful in buying or squaring off those who might have been most disaffected. He was also successful in 'building in' senior and influential staff into key positions within the new structures and in making them clearly accountable for key aspects of the work these entailed. This gave the structures an aura of power and officially-legitimated authority in the eyes of most staff. In some respects, for example, in his attempts to restrict the scope of staff meetings, Lucas might be thought to have been using an approach which reflected the kind of more-or-less manipulation which had characterized the Barber regime. On balance we felt that this was not an appropriate interpretation since given the overtness of his autocratic style of management, Lucas did not seem to require manipulation of any subtlety. Conversely, given the absence of opportunities for debate, discussion and consultation, he left himself little room to employ some of the strategies that Barber had used with such telling effect. The opportunities for advocating the normative grounds for the changes he wished to make were simply not there, and without them the kinds of attachment to his philosophy that Barber secured from many of his staff through strong moral appeals were almost impossible to achieve. If Barber surrounded himself with disciples at all levels amongst his teachers, the best Lucas could hope for were loyal line managers and an acquiescent staff. Insofar as this is what he wanted, the evidence suggests that he was successful both during an initial brief period of intense reform and in the many years of his regime that followed.

Peter Ribbins

Conclusions on a Case

As an illustration of the praxis of three educational leaders some may find the case of Rivendell makes for uncomfortable reading. It tells us of Mr Barber, who espoused a coherent and comprehensive set of egalitarian and democratic egalitarian philosophies that were at variance with the often calculating and manipulative managerial strategies which he employed with such telling effect to achieve his purposes. It also tells us of Mrs Sewell, who had no coherent educational philosophy or was unable to make clear what this was, lacked the will or the ability to be manipulative. Thus, while Barber merely espoused democratic managerial ideals, Sewell made a real effort to introduce democratic structures and processes, only to be accused of a lack of leadership and a poverty of philosophy. Seen as unsuccessful, she came to share this view and gave up headship. Rivendell teachers, it seemed, preferred strong leadership and a semblance of democracy, even when they knew this to be largely a sham. From their third head, Mr Lucas, they got strong and honest leadership without much manipulation and little attempt at even a facade of democracy. Again, they were not satisfied. Lucas was in a hurry and successfully drove through many major changes during his first year at the school yet, despite much passionate talk of opposition, very little came of any of this.

Final thoughts

In this chapter I have outlined a three level approach to the study of leaders, leading and leadership. I have sought to illustrate the merits of this approach in one of its third level ethnographic forms with reference to three successive, and very different, regimes of headship at a secondary school in the United Kingdom. I believe that this approach can be applied to good effect to research into the praxis of leaders and led within a wide variety of educational and other contexts and would wish to take this opportunity to call for more such studies. Those who are mad enough (Wragg, 1995) to want to be leaders, but who have no desire to be corrupted by the exercise of this 'moral art', need them. Hodgkinson (1991) notes that one of the functions of his book is to 'ground action on better theory, on the best theory available' (1991, 111). I believe it is also necessary to attempt to ground theory in action.

References

BEST, R., RIBBINS, P., JARVIS, C. and ODDY, D. (1983) *Education and Care*, Oxford: Blackwell.
GARDNER, H. (1995) *Leading Minds: An Anatomy of Leadership*, New York: Basic Books.
GREENFIELD, T. and RIBBINS, P. (1993) *Greenfield on Educational Administration: Towards a Humane Science*, London: Routledge.
GRONN, P. and RIBBINS, P. (1996) 'Leaders in context: Post-positivist approaches to understanding educational leadership', *Educational Administration Quarterly*, **32**, 3.

HODGKINSON, C. (1991) *Educational Leadership: The Moral Art*, Albany, New York: SUNY.

MORTIMER, P. and MORTIMER, J. (eds) (1991a) *The Primary Head*, Salisbury: Open Books.

MORTIMER, P. and MORTIMER, J. (eds) (1991b) *The Secondary Head*, Salisbury: Open Books.

RIBBINS, P. (1986) 'Qualitative perspectives in research in secondary education', in SIMKINS, T. (ed.) *Research in the Management of Secondary Education*, Sheffield: Sheffield City Polytechnic.

RIBBINS, P. and MARLAND, M. (1994) *Headship Matters: Conversations with Seven Secondary School Headteachers*, London: Longman.

RICHARDSON, E. (1973) *The Teacher, the School and the Task of Management*, London: Heinemann.

SEDDON, T. (1994) *Context and Beyond*, London: Falmer Press.

SOUTHWORTH, G. (1995) *Looking into Primary Headship: A Research-based Interpretation*, London: Falmer Press.

WRAGG, T. (1995) 'You don't *have* to be mad to try this . . .', *TES*, 20 October, p. 60.

9   Leadership From a Distance: Institutionalizing Values and Forming Character at Timbertop, 1951–61

Peter Gronn

Introduction

The mid- to late 1970s was a fecund period for leadership studies during which a number of seminal works challenged prevailing assumptions in the field. One such publication, deemed a leadership classic and the subject of a recent symposium in the *Leadership Quarterly*, was Kerr and Jermier's highly influential substitutes for leadership article. Kerr and Jermier (1978) proposed a matrix comprising 24 sets of contingent circumstances in which the direct or indirect leadership of an individual might comprise just one of a range of candidate explanations invoked to account for event outcomes and performance in organizations. Following some empirical work of their own Kerr and Jermier concluded that leadership counted on less than half of the posited occasions. Instead, the explanation for what transpired mostly lay with a range of substitute factors: characteristics inherent in the task, the subordinate and the organization. Probably the most significant implication of this substitutes finding is that in a number of instances the scope for the effective exercise of leadership is very likely to be minimal or neutralized by countervailing forces.[1]

    Almost immediately Kerr and Jermier's claim was taken up by Manz and Sims (1980) to propound an argument for employee self-management as one possible substitute for superordinate leadership – an area of scholarly endeavour which has subsequently blossomed – but, as Howell (1997, p. 114) notes, the full impact of the substitutes thesis across the field was partially blunted by the simultaneous publication of, and later reception accorded, James MacGregor Burns' (1978) magisterial study entitled *Leadership*. Burns' book, in turn, provided much of the stimulus for Bass' (1985) *Leadership and Performance Beyond Expectations* and the latter's subsequently influential research program with Avolio and others on transformational leadership. Nonetheless, Podsakoff and MacKenzie's (1997, p. 118) review of two decades of leader substitutes research in the same *LQ* symposium indicates the breadth and depth of impact of Kerr and Jermier's original argument in a range of disciplines and subfields. What is noteworthy, however, is that the body of findings reviewed by Podsakoff and MacKenzie emanates, almost without exception, from psychometrically designed studies. By contrast, in their symposium response Jermier and Kerr (1997, p. 98) query the search for substitutes in situations intended to yield 'a significant cross-sectional correlational effect involving leader behaviors'. Rather, they assert that:

> at the heart of the matter of leader substitutes is the typical situation where leader behavior and outcome variables are weakly related or unrelated. The substitutes model offers an explanation for this situation along the lines that leadership has already had its effects through the substitutes such that formal face-to-face interactions would be superfluous.

In short, to the extent that managerial leadership achieves its presumed effects then it is likely to do so in circumstances other than the deliberate, overt exercise of decision-making power in interpersonal interactions, viz. through 'technological, structural, and other impersonal processes in the organization'.

Jermier and Kerr (1997, p. 99) go on to lament not only the absence of any research into such processes but also the paucity of attention accorded contextual factors – as opposed to the psychometric preference for 'contextual variables' – and the subjective understandings of the actors in such contexts, a point developed at greater length elsewhere by this writer (see Gronn and Ribbins, 1996). For Jermier and Kerr, then, the utility and validity of cross-sectional research designs and questionnaire surveys of leadership appear to have gone way beyond the point of diminishing returns. Immediately following a confessional *mea culpa* for their sins of commission in this regard in their own work, they then make a forceful case for longitudinal fieldwork designed to permit an analysis of the development of substitutes over time and the understanding attached to them by participants in a variety of settings. This chapter takes up this challenge by providing a variant of the longitudinal qualitative approach sought by Jermier and Kerr – an historical case study relying on documentary sources and oral history interviews – which meets their criterion of minimized face-to-face interaction (i.e., an absence of bodily co-presence) between a leader and (in this instance) his subordinates: hence the title of the paper. The case documented is the first decade of Timbertop, the mountain school campus of the Geelong Grammar School, in Victoria, Australia, during the final years of the headmastership of its founder, James Ralph Darling.

This account of the evolution of Timbertop has the additional virtue of illustrating the importance of values in organizational life, something lying at the heart of a well-respected, alternative and longstanding approach to leadership which emphasizes the leader's moral authority – rather than her or his measurable behaviour – and generally associated with traditional theorists like Selznick and Barnard. The image of the leader in Barnard's (1982 [1938]) beehive-like, cooperative organizational system outlined in his classic, *The Functions of the Executive*, for example, is of a kind of great moral helmsman (and, by implication, helmswoman). Building on Barnard's work in *Leadership in Administration*, Selznick (1957, p. 17) stressed the importance of the leader in institutionalizing values, by which he meant 'to *infuse with value* beyond the technical requirements of the task at hand' (Selznick, 1957, p. 17, original emphasis; and see Selznick, 1992, p. 233; Terry, 1993). More recent commentators in this tradition have invoked the image of an organization as a 'moral order' and the leader as an 'entrepreneur for its values' (Greenfield and Ribbins, 1993, p. 222), and even go as far as typifying organizations as akin at times to 'moral primitives' (Hodgkinson, 1991, p. 190).

When institutionalizing values, according to Selznick (1957, p. 27), the leader exercises a 'guiding hand' – imagery consistent with the Barnardian idea of the hand at the helm, but contrasting with other hand metaphors such as the alleged 'dead hand' of the state and the 'invisible hand' of the market – yet what does such moral steering or guidance look like in practice? How, for example, does a leader invested with moral authority set about institutionalizing desired ends or purposes and then husbanding them? The recent literature on leadership is studded with normatively framed exhortations about the importance of charismatic and visionary thinking, consistent with the quest for excellence and new organizational heroes (Gronn, 1995), and usually set within a context of organizational restructuring and competitive economic advantage. Values are often claimed to figure prominently in the work of these new entrepreneurial leaders, yet longitudinal studies document-ing the perspectives of leaders and led, and unravelling the processes of wholesale structural change and accompanying shifts in values, tend to be thin on the ground – Roberts' (1985) work, perhaps, being a noteworthy exception (and see Roberts and Bradley, 1988).

Given these recent developments, and as an example of institutional leadership, stewardship, custodianship or what Terry (1990) refers to as 'administrative con-servatorship', Timbertop takes on added significance. First, it illustrates what might be termed leadership at a remove or from afar as part of which an innovation that is the brainchild of a highly esteemed educational leader (i.e. Darling) is implemented, but in the form of a satellite campus or an extension to an existing school, and physically distant from it, in which case the leader is in no position to exercise direct, day-to-day supervision over its development and implementation. Second, given that this particular project represented such a significant financial outlay and investment for the school concerned, and given that there was no precedent for Timbertop in Australia (and virtually none anywhere else in the world at the time) on which to fall back, Darling's leadership was not only ground-breaking, but also enshrined a reasonably high risk strategy in which the potential for things to go badly awry, and for him to experience a deep sense of personal failure, was genuine. Third, because of these possible eventualities, Darling's leadership was all the more remarkable given that the early years of the Timbertop experiment corresponded with the end of a long and illustrious career (1930–1961) – a twilight time for many leaders who tend to look back and consolidate their achievements, and minimize the possibility of being remembered for any humiliating and ignoble last hurrahs.

The chapter analyses the evolving delegated authority relationship between Darling and the first head of Timbertop whom he appointed, Edward Hugh Mont-gomery, and in doing so highlights the importance of a neglected substitute for the direct exercise of leadership, namely the leadership duo or couple. Couples typically comprise a partnership between the incumbents of a superordinate and a subordin-ate managerial role (Krantz, 1989), the kind of mutually supportive dual relation-ship formed by a focal leader and a sympathetic key figure in adjacent agency or instrumentality (Bryman, Gillingwater and McGuinness, 1996, pp. 859–60) or siblings in a family business (Bryman, 1993, p. 298). Like the increasingly popular senior level management team, a leadership couple is a species of Hodgson, Levinson and Zaleznik's (1965) executive role constellation, a leadership arrangement marked by a division of role tasks and responsibilities along specialized and complementary lines, and some type of negotiated understanding designed to maintain a requisite and robust psychological distance between its members. Yet couples are much more common in leadership and management than is normally acknowledged. They can be found in a variety of diverse contexts but particularly in multi-divisional corporate structures or instrumentalities (e.g. firms and transnational corporations) and in multi-site organizations (e.g. universities) in which the section, agency, campus, regional or divisional head acts on behalf of, or with a roving commission from, a CEO or equivalent executive officeholder.

Krantz (1989, p. 161) pointed to a paradox at the heart of the couple, namely that 'each [individual] must trust the other while coping with feelings of dependence on the other'. This chapter shows that the resolution of the paradox is itself paradoxical for, if the relationship between the substitute and the leader for whom he is a proxy is to be productive, then the duo might best comprise an 'odd couple' rather than a cloned or carbon copy pair of duplicate operational styles and evenly matched psychological temperaments. Moreover, the circumstances of institution-building or expansion – i.e., the foundation of a new organizational branch – it is argued, provide an ideal opportunity for the circumscribed autonomy of the substitute to flower. Wedded to an implicitly understood world view or framework of values, and with each partner in the couple knowing the mind of the other, both the senior of the two (as the founder and framer of the new vision), and the junior (as the keeper or guardian of his mandate), build a joint and evolving understanding in their separate spheres and bailiwicks as the enterprise to whose realization they are jointly committed is given shape. One final paradox, of course, is that in his new geographically isolated or distant realm the junior partner in the couple and substitute for the absent leader – the chief agent of influence – is himself both a follower and a leader.[2]

Methods and Sources

The following discussion of the Darling–Montgomery partnership arises from extended biographical work-in-progress on Darling's life and his contribution to Australian education. This research relies on a variety of documentary sources which, in the case of Darling's Timbertop years, include letters between Darling and Montgomery (classified annually as part of the headmasters' correspondence files) and Darling's monthly reports to the school council. Other documents comprise various school council records and individual files on Old Geelong Grammarians or old boys (i.e. alumni), all of which are housed in the Geelong Grammar School Archives. Other collections consulted include the Darling Papers, the bulk of which are retained by the Darling family and some of which are held in the National

Library of Australia (Canberra). Regular reports in the *Corian* – the magazine of the Geelong Grammar School – were also drawn on.

When drafting the chapter on Timbertop for the biography – on which this chapter is based – information from these sources and from publicly available records (e.g. newspapers) was classified into a number of initial, first-sort categories (103 in all) in broad conformity with the process of open coding outlined by Strauss and Corbin (1990, pp. 61–74). These were subsequently collapsed or consolidated into a small number of core or anchoring themes which were then interwoven selectively as part of a broad chronological narrative. What quickly became apparent from the coding process were two things: first, that as an instance of leadership it made little sense to think of the development of this educational innovation as a single-handed endeavour – rather Timbertop owed its successful evolution to the joint oversight of two men; second, the contours of the couple relationship between the two of them were formed when they worked their way through a series of incidents related to the moral welfare and character development of young men during the early years of Timbertop. These two points are elaborated in the following sections.

Timbertop and its Antecedents

The Timbertop campus is located on the slopes of Mt Timbertop, 140 miles northeast of Melbourne, the state capital of Victoria, and about 180 miles from the main (Corio) campus of Geelong Grammar School, a coeducational fee-paying boarding school founded in 1857. The new site was established in 1951 for a number of expedient and personal reasons. First, it was an attempt to solve problems arising out of increased school running costs and an acute shortage of boarding accommodation. Darling's main difficulty in the late-1940s and early-1950s was to contain rising costs during a period of sky-rocketing inflation in the Australian economy and recent hefty basic wage increases awarded as part of the national system of centralized wage fixation. His options were the usual (and to him distasteful) ones of either making economies and reducing enrolments or increasing tuition fees. But in a period of buoyant enrolments by far his most pressing immediate problem was the sheer pressure of pupils at Corio; he calculated that in 1952, for example, the school would be 53 boys over-capacity.

Second, the burgeoning demands of administering a school already occupying three sites (one in Melbourne, one in Corio and one six miles away in Geelong) were beginning to weigh heavily on him. He was, as he confessed to one of his old boys, becoming acutely conscious of his age:

> As one gets older I think one realizes more fully the truth that one 'can only light a little candle to the glory of God' and that adequate stewardship must probably be content with the sphere limited by one's personal contacts. While I may have had great ideas of being an influence in the educational and political life of the country I am now much more content to understand that the boys actually in the school at any given time are my main responsibility and opportunity.

Being 'very much older' meant that he could no longer 'work so quickly or recover so rapidly from crises'. So vast was the educational leviathan which he had created and which he now presided over 'that organization and administration tend to crowd out the more valuable personal work, and I find it very difficult to get out of the office'. 'I wage a continuous battle against the tentacles of the machine, examinations, public [i.e., independent, fee-paying] school sport, out of school activities all the result of enfolding and cramping the boy himself.' The only solution lay in still further expansion and thereby creating – ironically – yet one more school site: 'Briefly it is to take a whole year of boys ([aged] $14\frac{1}{2}$–$15\frac{1}{2}$ probably), buy a property just under the mountains in the real bush and send them there to do a year of the[ir] education in harder but more natural surroundings outside the claims of the machine.' Simultaneously, this 'epoch-making' idea would be of educational value because it would strengthen boys' bodies, their wills, and help conquer their physical fears; it would also satisfy 'the natural instinct for the earth', permitting him to alleviate general congestion at the main school.[3]

The school council subcommittee which oversaw the inauguration of the project in 1951 made an inspired choice of location. The site comprised about 500 acres with a leasehold of an additional 1200 surrounding acres and lay at about 2000 feet above sea level on the northern side of the Great Dividing Range (a spine of moderately high mountains sprawling across central and northeastern Victoria), which meant that it would be sunnier and less wet than a south-facing position. Moreover, the new site was within ready reach of a railway station, which alleviated the problem of transporting pupils (then solely boys) to and from Corio or Melbourne. A small mountain stream formed a natural boundary and guaranteed the school a regular supply of fresh water. From this stream the lightly wooded terrain initially rose gently and then more steeply on a forested slope back up the northern face of Mt Timbertop, a mountain slightly in excess of 4000 feet at its summit. To the immediate east was the Mt Buller alpine village, Victoria's premier skiing resort. It was a breath-takingly picturesque area comprising dense (but not impenetrable) bushland and pristine forest with superb, picture postcard views and vistas attainable in every direction from the surrounding peaks, virtually all of which were snow-capped in winter. Moreover, it was still substantially virgin countryside which provided the mountaineering enthusiast with an almost inexhaustible number of exhilarating walking tracks, both up and down the valleys and along the craggy escarpments, all of which were generously endowed with native flora.

Timbertop has become associated in the popular mind with the fact that the heir to the British throne, His Royal Highness, Charles, the Prince of Wales, spent two terms there on exchange from Gordonstoun School, near Inverness, Scotland, in 1966. Indeed it was Kurt Hahn,[4] the founder of Gordonstoun (and its headmaster when the Prince's father, the Duke of Edinburgh, was head boy there in 1939), whose educational efforts lay in the back of Darling's mind while the Timbertop scheme was taking shape. Like many educators in the English-speaking world, Darling knew of Hahn's famous work at Salem, a coeducational boarding school near Lake Constance, Baden, through a well-known article in *The Listener*[5] published shortly after Hahn fled Nazi Germany for Britain in 1933. It was not until

1955, however, that Darling and Hahn eventually met in England, but Darling already knew a good deal about Hahn's ideas from a Gordonstoun housemaster, F. Spencer Chapman,[6] who visited Corio in 1941 while on a military posting in Australia.

A Very Odd Couple

Timbertop opened in early 1953. In August of the previous year Montgomery had been detached from his duties at Corio and appointed as master-in-charge at Timbertop in order to oversee the implementation of the new scheme. There is some suggestion that Darling had toyed at first with offering the job to Spencer Chapman (recently resigned as head of the King Alfred School in Plön, West Germany) who confessed himself tired of working in England but a great enthusiast for Darling's new venture.[7] Despite this possibility, Montgomery – or 'Mont', but 'Basher' to the boys – was the obvious choice. Since his appointment to Corio in 1941, and except for three years (1948–1950) during which he was the state member for Geelong in the Victorian Legislative Assembly, Montgomery had been, as Darling later described him, his 'factotum when anything practical needed to be done'.[8] Montgomery himself wrote that he 'once told the Headmaster that I was never sure whether he had engaged me as a master or a labourer' (Montgomery and Darling, 1967, p. 19). An intensely practical man, Montgomery embodied those traits often remarked upon as being the hallmarks of the traditional Australian male character: a practical man, down-to-earth, laconic, stoical, direct in manner and devoid of any hint of affectation or pretence. A contemporary recalled Montgomery as a big man with a domineering manner and a straight, no-nonsense talker. He was an excellent organizer and supervisor of the various outdoor pursuits for which Geelong Grammar under Darling's tutelage had become renowned: the wartime national service scheme, school pageants and exhibitions, forestry camps, fruit-picking during Christmas vacations and building construction. Montgomery remained at Timbertop as master until his retirement in 1963. According to school folklore Montgomery is supposed to have harboured an intense dislike of all Englishmen – except, of course, for those whom he had met.

The contrast with his headmaster could not have been more dramatic. Darling was an upper middle-class Englishman. He was educated at a minor English public school (Repton, Derby) and, following brief war service in France and Germany, had gone up to Oriel College, Oxford, where he took a BA. He then became a history master at Merchant Taylor's School, Crosby (near Liverpool) and at Charterhouse, Surrey, prior to his arrival at Corio in February 1930. At 30 years of age, and a bachelor, Darling had been the youngest of the five heads appointed since 1857 to administer the school. A highly intelligent, erudite, cultured, urbane and intensely religious and moral man, Darling moved at will and with ease in the club and society world of the various Australian elite strata who enrolled their privileged offspring at the school. His restless, fertile mind displayed an extraordinary capacity for generating innovative and original educational ideas in what was a Church of England school established originally by an act of the Synod of the Diocese of Melbourne and governed by a council comprising (mainly) old boys and clergy. As the head of an institution standing four-square in the English public boarding school tradition – and which thought of itself as 'the Eton of the Antipodes' – Darling wielded enormous authority. By the eve of World War II he had lifted Geelong Grammar's public profile and enhanced its reputation amongst Australian boys' schools beyond all measure (Gronn, 1992, 1994). Amidst the privations and frustrating restrictions of war, however, Darling's innovative urge had been dampened somewhat (Gronn, 1991) and he experienced the post-war period as one of marking time, so much so that his career may be said to have reached a plateau. Timbertop, therefore, offered him a real chance to rekindle his reforming fervour and to quicken his innovative pulse.

Ever since mid-1951, when Darling was supposed to have told him, 'Montgomery, I want you to buy me a mountain' (Montgomery and Darling, 1967, p. 19), it had been the latter's job to try and give shape to Darling's newest and boldest scheme yet. The next decade bore witness to a most remarkable relationship between the two men. Montgomery's entire authority at Timbertop was delegated to him by his headmaster. Being on the spot, however, meant that he exercised the remarkable latitude to decide as he thought fit so that Darling had, in effect, placed himself in a position of near to absolute dependence on his underling for the success of his new venture. The irony was never lost on him. Moreover, given that the primary purpose of Timbertop was educational – i.e. its business was the traditional business of the school, which had always been character-building – the headmaster's influence on the boys for the year in which they were absent from Corio could only ever be indirect. This was an entirely new experience for Darling and one he was undergoing in the ebb-tide of a long and glittering career. On the other hand, because the two men had for some time had one another's measure and they trusted each other implicitly, Darling was able to put his mind to rest. The success of their relationship was founded on the need for absolute candour and a regular flow of information between them, yet – despite a number of early problems at Timbertop calculated to tax the most rock solid of unspoken understandings (and to be discussed shortly) – neither man ever really felt constrained to question the nature of their relationship.

'A Sort of Holy Madness'[9]

Darling launched the Timbertop scheme on speech (or prize-giving) day in December 1951 in an address to parents, pupils and old boys in which he made his strongest plea yet to the Geelong Grammar community to exercise moral leadership in the nation. His exhortation came shortly after the appearance in the jubilee year of the Commonwealth of Australia of *A Call to the People of Australia* – a well-publicized document endorsed by religious leaders and senior judges, and which was broadcast nationally on Remembrance Day (commemorating the World War I Armistice), 11 November. 'Now, more than ever, at a time in the history of

Australia when it has been judged necessary by the responsible leaders of the community to issue a Call to the Nation to abandon its selfish and unmoral materialism', Darling inveighed, 'it lies upon us whose education makes us capable of understanding that call to be the first to respond to it, and to accept the leadership which such a response involves.' The survival of democracy, he urged, required moral leadership. The real threat to the Australian social fabric was not revolutionary communism at all,[10] but 'selfishness in our personal ambitions and the refusal and fear of honest thinking'. To produce moral leaders, dedicated to the service of the community, some relief from the grip of 'the tightly-packed machine of school organization' simply had to be found. Leadership required courage and courage could come only from boys mastering their bodily weaknesses and fears, from going beyond fatigue, confronting error and then sticking to their ideals through thick and thin. What he wanted for Geelong Grammar, he told everyone present, was 'something different but at the same time something which is in the true tradition of its foundation'. The proposal, he continued, was consistent with the spirit of Hahn's work and the Outward Bound movement, except that Timbertop was to be incorporated, as he preferred to think of it, into the ordinary life of an ordinary school. It would be as self-supporting a settlement as possible, with the emphasis on the development of individual self-dependence and initiative, and a love of the land. Apart from these educational advantages, the sending of about 100 middle dormitory boys to Timbertop would, 'in one glorious hit', solve the school's 'desperate problem' of overcrowding. In order to continue to be 'an abiding influence in the life of Australia', therefore, Geelong Grammar had to change its form, while preserving 'its true spirit and tradition'.[11] His speech was a model of conservative reform: calculated institutional adaptation as a considered response to mounting pressures for change.

Site work got under way at Timbertop in Easter 1952 to prepare for the initial intake of boys the following year. The translation of his headmaster's ideas into the physical fabric and texture of a new school was Montgomery's essential brief, a difficult one given that building materials were in seriously short supply, and Darling and the school council were wholly intent on keeping expenses down (by the end of 1952 the estimated cost of Timbertop had blown out to £115,000). It was decided to accommodate the boys in separate, free-standing units, constructed from locally milled timber on partially excavated sites, to be built by the school using its own boy labour, and designed for 12 boys per unit – each unit comprising a living room and fireplace, dormitory, pantry, boiler room, changing room, bathroom and lavatory. There were also drainage and soil erosion problems to be dealt with and quite appalling weather conditions endured during the construction phase. Furthermore, the condition of the mountain roads and tracks was dreadful – mostly mud, slush, potholes and ditches. Until a telephone was installed in early 1953, communication with the outside world was extremely difficult. Despite these and numerous other seemingly insurmountable difficulties – not to mention his own recurring bouts of gloom and despondency – Darling insisted on speech day 1952 that his idea had been well and truly vindicated, astonishingly well supported by the parents, and that 'the back of it is broken and it is going to be a great success'.[12]

Regular school work began in earnest for the first intake of boys on 16 February 1953 while construction of the units and buildings continued round about them. Invoking the requisite spirit of school patriotism Montgomery reported in the *Corian* that Darling's experiment in boy governance was working:

> The first term has shown that the method of allowing boys to 'run themselves' as much as possible is most successful. Two boys are elected each month from each Unit, and act as spokesmen for their Unit, and are responsible for organization and general 'looking after' of their own interests. Much valuable information has been forthcoming in the form of suggestions and requests, all of which have gone towards the better working of the School . . . Because of this method of running, discipline, as such, is hardly apparent, and with the feeling that it is 'our' School and not 'the School', there is little necessity to suggest ways and means whereby boys should take more care of furniture, books, and a hundred and one things which are so often badly treated.[13]

Gradually, the customs and activities for which Timbertop would eventually become famous emerged. One of the earliest of these was the weekend camp in which groups of at least three boys were entrusted to hike and camp out on journeys in excess of 30 miles there and back to a favoured destination. It was to be three years before anything went badly amiss on any of these Timbertop expeditions but in mid-1956 during inclement weather four lads failed to arrive at their anticipated rendezvous on time. Eventually they did make it but only after a major public search had been organized. This resulted in some undesirable publicity for the school, including reports in the Melbourne press and an item on the Australian Broadcasting Commission radio news. Montgomery took some comfort that much was learned from the mishap, but his 'cross', as he termed it, was that he had had to request Darling to agree to the all-out search – 'I must confess that I honestly felt at the time that we could not afford to wait longer.' Thankfully, in the absence of the Timbertop masters during the crisis, the remaining boys had 'run the place unaided' for two days.[14]

Testing the Limits

By about 1954 some semblance of normality was taking root at Timbertop. The hectic pioneering period was substantially behind the two men and their new arms-length relationship had begun to regularize itself. In the early years Darling had involved himself directly in a hands-on way at Timbertop as much as he could in activities like work camps, site preparation and clearance. From this time on he visited Timbertop approximately once during a school term or whenever he accompanied important visitors and dignitaries. In between times he and Montgomery corresponded reasonably frequently, and Darling would report monthly to meetings of the school council, relying on Montgomery's lengthy hand-written summaries of developments. The two of them would usually only telephone one another sparingly – except in times of crisis (such as the emergency just referred to) – or whenever the circumstances were thought to have got sticky or out of hand and Montgomery felt he needed Darling's 'ruling', as he termed it. Then, provided the two of them agreed, or if Darling formally requested him or suggested that Montgomery might care to come down to Corio, the latter would undertake the long, time-consuming journey to confer with his headmaster.

This working division of labour between the two of them was roughly equivalent to the well-known distinction between policy and operations, with Darling making all staff appointments and curriculum decisions for Timbertop and Montgomery exercising control over the development and maintenance of the site, as well as discretionary authority in regard to the welfare and discipline of the boys. This arrangement suggests that, almost by definition, the idea of delegated responsibility for operational decision making would appear to be a perfect example of a substitute for leadership and, in this particular Timbertop instance of it, of the superfluousness of formal face-to-face interactions (Jermier and Kerr, 1997, p. 98). Equally, delegated authority seems to be a clear cut case of when a leader's so-called effects on organizational outcomes can only ever be indirect (i.e. mediated through a substitute). But delegation also raises questions to do with whether, in circumstances of substantial discretion to a subordinate substitute, effects or outcomes can be reliably predicted (Hambrick and Finkelstein, 1987, p. 394), and the very meaning of 'effects' and what it means to achieve effects directly or indirectly. A long time ago Friedrich (1963, pp. 199–200) pointed out how in instances of 'anticipated reactions' no action on the part of person A was necessary in order to influence B. All that B needed to do was to assume (possibly incorrectly) what A might do were a certain policy to be adopted and then to refrain from action, in which case B's expectation of A influenced B's resulting inaction or choice of an alternative. Thus, influence can prevent certain outcomes from occurring, as well as causing them to take place.

This point is especially germane to the way in which the Darling–Montgomery odd couple worked in operational matters, because it was precisely in fluid and ambiguous circumstances (such as at Timbertop where new behaviour codes were not yet absolutely clear) – the very opposite situation from those in which substitute leadership would be evident, as noted originally by Kerr and Jermier (1978, p. 398) – that Montgomery would seek his leader's 'ruling'. This was Montgomery's strategy despite there being evidence of Kerr and Jermier's (1978, p. 398) two necessary characteristics for the exercise of subordinate substitute influence – ability and 'professional' orientation – in his administrative makeup. There is another complicating point here as well. Krantz (1989, p. 16) notes that the price paid by leadership couples for the aforementioned irony of mutual-trust-but-also-mutual-dependence at the heart of their relationship is that 'the extent to which each [partner] relies on the other and can be let down by the other often touches upon deep-seated anxieties'. These two points (i.e. leader influence instead of substitute influence in ambiguous circumstances and the leader's anxiety) come together in consideration of this couple's handling of a number of incidents in which boys transgressed emerging Timbertop norms and values – bearing in mind that, of the more than 1000 boys who passed through Timbertop between 1953 and 1961, the examples cited represent a minuscule proportion (although some of the most difficult) of this overall number.

Misdemeanors

From the very beginning Darling had been sensitive to innuendo and mutterings at Corio that the standard of classroom work could be expected to decline and to the allegation later on that it was indeed worsening, amidst the novel environment of Timbertop. Much and all as Darling considered Montgomery to be 'never better when facing difficulties' and that he 'does succeed in passing on this spirit to the boys under him', he informed the council in late 1953 that he had told Montgomery that Timbertop 'must be regarded as a failure insofar as in the handling of it we have relapse[d] to making it just an ordinary part of the school, governed in the same way'.[15] But it was behaviour problems which really unleashed the headmaster's latent anxieties, and the factor which compounded matters here was Darling's understandable desire to secure the widest, maximum, positive publicity for his venture.

From a public relations perspective, Darling's experiment in boy democracy was undoubtedly one of Timbertop's great strengths. He knew this, admitted it publicly and was perfectly content for it to be the yardstick by which Timbertop would be judged (Darling, 1954, p. 225):

> For various rather complicated administrative reasons, the establishment of Timbertop will help the main school, but it is upon its educational merit that it is to be judged, and the verdict on that question will depend upon the degree to which it succeeds in answering the problems posed in the first part of this article [i.e. growing up into self-confident independence, which he had termed 'the core of the educational process']. So far it can be said at least that the results are promising.

In 1955, however, when he was on leave in England, there was a spate of bullying in three of the units, and because the unit system represented the heart of the boys' community life, such incidents meant that boy government was also likely to be Timbertop's feature of greatest vulnerability. More bullying followed in 1956. Reports of it 'frightened' him, Darling confessed candidly to Montgomery shortly after his return home in late 1955, because – while 'God knows I am in no position down here to throw any stones' – 'Timbertop is the very apple of my eye and anything which affects its reputation hits me very hard.' He was acutely conscious that 'we have staked our all' on the belief that the masters' supervision and vigilance could be dispensed with and exercised by the boys. Moreover, he confessed to being nagged by feelings of unease that he and Montgomery had been wrong 'in trying to pass the responsibility round, with the inevitable result of having on occasions very weak leaders'. 'Is it possible that we should try to achieve more continuity by holding back the twenty best boys of one year for a month or a term to introduce the new ones to the system, and how could we fit that into the school work programme?'[16]

One instance of bullying involved a boy who, for some reason, annoyed and irritated the other lads, yet who dismissed most of them as merely rough and uncouth. Late one evening his parents visited Timbertop and harangued Montgomery about the alleged iniquitous nature of the school. Offending words of a lavatory humour variety were said to have been uttered or written by some other boys and the parents were hellbent on travelling down to Corio to demand an audience with the headmaster because, Montgomery wrote (paraphrasing them), 'the whole thing must go to Council and be exposed'. Montgomery managed to dissuade them by pointing out that their son was by no means the only white sheep in an otherwise black flock; that whatever had taken place was mostly his own fault and that he simply had to learn that 'what he gave so must he take'. Their son's apparent lack of a sense of humour and his refusal to cooperate with the others had not helped his cause either. Eventually the parents calmed down, admitted that they had spoken rather hastily, expressed their complete confidence in Montgomery and departed. Montgomery then took the offending unit aside after chapel, gave them a 'fatherly and moral' talking-to and, unbeknownst to the others, appointed one of their number as the boy's guardian angel. 'Everything is in a stable position', he re-assured his chief.[17]

On the eve of his departure for England in March 1955 Darling had told Montgomery that what he had seen up there at Timbertop on his recent short visit was absolutely 'first-class' and that there was so much about which he felt 'greatly inspired and delighted'. But the reason he had now taken fright at incidents like this latest one, he explained, was not only because bullying was bad for the school's reputation but also because 'its appearance seems to undermine all our faith in the theory upon which Timbertop is based'. Boys who were bullied, he impressed on Montgomery, nearly always asked for it, and when trying to get to the truth of what exactly happened the bullied usually exaggerated and the bullies invariably minimized:

> If it is true, as it seems to be, that the victim is nearly always the boy who fails to do his share of the community's work, shouldn't we try to find a correct way of dealing with this problem? Are the masters on the spot enough? I mean, do they actually visit the units sufficiently at unexpected and dangerous times? [D]o they know the boys well enough to spot this sort of thing quickly enough? Thank Heavens that you have always been quicker on the mark than the complaint. That makes a very great difference in answering: but I am frightened nevertheless.

The next year Montgomery had to deal with a parent's allegations of boys' bad language and sexual talk, as well as sporadic bouts of cigarette smoking by boys in their units. Montgomery confessed himself at his wit's end in dealing with one offender who initially admitted to 'moral cowardice', despite an 'adamantine facade', but then subsequently transgressed again and who was also suspected of wilfully destroying school property. Having secured repentance from the boy after spending more than an hour with him, Montgomery admitted virtual defeat: 'I dressed him down hard but I might just as well have been talking to the Sphinx'; 'I am upset in that I feel I should have been able to do something with him.'[18]

Tensions

These incidents were isolated blemishes rather than signs of an epidemic, but so sensitive was Darling about his new scheme's reputation that he raised one case of bullying with the council. In the only direct evidence of possible strain in his relationship with Montgomery, he reported to council that he was 'a little afraid that the people up there [at Timbertop] are inclined to defend themselves and minimize the importance of such cases as are brought to their notice'. At least at Corio a bullied boy to some extent had the defence of the machine to fall back on, he argued to Montgomery, which was not the case at Timbertop. There had been similar trouble at Corio that year, he admitted, and preach, harangue and chase prefects and housemasters as much as he might, he still felt insecure. Could not some kind of haven or sanctuary be set aside at Timbertop where a boy would feel secure in the knowledge that he could get away from his oppressors? Perhaps the composition of the units should even be reshuffled. He was well aware of the difficulty of striking a balance between over-protection – and a consequent hopeless softness – on the one hand, and misery resulting from continual nagging on the other, but some safeguard simply had to be found.[19]

By late 1958 Montgomery was able to assure his headmaster that bullying had diminished. Over time the relationship between the two men had further matured, and a clearer understanding of their separate, far-flung bailiwicks and the ways in which these related had evolved in their minds. Arms-length administration and accountability had taken some adjusting for both of them, but when Montgomery could say that he liked the boys Darling had sent up to him or that 'you have certainly set me a problem with one named ["X"]', then this kind of expression was a sure sign that each had a firm sense of what they were doing, and knew exactly where they stood, in relation to the other. As regards 'X' Montgomery was alluding to another problem with which he had to deal: the difficulty experienced by some boys arriving from Corio in making the transition to their new surroundings. Apparently the boy in question had scarcely arrived before he was informing Montgomery that he wanted to leave. He was a lad who was 'far too old in his conversation', Montgomery thought and, in any case, he disliked boys 'who talk to me of complexes [as this boy was wont to] and then quote psychology at me'. Darling insisted that this particular boy's trouble was probably that he talked too much for his own good, but cautioned that he might need special care. True to his word the lad in question did walk out of Timbertop one day and was discovered trying to travel home to Melbourne. The problem for Montgomery and Darling, especially with cases of sensitive boys like this one, was that whenever a Timbertop contingent returned to Corio after their year away they were found to be 'not fitting [back] into the machine as well as they should', probably because stories were beginning to spread amongst the boys due to depart for Timbertop about the nature and demands of the experiences they would be likely to encounter there: 'I *am* annoyed at last year's boys talking to 3rd Form boys and putting them against Timbertop', Montgomery once complained.[20]

Another type of problem with which Montgomery had to deal was occasional lonely and homesick lads whose letters to their families, he considered, were intended to be used as ammunition to have them taken away from Timbertop, and whose parents (especially their mothers) were 'driven nearly crazy with them'. In lengthily written reports to Darling, Montgomery would lay out all the relevant details, provide his assessment of the case, and then offer to come down and meet the parents. Darling would then apologize in his reply for all the trouble to which Montgomery had been subjected, express his confidence in the way the matter was being handled and suggest any possible additional courses of action. Occasionally, accusations about the mismanagement of his Timbertop charges found their way back to Montgomery by the oddest and most circuitous network of informants. In one instance the 'idle words of a "prof" [i.e. professional] man' threw him into a complete flat spin. 'Unmerciful treatment' or some such expression had apparently been uttered at a dinner party by a Melbourne psychiatrist in regard to a Timbertop boy. After hours of investigation into the matter, however, Montgomery assured Darling, no evidence, neither physical nor psychological, had come to light to substantiate the allegation. 'Presumably medical ethics blew out with the Atom Bomb', he fumed.[21]

Substitute Effects and Outcomes

In respect of the exercise of influence on followers by leaders – which is far-and-away the overriding concern of commentators committed to facilitating leader effectiveness – it was pointed out earlier that two considerations complicate discussions of the relationship between causal influence and effects. The first was that while a leader's influence can indeed be exercised directly, it can also be indirect (or mediated) – one of the very possibilities allowed for by Kerr and Jermier's theory of leader substitutes. (And substitutes, of course, are but one type of circumstantial moderator of influence along with 'neutralizers', 'enhancers' and 'supplements' as well: see Bass, 1990, pp. 682–6; and Howell, Dorfman and Kerr, 1986.) The second was that influence may well yield inaction and, therefore, influence need not even be manifest in overt behaviour. An additional complication arises when influence is considered temporally. Clearly, some effects of leaders – including, for that matter, those of their substitutes, such as subordinate partners in leadership couples – only find expression over an extended period of time, analogous to the manner in which a greenish water stain eventually builds up on the side of an enamel bath tub, but which is not immediately evident when a tap is first seen to be dripping.

Elmore brings yet another angle to bear on the general problem when he demonstrates that a 'forward mapping' approach to policy-implementation – substantially like the typical search for effects which dominates leadership studies – makes no allowance for the possibility that 'most of what happens in the implementation process cannot be explained by the intentions and directions of policy-makers' (1979–80, p. 603). In short, reality frequently distorts intentions and produces unintended effects and consequences. In a 'backward mapping' approach, by contrast, the working assumption is that 'the closer one is to the source of a problem, the greater is one's ability to influence it'. Moreover, and again in a manner consistent with the significance accorded it in the Timbertop example being documented, backward mapping highlights the crucial role played by discretion in the accomplishment of outcomes; i.e., 'responsibilities that require special expertise and proximity to a problem are pushed down in the organization, leaving more generalized responsibilities at the top' (Elmore, 1979–80, pp. 606–7). Finally, implicit in this notion of delegated discretion is the kind of reciprocal view of authority relations lying at the heart of Barnard's (1982 [1938], p. 163) analysis – in which formal authority is exercised downwards and informal sanction for it flows upwards – and of the conception of leader-follower relations being outlined in this chapter. (Reciprocity as a property of leadership couples is taken up in the next section.)

In a recent interview Kerr – the originator with Jermier of the substitutes view – noted that their idea 'never had solid empirical support', although at the same time he had 'never waivered in [his] conviction that it's right'. Typically, he said, in quantitative studies of leadership 'we're bragging about the .3 correlation, which means we explain about 9 per cent of the variance. We never get curious about the 91 per cent unexplained' (Frost, 1997, p. 346). While accounting for statistically unexplained variance is firmly at odds with both the objective and the entire discursive cast of the account of leadership being developed in this chapter, there is nonetheless a body of evidence available about what Timbertop was thought to be achieving at the time which permits some estimation of the relative contributions made by its headmaster-founder and the man formally responsible for implementing the founder's ideal. A number of contemporary eye-witness accounts – and later recollections of Timbertop by individuals both directly involved in and around the periphery, as well as by those having only minimal or temporary contact with the headmaster and his scheme – provide sound, solid evidence of its effects and outcomes.

First of all there are the perspectives of those for whom 'seeing was believing' and who by and large acclaimed Timbertop to be a great success. These views varied only in the intensity with which they celebrated its triumph and were of two kinds: journalistic accounts and visitors' reflections. Thus, in October 1954, a lengthy report on Timbertop appeared in the prestigious *Times Educational Supplement (TES)* which (for the benefit of its mostly English readership) expatiated on the system of unit discipline. Timbertop's unit leaders, known as 'speakers', were elected monthly by secret ballot:

> These 'speakers' form a sort of democratic assembly with whom the master in charge confers about such matters that arise, but they have no powers or privileges conferred by authority and are very much leaders among equals. There being no prefectorial hierarchy the whole community really runs on trust and the essence of belief at Timbertop is that boys of this age can be trusted to be responsible for themselves. If they cannot the whole experiment fails.

Visitors might well have been struck by an apparent absence of organization and routine but, the *TES* report cautioned its readers, such an impression belied the reality of self-discipline.[22] Typical of those who did visit Timbertop were people like J.D.G. Medley, the recently retired vice-chancellor of the University of Melbourne, and Brian Hone, the headmaster of Melbourne Grammar School. But their euphoria for the scheme has to be tempered by the knowledge that they were also part of Darling's personal network of friends and acquaintances, and that Darling was a man who had always gone out of his way to bring important and eminent visitors to his school to meet the boys (including – although in this case he was unsuccessful – no less than Prince Philip himself, who was in Melbourne in 1956 for the Olympic Games).

Second, there are the retrospective testimonies of those who were either school masters at Timbertop or who were their pupils. The evidence here of the effects of the Timbertop year varies and is no doubt coloured by the informants' subsequent experiences, but a couple of examples are worth citing. For one boy – who later became a world renowned botanist – Timbertop was recalled as by far his most enjoyable year at school because for the very first time in his entire school life he was afforded the freedom to come and go and to pursue his hobbies like birdwatching.[23] Then, in 1956, the experience was sufficient to stimulate some of the boys to produce the *Timbertop Magazine*, which became an annual literary publication intended to record the various activities pursued at Timbertop, particularly those relating to natural history. Thus, the magazine published numerous accounts of journeys, noteworthy features of the surrounding terrain, photographs and articles on insects, birds and wildflowers. For other boys for whom the Timbertop experience was rewarding there were also occasional minor inconveniences experienced during the year away from Corio – like the interruption to one's musical studies (because no instruments were taught at Timbertop) or the temporary loss of former Corio friends (who were scattered across different units).[24] Third, there is additional evidence from people who were initially sceptical about Darling's idea but who later became enthusiasts for it. The general manager of a major Victorian paper manufacturing firm who advised Darling on tree planting at Timbertop, for example, was one example. He admitted that for some time he had been 'very doubtful about the whole Timbertop scheme' but that having seen it for himself 'I am well on the way to being converted'.[25]

Implicit in all these accolades is evidence of praise for the leader and the genius of his original conception, but only because that vision had been made real for the world to see by the efforts of Montgomery and the Timbertop masters; i.e. the positive outcomes referred to were principally contingent upon the work of a substitute leader. Two other compelling pieces of evidence further substantiate the point. The first triennial report compiled by inspectors from the Victorian Education Department in 1955 (and required of Geelong Grammar by virtue of its status as a registered school) noted of Timbertop that 'all the necessary equipment for effective work appears to be available'.[26] Better still, as part of a searching evaluation of the entire school (commissioned by Darling as part of Geelong Grammar School's centenary celebrations) Professor W.F. Connell and his University of Sydney team spent a week at Timbertop in early 1957 and evaluated its significance. Darling later reflected that Connell's overall report[27] of nearly 400 pages 'turned out to be rather shattering and seemed to leave us with hardly a feather to fly with', yet it was full of praise for Timbertop (1978, p. 202). According to the report Darling's innovation had been especially successful in fostering self-reliance and the development of non-authoritarian personalities among the boys. Connell's team also conducted an extensive sociometric analysis and concluded that 'there were very few isolates or rejectees, that "getting along with other boys" was the developmental task which caused the least amount of worry, and that the friendliness of other boys and the happy relationship between boys and masters were such as to call for special comment from the boys.'[28]

Not only did this particular passage utterly vindicate the success of Darling's idea of self-governing units, but Connell called Timbertop 'one of the best conceived and best executed developments in Australian education in recent years'. Its objects, he said, were 'wholly admirable' and were being implemented soundly. Educationally, Connell believed, Timbertop was 'the most exciting and provocative part of the School'.[29] Two aspects, however, were believed to require attention – both of which Darling and Montgomery had been grappling with already. The first was classroom work. Here Connell did not believe that 'a very good balance had been struck' and that insufficient advantage had been taken of Timbertop's uniqueness to permit masters to enable their subjects to 'grow out of the local situation' while retaining continuity with the curriculum at Corio.[30] The second concern was the readjustment of boys to normal school routines after their return from Timbertop. 'To attempt to discipline them into an earlier pattern of behaviour would seem to me to be quite wrongheaded', Connell noted, 'and a waste of much of the value and achievement of the Timbertop year.' Instead, he recommended changes at Corio to help further foster the personality development undergone during the year away.[31] These two caveats aside, considered as an example of dispassionate, objective evidence of outcomes and effects being generated through leadership the report's conclusions were as close to a ringing endorsement of the entire experiment as Darling was ever likely to get.

The Significance of Leadership Couples

To this point the discussion has documented a case of the kind of substitute leadership circumstances allowed for by Bass (1990, p. 685), namely 'selecting mature subordinates may provide a substitute for stable leadership' and 'assigning an assistant to a manager may act to supplement the manager's leadership'. By no means all of the details of the working relationship between Darling and Montgomery have been provided in the space available but on the basis of what their example reveals, it is possible to summarize some of the core attributes of leadership couples, to outline a few of the necessary and sufficient conditions for productive and successful coupling relationships and to suggest how a couple acts as a substitute.

The first distinguishing feature of the Darling–Montgomery relationship is that it was a hierarchical, rather than a peer or collegial, couple operating in a headquarters-field setting or context. Couples in such vertical line relationships, as Krantz (1989, p. 164) quite correctly points out, are required to transact their relations across an authority boundary and the superior is held accountable for both his or her own and the subordinate's work performance – two features which constitute the source of a couple's dependence on one another, and which may activate powerful, intensely experienced emotions with the potential either to facilitate or impede fruitful, positive exchanges. Next, provided couples manifest the three additional properties of specialization, differentiation and complementarity of role tasks in their internal dynamics then, suggest Hodgson et al. (1965, p. 486), they will form an integrated and effective work unit. Once more, on any reckoning of the evidence in the light of these three criteria, Darling and Montgomery's relationship passes muster. But the question still remains: what considerations lessen the likelihood of relations in a couple or a pairing turning psychologically sour? Or, expressed slightly differently, why do leadership couples gel?

Four additional factors made for a productive bonding between Darling and Montgomery and these can be generalized to other instances: theirs was a well-rehearsed working relationship, it was enshrouded in a reciprocal moral unity, there was sufficient space for each of them from within which to exercise their personal responsibilities and the balance of their temperaments was about right.

The Importance of Rehearsal

Although Hodgson et al. (1965) very carefully crafted the way in which an executive role constellation arose out of a particular management succession change-over at 'the Memorial Psychiatric Institute', the analytic model of constellations they generated from the case made no provision for their emergent properties. Thus, specialization, differentiation and complementarity are purely functional criteria and exclude the crucial element of time. Graen and Scandura's (1987, p. 179) dyad model, by contrast, incorporates such factors as the 'respective genetic endowment, past histories, and current circumstances' of both the member and the superior, and incorporates a phased, sequential development of the dyad's, or couple's, relationship, namely role taking, role making and role routinization. The critical point here is less whether the Darling–Montgomery case maps exactly onto these three developmental phases, but that: (a) their relationship did evolve over time, and (b) the crucial role taking (or sampling) phase in the partnership – 'wherein the superior attempts to discover the relevant talents and motivations of the member through iterative testing sequences' (Graen and Scandura, 1987, p. 180) – was an extended one. That is, because, as Montgomery later reflected, 'during my ten years or so at Corio, I had become accustomed to doing many things quite remote from teaching' (Montgomery and Darling, 1967, p. 19), both he and the headmaster had had ample opportunity by virtue of their involvement in numerous unstructured school tasks to rehearse the boundaries of their relationship.

What this period of rehearsal or pre-performance ensured was that by the time their roles formally interlocked in the pursuit of the new joint venture each man had a very sound understanding of the other's strengths and weaknesses, their potential for the exercise of discretion, their capacity to solve problems and the limit of each other's endurance when under pressure. The consequence of such rehearsed role performance for leadership couples is that if they have the prior opportunity to test themselves with one another then their eventual interlock is much less likely to degenerate into leadership gridlock.

Leader–follower Reciprocity

In the absence of the luxury of available time for key dyadic relationships to be rehearsed or apprenticed in advance, however, leaders may well have to rely on other arrangements if couples, dyads and constellations are to achieve a desired working symbiosis. Selznick (1957, pp. 14–15 and see Barnard, 1956, pp. 82–3, 88), for example, noted how a practice like the careful recruiting of members and successors from cohorts of specially trained, socialized and prepared elite cadres can facilitate commitment to, and the perpetuation of, institutional values. Both Darling and Montgomery were themselves products of English and Antipodean varieties of the boys' public boarding school system and were firmly dedicated to the pursuit and furtherance of the system's ideals. This mutuality of outlook created a kind of unspoken code which freed both men from the constant necessity of intuiting or having to second guess the thinking and motivation of the other. In addition, because the key component of that public school ideal was *noblesse oblige* or duty to serve and, given that values determine an individual's perceptions, preferences and behaviour (Hambrick and Brandon, 1988, p. 18), this unspokenness was cemented further by their shared canopy of values.

This line of reasoning suggests that at the heart of the leader–follower bond between a subordinate and his or her immediate superior may lie a version of Gouldner's (1960) 'norm of reciprocity'. The material exchange relationship which is the essence of transactional leadership (Bass, 1985, p. 11; Burns, 1978, p. 4) – the obverse of the currently popular model of transformational leadership – implies reciprocity, but often in the crude form of needs gratification. In that case the act of reciprocation is dictated by expediency: an implied social obligation to repay the benefits received. In the Darling–Montgomery couple, however, their reciprocity was less a matter of repayment than the expression of mutual obligations stemming from their commitment to a shared ideal and its realization. Stripped to its barest essentials, that Timbertop ideal was a simple one: 'building up of a true self-confidence based on competence' among adolescent boys (Montgomery and Darling, 1967, p. 140).

The Need for Space

Qualitatively, both role rehearsal and moral reciprocity represent the outcomes of substantial long-term institutional investments in leader formation (Gronn, 1993, pp. 345–8). Their advantage is that both are properties which institutional leaders may take as relationship givens. In that case, the principal way in which rehearsal and reciprocity may be capitalized on is that they create the kind of loosely-coupled leader–substitute relationship evident between Darling and Montgomery: both givens maximize the trust accorded the substitute in exercising discretionary decision making and widen the superior's 'zone of indifference' (Barnard, 1982 [1938], p. 169) to the substitute's actions. Discretion has been defined as 'latitude of managerial action' (Hambrick and Finkelstein, 1987, p. 371). Moreover, domains of discretion vary in their importance in respect of the accomplishment of organizational outcomes. At Timbertop, of course, the scope of Montgomery's discretion was extensive and his domain of discretionary latitude was significant because it entailed the custodianship of core institutional values. A rule of thumb for leadership couples, therefore, might be expressed as follows: the greater the significance of the substitute's domain of discretion, then the smaller the superior's zone of indifference. Given the existence of factors such as pre-role rehearsal and moral reciprocity, however, the more significant the domain of discretion, the greater the superior's zone of indifference.

Temperament and Disposition

The three role types which Hodgson et al. (1965, p. 482) distilled from their triadic constellation were 'paternal-assertive', 'maternal-nurturant' and 'fraternal-permissive' – perfectly understandable given their prior commitment to a psychoanalytic framework (Hodgson et al. 1965, p. 31). Yet none of these categories fits the Darling–Montgomery dyad. Certainly, Darling may well have been revered as a father-figure in the wider Geelong Grammar School community, but he was anything but a paterfamilias in his dealings with Montgomery. Rather, as was suggested earlier on in this discussion, given their different cultural backgrounds and personalities, they are best characterized as something of an 'unlikely lads' or an 'odd couple' combination. Their relationship was a blending, on the one hand, of an Englishman embodying the gentlemanly ideal and, on the other, a common sense, down-to-earth Australian; in short: a partnership between a man of ideas and a man of action. In their case the two of them clicked. That said, it would appear well nigh impossible to be prescriptive about the most advantageous combinations of personal factors. All that can be observed is that for the couple concerned, the interpersonal chemistry has got to feel right or, as an English headmistress once said at the conclusion of an applicant's interview for the vacancy of deputy in her school when discounting him as a possible colleague and potential substitute for her: 'I knew instinctively that (A) wasn't the right one' (Gronn, 1986, p. 14).

Couples as Substitutes

A precise understanding of the mechanisms through which couples operate as substitutes for single-handed leadership has so far proven elusive and is probably only accessible by the kind of extended participant observation and clinical interviewing utilized by Hodgson et al. (1965). As an alternative, historians who have described the dynamics of close collaborative leader relationships – such as the Georges' (1964) study of President Wilson and Colonel House – have mostly relied on inferences drawn from documentary sources. Thus, in her account of colonial Australian schooling Zainu'ddin (1981) provides an illustration of the hazards of dual control. She describes the typical nineteenth century Methodist pattern of school administration as a duumvirate comprising a ministerial president and an academic headmaster. In 1882, the founding year of the Methodist Ladies' College, Melbourne, for example, the Rev. W.H. Fitchett was appointed president and Mr F. Wheen as headmaster. With Fitchett maintaining that his decisions overrode those of Wheen and the latter seeing himself providing organizational continuity (given the Methodist tradition of itinerant ministry) and academic leadership, it was small wonder that conflict very soon erupted, as a fellow cleric noted (Zainu'ddin. 1981, pp. 72–3):

> We have the 'dual control' system here in Wesley [College – the Methodist boys' school] and the Methodist Ladies. Watkin D.D. [Wesley president] and Way M.A. [Wesley headmaster] seem to get on all right; but Fitchett and Wheen at the MLC are always on the verge of a big row; as they are both men of energy and strong will.

Some time later it became evident that Fitchett and Wheen were no longer merely on the verge of a big row but instead 'immersed in one' (Zainu'ddin, 1981, p. 77).

While no one in Darling's and Montgomery's case will ever know the exact details of their various telephone utterances, one-on-one conversations, site visits and the like, useful deductions can still be drawn from the rhetoric of their correspondence. Nowhere is there any evidence of Darling issuing his lieutenant with directions, commands and instructions, nor does he ever pretend to throw his weight about or try jousting with verbal flourishes. For his part Montgomery confined himself to relaying stories or little dramas in reassuring tones to his chief, which were spiced with occasional gripes about the deteriorating state of the world. Further, instead of adopting an urgent or insistent tone Darling's style was to drop gentle hints, to ask questions, to think out aloud and to commend moral rules of thumb. No doubt Darling would also cast a watchful eye around whenever he appeared in person at Timbertop but, because it was foreign to his nature ever to formally 'inspect' anything, his instinct was always to position himself at a respectable distance. It was the totality of these kinds of qualitative attributes which betokened a commitment by both men to the welfare and advancement of a common enterprise.

Future Research

The field of leadership is currently witnessing a rethink of some of its conventional approaches. Two examples are recent pleas to pay more attention to the contexts of leadership (e.g., Bryman et al. 1996; Gronn and Ribbins, 1996) and for follower-centric approaches to understanding leader-followership (Meindl, 1993, 1995). The Timbertop case suggests the need for an additional rethink: how best to re-conceptualize the unit of leadership analysis. This point represents a modification of the original argument about substitutes because the focus there was still on 'a leader' – i.e., an individual unit of analysis – and Kerr and Jermier's concern was to query the legitimacy of invoking the paramountcy of that leader's leadership on every conceivable occasion.

Despite such recent rethinking, methodological individualism still pervades much of the field. Thus, Bryman (1992, p. 153) has pointed out how commentators tend to 'overstate the importance of individual leaders' to the detriment of alternative arrangements. Clearly there are circumstances in which the appropriate unit of analysis is the stand-alone, solo performer leader, but equally there are many other occasions in which that unit of analysis is some kind of collective conception of leadership. A helpful starting point here might be to devise a spectrum or template of possible leadership forms and their distinguishing criteria against which to more accurately define cases and contexts nominated by commentators for scrutiny. One useful generic term for such leadership possibilities might be the 'leadership regime'. A continuum of likely regime types can be conceived of as ranging from single-handed leadership on the one hand, through constellations of close associates like couples and dyads, triads and even quartets (Murnighan and Conlon, 1991) to senior management teams or top management groups and on to entourages of advisers and opaque institutional entities captured by locutions like 'the Kennedy administration' or even 'the establishment', on the other.

Ironically, one consequence of adherence to such a scheme would be to render the very claim about substitutes redundant because the substitution idea really only has argumentative currency in a context in which the explanatory fascination is with individuals. The reason is that implicit in the acknowledged likelihood of there being a range of possible leadership forms is the recognition that phenomena like organizational outcomes and effects are potentially attributable to causal entities other than single leaders (i.e. to substitutes for, or alternatives to, individuals) or to a matrix of causal factors in which a leader comprises but one element. Further, such a continuum also acknowledges, by definition, that there are likely to be cases in which it is impossible not only to track through (or map back) causal flows of influence directly attributable to individuals but indirect and mediated forms as well. The point of such reasoning is less to invalidate the claim that it is individual leaders who count or make a difference, in the end, than to require all students of leadership to accord due recognition to the constraints on, as well as the opportunities for, various forms of leadership and to better justify their choice of a particular possibility. As has already been suggested elsewhere (Gronn and Ribbins, 1996, pp. 453–4, 456), these considerations lead us immediately into the realm of epistemological debates about the relationship between agency and structure. But that has to be the subject matter for another occasion.

Conclusion

This chapter has addressed a largely neglected but significant aspect of leadership: the possibility that on some occasions and in some contexts the direct exercise of leadership might be redundant or be substituted for by an alternative medium or vehicle. The immediate stimulus for the discussion was the recent *LQ* symposium which revisited the substitutes thesis, and the two decades of published research subsequent to its original articulation by Kerr and Jermier (1978). The focus of the analysis was on the leadership couple as just one exemplar of a range of possible leader substitutes and, in particular, on the leadership attributes and actions of a superior and his immediate subordinate as evident in one historical case study. The case – the establishment and first decade of the famous Timbertop school – was used to elucidate the work of the couple, to demonstrate a range of leader effects and outcomes attributable to that particular leadership unit, and to augment a number of the defining properties of couples and dyads previously reported in the literature. In essence, the chapter documents an example of the exact challenge proposed by Graen and Scandura (1987, p. 195) in their exposition of dyadic relations in leadership settings; i.e., 'to find organizations that are faced with the task of producing new dyadic structures, and intensively research the development of these structures over time from a number of different points of view'. Furthermore, because the wider context of the dynamics of the substitute couple documented was one in which values and their institutionalization were paramount, the chapter has also provided the kind of 'temporal, dynamic view of discretion' for which Hambrick and Finkelstein (1987, p. 403) have recently appealed, in that the latitude and leeway accorded the subordinate substitute member of the couple in respect of attaining highly valued outcomes was central to the analysis.

In the opening paragraphs of their original discussion, Kerr and Jermier (1978, p. 375) drew attention to the fixation of the field of leadership studies with positional, hierarchical leadership. Little appears to have changed in the period since they wrote. Indeed, by focusing on a line management example (a school head and his newly-appointed master-in-charge) the present discussion has perhaps helped to further substantiate the validity of Kerr and Jermier's observation. On the other hand, Kerr and Jermier also noted the preference of leadership commentators for the statistical, rather than the practical, significance of their conclusions. While this chapter has not sought to distill a detailed set of recommendations – in the practical, real-world sense implied by Kerr and Jermier – its conclusions nonetheless have serious everyday import. It is remarkable how relatively few commentators in the past two decades have taken up Kerr and Jermier's challenge to the received wisdom on the effects achieved by leadership (see, e.g. the moderately long reference list on substitutes in the review by Podsakoff and MacKenzie, 1997). What is even more remarkable is how reluctant those same commentators have been to undertake the kind of holistic, in-depth, highly contextualized analysis documented in this chapter. This discussion has provided a modest starting point for further qualitative analyses of the manifold forms taken by leadership substitutes, as well as the investigation of additional examples of leadership couples – as but one of a range of leader regimes – and a comparative, case by case consideration of their defining properties and significance.

Notes

1 Other influential publications from this period included Burns (1978); Calder (1977); House (1977); Pfeffer (1977) and Zaleznik (1977).

2 Bass (1990, p. 686) notes a slightly different paradox: that of self-managing, autonomous work groups which, he believes, 'require' the delegated authority of an external, higher-up leader.

3 Darling to Gatenby (1951) 30 May, Old Geelong Grammarian files, Geelong Grammar School Archives (hereafter GGSA).

4 Kurt Matthias Robert Martin Hahn (1886–1974): private secretary to Prince Max of Baden, Imperial Chancellor of Germany, 1918; headmaster of Schule Schloss Salem (1920–33), founder and headmaster of Gordonstoun (1934–53); founder of the Outward Bound Sea School (1941) and the Duke of Edinburgh's Award Scheme (1956).

5 Hahn, K. (1934) 'A German public school', *The Listener*, 17 January.

6 Frederick Spencer Chapman (1907–1971): adventurer, explorer and author: member of the British Arctic Air Route Expedition (1929–31); first paid executive of the Outward Bound Trust (1946).

7 Chapman to Darling (1952) 14 September, and Darling to Chapman (1952) 27 October (incomplete draft letter), ms 7826, series 7, box 15, folder 6, Darling Papers, National Library of Australia.

8 Darling, J.R. (1987–88) 'Edward Hugh Montgomery', *Corian*, Nov.–Jan., p. 15.

9 Darling to Bickersteth (1953) 13 November, Geelong Grammar School, Headmasters' Correspondence (hereafter GGSHMC), GGSA.

10 Two months previously a federal referendum seeking Commonwealth power to ban the Communist Party had failed to pass.

11 Darling, J.R. (1951) *Corian*, December, pp. 148–154.

12 Darling, J.R. (1952) *Corian*, December, pp. 160–1.

13 Darling, J.R. (1953) *Corian*, May, p. 15.

14 Montgomery to Darling (1956) 19 June, GGSHMC Timbertop file (hereafter GGSHMCTT), GGSA.

15 Darling (1954) Reports to council, 20 September and 15 March, GGS Headmasters' Reports to Council file (hereafter GGSHMRC), GGSA.

16 Darling to Montgomery (1955) 14 November, GGSHMCTT, GGSA.

17 Montgomery to Darling (1955) 7 November, GGSHMCTT, GGSA.

18 Darling to Montgomery (1955) 10 March, GGSHMC; 14 November, GGSHMCTT; Montgomery to Darling (1956) 21 March, GGSHMCTT, GGSA.

19 Darling (1956) Reports to council, 8 October, p. 2, GGSHMRC; Darling to Montgomery (1956) 17 October, GGSHMCTT, GGSA.

20 Montgomery to Darling (1957) 28 March, 15 February; Darling to Montgomery (1957) 20 March, GGSHMCTT; Darling (1956) Reports to council, 8 October, p. 2, GGSHMRC; Montgomery to Darling (1956) 24 October, GGSHMCTT, GGSA.

21 Montgomery to Darling (1959) 9 March, 3 May, GGSHMCTT, GGSA.

22 'Where men and mountains meet: Geelong's settlement in the bush' (1954) *Times Educational Supplement*, 15 October, p. 964.

23 Pickett-Heapes, Professor J. to the author (1985) 20 May.

24 MacKnight, Dr C.C. to the author (1985) 24 May.

25 Brookes to Darling (1954) 18 March, GGSHMC, GGSA.

26 Victoria Education Department (1955) *Inspector's Report Book, G.G.S.Timbertop*, Timbertop Archives, pp. 2–3.

27 GGSA (1957) *Evaluation of Geelong C. of E Grammar (Secondary) School.*
28 GGSA (1957) *ibid.*, pp. 282–3.
29 GGSA (1957) *ibid.*, p. 280.
30 GGSA (1957) *ibid.*
31 GGSA (1957) *ibid.*, p. 283.

References

BARNARD, C. (1956) *Organization and Management: Selected Papers*, Cambridge, MA: Harvard University Press.
BARNARD, C. (1982 [1938]) *The Functions of the Executive*, Cambridge, MA: Harvard University Press.
BASS, B.M. (1985) *Leadership and Performance Beyond Expectations*, New York: Free Press.
BASS, B.M. (1990) *Bass and Stogdill's Handbook of Leadership: Theory, Research and Managerial Applications*, 3rd edn, New York: Free Press.
BRYMAN, A. (1992) *Charisma and Leadership in Organizations*, London: Sage.
BRYMAN, A. (1993) 'Charismatic leadership in business organizations: Some neglected issues', *Leadership Quarterly*, **4**, pp. 289–304.
BRYMAN, A., GILLINGWATER, D. and McGUINNESS, I. (1996) 'Leadership and organizational transformation', *International Journal of Public Administration*, **19**, 849–72.
BURNS, J.M. (1978) *Leadership*, New York: Harper and Row.
CALDER, B.J. (1977) 'An attribution theory of leadership', in STAW, B.M. and SALANCIK, G.R. (eds) *New Directions in Organizational Behavior*, Chicago, IL: St. Clair, pp. 179–204.
DARLING, J.R. (1954) 'Timbertop, an experiment', *Educational Magazine*, **11**, 5, pp. 223–5.
DARLING, SIR JAMES (1978) *Richly Rewarding*, Melbourne: Hill of Content.
DARLING, J.R. (1987–8) Edward Hugh Montgomery, Corian, Geelong, Victoria: Geelong Grammar School, Nov.–Jan. p. 15.
ELMORE, R.F. (1979–80) 'Backward mapping: Implementation research and policy decisions', *Political Science Quarterly*, **94**, pp. 601–16.
FRIEDRICH, C.J. (1963) *Man and his Government*, New York: McGraw-Hill.
FROST, P. (1997) 'Bridging academia and business: A conversation with Steve Kerr', *Organization Science*, **8**, pp. 333–47.
GEORGE, A.L. and GEORGE, J.L. (1964) *Woodrow Wilson and Colonel House: A Personality Study*, New York: Dover Publications.
GOULDNER, A.W. (1960) 'The norm of reciprocity: A preliminary statement', *American Sociological Review*, **25**, pp. 161–78.
GRAEN, G.B. and SCANDURA, T.A. (1987) 'Towards a psychology of dyadic organizing', in CUMMINGS, L.L. and STAW, B.M. (eds) *Research in Organizational Behavior*, Greenwich, CT: JAI Press, pp. 175–208.
GREENFIELD, T. and RIBBINS, P. (eds) (1993) *Greenfield on Educational Administration: Towards a Humane Science*, London: Routledge.
GRONN, P. (1986) 'Choosing a deputy head: The rhetoric and reality of administrative selection', *Australian Journal of Education*, **30**, pp. 1–22.
GRONN, P. (1991) 'A drag on the war effort?: Geelong Grammar School, 1940–45', *Journal of the Royal Australian Historical Society*, **77**, 2, pp. 53–76.
GRONN, P. (1992) 'Schooling for ruling: The social composition of admissions to Geelong Grammar School, 1930–39', *Australian Historical Studies*, **98**, pp. 72–89.

GRONN, P. (1993) 'Psychobiography on the couch: Character, biography and the comparative study of leaders', *Journal of Applied Behavioral Science*, **29**, pp. 343–58.

GRONN, P. (1994) 'Will anything ever be done?: Geelong Grammar School and the Associated public schools head of the river in the 1930s', *Australian Historical Studies*, **103**, pp. 242–61.

GRONN, P. (1995) 'Greatness revisited: The current obsession with transformational leadership', *Leading and Managing*, **1**, pp. 14–27.

GRONN, P. and RIBBINS, P. (1996) 'Leaders in context: Postpositivist approaches to understanding educational leadership', *Educational Administration Quarterly*, **32**, pp. 452–73.

HAHN, K. (1934) *The Listener*, BBC, January 17.

HAMBRICK, D.C. and BRANDON, G.L. (1988) 'Executive values', in HAMBRICK, D.C. (ed.) *The Executive Effect: Concepts and Methods for Studying Top Managers*, Greenwich, CT: JAI Press, pp. 3–34.

HAMBRICK, D.C. and FINKELSTEIN, S. (1987) 'Managerial discretion: A bridge between polar views of organizational outcomes', in CUMMINGS, L.L. and STAW, B.M. (eds) *Research in Organizational Behavior*, **9**, Greenwich, CT: JAI Press. pp. 369–406.

HODGKINSON, C. (1991) *Educational Leadership: The Moral Art*, Albany, NY: SUNY Press.

HODGSON, R.C., LEVINSON, D.J. and ZALEZNIK, A. (1965) *The Executive Role Constellation: An Analysis of Personality and Role Relations in Management*, Boston, MA: Graduate School of Business Administration, Harvard University.

HOUSE, R.J. (1977) 'A 1976 theory of leadership', in HUNT, J.G. and LARSON, L.L. (eds) *Leadership: The Cutting Edge*, Carbondale, IL: Southern Illinois University Press, pp. 189–207.

HOWELL, J.P. (1997) 'Substitutes for leadership: Their meaning and measurement – an historical assessment. *Leadership Quarterly*, **8**, pp. 113–16.

HOWELL, J.P., DORFMAN, P.W. and KERR, S. (1986) 'Moderator variables in leadership research', *Academy of Management Review*, **11**, pp. 88–102.

JERMIER, J.M. and KERR, S. (1997) 'Substitutes for leadership: Their meaning and measurement – contextual recollections and current observations', *Leadership Quarterly*, **8**, pp. 95–101.

KERR, S. and JERMIER, J. (1978) 'Substitutes for leadership: Their meaning and measurement', *Organizational Behavior and Human Performance*, **22**, pp. 374–403.

KRANTZ, J. (1989) 'The managerial couple: Superior-subordinate relationships as a unit of analysis', *Human Resource Management*, **28**, pp. 161–75.

MANZ, C.C. and SIMS, H.P. (1980) 'Self-management as a substitute for leadership: A social learning theory perspective', *Academy of Management Review*, **5**, pp. 361–7.

MEINDL, J.R. (1993) 'Reinventing leadership: A radical, social psychological approach', in MURNIGHAN, J.K. (ed.) *Social Psychology in Organizations: Advances in Theory and Research*, Englewood Cliffs, NJ: Prentice Hall, pp. 89–118.

MEINDL, J.R. (1995) 'The romance of leadership as a follower-centric theory: A social constructionist approach', *Leadership Quarterly*, **6**, pp. 329–41.

MONTGOMERY, E.H. and DARLING, J.R. (1967) *Timbertop: An Innovation in Australian Education*, Melbourne: Cheshire.

MURNIGHAN, J.K. and CONLON, D. (1991) 'The dynamics of intense work groups: A study of British string quartets', *Administrative Science Quarterly*, **36**, pp. 165–86.

PFEFFER, J. (1977) 'The ambiguity of leadership', *Academy of Management Review*, **2**, pp. 104–13.

PODSAKOFF, P.M. and MACKENZIE, S.B. (1997) 'Kerr and Jermier's substitutes for leadership model: Background, empirical assessment, and suggestions for future research', *Leadership Quarterly*, **8**, pp. 117–25.

ROBERTS, N. (1985) 'Transforming leadership: A process of collective action', *Human Relations*, **38**, pp. 1023–46.

ROBERTS, N. and BRADLEY, R.T. (1988) 'Limits of charisma', in CONGER, J.A. and KANUNGO, R.M. (eds) *Charismatic Leadership: The Elusive Factor in Organizational Effectiveness*, San Francisco, CA: Jossey-Bass, pp. 253–75.

SELZNICK, P. (1957). *Leadership in Administration: A Sociological Interpretation*, Evanston, IL: Row, Peterson and Co.

SELZNICK, P. (1992) *The Moral Commonwealth: Social Theory and the Promise of Community*, Berkeley, CA: University of California Press.

STRAUSS, A. and CORBIN, J. (1990) *Basics of Qualitative Research: Grounded Theory Procedures and Techniques*, London: Sage.

TERRY, L.D. (1990) 'Leadership in the administrative state: The concept of administrative conservatorship', *Administration and Society*, **21**, pp. 395–412.

TERRY, L.D. (1993) 'Withstanding the test of time: Philip Selznick's Leadership in Administration', *Leadership Quarterly*, **4**, pp. 361–5.

ZAINU'DDIN, A.T. (1981) 'The career of a colonial schoolmaster: Frank Wheen Esq. BA (1857–1933), in MURRAY-SMITH, S. (ed.) *Melbourne Studies in Education 1981*, Melbourne: Melbourne University Press pp. 60–97.

ZALEZNIK, A. (1977) 'Managers and leaders: Are they different?', *Harvard Business Review*, **55**, 3, pp. 67–78.

Part III

Value Praxis and Other Ethical Issues

10 The Meaning of Time: Revisiting Values and Educational Administration

Clay Lafleur

> Everything seems so hurried. I rush from meeting to meeting. I often arrive late or not completely prepared . . . The pace of living also results in my spending less time doing the things that I value. Being with friends and family, for example, are treasured occurrences that are the stuff of meaningful memories, but which represent increasingly smaller portions of my daily living. And contributing in a quality way to events and projects in my own community are rare possibilities these days. (Personal Journal Entry)

> Time is sort of absolute. I can't overcome the obstacle of time. Yes I can. I put priorities on things, on what I want to accomplish and what I want students to accomplish. I prioritize. (Grade 7 Teacher)

Introduction

Time affects everyone. It is part of the social ethos of our daily experiences. In education, time is often viewed as a commodity to be managed, a limited resource with financial implications. Organizational time is characteristically monochronic, future-oriented, compartmentalized and calendar based. Time is a regulator that is linked with ways of managing and manipulating our environment; time is also a controller that confers power and status to individuals. This objective notion of time stands in contrast to a more subjective and situated view of time. There is, for example, a variety of situations, e.g. within classrooms and contexts of continuous change, where time is distinctively polychronic, rhythmic and directly linked to individuals' emotions. These more subjective views of time are often very personal and meaningful, supporting connection and engagement with the learning enterprise. Educators require many kinds of time and they often construct and make meaning of time differently.

Understanding the value perspectives underlying the meaning of time has a direct bearing on how time is featured, or could be featured, in an organization. In this chapter, a first step is made towards understanding better the relationship between time and values. Heightening the awareness of educational administrators on this topic will not necessarily save time, but it may make the vanishing 'now' a little more palatable.

How we use time is a reflection of the quality of our life. Our views of time and the decisions we make about our use of time are integrally connected to what we value and believe. Sometimes, however, we find ourselves victims of circumstances. We may find ourselves in time binds that define our day-to-day existence and limit our freedom to be ourselves. Consider, for example, the teacher whose time is increasingly colonized for administrative tasks, or the principal who must spend time implementing a number of mandated educational changes without sufficient resources and support, or the administrator who must develop a new policy within a few days and then wait weeks for approval only in the end to have significant changes made to that policy within hours or minutes. In these instances, our efforts to practice what we value are warped by time. Tension, anxiety, frustration and stress are common features of today's hectic pace of living. In a period of rapid change, chaos and uncertainty the optimal use of time can be a challenging and complex undertaking.

There are many ways to view time that help us make decisions about what we do. However, we need discerning eyes to plan for and anticipate the future. Organizing our time so as to enhance the quality of our efforts is complex. We can, however, learn from the experience. Time is the compass for defining who we are and who we can become. By understanding better how we use our time, we can add renewed purpose to our daily tasks. Time is a window to our values; it is a lens for improving our personal and professional lives.

In this chapter I want to invite the reader to make connections between values and time – to see how these connections enhance our understanding of ourselves and what we do in the workplace. What I offer is not particularly new. It may, however, add a new twist or a fresh perspective for explaining issues related to educational administration.

The study of values is foremost in the study of leadership and organizations. As Corson (1989) indicates, 'There is not much that we can know about the policy needs of organizations without finding out about the values, the inclinations and the motives of the people within them (p. 54).

Organizations are people places. Individuals come together to pursue common purposes. Relationships, schedules, meetings, deadlines are the stuff of day-to-day realities. Developing individual and organizational capacity to deal with change and reform is essential. Fundamental to such learning are our understanding and use of time and a commitment to broaden our knowledge base of temporal issues. Schein, for example, reminds us that time is central to who we are and how we act in the workplace. 'The perceptions and experience of time are among the most central aspects of how any group functions; when people differ in their experience of time, tremendous communication and relationship problems typically emerge' (1992, p. 105).

Developing an Awareness of Time

Individuals respond in different ways to temporal conditions that shape their very being. Our conditioning to time, our perception of time, and our control over time affect how we adapt to the succession, duration, rhythm, order and pressures of time (Fraisse, 1963). An example of the importance of time in education is posited by Lubeck (1985). She indicates how time affects life in schools when she says, 'Different uses of time suggest different conceptualizations of time . . . time is perceived differently and used differently . . . because it serves different purposes' (p. 69).

Giddens (1984, 1987), provides a cogent exploration of time and space patterns. Time as a commodity – a resource to be used, consumed and invested – is posited as a dominant and valued feature of our society that is reflected in the time-tabled structure and organization of schools. From this perspective the linear, objective and clock-dominated view of time becomes a necessary organizing device in schools. In other words, time controls life in schools. Giddens also suggests that the time and space patterns of staff and students in schools characterize power relations.

The predominant concern about scheduling and linear time has prompted Slattery (1995b) to respond critically. He suggests that perspectives which focus on linear, objective and managed time as ways of achieving maximum efficiency are inappropriate. Education today is more apt to be characterized by chaos, non-rationality and zones of uncertainty. Furthermore, social systems are much more open and interactive. The integration of time, place and self in contexts of relatedness, complexity, interconnections and subjectivity, for example, provide new temporal possibilities in education. As such, organizations need to work with time rather than in time. In other words, clock time rarely signals the starting time of real learning. Such learning often occurs when teachers and students are ready – when past experiences and the anticipation of future visions are unified in the present. In Slattery's terms, we need to understand time as proleptic. In other words, the past and the future have meaning only in the context of the present. For example, having students relate their own personal and family history with a current science, history or literature project and creatively explore future possibilities helps them develop significant connections. In this sense, time offers an opportunity for curriculum to have meaning for students and unfold in an environment of unpredictability, dynamic change and the natural flow of learning activities.

Hargreaves (1994) identifies four dimensions of time and their implications for educators' work. *The first dimension is technical-rational time.* Reminiscent of *Prisoners of Time*, this type of time is 'a finite resource or means which can be increased, decreased, managed, manipulated or reorganized in order to accommodate selected educational purposes' (p. 96). Since more time or how time is scheduled is no guarantee of educational change, other notions of time are important. *The second dimension is micro-political time.* This view complements Giddens' (1987) views and considers issues related to power and status. The notion of teachers' work being classroom work and time outside of the classroom becoming a competing status claim are examples of the discussion of issues having micro-political significance. *The third dimension of time is phenomenological time.* This subjective, lived time comes alive with the integration of Hall's concepts of monochronic and polychronic time-frames into the explanation of phenomenological time. For example, educational administrators often find themselves at a distance from the classroom and see the implementation of a new curriculum from the standards of their own administrative context. Their singular, monochronic view of time often results in more immediate expectations for implementation that frequently do not match the realities of classroom life. Teachers, on the other hand, experience the chaos, unpredictability and excitement of classroom life on a daily basis as they try to deal with numerous demands of students. Their polychronic view of time usually means that external demands to implement curriculum expectations are not viewed with a similar urgency (see Werner, 1988). *The fourth dimension of time is socio-political time.* Two novel concepts are posited – separation, based on an analogy of Hawkings's (1988) description of physical properties, where time moves more slowly the further one is away from the classroom and colonization where administrators use teachers' time for their own purposes. The completion of large-scale assessments, for example, is often dependent on colonizing teachers' time for administrative purposes. Of particular relevance when considering temporal issues in a context of educational reform is the concept of intensification. The stress on educators, caused by increased workload and workplace pressures, is intricately connected to this notion of intensification.

Gurvitch's (1971) typology of social time provides a useful framework and a possible strategy for considering the social content of temporal practices. He posits eight types of time: enduring time, deceptive time, erratic time, cyclical time, retarded time, alternating time, time in advance of itself, and explosive time. His primary thesis is that every social relation contains its own sense of time. A number of possibilities exist for examining the practices of educators. For example, the notion of enduring time (where established structures and organizational stability are featured) stands in contrast to alternating time (where past and future compete in the present) and explosive time (where radical transformations are commonplace).

In an effort to make sense of the vast literature on time and to make connections to educators' practice, I have begun to develop a similar working typology of time. Several categories of time in this typology include: technical-rational time, cyclical time, experienced time, cultural time, proleptic time, focused time, political time, technological time and reflective time. For each of these general categories I have clustered several related dimensions of time so as to provide a range of similar perspectives. Sample workplace practices clarify further these categories of time (see Figure 10.1). The intriguing aspect of the table is the explanatory and discursive potential for exploring individual action and, for example, the underlying values of educators. This working typology serves to consolidate a great deal of research and polemics about time that appear in a number of different disciplines.

Wide ranging curriculum changes that are occurring within many jurisdictions world wide have implications for the meaning of and the ways that we use time in schools. How, for example, will planning time and staff development time be accommodated by educational administrators? What are the implications of an increased focus on assessment and accountability ? How will parents be meaningfully involved in the education of their children? What impact will technology have on how schools are organized, how teachers teach and how students learn?

Answers to these questions will require clarity of purpose. Knowing what we value will become more apparent as we are forced to deal with these changes. At the very least, the discourse about values will become critical in shaping our direction and actions.

Figure 10.1 Typology of time in the lives of educators

Category	Time Dimensions	Evidence in Workplace
1. Technical-Rational Time	Organizational time, linear time, objectified time, clock time, scheduled time, quantifiable time, commodified time	Timetables, deadlines dominate – time provides an absolute framework for referencing all events – time moves forward and is a commodity, a scarce resource to be used, consumed, invested.
2. Cyclical Time	Biological time, rhythmic time, calendar time, repetitive time	Time is connected to the biological, cyclical rhythms of life, e.g. day, season, year – time is viewed in relation to important activities rather than 'clock' time – social behaviour is influenced by entrainment, e.g. overlapping rhythms of individuals – there is a sense of security in the repetitiveness and cyclical nature of tasks and activities.
3. Experienced Time	Personal time, social and group time, sharing time, subjective time, phenomenological time, private time, situated time, reflective time	Personal, situated experiences are often very meaningful – emotional and personal experiences influence daily activities – social and group time permeate our family, work and community lives – opportunities for reflection support personal histories and narratives in workplace endeavours. Time 'drags or flies' according to the nature of the activity and relationships in which one is engaged.
4. Cultural Time	Sacred time, profane time, monochronic time, polychronic time	In some cultures time is a dominant and central feature of daily life; in other cultures time has a less significant role. A rapid, hectic pace may characterize one culture; in another movement is slow and casual. Time may be monochronic or polychronic, sacred or profane. How time is perceived and used represents way life is experienced in cultures.
5. Proleptic Time	Transformational time, 'becoming' time, connected time, hermeneutic time, praxis time	Time, self and place are integrated in curriculum and learning activities. There is a focus on transformational practices in learning or leadership. Interconnections are featured and the importance of understanding is emphasized.
6. Focused Time	Engaged time, managed time, intense time, academic time, learning time, practice time, visualized time	Time becomes a strategy for improvement and developing excellence – time is viewed relative to the completion of a task rather than being regulated by the clock – time is a program not a structure.
7. Political Time	Culturally conditioned time, colonized time, gendered time, proximal time, accountability time, time and power, time and status	How we use time in the workplace is conditioned over time – time is a way of controlling/regulating behaviour – time may have gender specific implications depending on roles and private time dimension – time perspectives vary in proportion to the distance from an innovation/activity.
8. Technological Time	Real time, compressed time, networked time, instant time, simulated time, time and space distanciation	The use of telecommunications and computer technologies, for example, shrink and compress distances/space – instantaneous networks and real time communications are supported – individuals are able to simulate conditions as if they were in the present.
9. Reflective Time	Collaboration time, volunteer time, action-research time, out-of-work time, professional development time	Participation in formal and informal in-service sessions during work time. Colleague-to-colleague talk and planning time. After work training activities, university courses and informal after hours study groups. Volunteer activities within the community.

An Initial Glance at the Values Landscape

There is general agreement that values play a key role in education. Because moral choices are made daily within the workplace, it is appealing to opt for a traditional view that supports the universality of fundamental values as a way of sorting out right from wrong (Campbell, 1994). Unfortunately, such a position does little to assist individuals to resolve moral and ethical dilemmas when the world around us is characterized by indeterminacy, diversity, difference and complexity.

When discussing values in education there is a danger in adopting a discourse of clarity. It may be necessary to be more critical about the partiality of theoretical language – particularly with respect to who speaks, under what conditions and for whom? We need to increase our awareness of private consciousness. In doing so, we also need to invest in wise eyes, learn how to focus on the unknown and to listen to unheard voices. To ensure that 'populist elitism' does not occur in writing about values, it may be necessary to find elegance in communication while at the same time acknowledging Giroux's warning to adopt a language:

> ... that not only recognizes the importance of complexity and difference but also provides the conditions for educators to cross borders, where disparate linguistic, theoretical, and political realities meet as part of an ongoing attempt to engage in a 'continual process of negotiation and translation between a series of individual and cultural positions'. (1993, p. 157)

Squires' (1993) collection of essays challenge the postmodern deconstruction of *principled positions*. Contributors to her text attempt to reconnect absolutes of truth and values to the postmodern preference for fragmentation, uncertainty, difference and partial truths. Squires believes that we must start rethinking our values by exploring plurality and learning how to 'negotiate the social hazards of social complexity and moral diversity' (p. 189). She explains, 'The challenge is to construct that unity in a way which achieves (invents or imagines) a sense of universal human values while respecting human variety and difference' (p. 199).

Research methods for the study of values have ranged from those used in the behavioural and social sciences, cybernetics, several branches of the biological and physical sciences to philosophy (Rokeach, 1979). In spite of previous efforts, the 'discourse on the subject of values remains clouded by conceptual difficulties and epistemological wrangling' (Begley, 1996, p. 3).

Often we are locked into established ways of doing things because of power relations, job expectations and historical precedents. It is widely agreed that the world of the twenty-first century will require citizens who must face an array of unpredictable and unknown challenges. For example, today's students require knowledge and skills that will enable them to perform multiple tasks, to be self-directed learners, to understand the importance of lifelong learning, to be resourceful problem-solvers, to be competent users of technology and to understand themselves, their culture and the culture of others. Learning how to think critically, to work in social and emotional contexts, to manage information technologies, to communicate effectively and to solve problems meaningfully are increasingly accepted as essential graduation requirements.

Organizations in Postmodern Society

By focusing on organizations in a postmodern society, I hope to provide a context for examining values and time. Teachers and educational administrators can no longer float on comforting clouds of certitude. They must begin to critically examine who they are, what they believe and value, how time influences their decisions and how they can make a difference in turbulent times. The ability to reflect must be complemented with a strategic agency that shapes social, cultural and political structures.

The changes from modernity to post modernity, or perhaps to a more radical or different form of modernity, are often reflected in the turbulence, complexities, uncertainty, ambiguity, fragmentation and messiness of day-to-day realities. Whether these occurrences are the result of global trends, the implementation of market-driven principles, the exponential developments in technology, changing demographics, or economic and political changes, the fact is they are having a dramatic impact in education. In my current position as Manager of Standards and Assessment in the Ontario Ministry of Education and Training, I can personally testify to daily life in an organization that is characterized by profound change, complexity, intensity, high levels of stress and unpredictability.

Shifts in thinking about what organizations are and how they can best function in a postmodern society are central to the work of educational administrators. Organizations are places where individuals collectively pursue common purposes. Consequently, there are certain dynamics such as those involving values, time, relationships and power that influence and frame how individuals and groups work together.

The evolution of thought about organizations parallels the history of ideas associated with the field of inquiry. Slattery, for example, characterizes the shift from traditional perspectives of organizations when he writes: 'At the root of modernity and its discontents is a disenchanted and mechanistic world view that denies the qualities of subjectivity, experience, and feeling' (1995a, p. 624). Increasingly organizations are characterized by turbulence, chaos, complexity, and 'zones of uncertainty'. There is also a tendency for social systems to be more open and interactive.

In his delightful book, *The Empty Raincoat*, Handy (1995) indicates that turbulence and paradox are features of our life. He captures the possibilities of this condition in the following passage:

> The world is up for re-invention in so many ways. Creativity is born in chaos. What we do, what we belong to, why we do it, where we do it – these may all be different and they could be better. Our societies, however, are built on case law. Change comes from small initiatives that work, initiatives which, imitated, become fashion. We cannot wait for great vision from great people for they are in short

supply at the end of history. It is up to us to light our own small fires in the darkness. (pp. 270–1)

Organizations today are complex, turbulent, practical, unpredictable, deceptive, and ambiguous places (Bolman and Deal, 1991; Evans, 1996). In one sense, the idea of organization tends to be a much harder concept to understand than disorganization. Said another way, the whole is greater than its parts; however, often we can only begin to understand the whole by understanding little pieces of the puzzle. As places where complexity thrives, organizations embody a notion of progress that involves emergent structures – with feedback loops for stability – that were not present in what went before (Waldrop, 1992, pp. 294–9). Complex organizations possess a kind of dynamism that makes them qualitatively different from static objects; they are more spontaneous and more disorderly.

The concept of the learning organization (Cohen and Sproull, 1996; Senge, 1990) has increasingly emerged in the literature as a way of developing organizational capacity, including emergent structures, that enable it to deal with change. Or, as Watkins and Marsick more clearly write: 'To survive in the turbulent environment created by (several external) forces, organizations and their workplaces must be flexible, far-sighted, and able to learn continuously' (1993, p. 5). It is in this context of a learning organization that many of the shifts in thinking about what organizations are and how they can best function in a postmodern society can be found.

The Overwhelming Impact of Change

There is little question that worldwide trends are impacting today's education. The outstanding debts of third world countries and the role of credit are, for example, critical determinants of global economic behaviour and political action (Harvey, 1990). These conditions are often manifested in systems and approaches to labour control that may include mandated restructuring, unemployment or curbs on unions. In addition, the impact of new technologies and the intense emphasis on marketing as a way of generating money – and saving jobs or programs – are influencing decisions in educational organizations.

I am not implying that global changes occurring today are more challenging than those of previous periods in our history – they are, however, uniquely ours to resolve. Crises of capitalism, ecological calamities, gender and racial discrimination, religious differences, social injustices and oppression are daily occurrences that eventually impact education.

It is no wonder then that today's workplace is often characterized by a turbulent policy environment, a hectic and often unmanageable pace of change, an increase in workload, access to fewer resources, and a new view of role and expertise. The resultant overload and role ambiguity contribute to an increase in stress and a loss of control and professional identity (Murphy, 1994, pp. 24–5). Along with a continuing focus on standards and assessment, results-driven systems – with a concomitant push for value-added education, Marsh believes that the next decade will be characterized by 'political, economic and social issues of stunning complexity and tenacity . . . [which] will evolve with rapid speed, but are likely to accelerate the reshaping of schools themselves as well as the world "beyond" the school' (1997, p. 4). In this context the role of teachers and administrators will assume greater importance, but will require a modicum of reinvention.

Although writing about multiculturalism and children's literature, Elaine Schwartz's (1995) closing comments to her essay review might equally apply to those interested in the future of education. She writes:

> This shift to postmodernism carries within it a sense of urgency. Culture, as our ancestors have experienced it, no longer reflects the immediate realities of daily life. Culture as we know it is now greatly impacted by global, political, and economic issues, the accessibility of international travel and communications. Technology has metaphorically shrunk our world, while simultaneously devaluing the signifi-cance of our independence with our borderlands. Meanwhile, those borderlands have grown exponentially, both in size and in number. This growth, as represented by the current transition from a late twentieth-century culture of modernism to the postmodernism of the twenty-first century, requires that educators fully grasp these dramatic changes and interrogate their own place within this transition. (p. 646)

The sense of *urgency* and *immediacy of daily realities* serve to highlight the time demands that educators face. The challenge to *interrogate their own place within this transition* puts educators on notice to examine their life – to take stock of what they value.

There is little question that many educators are becoming overwhelmed with the scale and pace of educational change. The literature on change in education has assumed a stature deserving study in its own right. Fullan's (1991) treatise on the meaning of educational change, for example, provides a comprehensive review of the issues. Whether the focus is on restructuring, planned educational change, or the improvement of organizations educators have come to accept change as a way of life – not, however, without some pain and anguish. Years of change and reform initiatives have left many educators confused, exhausted, angry and disillusioned. The challenge then is to provide a sense of certitude and stability in a sea of tur-bulence and mandated uncertainty so that the primary purposes of schools remain clear – where learning permeates the total school community.

Rethinking Time

There is little question that schools operate within the precise economy of time. Time is often viewed as a commodity – a resource to be used, consumed and invested (Giddens, 1984, 1987). The Report of the National Education Commission on Time and Learning (1994) identifies traditional time tabling and scheduling practices as obstacles to learning. Hargreaves (1994) refers to technical-rational time as a finite resource that is regarded by educational administrators as being able to be managed and manipulated. This commodified concept of time can be found in a variety of metaphorical expressions such as: 'I never have enough time', 'you have to manage time', and 'time is money' (Lakoff and Johnson, 1980; Lakoff and Turner, 1989).

In an era of limited resources it becomes increasingly important for teachers and educational administrators to work cooperatively and collaboratively together as they provide the best learning opportunities for their students. This may necessitate reculturing, restructuring and retiming (Fullan, 1995). However, as Hargreaves (1996) clearly demonstrates, this task must acknowledge the ways that school and teacher cultures are being increasingly colonized by government and management. 'Manufactured uncertainty', paradoxes related to educational expectations, and the 'interior turn towards the self, personal relationships and lifestyle choices as a focus for empowerment and change' (p. 8) represent challenges to cultural approaches to educational change. How can we, as Hargreaves suggests, 'recognize and support teachers as active agents in developing and maintaining their own cultures' while at the same time assist teachers and school administrators to turn 'outwards in their change strategies to fight the assault on public education' (p. 24)? One possibility is to examine the different *time tracks* found in teachers' and educational administrators' work and to investigate how teachers and administrators respond to different *time binds* and pressures. Understanding how time is used and the different meanings given to temporal issues can clarify the competing approaches to and expectations for the school as a learning organization.

Legislation aimed at reforming educational governance, education finance or education labour relations often touch upon matters related to instruction and usually involve matters with direct temporal implications, e.g. reduce teacher preparation time, extend the length of the school year, and increase class size. Clearly time is a contested commodity – a costly resource that affects not only working conditions, but also determines the very existence of people's careers. Underlying these temporal issues are more fundamental questions related to control and power.

Educators require many kinds of time and they often experience and construct meanings of time differently. Yet existing structures and administrative assumptions frequently limit the meanings of time to notions of time as a commodity or regulator. The rhythms of schools and teachers are often interlocked. In a season of pronounced curriculum reform it may be necessary to review the nature of time, including how it is organized and expressed, in a school before making changes. Increasingly the pressure to do more with less, and more quickly, affects how we feel, think and behave. Conflicting views about how to respond to these changes may result in organizational disharmony – often with worrying implications. When, for example, do expectations by government and educational administrators for teachers to act more professionally become exploitation? Time to plan and practise, time for curriculum development, time to turn policy into practice, time to teach mandated curriculum expectations, time to assess and report learning, time to support extra-curricular activities, time to share successful practices, time to communicate with parents, time to sell reform, and time for vigilance about the primary purposes of education are concerns commonly encountered by teachers.

Values and Public Education in a Context of Educational Change

More than ever public education is coming under close scrutiny. In a context of rapid economic, political, social and educational change, the future is no longer as predictable as it used to be. As educators we must respond and rally on behalf of our children to ensure that each receives the best education possible. In order to do so, however, it is important that teachers, students, parents, business and the community engage in an open dialogue. One that encourages debate and clarification of the purposes of public education.

Such a discussion must include the examination of values underlying public education. A cursory review identified several common qualities that people consider important as principles for conduct and as major aims of existence. Some of these standards that guide actions and judgments will be presented later in this section. Rather than attempting to provide a definitive listing, the intent here is to challenge you to ponder and reflect. How exactly are values presented in the curriculum? Are they dealt with in an explicit or implicit manner? To what extent do we talk about the importance of values? How do we practise values in our classrooms and schools? In an era of exponential change do values remain stable? Do they retain their relevance? Are there new and emerging values?

The concept of the 'hidden' curriculum permeates our day-to-day interactions. As one of my colleagues is prone to say, we have become more sophisticated in talking the talk, however we still do not walk the talk very well. We get preoccupied with the day-to-day realities of implementing the mandated curriculum and sometimes we loose sight of the issues which form the foundation of public education. In addition, the dominant need for business to be competitive and on the technological critical edge extend 'hidden' curriculum concepts such as those involving power and control even further.

Before we get caught up in the excitement of the chase let us make sure that we ask ourselves some hard questions. Let us revisit the discussion about what we value in public education. Let us critically clarify and understand the purposes of public education and the new roles and responsibilities that all of us must play. Hopefully in this way we can ensure value added education for all.

In the next section an attempt is made to clarify the meaning of values in education and to provide examples from a few selected sources as to what these values might include. The intent is to initiate discussion and reflection rather than to provide the 'correct' set of values that underlie public education.

Getting a Handle on the Meaning of Values

The Oxford English Dictionary refers to values as those qualities that are 'worthy of esteem for [their] own sake' or have 'intrinsic worth'. Used by itself and in the plural, the word values refers to a code of behaviour, principles or 'moral' values, where moral pertains to what is right, proper and good.

Kluckhohn (1951) provides a helpful starting point for any discussion of values by offering this definition: 'A value is a conception, explicit or implicit, distinctive of an individual or characteristic of a group, of the desirable which influences the selection from available modes, means, and ends of action' (p. 395).

In his seminal work entitled, *Beliefs, Attitudes and Values: A Theory of Organization and Change*, Rokeach (1972) posits a definition that helps clarify the meaning of values:

> Values . . . have to do with modes of conduct and end-states of existence. To say that a person 'has a value' is to say that he/she has an enduring belief that a specific mode of conduct or end-state of existence is personally and socially preferable to alternative modes of conduct or end-states of existence. Once a value is internalized it becomes, consciously or unconsciously, a standard of criterion for guiding action, for developing and maintaining one's own and others' actions and attitudes, for morally judging self and others, and for comparing self with others. Finally, a value is a standard employed to influence the values, attitudes, and actions of at least some others – our children's, for example. (p. 159)

Rokeach provides further clarification of the meaning of values when he explains how values differ from attitudes:

> While an attitude represents several beliefs focused on a specific object or situation, a value is a single belief that transcendentally guides actions and judgments across specific objects and situations, and beyond immediate goals to more ultimate end-states of existence. Moreover, a value, unlike an attitude, is an imperative to action, not only a belief about the preferable but also a preference for the preferable . . . Finally, a value, unlike an attitude, is a standard or yardstick to guide actions, attitudes, comparisons, evaluations, and justifications of self and others. (p. 160)

In an attempt to uncover a core set of universal values, Rushworth Kidder travelled the world to interview leading thinkers, artists, writers, educators, business people and religious and political leaders. *Shared Values for a Troubled World* (1994), describes his conversations with men and women of conscience. Based on twenty-four interviews Kidder identified eight universal values necessary to create the moral conditions for sustaining our future. These eight universal values that represent a kind of global code of ethics are: love, truthfulness, fairness, freedom, unity, tolerance, responsibility and respect for life.

In a discussion of moral values, Thomas Sergiovanni (1992) writes:

> Certain ideals enhance human life and assist people in fulfilling their obligations to one another: These should be served whenever possible. Among the most important ideals are . . . tolerance, compassion, loyalty, forgiveness, peace, brotherhood, justice (giving people their due), and fairness (being impartial, as opposed to favouring selected people). (p. 110)

Stephen Covey's (1989) philosophy for creating more meaningful relationships and success in the workplace has recently had a significant impact on educational change and leadership initiatives. He advocates that principles rather than values are the true enduring standards. Covey believes that principles are less subjective than values. Covey suggests that our values are developed 'with deep respect for principles'. He writes:

> Principles are guidelines for human conduct that are proven to have enduring, permanent value. They're fundamental. They're essentially unarguable because they are self-evident . . . consider the absurdity of trying to live an effective life based on their opposites. I doubt that anyone would seriously consider unfairness, deceit, baseness, uselessness, mediocrity, or degradation as a solid foundation for lasting happiness and success. (p. 34)

If, indeed, principles are more objective and unarguable, would it be less problematic and controversial for public education to embrace a clear set of principles rather than debate the suitability of more subjectively based values? What, indeed would the impact be on educational reform? In a consideration of restructuring initiatives in education, David Conley (1993) addresses the problematic. He states:

> Changes in the values of society inevitably have profound effects on education. Although schools profess to attempt 'neutrality' on issues of values and morals, all schools possess implicit value and moral structures. These structures generally mirror the community in which the school exists. Such an arrangement makes perfect sense. What happens, though, when value and moral systems are in flux? The compass does not point north with consistency. What are schools to do in an environment of conflicting signals? (p. 43)

Conley continues:

> Much of the restructuring movement has concerned itself with changing the structures of education rather than examining its values. However, structural changes carry with them implied moral and ethical assumptions. It is worthwhile to examine some of these implicit assumptions embedded in the goals of school restructuring. (p. 43)

Recent emphasis on the need for reflective practice comes from the seminal work of Schon (1983, 1987). The concept of the 'reflective turn' makes research into a reflective practice in its own right. Central to this process are key questions such as: What is it appropriate to reflect on? What is an appropriate way of reflecting on practice? How is rigour achieved? Three types of reflective practice are posited by Brubacher, Case and Reagan (1994): reflection-on-practice, reflection-in-practice, and reflection-for-practice. While all three forms of reflective practice have merit, reflection-for-practice is proactive – it is more conducive to guiding future action and supporting development in a context of change.

Beck supports learning values through dialogue. Citing contemporary thinkers from the hermeneutic school of thought, Beck makes a cogent case for the dialogical approach. Key aspects to the dialogue model are, '(a) respect for each other's insights; (b) respect for each other's tradition or "story"; (c) freedom of speech, belief, action; (d) shared control of the form and content of dialogue; (e) focus on concrete, lived experience; and testing through action ("praxis")' (1993, p. 266).

The unexamined life is not worth living. Socrates' maxim '. . . invoke[s] and inspire[s] introspection, reflection, intensification and heightening of consciousness' (Hodgkinson, 1996, p. 8). As educational administrators we have a responsibility to engage in self-reflective practice, to assess our own value inventory, to take stock. 'A value audit is a stock-taking of one's own values. It is a reflective and contemplative effort which seeks to bring into the light of consciousness the range, depth and breadth of one's preferences, conditioning and beliefs' (Hodgkinson, 1991, p. 136). Through this value analysis, a more thorough realization and understanding of one's values and the crucial role that they play in decision making should be possible. Although this analysis can be done hypothetically, ideally '. . . it is done with a specific focus on a praxis problem which is being faced in a real situation' (Hodgkinson, 1991, p. 136).

Our use of time is one such praxis problem. An awareness of our own values and how they interact with those of another or the collective ethics of the external environment be it the school, board or community has the potential to improve our individual decision making practices.

Rokeach's (1979) assertion that a value is an imperative to action, provides a remarkably useful connection to Argyris and Schon's (1974) concept of theory-in-action. In addition, Rokeach makes a distinction between instrumental values that focus on means such as honesty and courage, and terminal values that focus on ends such as salvation or peace. He also suggests that values are hierarchical with a rank-ordering structure.

Noteworthy in current discussions about values is Hodgkinson's (1991) tripartite value model – a model that facilitates the classification of values into three types of values: Type III (Preference) values, Type II (Consensus and Consequence) values and Type I (Principle) values. Type III values are based on individual preferences and refer to what is enjoyable. They tend to be rooted in the emotions and the affective. Type IIb values are next in the model and include values concerned with what is right or ought to be. They also focus on collectivity and context; they deal with consensus. Type IIa values are also concerned with what is right, however, they presuppose a social context with social norms. And, Type I values are grounded in the metaphysical; principles dominate. They require an act of faith or commitment.

Distinctions involving the 'good' and the 'right' or the 'desirable' and the 'desired' constitute one way of differentiating these three value types. Distinctions indicating how values are distinguished or grounded provide a further way of differentiating these value types. Hodgkinson identifies four grounds for value judgments: preference, consensus, consequence and principles (1991, pp. 96–101).

In Feather's (1975) view 'any model that attempts to relate action simply to general values alone is doomed to failure because it has left out of consideration the important role of the situation in which the behaviour occurs' (p. 297). And, commenting on the conditions under which values lead to action, Feather identifies the central role of motives. He explains:

Values may then be seen as a particular class of motives: those tied to a normative base relating to an evaluative dimension of goodness–badness. Thus, motive would be the more inclusive concept and value would be a member of this general class. There may therefore be some motives that are not values but no values that are not motives. (p. 300)

How we perceive and use time often requires some hard choices. Making decisions is largely value-based. Like Hodgkinson (1991), it is posited here that an assessment of one's own values can further one's self-awareness, individual understanding, and moral responsibility in decision making. 'Values are seen as inferable from behaviour [and dialogue], or predictive of behaviour, when the individual is aware of all available alternatives, can freely choose any particular one, and knows the probabilities of outcomes occurring' (Churchman, 1961, cited in Rokeach, 1979, p. 73).

Concluding Comments

How we perceive time, how we construct time and how we use time provide a lens for seeing who we are and what we value. Educators are affected by many kinds of time – including, for example, timetables, planning time, administrative time, report-card time, teaching time, assessment and reporting time, parent time, community time, professional development time and extra-curricular time. They often construct and make meaning of time differently. Existing structures, however, frequently limit the development of alternative shared meanings of time. The rhythms of schools and educators are often interlocked. During extensive, mandated curriculum reform it may be necessary to review the nature of time in a school before making changes. What is the best way to maintain teaching time as sacred time and ensure that planning time is also available? What amount of teacher time should be spent on extracurricular activities – and which ones? What are the implications of intensified working conditions and concomitant stress for re-culturing, restructuring and retiming? How do educators find time to learn new skills and ideas? How can the monochronic view of time often held by educational administrators accommodate better the polychronic framework of teachers? Are there ways to resolve such temporal dilemmas and tensions? How can the concept of proleptic time be seriously considered during periods of fundamental educational change?

In a recent interviews with Grade 7 and 8 teachers, principals and administrators, I have been particularly struck by the references to their own set of personal values when confronted by so much change and confusion in education. Values have always been powerfully and decisively operative both in societies and in the lives of individuals. People become what they choose. Conversely, what a person is and does provides us with a glimpse of their values. Values determine purpose and policy; they give direction and motivation to human activity. Values serve as criteria of judgment enabling us to determine the comparative worth of our experiences.

As we rapidly approach the millennium there are pressures to rethink the purposes of schools and the ways in which they operate as learning organizations.

Stretching our understanding of time can create possibilities and enable educators to make leaps of imagination. By looking through the unaccustomed lenses of time, then we will be able to view anew the relevance of current and emerging practices and the values we espouse.

References

ARGYRIS, C. and SCHON, D.A. (1974) *Theory in Practice: Increasing Professional Effectiveness*, San Francisco, CA: Jossey-Bass.

BECK, C. (1993) *Learning to Live the Good Life: Values in Adulthood*, Toronto: OISE.

BEGLEY, P.T. (1996) 'Cognitive perspectives on the nature and function of values in educational administration', in LEITHWOOD, K., CHAPMAN, J., CORSON, D., HALLINGER, P. and HART, A. (1996) *International Handbook of Educational Leadership and Administration*, Dordrecht/Boston/London: Kluwer.

BOLMAN, L.G. and DEAL, T.E. (1991) *Reframing Organizations: Artistry, Choice and Leadership*, San Francisco, CA: Jossey-Bass.

BRUBACHER, J.W., CASE, C.W. and REAGAN, T.G. (1994) *Becoming a Reflective Educator*, Thousand Oaks, CA: Corwin.

CAMPBELL, E. (1994) 'Personal morals and organizational ethics: A synopsis', *The Canadian Administrator*, **34**, 2, November, pp. 1–10.

COHEN, M.D. and SPROULL, L.S. (eds) (1996) *Organizational Learning*, Thousand Oaks, CA: Sage.

CONLEY, D.T. (1993) Roadmap to restructuring: Policies, practices and the emerging visions of schooling', *ERIC Clearinghouse on Educational Management*, Eugene, OR: University of Oregon.

CORSON, D. (1989) *Language Policy Across the Curriculum*, Philadelphia, PA: Multilingual Matters Ltd.

COVEY, S.R. (1989) *The Seven Habits of Highly Effective People*, New York: Fireside.

EVANS, R. (1996) *The Human Side of School Change*, San Francisco, CA: Jossey-Bass.

FEATHER, N.T. (1975) *Values in Education and Society*, New York: Free Press.

FRAISSE, P. (1963) *The Psychology of Time*, New York: Harper and Row.

FULLAN, M. (1991) *The New Meaning of Educational Change*, with STEIGELBAUER, S., New York: Teachers College.

FULLAN, M. (1995) 'The school as a learning organization: Distant dreams', *Theory Into Practice*, **34**, 4, 230–5.

GIDDENS, A. (1984) *The Constitution of Society*, Berkeley, CA: University of California Press.

GIDDENS, A. (1987) *Social Theory and Modern Sociology*, Stanford, CA: Stanford University Press.

GIROUX, H.A. (1993) *Living Dangerously: Multiculturalism and the Politics of Difference*, New York: Peter Lang.

GURVITCH, G. (1971) *The Social Frameworks of Knowledge*, New York: Harper and Row.

HANDY, C. (1995) *The Empty Raincoat: Making Sense of the Future*, Reading: Arrow.

HARGREAVES, A. (1996) 'Cultures of teaching and educational change.' Paper presented to the American Educational Research Association, New York.

HARGREAVES, A. (1994) *Changing Teachers, Changing Times: Teachers' Work and Culture in the Postmodern Age*, New York: Teachers College.

HARVEY, D. (1990) *The Condition of Postmodernity*, Cambridge: Blackwell.

HAWKINGS, S. (1988) *A Brief History of Time*, Toronto: Bantam.

HODGKINSON, C. (1991) *Educational Leadership: The Moral Art*, Albany, NY: State University of New York Press.

HODGKINSON, C. (1996) *Administrative Philosophy: Values and Motivations in Administrative Life*, Oxford: Pergamon Press.

KIDDER, R.M. (1994) *Shared Values for a Troubled World: Conversations with Men and Women of Conscience*, San Francisco, CA: Jossey-Bass.

KLUCKHOHN, C. (1951) 'Values and value orientations in the theory of action', in PARSONS, T. and SHILS, E.A. (eds) *Toward a General Theory of Action*, Cambridge, MA: Harvard University Press.

LAKOFF, G. and TURNER, M. (1989) *More than Cool Reason: A Field Guide to Poetic Metaphor*, Chicago, IL: University of Chicago Press.

LAKOFF, G. and JOHNSON, M. (1980) *Metaphors We Live By*, Chicago, IL: University of Chicago Press.

LUBECK, S. (1985) *Sandbox Society*, London: Falmer Press.

MARSH, D.D. (1997) 'Educational leadership for the twenty-first century: Integrating three emerging perspectives.' Paper presented at the annual meeting of the American Educational Research Association, Chicago, IL.

MURPHY, J. (1994) 'Transformational change and the evolving role of the principal: Early empirical evidence', in MURPHY, J. and LOUIS, K.S. (eds) *Reshaping the Principalship: Insights from Transformational Reform Efforts*, Thousand Oaks, CA: Corwin.

PRISONERS OF TIME (1994) Report of the National Education Commission on Time and Learning, Washington, DC: US Government Printing Office.

ROKEACH, M. (1972) *Beliefs, Attitudes and Values: A Theory of Organization and Change*, San Francisco, CA: Jossey-Bass.

ROKEACH, M. (1979) *Understanding Human Values*, New York: Free Press.

SCHEIN, E.H. (1992) *Organizational Culture and Leadership*, 2nd edn, San Francisco, CA: Jossey-Bass.

SCHON, D.A. (1983) *The Reflective Practitioner: How Professionals Think in Action*, New York: Basic Books.

SCHON, D.A. (1987) *Educating the Reflective Practitioner*, San Francisco, CA: Jossey-Bass.

SCHWARTZ, E.G. (1995) 'Crossing borders/Shifting paradigms: Multiculturalism and children's literature', *Harvard Educational Review*, **65**, 4, pp. 634–50.

SENGE, P.M. (1990) *The Fifth Discipline: The Art and Practice of the Learning Organization*, New York: Doubleday.

SERGIOVANNI, T.J. (1992) *Moral Leadership: Getting to the Heart of School Improvement*, San Francisco, CA: Jossey-Bass.

SLATTERY, P. (1995a) 'A postmodern vision of time and learning: A response to the National Education Report, Prisoners of Time', *Harvard Educational Review*, **65**, 4, pp. 612–33.

SLATTERY, P. (1995b) *Curriculum Development in the Postmodern Era*, New York: Garland.

SQUIRES, J. (1993) *Principled Positions: Postmodernism and the Rediscovery of Values*, London: Lawrence and Wishart.

WALDROP, M.M. (1992) *Complexity: The Emerging Science at the Edge of Order and Chaos*, New York: Simon and Schuster.

WATKINS, K.E. and MARSICK, V.J. (1993) *Sculpting the Learning Organization: Lessons in the Art and Science of Systemic Change*, San Francisco, CA: Jossey-Bass.

WERNER, W. (1988) 'Program implementation and experienced time', *The Alberta Journal of Educational Research*, **34**, 2, pp. 90–108.

11 Leadership and Management in Education: Restoring the Balance in Pursuit of a More Just and Equitable Society

Paul Carlin and Helen Goode

The more recent developmental perspective asserts that as individuals we can be participants in the making of our history . . . This bias in our culture which is relatively recent, has profound implications for how we view and act on the world. It enables us to entertain the possibility that we might reconstruct our worlds, makes us responsible for the values which we choose to pursue, and holds us accountable for the consequences of our choices. Persons who would make history must also assume its burdens and accept responsibility for failures to realize their best values. (Riffel, 1986, pp. 164–5)

Introduction

As people and institutions in nations across the world attempt to adjust and respond to the pervasive change forces of the modern world, the concepts of leadership and management, and the relationship between them, need to be redefined. A key element of the change process is the dominant policy of 'the market' with its emphasis on choice, competition, outcomes and efficiency, and this is having a major impact on all areas of social policy, including education. Commenting on these impacts on education, Hughes reports on the Jomtien *World Conference on Education for All* sponsored by UNESCO, and he makes the point that, 'Jomtien marked a crucial realisation: that a major effort was required if the divisions which mark our world were not to become deeper and more unbridgeable' (1997, p. 2). Because leadership must address areas of values, equity and fair distribution of material and cultural resources and capacity, this chapter argues that, at the present time, the balance between leadership and management needs to be realigned because, as we become more deeply embedded in the global economy, management is being given pre-eminence when in fact *leadership* is being demanded.

An Overview of the Research on the Social-cultural Context of Education

According to Mackay Australia has been experiencing and struggling with a sustained period of major discontinuity and dislocation for the past 20 years.

There could hardly be a more fascinating time to be studying Australia than in the 1990s and yet, at the same time, it is a period in which most of the traditional landmarks, signposts and reference points no longer define the Australian way of life. We are living in a period of such radical social, cultural, political, economic and technological change that it is not going too far to suggest that Australian society is actually in the process of being redefined. (1993, p. 1)

These changes reach into most aspects of our personal and social lives. Lepani (1994) commenting on Mackay's work contends that the stresses of these multi-faceted changes are contributing to a more confused and fragile sense of identity, the loss of a coherent sense of purpose and a growing sense of alienation for many people. That is, they are reaching into the nation's psyche.

Reich reporting on the transformation of nations across the world as a consequence of the moves to global economies and instant communication facilities comments that:

Each nation's primary assets will be its citizen's skills and insights. Each nation's primary political task will be to cope with the centrifugal forces of the global economy which tear at the ties binding citizens together – bestowing ever greater wealth on the most skilled and insightful, whilst consigning the less skilled to a declining standard of living. (1991, p. 3)

For many people, and especially for young adults, these symptoms are very real. They are part of a common reality – periods of unemployment, boredom, financial difficulties and being neglected and alienated. But more importantly these experiences become a significant part of their psyche, which is characterized by little hope, tension and a sense of being powerless. Yet, in this fragmented state, a media that incessantly promotes images of glamour, excitement, living for the moment and taking charge bombards them. There is little in the media that offers incentives to encourage people to invest time and effort in education and learning. Eckersley articulates starkly the nature of the emerging crisis.

The growing crisis facing western societies is, then, deeply rooted in the culture of modern western societies: in the moral priority we give to the individual over the community, to rights over responsibilities, the present over the future (and the past), the ephemeral over the enduring, the material over the spiritual. (1992, p. 19)

It is now beyond doubt that these symptoms, this pervasive level of illness, has crept into the lives of individuals, communities and nations. For many, they are an integral part of their lived experience, they are the lens that are used often to view and interpret the world, its possibilities and constraints. Then depending on how they see and feel about themselves and their world, they make decisions, safe or enterprising, informed or uninformed. This climate poses real challenges for the capacity of schools to meet the needs of students and their families. How can schools provide the safe emotional environment and the range of services students and families require, if they are to be encouraged and assisted to participate successfully in the formal and informal learning program?

It is in this context that Cox, in the 1995 Boyer Lectures, argues that we need to rediscover and give priority to the building of a 'civil society'. She maintains that there needs to be a priority and an urgency given to rebuilding relationships and community. To achieve this, much more attention needs to be invested in the nurturing and enhancement of social capital. She defines social capital by saying: 'Social capital refers to the processes between people which establish networks, norms and social trust and facilitate co-ordination and co-operation for mutual benefit. These processes are also known as social fabric or glue . . .' (p. 15). This is one of four forms of capital identified by Cox (1995). She asserts that although social capital is extremely important, because it constitutes the essence of our humanity, it is frequently the one that is overlooked. Within the current political and economic framework, financial capital has priority and takes up a very large part of the decision-making agenda. Environmental capital also receives considerable political attention as a consequence of the work done by several committed lobby groups who have captured considerable support. Because of the emphasis given by governments to 'international competitiveness', human capital, that is the aggregate of our skills and knowledge, is also given prominence. But Cox (1995) argues that in this period of deep insecurity and loss of meaning, that unless the issue of social capital is adequately resourced, then our capacity to develop and maintain the levels of the other forms of capital will be diminished.

Beare, in reference to the work of Joseph Campbell, refers to the need for a fifth form of capital, namely spiritual capital. However, it does not lend itself to measurement, but it does go to the heart of what it is to be human.

> What has mythmaking got to do with a program budget, with performance indicators and outcome measures, with efficiency and economics? A great deal, for to redefine education in business terms, in an economic or instrumental way, belittles one of the most significant aspects of all education. The question, then, is whether any new mythology about education is 'life amplifying', whether it substitutes the trivial for the profound, the banal for the transcendental, the cheap for what is culturally rich. (1987, p. 82)

The whole question of capacity is addressed by Baldwin in reference to the area of social security. He argues that unless those with the least resources and the least capacity are taught how to increase and apply their capability levels, then little return will be achieved for the allocation of scarce resources.

> Those concerned with equity and justice in modern developed countries should increasingly focus their efforts on achieving a fairer distribution of the capability, the freedom to achieve . . . We should focus on both providing an adequate level of resources to those getting our payments and on enhancing their ability to make the most of these entitlements. Individual's living standards are not just a function of the availability of cash and other resources, but also of having the wherewithal to effectively utilise these resources. Those with the least resources often also have the least capacity to make the most of them. (1995, p. 39)

I suggest that this principle has important implications for education. In a time of global economies and fragile identities and self-esteem, the provision of educational passports to young people will still leave many of them vulnerable, unless they also learn how to apply them in order to make a difference in their lives. This has important ramifications for the way in which teaching, learning and assessment are structured, especially for those students who may be at risk – academically or socially.

The issue of social capital raises important questions related to the concepts of wealth distribution and utilization, and community. Colebatch (1996, p. A 23) commenting on the United Nations *Human Development Report* (1996) states that: 'Over the past 30 years, the world's poorest 20 per cent of people have seen their share of global income fall from 2.3 to 1.4 per cent, while the richest 20 per cent rose from 70 to 85 per cent of world income.' Starratt (1992, p. 4) exhorts us to reconsider what counts as wealth. 'I believe we need to rethink the definitions of wealth and prosperity. Time is wealth. Friends and family are wealth. Experience of the sacred is wealth.'

However, unless these features are perceived to be of worth and value, they will not be nurtured and sustained, and consequently will continue to decline. Much of the work cited in this chapter suggests strongly that in the current culture, individual rights and wants continue to be given priority over communal well being and the common good. This tends to reinforce and exacerbate existing divisions in local communities and across nations. The growing trend towards more urbanization, changed employment patterns and family structures, within a framework of multicultural and pluralist societies, is placing increasing pressure and tension on individuals and groups. As a consequence, many people are having difficulty coping and are resorting to unhealthy ways of dealing with these problems, for example, increased substance abuse. This in turn leads to higher levels of social problems, crime and violence. Barker terms it the great divide:

> The social and economic consequences of this phenomenon have, in different degrees, been universal throughout Western societies. High unemployment, especially among the young and the ageing, has left millions feeling vulnerable or, worse, alienated. Millions more are socially marginalised or excluded as inequality and poverty increases. (1997, p. 32)

It is the support that comes from belonging to life-giving communities of agreed values, trust and mutual benefit that can carry members through the difficult periods and help to restore them to health.

It is in this regard that the role of schools as vital elements and an integral part of modern communities needs to be examined. With the decline of churches as centres of community and the significant changes to the provision of services by local government, the role of schools working with families and other social agencies becomes a crucial part of community infrastructure and well being. One example of the contribution that many schools are making to community coherence and well being is the provision of after-school care programs for many children. However, with the devolution of increased responsibilities to schools across most countries in the western world, their capacity to be both centres of academic excellence and centres of community support in periods of radical social and economic change is becoming increasingly demanding and difficult.

Selected Insights into the Research on Leadership and Management

The research literature on the topic of leadership and management as it applies to educational institutions is extensive. Burns (1978) was one of the early researchers to introduce the terms 'transactional' and 'transformational' in an attempt to distinguish between what he considered to be qualitatively different forms of leadership. Silins (1994, p. 274) describes the difference in this way.

> Transformational leadership bonds leaders and followers within a collaborative change process that impacts on the performance of the whole organisation resulting in a responsive and innovative environment. In contrast, transactional leadership does not bind leaders and followers in any enduring way and promotes a routinised, non-creative but stable environment.

Following on from the work of Burns, Bass (1985) argued that transformational leadership is required if schools and organization are to respond to change initiatives – both internal and external. Schools will need purposeful and courageous leaders if they are to achieve improved student learning outcomes and create an organization that operates and develops in ways that are consistent with the core values of its mission statement or charter.

Kotter (1990, p. 3) describes *leadership* as an ageless topic, whereas he claims that *management* has emerged in the last century in response to the significant increase in the number of complex organization. He maintains that modern management essentially involves three processes: 'planning and budgeting; organizing and staffing; and controlling and problem solving'. With regard to leadership, he asserts that it is about achieving 'constructive or adaptive change', that is, creating a world 'in which both they [leaders] and those who depend on them are genuinely better off' (p. 5). This leadership function he maintains is comprised of three sub-processes, which he describes as establishing direction, aligning people, and motivating and inspiring people. He then makes the point that within complex organization:

> Management and leadership, so defined, are clearly in some ways similar . . . They are both, in this sense, complete action systems; neither is simply one aspect of the other. People who think of management as being only the implementation part of leadership ignore the fact that leadership has its own implementation processes: aligning people to new directions and then inspiring them to make it happen. Similarly, people who think of leadership as only part of the implementation aspect of management (the motivational part) ignore the direction-setting aspect of leadership. (Kotter, 1990, p. 5)

Drucker (1990) in his work on management, describes management as both a social function and a liberal art (Chapter 15). He contends that within the last 150 years, 'management has transformed the social and economic fabric of the world's developed countries' (p. 213). In answer to his own question 'What is management?' Drucker 1990 (pp. 220–3) makes the following points.

- Management is about human beings . . .
- because management deals with the integration of people in a common venture, it is deeply embedded in culture . . .
- every enterprise requires commitment to common goals and shared values . . .
- management must also enable the enterprise and each of its members to grow and develop as needs and opportunities change . . .
- it [every enterprise] must be built on communication and on individual responsibility.

However, in reference to management as a liberal art (p. 223), he adds the dimension that many other writers ascribe to leadership: '. . . management is deeply involved with spiritual concerns – the nature of man, good and evil'.

Starratt (1993) also uses Burns' (1978) categories of transactional and transformational leadership to investigate the nature of leadership behaviours and processes in periods of significant political and educational reform. He argues that the pervasive nature of current reform initiatives and their political impact on individuals and groups requires a concerted moral response from political and educational leaders. The management of the implementation of these reforms is both important and legitimate, but on its own it is not sufficient. These reforms require leadership that will question, challenge and advocate where necessary to ensure that the processes and outcomes of these reforms are based on the values of fairness, justice and dignity for all.

Murphy (1995, p. 14) in a paper presented at the ACEA international conference, put forward a notion of 'creative leadership', in which he argued that tomorrow's leaders will be required to design, articulate and put into operation an educational vision which will help to bring about a new and better society. He uses a set of metaphorical lens to redefine the kind of leadership to be exercised if a better society is to be achieved. These include: leader as community servant; leader as organization architect; leader as social architect; and leader as moral educator. An example of what this means for the practice of leadership is set out below.

> The leadership challenge for administrators is quite complex . . . They must learn to lead not from the apex of the organisation pyramid but from the nexus of a web of interpersonal relationships (Chapman and Boyd, 1986) – with people rather than through them. Their base of influence must be professional expertise and moral imperative rather than line authority. (Murphy, 1995, p. 14)

Because of the rapidly increasing diversity of student populations in most western countries, and the fact that approximately 80 per cent are staying on to complete a full secondary education, Murphy (1995, p. 19) maintains that:

... school leaders, in their role as social architects in the post-industrial age, must see schooling as one element of a larger attack on the problems facing youth: School leaders need to have an expansive view of the change to and the possibilities of schooling. Instead of trying to artificially limit the roles of schools, they need to expand the influence of schools to each child, each family, the community, the political infrastructure (Murphy, 1995, p. 19, citing Astuto (1990)).

This brief review of the research findings cited above makes two points very powerfully.

- As the student population becomes more diverse in terms of language, culture and socio-economic background, and the range of abilities and needs increase, leadership practices in schools will have to make the necessary adjustments if schools are to continue to be important vehicles for meeting human needs and for bringing about a better and more just society.
- Because of the impact of multidimensional change on people of all ages, including teachers, students and their families, schools will need to be part of an integrated policy and service provision if these opportunities and needs are to be addressed, and if they are to become a source of meaning, hope and empowerment to their communities.

DePree captures one of the ways in which leadership is fundamentally different from management when he comments that, 'It is more difficult, but far more important, to be committed to a corporate concept of persons, the diversity of human gifts, covenantal relationships, lavish communications, including everyone, and believing that leadership is a condition of indebtedness' (1989, p. 72)

What are the Challenges for Leaders in Schools?

The issue of the capacity of schools to meet the needs and expectations placed on them by governments as the key unit for the delivery of education policies and programs, and at the same time be an important centre for community support, is a complex and demanding one. Particularly, as government, business and community leaders are identifying schools as probably the most effective agency for addressing issues of concern, such as drug education, sex education, road traffic safety. This has led to a situation that continues to be a source of tension and demand for school leaders.

Sergiovanni (1994, p. 217) poses the question as to whether schools are organizations or communities. He asserts that operating out of each metaphor has critical implications for the definition and nature of leadership in schools, and for the kinds of values, relationships and working patterns that are honoured in schools. He makes the distinction in this way.

Life in organization and life in communities are different in both quality and kind. In communities, we create our social lives with others who have intentions similar to ours. In organization, relationships are constructed for us by others and become codified into a system of hierarchies, roles, and role expectations.

In my experience, this dual metaphor is one of the greatest sources of tensions for schools. Since the late 1980s, the international moves towards devolution of responsibility and more explicit accountability demands have required schools to enact operational procedures that make them indistinguishable from many other kinds of organization. But at the same time, referring back to Mackay's (1993) work that highlights an increasing loss of identity and hope, the demands on schools to be centres of community support continues to grow. The capacity of school leaders and staff to cope with these demands from both sources, meet expected standards of excellence and cope with the emotional demands of social fragmentation has, for many, reached a critical point. It is a situation that is forcing school leaders to address and attempt to resolve an increasing number of decisions that involve significant moral dilemmas.

The factors upon which reforms to schools in the public sector have been based is well documented by Caldwell. In a review of developments across six nations, he identifies five themes which are common to all:

(1) efficiency and effectiveness in the delivery of public services; (2) ideology that embraces a faith in the market mechanism as a means of securing improved outcomes; (3) equity in the allocation of scarce resources; (4) empowerment of the school community; and (5) research on school effectiveness and improvement. (1996, p. 416)

A key feature of these reforms within Victoria's Schools of the Future program has been the requirement for schools to develop and articulate a charter, which sets out the goals and priorities for the next three years, the allocation of a school global budget according to the goals and priorities of the charter and the provision of a comprehensive annual report. The global budget consists of per capita core funding which constitutes approximately 86 per cent of the budget, and added to this is needs-based funding for students at risk, students with disabilities and impairments, students from non-English speaking backgrounds, rurality and isolation, and priority programs such as early literacy.

Perhaps for the first time, school budgets and their component parts have been defined, including core and needs-based elements, and the basis for determination has been made public. The fact that the principles underpinning this process are explicit is a major attempt by the government to adhere to the values of openness, fairness and equity. The allocation of this level (approximately 90 per cent) of recurrent expenditure to schools gives both the staff and the school community, through the constitution of the school council, the decision-making capacity and authority to employ the appropriate resources to most effectively meet the goals and priorities agreed to in the charter.

However, greater decision-making authority is always accompanied by increased responsibility for the processes and outcomes that flow from these decisions.

Schools, as part of the public administration framework, are now subject to the same accountability requirements related to effectiveness, efficiency and equity as other portfolios (e.g. health). This not only increases, and changes in important ways, the role of the principal and other school leaders, including that of the voluntary position of school council chairperson, it also means that many of the decisions they have to make involve significant moral dilemmas. The impact of public education now being located within the public administration framework is very clear. Following on from the report of the Victorian Commission of Audit (1993), several other initiatives were introduced. One was the government's 'Management Improvement Initiative', and the second was the 'Integrated Management Cycle'. Elvins describes the principles underpinning these initiatives in these terms.

> In future, Treasury will be allocating larger parcels of money which managers will be expected to manage, without being hamstrung by the central controls which existed in the past. As a counterbalance, it will be necessary to improve performance reporting and accountability. This is where performance measurement systems, especially program evaluation, are going to become more important. (1995, p. 55)

Given this pressure on the public sector to provide an increasing level of service, the intentions of these initiatives clearly are legitimate and important. However, issues of performance management and measurement in human service organization are complex, and a number of writers, such as Wyatt (1995) and McMorrow (1995), argue that whereas these processes are important to ensure the appropriate use of public funds, further significant development work needs to be undertaken in some of these areas before too much confidence can be attributed to the findings. For schools, and in particular school leaders, I suggest there are three issues in Elvins' statement which should be noted. The first is the use of the term 'managers', because I believe it is instructive in terms of the changing role of principals, and following that are performance management and performance measurement.

However, a number of writers including Greenfield argue that the demand environment encountered by principals in schools prior to these most recent changes makes considered decision making very difficult.

> The work of the school administrator involves extensive face-to-face communication, is action oriented, is reactive, the presented problems are unpredictable, decisions frequently are made without accurate or complete information, the work occurs in a setting of immediacy, the pace is rapid, there are frequent interruptions, work episodes themselves tend to be of very brief duration, responses often cannot be put off until later, resolution of problems often involve multiple actors, and the work is characterized by a pervasive pressure to maintain a peaceful and smoothly running school in the face of a great deal of ambiguity and uncertainty. (1995, p. 63)

In essence, it would be fair to conclude that for school administrators at this time the overall management load has never been greater, the demand for schools to be centres of community support and identity is very high, and as a consequence the demand for leadership integrity, courage and stamina is at an all time high.

Greenfield accepts this demand environment as a given, but asserts that there are critical differences between the workplaces of schools and other kinds of organization.

> Three conditions distinguish the work of school administrators from that of their colleagues in non-school contexts: the uniquely moral character of schools; a highly educated, autonomous and permanent workforce; and regular and unpredictable threats to organization stability. The resultant demand environment requires school administrators to rely more extensively on leadership than routine administration to influence teachers and to negotiate the complex interplay among the five situation imperatives of school administration; moral, instructional, political, managerial and social/interpersonal role demands. (1995, p. 61)

This work captures in a sophisticated way the conditions and complexity of schools as both vital educational communities and as organization workplaces. In the workplace of schools, characterized to this point by a well-educated and relatively permanent workforce, leaders will need to employ an appropriate balance of motivating staff to perform in expected ways through a commitment to agreed values and processes, and by reference to system requirements and regulations. The nature of this balance strategy is often very fluid requiring adjustment for both individuals and groups, according to the issue being addressed. Management on its own will often gain high levels of compliance, but leadership seeks and expects much higher levels of performance given out of commitment to the mission of the school. Gaining this level of trust and commitment from a majority of staff, especially during periods of sustained major change, is one of the essential challenges for leadership teams in schools.

When the 'uniquely moral character of schools' referred to by Greenfield (1995) is understood in terms of the many issues that need to be resolved by teachers and school administrators, together with the constancy and sometimes unpredictable nature of life in schools, the challenge for school leaders is immense. For schools to be centres of well being, leaders must give priority to attending to, monitoring and building quality relationships: administration and staff; staff with staff; staff and students; students with other students; and staff with parents and the community. The issues of relationships, well being and community are particularly important dimensions of the purpose and experience of schooling. Because the quality of relationships impacts in significant ways on the identity and self-esteem of both teachers and students, it has the capacity to limit or enhance teacher availability and motivation for teaching, and student availability and motivation for learning. But it requires energy, time and follow-up, which in the demand environment of schools can be very challenging, particularly when charter targets have to be met.

This is not to suggest in any way that these two aspects are not mutually supportive, but rather that the formal and co-curricula demands of schools are difficult to achieve within the hours available in the school year. For students who require additional time and support to ensure they receive their entitlements, it often confronts teachers with difficult choices to make between the resources and time available. Thus the need to support all students and staff to achieve charter goals and priorities requires not only effective management, but also insightful and courageous leadership.

What are the Implications for Decision Making in Schools?

The critical issue of decision making in schools has for some time been the subject of extensive research. According to Maguire and Ball shared decision making (SDM) in the USA is about achieving radical change and creating a preferred future. 'The thrust of SDM is the recreation of schools as "moral communities" but such reforms (unless in practice they are no more than cosmetic) also have significant implications for the power relations of education' (1994, p. 8). But how does this work in practice, especially within a policy framework of local management of schools with its emphasis on quasi-markets, performance management, and high accountability for efficient and effective use of resources, and the achievement of charter goals and government priorities? In what ways does this framework shape the scope and nature of decision making in schools?

In terms of the scope of decision making available to school leaders, it is important to note that under Victoria's Schools of the Future program, schools are allocated a global budget to support the implementation of a charter of which the Minister of Education is one of the signatures, and against which the school must provide a comprehensive annual report to all its constituents. Given that the Minister is responsible through the Parliament to the people of Victoria for the provision of a quality education, this is quite appropriate. In addition, schools are required to develop, implement and report student achievement against a curriculum that is informed by and can be justified in terms of outcomes specified in the curriculum and standards framework approved by the Board of Studies. Thus while there is considerable scope for decision making within the areas of budget allocation and distribution, curriculum content and teaching, learning and assessment processes, two things become very clear. The first is that the central policy framework is much more explicit and reaches more extensively into school operational levels than ever before; and second, with regard to budgeting, resource management and performance management, the management dimension of the role of school leaders has been expanded considerably.

Within this policy framework, it becomes vitally important that principals be enterprising in building a positive image of the school. One that is aware of and responds to community aspirations, because maintaining and enhancing enrolments in part determines the size of the global budget, and this in turn determines to a significant degree the quality and range of programs and services the school can offer and service adequately. These features play an important part in influencing the kinds of students and their families the school can attract to contribute to its performance and development. In order that quality programs and high results can be achieved, the principal needs to ensure that other members of the leadership team are attending to and monitoring the core elements of the school's operation.

With reference to the nature of decision making in schools, not only has the range of decisions required under local management of schools increased significantly, but the major decision-making responsibilities are now shared at a number of levels. At the level of policy-making, evaluation and budget distribution, the school council or board of governors now has responsibility for these decisions. With regard to curriculum, teaching, learning and assessment, and student welfare provision, the principal and staff are the key decision makers.

Weiss (1995) in a longitudinal study of shared decision making in 12 American public high schools, developed a conceptual framework to investigate decision outcomes. According to this theory, people bring different interests, ideologies and information levels to the decision-making process, and that the interaction of these three elements determines the position that an individual takes on any given issue. Weiss defines interests as self-interests, and she points out that these can be in harmony or in conflict with organization interests and goals; in ideology she includes principles, values and political orientation that can have a powerful impact on decision making; information refers to knowledge about an issue – its context and content, how it relates to regulatory requirements, and the likely consequences of various decision options. But she reminds us that it is the fourth 'I' that is most important, because these decisions are taken in an institutional setting. She asserts that there are two ways in which an institution can impact on decision making.

> First, the institutional environment shapes the way in which participants interpret their own interests, ideology and information. Thus, policy decisions are not just the summation of participants' preferences, but are molded by the structures (e.g. of participation), the rules (e.g. of access to information), and the norms (e.g. of appropriate behaviour) in the institution. Second, organization arrangements affect the decision process itself, such as who is empowered to make decisions. (1995, p. 574)

The role of institutions as builders and guardians of values is a powerful one. Institutional values operate at many levels ranging from the espoused values of mission statements and those that characterize regular decision-making procedures and everyday relationships and practices. The presence and consistent application of the values of integrity, inclusiveness and justice will be critical indicators of the prevailing culture. The preservation of these values is being challenged by the dominant economic paradigm with its emphasis on markets, competition and privatization. Social institutions, including schools, are also required to operate in these reformed frameworks of public administration. The critical question is whether the decisions and practices associated with this paradigm result in a fairer and more equitable distribution of the knowledge, cultural and economic wealth to all citizens, or is it in fact exacerbating the current imbalances.

Conclusion

Western society, indeed the whole world, is presently in the deep throes of a cultural and economic turning point, with all the threats and opportunities that characterize these transitions. In these times of global and national turbulence, the fundamental anchor for survival and renewal will be the core values that are articulated and reinforced by communities and institutions. Schools working with families play a vital role in enculturing tomorrow's citizens and leaders into the values and meanings that constitute our essential humanity. For this to be achieved, leadership will need to be developed and exercised. However, Grace expresses grave concerns about the message that current leadership programs in the UK are instilling in present and future leaders of school communities:

> There is now a sense in contemporary English state schooling that the moral and spiritual capital of leadership which has been a cultural resource of school leaders in the past is weakening because the sources for its renewal are also weakening . . . In preparing individuals for school headship an emphasis upon finance, management and marketing is clearly insufficient, if society expects schools to have moral and ethical purposes. (1996, p. 155)

References

ASTUTO, T.A. (1990) 'Reinventing school leadership.' Working memo prepared for *Reinventing School Leadership Conference*, Cambridge, MA: National Center for Educational Leadership, pp. 2–5.

BALDWIN, P. (1995) 'Beyond the safety net: The future of social security.' Paper by Hon Peter Baldwin, Minister for Social Security, Canberra: AGPS.

BARKER, G. (1997) 'The great divide', *The Australian Financial Review Magazine*, June, pp. 30–33.

BASS, B.M. (1985) *Leadership and Performance Beyond Expectations*, New York: Free Press.

BEARE, H. (1987) *Shared Meanings about Education: The Economic Paradigm Considered, The Buntine Oration*, Carlton, Victoria: Australian College of Education.

BURNS, J.M. (1978) *Leadership*, New York: Harper and Row.

CALDWELL, B.J. (1996) 'School reform for the knowledgeable society', *The Australian Economic Review*, 4th quarter, pp. 416–22.

CHAPMAN, J. and BOYD, W.L. (1986) 'Decentralization, devolution and the school principal: Australian lessons on statewide educational reform', *Educational Administration Quarterly*, **22**, 4, pp. 28–58.

COLEBATCH, T. (1996) *The Age*, Saturday 20th July, Melbourne, Australia, p. A 23.

COX, E. (1995) 'A truly civil society', 1995 Boyer Lectures, Sydney, Australia: Australian Broadcasting Commission.

DEPREE, M. (1989) *Leadership is an Art*, New York: Doubleday.

DRUCKER, P.F. (1990) *The New Realities*, London: Mandarin.

ECKERSLEY, R. (1992) *Apocalypse? No! Youth and the Challenge to Change*, Melbourne, Australia: Australia's Commission for the Future.

ELVINS, R. (1995) 'Program evaluation in the budget sector in Victoria', in GUTHRIE, J. (ed.) *Making the Australian Public Sector Count in the 1990s*, Sydney, Australia: I I R Conferences Pty Ltd.

GRACE, G. (1996, September) 'Educational leadership and the moral environment of the market: Document B, The moral, ethical and professional dilemmas of headteachers.' A keynote address given to the British Educational Management and Administrators Society (BEMAS) conference, Coventry, UK.

GREENFIELD, W.D. (1995) 'Toward a theory of school administration: The centrality of leadership', *Educational Administration Quarterly*, **31**, 1, pp. 61–85.

HUGHES, P. (1997) 'Learning: A broader agenda – New demands for a new century', *IARTV Occasional Paper*, July, 51, Melbourne, Australia.

KOTTER, J. (1990) *A Force for Change: How Leadership Differs from Management*, New York: Free Press.

LEPANI, B. (1994) 'The new learning society: The challenge for schools', IARTV Seminar Series, Melbourne, 24th March.

MACKAY, H. (1993) *Reinventing Australia: The mind and mood of Australia in the 90s*, Pymble, Australia: Angus and Robertson.

MAGUIRE, M. and BALL, S.J. (1994) 'Discourses of educational reform in the United Kingdom and the USA and the work of teachers', *British Journal of In-Service Education*, **20**, 1, pp. 5–16.

MCMORROW, W.J. (1995) 'Performance indicators in policy', in GUTHRIE, J. (ed.) *Making the Australian Sector Count in the 1990s*, Sydney, Australia: I I R Conferences Pty Ltd.

MURPHY, J. (1995) 'Creative leadership.' Paper presented to the ACEA National Conference, July, Sydney, Australia.

REICH, R.B. (1991) *The Work of Nations*, London: Simon and Schuster.

RIFFEL, J.A. (1986) 'The study of educational administration: A developmental point of view', *The Journal of Educational Administration*, **24**, 2, pp. 152–72.

SERGIOVANNI, T.J. (1994) 'Organisation or communities? Changing the metaphor changes the theory', *Educational Administration Quarterly*, **30**, 2, pp. 214–26.

SILINS, H.C. (1994) 'The relationship between transformational and transactional leadership and school improvement', *School Effectiveness and School Improvement*, **5**, 3, pp. 272–98.

STARRATT, R.J. (1992) 'Leadership, vision and the life world.' Paper presented to the ACEA National Conference, July, Darwin, Australia.

STARRATT, R.J. (1993) *Transforming Life in Schools*, Hawthorn, Australia: ACEA.

VICTORIAN COMMISSION OF AUDIT (1993) *Report of the Victorian Commission of Audit*, Melbourne.

WEISS, C.H. (1995) The four 'I's of school reform: How interests, ideology, information and institution affect teachers and principals', *Harvard Educational Review*, **65**, 4, pp. 571–92.

WYATT, T. (1995) 'Developing performance indicators to improve quality performance in education', in GUTHRIE, J. (ed.) *Making the Australian public sector count in the 1990s*, Sydney, Australia: I I R Conferences Pty Ltd.

12   Poietic Leadership

Don Shakotko and Keith Walker

While most philosophers acknowledge a role for imagination in their moral frame-works, this role has typically been qualified by caution and a deep suspicion that the imagination and the affective domain will lead thinkers away from truth (Kearney, 1991, p. 3). As a result, imagination is banished to a sort of 'ontological homelessness' (Seerveld, 1987, p. 43), from whence modern philosophers regard her with scorn, condescension or averted gaze. Her epistemological offspring suffer a similar fate; imaginative vehicles such as narrative, metaphor and irony are seldom acknowledged as essential components of the moral reasoning process. Recently, a growing number of 'voices in the wilderness' have acknowledged a role for imagination in critical thought, and interest in the relationship between imagination and moral reasoning is increasing. For over three decades, Iris Murdoch, a con-temporary novelist, moral philosopher and critic, has been at the vanguard of this movement. In an early critique of Stuart Hampshire's *Freedom of the Individual*, she argued for an active role for imagination in moral judgment, stating that 'we evaluate not only by intentions, decisions, choices (the events Hampshire describes), but also, and largely, by the constant quiet work of attention and imagination' (Murdoch, 1966, p. 49).

It is beyond the scope of this chapter to explore the ontological roots and debates entailed in this issue; rather, we have chosen to enter the dialogue at epis-temological and methodological levels. We do so, trusting that an exploration of the ways that imagination is engaged in moral reasoning will form part of the valida-tion platform for an appreciation of its actual and potential roles. Our thesis may be stated as follows: to the extent that it involves interaction with others, leadership is a moral activity. Leadership has a poietic (creative) dimension that complements leadership, which is a moral activity; leadership has a poietic (creative) dimension that complements and completes the traditional theoria-praxis grid on which most leadership models have been plotted; the imagination plays a crucial role in the enactment of this poietic process; and hence, engagement of the imagination is an integral aspect of leadership.

Our thesis is advanced through the following strategy: first, we develop a poietic for leadership within which the imagination is firmly situated; second, we briefly explore five poietic devices through which the imagination is engaged in moral reasoning; and finally, we discuss several implications of this model for the preparation of educational leaders. We begin by presenting a trinary view of the leader as human being which includes a poietic component.

Figure 12.1 A trinity of human operations

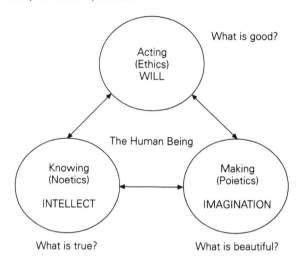

A Poietic for Leadership

Notable leaders throughout history have demonstrated an artistic flair; this quality has most often been associated with charismatic leadership and treated with some suspicion in leadership theory (Gronn, 1995; Gurr, 1996; Kets De Vries, 1995; Lakomski, 1995; Rejai and Phillips, 1997). Recently, however, writers have begun to acknowledge the significance of an aesthetic dimension of leadership. DePree (1997, 1992, 1989) and Pitcher (1995), among others, have drawn our attention to the artistic, as opposed to the technical-rational dimensions of leadership. Duke (1989, p. 351) focused on the symbolic aspects of leadership when he suggested that 'an aesthetic perspective on leadership would be concerned with the meaning attached to leaders and what they do'. We adopt a similar position by suggesting that leaders create a moral clearing or common arena within which individuals can come together to discover and create meaning. The relationship between art and leadership is not presented as simply metaphorical; but rather, leadership is a productive (poietic) enterprise which parallels the artistic process. Indeed, leadership is art.

In developing his poietic model for sociological inquiry, Brown (1977, pp. 26–27) advances a 'cognitive aesthetic', grounded in symbolic realism, which transcends the dualisms of science and art, truth and beauty, reality and symbols, explanation and interpretation. For him, both artists and scientists are makers 'not merely as craftsmen but now in a cognitive and ontological sense' (p. 34), and what they make is 'space for the act of ciphering, surface for the enactment of trans-formations' (p. 35). We suggest that leaders also are makers. They are makers who work with symbols and interpretations.

In relation to the fundamental beingness of humanity, Gilson (1965, p. 17) distinguished a trinity of operations: knowing, acting, and making (Figure 12.1).

Figure 12.2   A tripartition model of art

The three operations are intimately related and mutually dependent, yet each is associated with a distinct domain of human reasoning and poses an unique onto-logical question. The study of knowledge (noetics) is related to the intellect and asks the question 'What is true?' The study of action (ethics) is related to the will and asks the question 'What is good?' The study of production (factivity) is related to the imagination and the senses and asks the question 'What is beautiful?' Gilson related the three operations through rational activity by the suggestion that 'since man's nature is to be a living creature endowed with reason, rational activity is necessarily included in every human operation as a condition of its very possibility' (p. 18). However, he drew a clear distinction among the three domains; knowing and acting can subsist only in relation to the subject, while making produces some-thing distinct from the subject and is perhaps capable of subsisting independent of the maker (p. 19).

This trinity of beingness corresponds loosely to the three fundamental ways of knowing identified by Aristotle as *theoria, praxis* and *techne*. Ideas about leader-ship have tended to focus on the first two of these modes, on noetics and ethics, on converting theoria into praxis, while largely ignoring the more imaginative and affective domain of making. We maintain that this third domain is not merely a metaphor for leadership but, in fact, is the vital pathway between the other two.

A closer examination of this productive domain reveals another trinity of con-cepts which define the artistic experience. Nattiez (1990, pp. 10–12), drawing on the writing of C.S. Pierce and J. Molino, in the area of semiotic analysis, identifies three dimensions (the poietic, the aesthetic, and the trace) of any symbolic produc-tion. He refers to these three dimensions as the 'semiological tripartition' and offers this trinity as the basis for a theory of communication in general and of art in particular. For Nattiez, the poietic and the aesthetic are processes clearly distin-guished from each other in their relationship to 'the material reality of the work (its live production, its score, its printed text, etc.) – that is, the physical traces that result from the poietic process' (p. 15). Figure 12.2 illustrates the relationship between the three dimensions.

Duke (1989, p. 353) applied aesthetic principles to leadership by proposing a four-component leadership model (Figure 12.3) which moves from the poietic

Figure 12.3   An aesthetic model of leadership

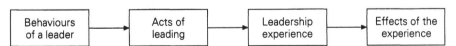

Source: Duke, D. (1989) 'The aesthetics of leadership', in Burdin, J. (ed.) *School Leadership: A Contemporary Reader*, Newbury Park, CA: Sage.

Figure 12.4   A poietic model for leadership

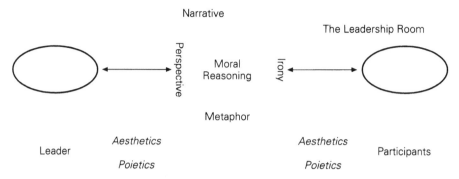

behaviour to the aesthetic experience in essentially a linear progression. Two distinctions between these two models will serve to define the position we advance. First, the direction of the arrows implies an active role for the 'audience' in Nattiez's model; in fact, a case might be made for the aesthetic experience being effectively a poietic process whereby the audience 'recreates' the work from their own unique perspective. In Duke's model, the direction of the arrows suggests that the leader is the sole active agent while the followers assume a passive role in the experience. We suggest that an artistic model of leadership entails consideration of the active role which the 'audience' plays in the process; rather than a passive or an independently active role for the audience, we see the artist (leader) and the audience (followers) interacting to create a common meaning from the work. The role of the artist (leader) is to define the arena within which the creative process can happen.

A second distinction involves the relationship between process and product. Nattiez clearly identifies the 'poietic' and the 'aesthetic' as dynamic processes while the 'work' is a neutral, symbolic form which is both the result of a complex process of creation (the poietic), and 'the point of departure for a complex process of reception (the aesthetic process) that reconstructs a "message"' (p. 17). However, Duke's model does not clearly distinguish process and product. As we interpret it, the 'behaviours of a leader' (poiesis) result in 'acts of leading' (the work) from which the spectator derives a 'leadership experience' (aesthetics) resulting in specific 'effects of the experience' (p. 353). Such a model leaves little room for artist–audience interaction in the process and seems to suggest that two independent products result, one created by the leader, the other by the spectator. We suggest that the product (the work) is both particular and singular, being created and recreated continuously by the interaction between artist and audience in the space that they share (Figure 12.4). Leadership closely resembles the ideal in the performing arts where the artist, the work, and the audience are all involved in the creative process.

Such a model tends to blur the distinction between aesthetics and poietics, between artist and audience, between leader and follower. However, even in the performing arts, there is a necessary distinction between artist and audience. The artist is the initiator of the work, inviting the audience to share in the poietic process with him or her.

In the expansion of his model, Duke (1989, pp. 353–8) identified four aesthetic properties of leadership: direction, engagement, fit and originality. These four characteristics conform closely to the model we advance as they suggest a leadership in which the leader shares the poietic process with the audience. We agree with Duke's assessment that while these do not constitute sufficient criteria for artistic leadership, they are certainly necessary and typical. Further, Duke identified three categories of creative acts, dramatics, design and orchestration by which the leader as artist creates leadership (pp. 358–62). We interpret these as at least partially definitive of the actual poietic process; however, as these three categories tend to focus on the leader as active agent and the followers as passive receivers, we propose a somewhat different approach.

While Duke concentrated on specific leadership attributes and behaviours required of leaders in the poietic process, we would shift the focus slightly and suggest that there are several identifiable poietic devices which the artistic leader employs in the making of leadership. Brown (1977) has proposed that sociological inquiry makes use of resources more frequently associated with the artist rather than the investigator wedded to scientific procedures. He suggests three such resources, point of view, metaphor and irony, which mark at least the beginning of a cognitive aesthetic. We maintain that the poietics of leadership involve five artistic resources: perspective, metaphor, narrative, the fine arts and irony. As with Duke's (1989) criteria, we make no claims of sufficiency; however, we maintain that a strong case can be made for the necessity of engaging each of these resources in the poietic process of creating the space within which moral discourse and the making of meaning can occur. In the following section, we explore the ways in which each of these contributes to that process.

Poietic Leadership Resources

The leader, as artist, creates a *room* into which participants are invited, to share in the experience of moral intercourse. In the place of a guitar or musical voice, the leader draws on a variety of poietic resources to create this space, and to allow others to share it with her. We introduce five of these resources: perspective, metaphor, narrative, the fine arts and irony. These should be considered as the kernel of a poietic model rather than as a definitive list; hopefully further thinking in this area will refine and supplement these resources.

Perspective

In his timely and elegant critique of contemporary art, Gardner (1977) employs a legend from Norse mythology to lament the failure of art, particularly fiction, to live up to its moral mandate. We employ the same legend to point to a similar, and perhaps more critical, failure on the part of modern philosophy.

> It was said in the old days that every year Thor made a circle around Middle-earth, beating back the enemies of order. Thor got older every year, and the circle occupied by gods and men grew smaller. The wisdom god, Woden, went out to the king of the trolls, got him in an armlock, and demanded to know of him how order might triumph over chaos. 'Give me your left eye,' said the king of the trolls, 'and we'll tell you.' Without hesitation, Woden gave up his left eye. 'Now tell me.' The troll said, 'The secret is, *Watch with both eyes!*' (p. 3)

While Gardner compared the state of contemporary art to Thor's hammer 'abandoned beside a fencepost in high weeds' (p. 4), we interpret this legend as a condemnation of the 'one-eyed' vision which seems to characterize modern thought. The loss of Woden's left eye may be representative of an inability to perceive the world with that essential breadth which Berggren (1962) referred to as 'stereoscopic vision: the ability to entertain two different points of view at the same time' (p. 243). Ricoeur (1978, p. 154) employed this same concept in his explication of the metaphorical process. He suggested that the meaning of a metaphor can only be comprehended if the imagination is employed to simultaneously hold the two perspectives presented by the metaphor in mental view. From a broader reasoning perspective, this same breadth of vision is absolutely essential in understanding the significance of a moral situation.

The modern world is characterized by false dichotomies (Johnson, 1989, p. 363) which force us to think in either-or dualities. Renihan (1985) argued for a more open view of reality called 'disciplined naivete' which allows one to explore the middle ground between extremes and find truth in that ambiguous in-between zone. This, we contend, is possible only through the exercise of both reason and imagination as complementary and equally valid offices, a process which Schon and Rein (1994) have called 'creative rationality'.

Brown (1977, p. 52) suggested that a similar attitude, which he identified as aesthetic perception, not only has application in the fine arts but also is useful for 'illuminating the nature and processes of nonartistic modes of creation'. Brown was concerned mainly with the application of this concept to sociological inquiry; however, its implications for other creative disciplines cannot be ignored. In aesthetic perception or di-stancing the 'distinction between strict objectivity and strict subjectivity are put aside . . . [and] . . . both ideas and feelings become ways of knowing and expressing the world' (Brown, 1977, p. 52). In effect di-stancing places one in an ambiguous state between apparently opposing di-poles and requires that judgment be suspended indefinitely.

The acknowledgment of such a third state, which Fulghum (1993) referred to as 'maybe', opens up a world of possibilities to explore. In a whimsical discourse on the concept of indeterminacy, Madeleine L'Engle speculated on the future of computers which operate in trinary rather than binary mode. The third condition between on and off, yes and no, positive and negative, she calls mu. 'Mu means that neither yes nor no is a workable answer' (1986, p. 204). While it is difficult for us to conceive of a computer that could function in an indeterminate state, we contend that for the largest part of our lives, this is the human condition.

The possibility of engaging in 'creative ambiguity', as a component of moral reasoning, is an attractive one. Davies (1982) claimed that positive moral action is related to a tolerance for ambiguity in several ways. First, it enhances an appreciation for the complexity of the variables involved in a moral judgment. A person who is tolerant of ambiguity will be much more willing to particularize social issues such as abortion and capital punishment and entertain alternative perspectives on them. Second, it 'affirms that even though we cannot fully comprehend life . . . the search for meaning can be fruitful' (p. 650). Third, comfort with ambiguity promotes hope. We are not condemned to live out a deterministic existence; there are always alternative possibilities to consider. Fourth, 'an appreciation of ambiguity leaves our evaluation of the other person open' (p. 652). Moral judgments are much more difficult and complex when the agent is tolerant of ambiguity; however, they are certainly more morally sound since they are based on the incongruence from a prototype rather than similarity with it. By focusing on similarities, we are apt to generalize and overlook the significant differences which particularize the decision-making situation. Certainly some personality types are more predisposed to tolerate ambiguity than others; however, Davies (p. 653) suggested that it may be possible to develop, or at least enhance, an appreciation for ambiguity regardless of personality type.

Conscious exposure to, interaction with, and reflection on ambiguous situations may increase one's confidence in making choices under ambiguous conditions. Dialogue and role playing may also increase one's comfort level. Perhaps one of the most significant ways of enhancing one's tolerance is engagement with works of fiction. Davies (p. 649) cites John Steinbeck's *East of Eden* as a prime example of a narrative fiction that provides an arena for the reader to wrestle with ambiguity and appreciate that meaning comes from just such conflict. As the parables of Jesus illustrate, storytelling can provide opportunity for one to imaginatively engage in dissonant situations thereby increasing one's capacity to see the world through more than one window. A recent movie, *Dead Man Walking*, effectively employs dramatic ambiguity to explore the issue of capital punishment. In the movie, a nun finds herself caught between her concern for a convicted murderer on death row and the agony of the parents of the murderer's victims. The director maintains a dynamic tension between the two perspectives throughout, with no attempt at resolution. In the end, the audience is left with the disquieting task of reconciling or accepting the ambiguity on a personal level. The experience is unsettling, to say the least; however, it has the effect of increasing one's tolerance for the complexity of moral issues beyond the scope of the issue addressed.

Similarly leaders must not only be willing to tolerate moral ambiguity in and amongst their roles, they must also find ways of modelling and encouraging that tolerance in others. This notion seems to fly in the face of conventional models of assertive leadership; however, a moral arena which is intolerant of ambiguity and which discourages stereoscopic vision leaves no room for poietic moral intercourse.

Metaphor

It would not be an overstatement to claim for metaphor the pre-eminent position in imaginative moral reasoning. Following Johnson's (1993, p. 33) argument, we propose that moral reasoning and discourse is metaphorical through and through; hence an awareness and appreciation of the metaphor as a poietic device is essential in creating a moral arena. This argument for metaphor is engaged on two levels: first, our most fundamental moral concepts are defined by systems of metaphors (Lakoff and Johnson, 1980); and second, we understand moral situations by way of the metaphorical mapping process (Johnson, 1993).

Received wisdom is largely antagonistic to reasoning based on metaphor. The positivist understanding of metaphor is that the concept is too cognitively indeterminate and unstable to be employed in the service of moral judgment. This thinking results from a misconception that metaphors generate an indefinite, context dependent and subjective meaning which is useless in practical moral reasoning. Johnson (1993) counters these claims by demonstrating that metaphors form the very core of our moral reasoning, and that, rather than leading to error, they are the very basis of sound moral judgments.

Regarding the first claim that our moral concepts are rooted in metaphorical language, Johnson (1993, p. 36) identifies three primary clusters of metaphors that we use to define our moral concepts: those concerned with actions, those concerned with obligations and those by which we evaluate moral character. In the action cluster, we employ metaphors which describe events as motions along paths, as in 'We're getting nowhere in solving this bullying problem – we're just plodding along.' States are metaphorical locations, as in, 'He's in love with ideas' or 'Stay out of trouble!' Difficulties are impediments to motion, as in 'He's trying to get around the school regulations' or 'She just went through a terrible experience with that class of students.' Long term purposeful activities are journeys along a path, as in 'We started out to help the underachieving student, but along the way we got sidetracked.'

In the obligation cluster we encounter metaphors that conceptualize rights and duties as commercial transactions. Causal relationships are often portrayed as involving a financial exchange, as in 'She was enriched by her experience with the peer coaching module' or 'He paid dearly for his mistake.' Rights and duties are conceived through a social accounting metaphor where a prisoner is required to 'pay his debt to society' and we 'owe allegiance to our family'. The conceptualization of moral obligation in terms of a monetary debt is perhaps the most prevalent moral metaphor in our culture.

The moral character cluster provides us with metaphors that we employ in evaluating human personhood. These metaphors reinforce the duality of the self by conceptualizing human nature in pairs of incompatible warring elements. Character is portrayed in terms of strength and weakness, as in 'The spirit is willing, but the flesh is weak' and 'You've got to control your passions.' Righteousness and evil are conceived of as up and down, as in 'That was a low thing to do' and 'I thought you were above such an act.' The up/down, high/low metaphors have come to be associated with a mind/body dichotomy which is closely associated with purity and pollution, as in 'That was a dirty trick' and 'Her motives were pure.'

These examples suggest that our language, and therefore our reasoning, is largely metaphorical. We would also submit that these metaphors affect the quality of our moral reasoning. Whether or not we are aware of the metaphors which influence our reasoning, their necessity and ubiquity serve to perpetuate the prevailing attitudes and values which enter into our moral judgments.

Johnson (1989) stated that these innate metaphors form part of our 'image schemata' by which the imagination makes sense of the external world. He described an image schema as 'a recurring pattern in the imaginative process by which we experience recognizable order in our understanding, cognition, and knowledge' (p. 370). Our imagination, acting as the translator, anticipates recognizable forms in reality and maps them onto our schemata.

The good news is that these schemata are not rigid; rather they are continually in process and are reformed as they interact with particular situations (Johnson, 1989, p. 370). This would imply that experience and awareness may act to enhance these metaphorical structures. Johnson (1993, pp. 193–5) suggested several positive outcomes resulting from an awareness of the metaphorical nature of reasoning. First, knowledge of the metaphors that we use helps us to understand ourselves. Second, this awareness aids us in the search for universals. For example, it allows us to examine moral reasoning across cultures by comparing the metaphors used by other people. Third, awareness of metaphorical reasoning is the starting point for changing or improving our moral reasoning. Finally, this knowledge helps us to understand others; by recognizing the metaphors and schemata that others use, we are able to communicate with others more effectively.

Narrative

> Deprive children of stories and you leave them unscripted, anxious stutterers in their actions as in their words. (MacIntyre, 1981, p. 216)

Second only to the power of the metaphor, is the role of narrative in engaging the imagination in moral reasoning. Johnson (1993, p. 11) claimed that narrative is a fundamental mode of understanding human action, evaluating moral character and projecting possible solutions to moral dilemmas. His argument takes the form of the four propositions summarized here: (1) we are beings in process, seeking to synthesize meaning, situated within a complex of physical, social, moral and political influences; (2) our culture supplies a stock of roles, scripts, metaphors, schemata which we use to understand and reason about the world; (3) within this milieu, moral judgments are made with the aid of the imaginative tools described in (2); and (4) narrative is a comprehensive synthesizing process which helps us organize our identity and test scenarios in making moral choices (Johnson, 1993, pp. 165–6).

Johnson's propositions are clearly illustrated in this short narrative which he has called *The Hooker's Tale*.

I was about fifteen, going on sixteen. I was sitting in a coffee shop in the Village, and a friend of mine came by. She said, 'I've got a cab waiting. Hurry up. You can make fifty dollars in twenty minutes.' Looking back, I wonder why I was so willing to run out of the coffee shop, get in a cab, and turn a trick. It wasn't traumatic because my training had been in how to be a hustler anyway.

I learned it from the society around me, just as a woman. We're taught how to hustle, how to attract, hold a man, and give sexual favors in return. The language that you hear all the time. 'Don't sell yourself cheap.' 'Hold out for the highest bidder.' 'Is it proper to kiss a man goodnight on the first date?' The implication is it may not be proper on the first date, but if he takes you out to dinner on the second date, it's proper. If he brings you a bottle of perfume on the third date, you should let him touch you above the waist. And go on from there. It's a market place transaction.

Somehow I managed to absorb that when I was quite young. So it wasn't even a moment of truth when this woman came into the coffee shop and said, 'Come on.' I was back in twenty-five minutes and I felt no guilt. (Cited in Johnson, 1993, pp. 154–5)

This woman is explaining her story to another and in so doing is trying to understand herself. She has a clear understanding of the ways in which cultural metaphors influence her actions and she is attempting to justify her actions in terms of those metaphors. Johnson regarded this narrative as typical of what each of us continually does. 'We live out narratives in our lives, we reconstruct them for our self-understanding, we explain the morality of our actions, at least partly in terms of them, and we imaginatively extend them into the future' (p. 155).

An individual's actions can only be made sense of when they are placed within a coherent narrative. As *The Hooker's Tale* illustrates, the woman's decisions and subsequent actions required a context through which she and her audience could understand the action. While this example is largely a justification of past actions, it also reinforces the schema through which she will make future decisions. MacIntyre explained:

I can only answer the question 'What am I to do?' if I can answer the prior question 'Of what story or stories do I find myself a part?' We enter human society, that is, with one or more imputed characters – roles into which we have been drafted – and we have to learn what they are in order to be able to understand how others respond to us and how our responses to them are apt to be construed. (1981, p. 216)

Narrative, then, situates an agent within a context and clarifies the roles and scripts within which human action can take place. We learn how to act through stories which we tell and which we share with others. As Johnson (1993, p. 172) explained, 'We make our first struggling, halting attempts at rational explanation by constructing narrative unities out of our confusing experience, in response to the recurrent who, what, when, where, why, and how questions that haunt us throughout our childhood and into our adulthood.'

Moral deliberation begins with the perception of the moral significance of a situation; it proceeds to an imaginative exploration of the possibilities for appropriate action in the particular situations, the formulation of an appropriate course of action, the formulation of intent to act in a moral way, and concludes with the perseverance to carry out the moral action. Narrative plays a crucial role in each step of the process. Whether the narrative is an internal dialogue or a verbalization shared with others, the attention, envisioning, intending and hoping that are the imaginative components of the deliberation are all fuelled by narrative.

From *Peter Pan*, to *The Brothers Karamazov*, to *The Prodigal Son*, people rely on a common stock of stories to particularize and complete their lives. Not only do we create and act out our own narrative, we also participate in a common human narrative represented by the wealth of stories we share. Shared stories, whether they be oral (as in a Garrison Keiler monologue), written (as in a John Irving novel) or visual (as in a Robin Williams movie), engage the imagination in at least three ways.

In the first instance, fictional narrative particularizes abstract concepts thereby providing a concrete frame from which to think about the concept and hopefully extend the thinking to one's own life. On the communal level, good movies often provide a particular context to think about concepts such as forgiveness and grace (*The Fisher King*) or social issues (*Philadelphia*). On the private level, novels such as John Irving's *Cider House Rules* create a powerful frame through which to examine the abortion issue. The characters and situations provide the particular images onto which our own thoughts and feelings can be mapped.

A second way in which fictional narrative engages the imagination in moral reasoning is in the presentation of alternative possibilities which we may safely explore. By playing out one possible course of action 'before the mind's eye', the narrative allows us to explore that possibility but also to engage in 'What would I have done?' thinking. By identifying with the protagonist we are able to enter into the moral reasoning process with her but we are also free to explore other alternatives and imagine other endings.

Finally, fictional narrative creates a space for shared dialogue. We are strong advocates of public readings and shared movie experiences, largely because these provide an immediate communal space for dialogue. If we share a narrative, then we share a context, an arena, where productive discourse can occur. Whether or not people agree on the position presented in the story, it nevertheless provides a common frame within which dialogue can proceed. To read a book or watch a movie alone is to miss out on the opportunity for expanding or affirming one's perspective through shared discourse (see English and Steffy, 1997, pp. 107–8). Narrative, then, is a primary vehicle for engaging the imagination in moral reasoning. Not only does it enrich and expand our perspective, it also provides the shared meeting place where people may engage in moral conversation.

Don Shakotko and Keith Walker

The Fine Arts

The preceding discussion of the relationship of fictional narrative to moral discourse leads naturally to a fuller exploration of the role of the arts in moral reasoning. Rorty (1989) has remarked that people who care about moral development turn, not to philosophical texts but to novels, short stories and plays. We suggest that the arts, in all their diversity, have much to teach us about the way we should be as human beings.

We live in a culturally deprived society; however, critics such as Gardner (1977) and Turner (1995) claim that this deprivation is as much due to the artistic community's abandonment of its moral responsibility as the apathy and ignorance of the broader community. Turner (1995) believes that the arts have been expropriated by political forces at both extremes of the spectrum creating the conditions for a cultural war.

> The Right believes that art should help maintain and preserve the order of the past against the ravages of dissolution and cultural decline ... The avant-garde, on the other hand, observes that natural physical order ... is deterministic and opposed to human freedom. Thus the only course for art to take must be that of disorder, of constant dissent, disruption, and rebellion against order. (p. 6)

Both the conservative right and the radical left are bound to a particularly modernistic view of nature; the conservatives wish to maintain it, the avant-garde wish to overthrow it; but both camps are locked into the same paradigm. Turner argued for a position in the 'radical center' (p. 6) that is essentially a 'natural classicism' based on the values of truth, goodness, and beauty. For Turner, redeeming the radical centre involves a recognition of the centrality of beauty in art and morality. It is the search for beauty that reunites art and morality – 'the greatest epistemological beauty, that is, truth; and the greatest ethical beauty, that is goodness' (p. 229).

Gardner (1977) posited that Thor's hammer is abandoned beside a fencepost in high weeds; Turner (1995) claimed that the conservative right and the radical left are using Thor's hammer to bludgeon our culture rather than to guard it. In either case, it is time for responsible efforts on our part to restore the arts to their rightful place in our culture. The following is a modest proposal of the ways in which the arts contribute to moral reasoning. We maintain that each is a rationale for the fine arts as a poietic resource.

First, 'true art is by its nature moral. We recognize true art by its careful, thoroughly honest search for and analysis of values' (Gardner, 1977, p. 19). Without being didactic, true art encourages us to clarify our values. Perhaps the difference between propaganda and art might be that propaganda forces, manipulates and destroys our freedom, while art invites us to question our thinking and liberates us to choose freely.

Second, art awakens us. Greene (1977, p. 43) claimed that the opposite of morality is indifference, a lack of concern. Art heightens our consciousness, makes us more aware of the moral significance of the world that we perceive. Active engagement with a work of art whether that be *Hamlet*, *Antigone*, or Bruce

Cockburn's *If I had a Rocket Launcher*, awakens in us a sensitivity to and aware-ness of moral issues which we may have ignored or conveniently forgotten.

Third, art encourages the actualization of potential. Relying on Tolstoy's eloquent defense of art, Gardner (1977, p. 27) states that one's imagination can translate the ideals expressed in art into moral action in the world. Art provides the ideal and invites us to actualize that ideal in our particular situation.

Fourth, art instructs. We find ourselves mired in an intractable dilemma; having abandoned our trust in God, and being unwilling to accept a relativistic view of the universe, we seemingly have no recourse but to reluctantly abandon the search for truth. Gardner suggests that we can trust art

> to make alternatives intellectually and emotionally clear, to spotlight falsehood, insincerity, foolishness – art's incomparable ability, that is, to make us understand – ought to be a force bringing people together, breaking down barriers of prejudice and ignorance, and holding up ideals worth pursuing. (p. 42)

Art, as an instructor, is not didactic and authoritarian, but rather Socratic, ironic, invitational. It creates the space for questioning that leads to sense-making.

Finally art is transcendent. The Teacher proclaims that '[God] has set eternity in the hearts of men' (Ecclesiastes 3:11); although our present age has largely abandoned God as the source, we nevertheless continue to seek and yearn for that lingering precious echo of eternity which seems to infuse our world, the something beyond us which Gardner calls 'the sad music of humanity' (p. 36). Art speaks to that level of our experience which we share with all the world; one cannot look at Van Gogh's *The Starry Night* without acknowledging the infinite, continuous creativity that transcends mortality.

Irony

> Just as philosophy begins with doubt, so also a life that may be called human begins with irony. (Kierkegaard, 1992)

While irony is most often understood as a rhetorical or literary device, it may also be understood as a philosophical stance or attitude toward life. Vlastos (1987) referred to someone who adopts such a stance as a 'life-long ironist' and cites Socrates as the exemplar (p. 88). In a similar vein, Kierkegaard (1992) proposed a significant role for the ironist personality in the development of the world spirit as it moves from present to future actuality (p. 260). In this section, we consider several characteristics of this ironist position which contribute to the creation of a moral arena.

Buechner (1990) developed a character in his novel *The Book of Bebb* which typifies the role of ironist as facilitator of wisdom. John Turtle, 'The Joking Cousin', plays a unique and vital role in the culture of a small Indian band in the American Southwest. We take up the story in the midst of a solemn funeral ceremony for the highly respected and recently deceased Chief of the tribe.

'I am the resurrection and the life,' Bebb said from the pulpit pale as death, and John Turtle stood behind him holding two fingers up over Bebb's head like rabbit ears. When Bebb was winding up his eulogy of Herman Redpath by giving out the details of the will – explaining how even from the grave Herman Redpath would continue to finance the ranch indefinitely and everyone was going to have his share including Jesus – John Turtle picked his nose on the chancel steps. At several points in the service he even tried to get Bebb to enter into dialogue with him.

'The Lord is my shepherd, I shall not want,' Bebb read from the lectern, his face glistening with perspiration, and 'I know what you want right enough,' John Turtle said from the foot of the casket.

Bebb said, 'He maketh me to lie down in green pastures, He leadeth me beside the still waters,' and John Turtle said, 'I know a girl what lives on a hill. If she won't do it her sister will.' You have to hand it to Bebb. He never batted an eye.

Unlike the small boy in the orange life preserver, nobody came up to snatch the Joking Cousin away when just after the benediction he walked over and either took or pretended to take a leak into Herman Redpath's open coffin. (Buechner, 1990, p. 150)

This unusual narrative aptly illustrates the role of the ironist as fool or deceiver. While the ironist in this case is as 'subtle as a chainsaw', he nevertheless serves a purpose much more profound than simply providing comic relief at a sombre occasion. The incongruity of the ironist's behaviour and his opposition to the solemnity of the circumstances seems to be pointing to some transcendent truth beyond. The fact that his role was accepted as a vital part of the tribe's culture indicates that something more profound than crude humour was taking place. This 'something' is the essence of irony, an indirect pointing toward deeper understanding while allowing that understanding to reveal itself to the audience in an intensely personal and subjective fashion.

It is this dramatic tension between two positions, the 'clash of the painful with the comic' (Duke, 1985, p. 17), that moves the observer beyond either position to a deeper understanding. Knox (1961, p. 4) attributes an analogous interpretation to Aristotle's 'mean of Truth' created in the tension between the eiron and the alazon. The ironist's role is to create the tension between ignorance and presumed wisdom, between comedy and tragedy, between perception and reality that will free the observer to move to a deeper, richer level of understanding.

The ironist as fool or clown invites us to explore boundaries, particularly the boundary between order and chaos. Two Charlie Chaplin movies, *Limelight* (1952) and *A Dog's Life* (1918) illustrate the ambiguity and discomfort which we experience in the presence of chaos. In the former, Chaplin and Buster Keaton are music hall clowns performing a skit; as the performers doggedly pursue their task, chaos erupts around them. In analyzing the skit, Willeford (1969, p. 108) explains that 'the fool breaks down the boundary between order and chaos, but he also violates our assumption that the boundary was where we thought it was and that it had the character we thought it had: that of affirming whatever we have taken for granted and in that way protecting us from the dark unknown.' Chaplin plays with this relationship again in *A Dog's Life* where the boundary is a fence that he uses to avoid the forces of law and order. In this breaking down of the boundary, the fool holds the social world open to values which transcend it and points to the potential for a new higher order which embraces both the order and chaos defined by our social world. Parallels between the truth conveyed by the ironist/fool and recent advances in our understanding of the relationship between order and chaos (Gleick, 1987) are too striking to be ignored.

The ironist's mission is to stand in perpetual opposition to the presumed wisdom of her age in order to create the incongruity necessary for liberation or enhanced perception. The difference between the ironist and the conventional critic is the way in which the ironist performs this role. Rather than adopting the condemnatory stance of the prophet, the ironist plays the fool, the joking cousin, the fox, and in so doing frees the object to become the subject in choosing its own pathway toward a higher level of understanding.

The ironist as jester, trickster, or holy fool can be found in virtually every culture. Among some North American Aboriginals he is known as Coyote; in Buddhism we find Pu'tai, a wandering monk who carries a bag of trash on his back; Islam has had numerous holy Sufi clowns; St Francis of Assisi took very literally St Paul's injunction to be 'fools for Christ' (Hays, 1993, p. 24).

Bakhtin (1981, p. 158) illuminates the roles of three archetypal literary figures, the rogue, the clown and the fool, who play a similar significant role in the literature of all cultures. Essentially the novelist employs these three figures to expose the conventional and all that is vulgar and falsely stereotyped in human relationships. In the novel, these figures are granted

> the right not to understand, the right to confuse, to tease, to hyperbolize life; the right to parody others while talking, the right to not be taken literally, not 'to be oneself'; the right to live a life in the chronotope of the entr'acte, the chronotope of theatrical space, the right to act life as a comedy and to treat others as actors, the right to rip off masks, the right to rage at others with a primeval (almost cultic) rage – and finally, the right to betray to the public a personal life, down to its most private and most prurient little secrets. (Bakhtin, 1981, p. 163)

This role is similar to that of the court jester whose function was to remind the king to laugh at himself, 'reminding the king of his follies, being his security guard against the loss of his humanity to the thieves of pride and power' (Hays, 1993, p. 25).

The jester employed irony to create a dynamic tension between wisdom and folly, thereby extending moral reasoning beyond the narrow confines of tradition and rationality. In a similar way, irony may be employed to broaden and redefine the boundaries of the moral arena. While the traditional jester's role may no longer be relevant, we suggest that a corresponding, albeit more subtle, role be encouraged and embraced by contemporary leaders.

In this section, we have proposed five poietic resources which leaders might employ in the creation of an arena for moral discourse. We offer these, not as a definitive model for artistic leadership, but rather as evidence for the essential role which imagination plays in the leadership practice. If we have been successful in this project, the obvious question to consider would be 'How then might we equip leaders with these poietic resources in our preparation programs?' We conclude this chapter with several exploratory responses to that question.

Redeeming the Imagination in Educational Leadership

In a thorough critique of the current practices in educational leadership development, Stout offers the following context for the principal's work:

> The general picture which emerges is of (typically) a harried man interacting in short episodes over trivial (or at least noninstructional) matters. In the course of a day, a school principal might engage in 150 or so different and disparate activities . . . School principals are most criticized for their lack of technical competence and for their arbitrariness in decision making. (1989, p. 393)

W.D. Greenfield (1988, p. 220) confirms this portrayal, suggesting that both moral and technical outcomes should be considered in the principal socialization process (see Eraut, 1994, pp. 50, 54–6). We maintain that the emphasis has been largely on the technical outcomes to the detriment of the moral (decision-making) outcomes (Beckett, 1996; Foster, 1986; Hodgkinson, 1991). Kets De Vries points to the disjunctive nature of leadership literature and, indirectly to professional education of administrators, through the following comment:

> When we plunge into the organizational literature on leadership we quickly become lost in a labyrinth: there are endless definitions, countless articles and never-ending polemics. As far as leadership studies go, it seems that more and more has been studied about less and less, to end up ironically with a group of researchers studying everything about nothing. It prompted one wit to say recently that reading the current world literature on leadership is rather like going through the Paris telephone directory while trying to read it in Chinese. (1995, p. 193)

Stout (1989, pp. 398–401) claims that one of the common criticisms of the professional training of educational administrators is that the content of preparation is often lacking in 'the study of values and ethics, the study of alternative futures'. How, then, may leadership preparation courses attend more specifically to this important dimension?

We suggest several ways in which professional education programs might begin to move our future administrators down the avenues of imagination. We qualify our speculations by acknowledging that creative educators are already making bold ventures in these areas. Personal experiences with creative professors as well as extensive reviews of the current literature give reason for optimism; however, we expect that an articulation of these ideas may provoke increased awareness and a commitment to attend more closely to their fulfilment.

1. The humanities need to be given a more prominent place in administration courses. This is by no means a novel idea. Popper (1989) reminds his readers that the University Council for Educational Administration (UCEA) has long sought to integrate the humanities into educational administration programs. As early as 1965, a Humanities Task Force was struck to support the use of humanities in educational administration. Unfortunately, this effort has met with less success than the corresponding efforts to incorporate the social and behavioural sciences. Popper offered two explanations for this lack of success.

> First, the pervasive attitude seems to be that the humanities as high culture are of consummatory value only for school administrators . . . Second, advocates of the humanities in educational administration have not presented ways-and-means models of how humanities content might be integrated with other components of education programs. It is one thing to say 'yes' to the humanities, but quite another to find instrumental applications for their content in program contexts. (p. 369)

It is beyond the scope of this chapter to present a comprehensive 'ways-and-means' model for the use of the humanities in preparation programs; however, this is certainly one of the most significant ways in which the moral imagination can be developed in educational leaders. We suggest that professors should make concerted efforts to incorporate classical and contemporary literary works which speak directly to the issues addressed in the course. Poetry, music and literary works could be employed to create space for dialogue between professor and students, thereby modelling the moral arena which these prospective leaders might create. For some professors this would involve a radical restructuring, not only of their courses, but also of their fundamental orientation toward leadership.

2. The role of metaphors in our thought and discourse should be clearly acknowledged and discussed. We have previously argued that metaphor is a predominant vehicle for engaging the imagination in moral reasoning. The diversity of metaphors which participants bring to the dialogue and which guide their worldview should be explored.

The metaphors which principals bring to their roles vitally influence the kinds of decisions they make. In an analysis of the metaphorical schemata employed by school administrators, Bredeson (1985) identified three distinct metaphorical themes in common use: maintenance, survival and vision. The five administrators studied used a particular metaphorical theme to interpret their role, conceptualize the education process, and put their beliefs and values into practice. Administrators with an internalized survival metaphor operated from a reactive posture characterized by crisis management with little or no concept of the broader, long term implications of their decisions (p. 47). Administrators with a maintenance metaphor saw the future as 'inexorably linked closely to the acceptance and continuance of what is.' Administrators with a vision metaphor maintained a holistic view and were concerned about using imagination and perceptual skills to think beyond the immediate to preferable, possible futures (p. 43). Bredeson concluded that administrators need help in redefining the nature of their roles. He suggested that this may be possible by awareness of and reflection on the metaphors which guide our reasoning (p. 48).

With this in mind, we suggest that it would not be unreasonable to offer a course directed specifically at metaphorical understandings of educational leadership. Included would be an epistemology of metaphor as well as an in-depth analysis of the personal, professional and organizational metaphors which guide the student's moral reasoning.

3. One of the most important attributes of contemporary leadership is a tolerance for ambiguity. W.D. Greenfield (1988) stated that the work situation of principals, in particular, is characterized by a high degree of ambiguity. Our present leadership philosophies tend to downplay the significance of ambiguity as it is often nega-tively associated with uncertainty, ambivalence and lack of conviction. Professional development courses should address this crucial imaginative capacity of moral reasoning. Moral dilemmas should be employed extensively to provide students with opportunities to hold conflicting positions in dynamic tension without feeling the urgency to resolve dissonance. Bebeau (1993) recommended extensive use of cases of this type to enhance ethical sensitivity. We have described narrative works which specifically address the complexity and ambiguity of moral issues. Student interaction with such fictional narrative would promote the tolerant attitude neces-sary to consider situations with stereoscopic vision. Furthermore, students should learn dilemma discussion techniques which promote imaginative moral reasoning.

4. Irony should be redeemed in professional education. Our politically correct academic discourse has sterilized language to the point where irony has either disappeared from view, or, equally as disastrous, it has been trivialized to the level of vulgar drivel found in situation comedies such as *Married with Children*. The ironists no longer has a voice in our discourse; they should be welcomed back to the table.

Torbert (1994, p. 39) describes four complementary leadership roles in tradi-tional societies. These are the Chief, the Warrior, the Priest and the Clown. While our modern institutions have embraced the first three of these roles, they have, sadly, neglected the fourth. Torbert calls for a redemption of this role.

> it is the presence of the fourth character on the team – the Clown or Court Jester – that goes farthest to assure that not just short-term action but also fundamental inquiry occurs among the four. His presence cheerfully forces each to extend his vision beyond himself and – even rarer – to extend his vision, often laughingly, to himself. Like a court jester, this person finds ways to assure that truth will be spoken in the corridors of power. (p. 39)

Not all leaders will be ironists of this dimension; yet it is crucial that future leaders appreciate and embrace the ironists in their midst.

Lichtenstein, Smith, and Torbert present a developmental model of ethical leadership which includes eight stages: impulsive, opportunist, diplomat, technician, achiever, strategist, magician and ironist. They draw parallels with moral development theorists such as Kohlberg and provide quantitative results of studies conducted with managers at various organizational levels. Among other things, their findings indicated that, 'as one matures developmentally, one becomes increasingly able to (a) accept responsibility for the consequences of one's actions, (b) empathize with others who hold conflicting or dissimilar worldviews, and (c) tolerate higher levels of stress and ambiguity' (1995, p. 100).

Lichtenstein et al., p. 101, found that, while a number of leaders had reached the strategist stage of development (wherein universal ethical principles govern and collaborative inquiry join with mutual influence), none had progressed to the ironist stage (wherein intersystemic development rules processes, and the leader wears a mask to expose others and self to new realities). We suggest that those involved in leadership development might consider the implications of this model for their practice.

5. The role of imagination should be made explicit in decision-making and policy-making processes. Creative rationality, rather than being perceived as an oxy-moron, should be the norm. Students should be encouraged to exercise their imagination in problem solving exercises.

Schon (1979) and Schon and Rein (1994) take this notion a step backward by suggesting that the imagination plays a role in the problem setting process prior to the decision-making moment. They claimed that intractable dilemmas often result because of two or more conflicting frames which the participants bring to the decision arena. The imaginative process of reframing provides a new perspective, a mutually acceptable frame which redefines the problem and creates a new solution set. This approach to policy making and problem solving involves many of the aspects of moral imagination we have discussed and warrants serious consideration in any leadership course.

6. The skills of moral perception and attending to the world should be explicitly taught and practiced (Blum, 1988; Murdoch, 1971). The increased influence of women in administration has certainly contributed to an enhanced awareness of this skill (Bateson, 1994); however, we maintain that there should be movement beyond awareness to the celebration and active pursuit of moral perception skills.

7. Interdisciplinary collaboration should be encouraged. Exposure to the humanities through contact with professors representing all the diversity of the arts should be an essential component of any leadership development program. Popper (1989, p. 382) claimed that 'program initiatives of this kind will not be easy to implement, given the ingrained reticence toward interdisciplinary collaboration in academia, but the promise of attractive rewards makes the investment of effort well worth the risk.' He proposed three ways in which interdisciplinary collaboration might be undertaken:

    (a)   a seminar by a humanities faculty which has been prepared especially for students in all administrative fields;

    (b)   a regularly scheduled cross-listed catalogue offering between educational administration and some department in the humanities group; and/or

(c) a short-term, but time intensive humanities institute, on or away from campus, modeled after the Executive Development Program at Harvard, Columbia, and other universities. (p. 382)

We would add that executive development strategies undertaken by organizations such as The Aspen Institute, The Trinity Forum, The Greenleaf Center and the National Leadership Group of American Council on Education provide some examples of practice which resonates with our thesis.

Concluding Remarks

In this chapter, we have argued that leadership involves an artistic, imaginative dimension which completes and enriches the traditional theory-practice perspective. It is only through the engagement of the imagination in the poietic process that a moral arena may be created; an arena in which all involved can engage in discourse, create common meaning, and make decisions which are both creative and rational. An awareness of the importance of imagination in moral reasoning should motivate us to engage this capacity more fully in our personal and professional lives. We strongly urge those who are involved in the education process to consider ways in which they may instill in their students a creative rationality which embraces their imaginative capabilities.

We have proposed several generic ways that the imaginative, poietic resources might be nurtured and developed in a professional development program for educational leaders. The success of such initiatives will depend largely on the commitment and mental disposition of the professors and students involved in the processes. We have suggested that, for many, this will involve an extraordinary imaginative leap and an envisionment of possibilities not before considered. The hope is that the fruits of these efforts will be educational leaders who are guided, in their personal and professional lives, by a practical wisdom which incorporates both reason and imagination in a creative praxis.

References

BAKHTIN, M.M. (1981) *The Dialogic Imagination*, Austin, TX: University of Texas Press.
BATESON, M. (1994) *Peripheral Visions*, New York: HarperCollins.
BEBEAU, M. (1993) 'Designing an outcome-based ethics curriculum for professional education: Strategies and evidence of effectiveness', *Journal of Moral Education*, **22**, 3, pp. 313–25.
BECKETT, D. (1996) 'Critical judgment and professional practice', *Educational Theory*, **46**, 2, pp. 135–49.
BERGGREN, D. (1962) 'The use and abuse of metaphor', *Review of Metaphysics*, **16**, pp. 237–58.
BLUM, L. (1988) 'Moral perception and particularity', *Ethics*, **101**, pp. 707–25.
BREDESON, P. (1985) 'An analysis of the metaphorical perspectives of school principals', *Educational Administration Quarterly*, **21**, 1, pp. 29–50.

Brown, R.H. (1977) *A Poietic for Sociology*, Cambridge: Cambridge University Press.

Buechner, F. (1990) *The Book of Bebb*, San Francisco, CA: Harper and Row.

Davies, R. (1982) 'Creative ambiguity', *Religious Education*, 77, 6, pp. 642–56.

DePree, M. (1989) *Leadership is an Art*, New York: Doubleday.

DePree, M. (1992) *Leadership Jazz*, New York: Doubleday.

DePree, M. (1997) *Leading Without Power: Finding Hope in Serving Community*, San Francisco, CA: Jossey-Bass.

Duke, D. (1989) 'The aesthetics of leadership', in Burdin, J. (ed.) *School Leadership: A Contemporary Reader*, Newbury Park, CA: Sage, pp. 345–65.

Duke, P. (1985) *Irony in the Fourth Gospel*, Atlanta, CA: John Knox.

Eraut, M. (1994) *Developing Professional Knowledge and Competence*, London: Falmer Press.

English, F. and Steffy, B. (1997) 'Using film to teach leadership in educational administration', *Educational Administration Quarterly*, 33, 1, pp. 107–15.

Foster, W. (1986) *Paradigms and Promises: New Approaches to Educational Administration*, Buffalo, NY: Prometheus.

Fulghum, R. (1993) *Maybe (Maybe Not)*, New York: Villard Books.

Gardner, J. (1977) *On Moral Fiction*, New York: Basic Books.

Gilson, E. (1965) *The Arts of the Beautiful*, New York: Charles Scribner's Sons.

Gleick, J. (1987) *Chaos: Making a New Science*, New York: Penguin Books.

Greene, M. (1978) *Landscapes of Learning*, New York: Teachers College Press.

Greenfield, W.D. (1988) 'Moral imagination, interpersonal competence, and the work of school administrators', in Griffiths, D., Stout, R. and Forsyth, P. (eds) *Leaders for America's Schools*, Berkeley, CA: McCutchan Publishing Co, pp. 207–32.

Gronn, P. (1995) 'Greatness re-visited: The current obsession with transformational leadership', *Leading and Managing*, 1, 1, pp. 14–27.

Gurr, D. (1996) 'On conceptualizing school leadership: Time to abandon transformational leadership', *Leading and Managing*, 2, 3, pp. 221–39.

Hays, E. (1993) *Holy Fools and Mad Hatters*, Leavenworth, KS: Forest of Peace Books.

Hodgkinson, C. (1991) *Educational Leadership: The Moral Art*, Albany, NY: State University of New York Press.

Johnson, M. (1989) 'Embodied knowledge', *Curriculum Inquiry*, 19, 4, 361–77.

Johnson, M. (1993) *Moral Imagination: Implications of Cognitive Science for Ethics*, Chicago, IL: The University of Chicago Press.

Kearney, P. (1991) *Poetics of Imagining*, London, HarperCollins.

Kets De Vries, M. (1995) 'The leadership mystique', *Leading and Managing*, 1, 3, pp. 193–210.

Kierkegaard, S. (1992) *The Concept of Irony With Continual Reference to Socrates* (Hong, H. and Hong, E. transl.), Princeton, NJ: Princeton University Press.

Knox, N. (1961) *The Word Irony and its Context, 1500–1755*, Durham, NC: Duke University Press.

L'Engle, M. (1986) *A Stone for a Pillow*, Wheaton, IL: Harold Shaw.

Lakomski, G. (1995) 'Leadership and learning: From transformational leadership to organisational learning', *Leading and Managing*, 1, 3, pp. 211–25.

Lakoff, G. and Johnson, M. (1980) *Metaphors We Live By*, Chicago, IL: University of Chicago Press.

Lichtenstein, B., Smith, B. and Torbert, W. (1995) 'Leadership and ethical development: Balancing light and shadow', *Business Ethics Quarterly*, 5, 1, pp. 97–116.

MacIntyre, A. (1981) *After Virtue*, Notre Dame, IN: University of Notre Dame Press.

MURDOCH, I. (1966) 'The darkness of practical reason', *Encounter* 27, July 46–50.
MURDOCH, I. (1971) *The Sovereignty of Good*, New York: Schocken Books.
NATTIEZ, J. (1990) *Music and Discourse: Toward a Semiology of Music*, Princeton, NJ: Princeton University Press.
PITCHER, P. (1995) *Artists, Craftsmen and Technocrats*, Toronto, Canada: Stoddart Publishing Co.
POPPER, S.H. (1989) 'The instrumental value of the humanities in administrative preparation', in BURDIN, J. (ed.) *School Leadership: A Contemporary Reader*, Newbury Park, CA: Sage, pp. 366–89.
REJAI, M. and PHILLIPS, K. (1997) *Leaders and Leadership: An Appraisal of Theory and Research*, Westport, CT: Praeger Publishing.
RENIHAN, P. (1985) 'Organizational theory and the logic of the dichotomy', *Educational Administration Quarterly*, **21**, 4, pp. 121–34.
RICOEUR, P. (1978) 'The metaphorical process as cognition, imagination and feeling', *Critical Inquiry*, **5**, 1, pp. 143–59.
RORTY, R. (1989) *Contingency, Irony and Solidarity*, New York: Cambridge University Press.
SCHON, D. (1979) 'Generative metaphor: A perspective on problem-setting in social policy', in ORTONY, A. (ed.) *Metaphor and Thought*, Cambridge: Cambridge University Press, pp. 254–83.
SCHON, D. and REIN, M. (1994) *Frame Reflection: Toward the Resolution of Intractable Policy Controversies*, New York, Basic Books.
SEERVELD, C. (1987) 'Imaginativity', *Faith and Philosophy*, **4**, 1, pp. 43–57.
STEVENS, W. (1993) *Stevens Poems*, Toronto, Canada: Knopf.
STEVENS, W. (1997) *Stevens: Collected Poetry and Prose*, New York: Library of America.
STOUT, R. (1989) 'A review of criticisms of educational administration: The state of the art', in BURDIN, J. (ed.) *School Leadership: A Contemporary Reader*, Newbury Park, CA: Sage, pp. 390–402.
TORBERT, W. (1994) *The Power of Balance*, Newbury Park, CA: Sage.
TURNER, F. (1995) *The Culture of Hope*, New York: The Free Press.
VLASTOS, G. (1987) 'Socratic irony', *Classical Quarterly*, **37**, 1, pp. 79–96.
WILLEFORD, W. (1969) *The Fool and his Scepter*, Evanston, IL: Northwestern University Press.

13 Values, Leadership and School Renewal

Clive Beck

Educational administrators already act out of a set of values and make many wise decisions. Our purpose then in considering values in educational leadership is not to introduce values into educational leadership for the first time, but rather to find ways to help administrators assess and enhance their approach to values in the school context.

Some of the values which guide administrators are *institutional*. Administrators are trained and socialized into distinctive 'administrative values', many of which they may not practice in everyday life, for example, with their family or friends or at their local health club or place of worship. They are also constrained by 'systemic values' which permeate the structure of schooling and push them in certain directions. These values are usually not consciously embraced or openly discussed but are nevertheless very influential.

Other values which guide administrators are *personal*: they do indeed reflect their everyday approach to life. Many of these values are derived from the ethos of the broader society, but have been adopted (whether consciously or not) by the individual for general life purposes. Others are largely individual creations appropriate to individual needs and circumstances. Personal values of either of these kinds are often relevant to the school situation; as Thomas Greenfield said, 'The error most theorists make in thinking about organizations and the administration of them is to conceive them as somehow separate from life, love, sex, growth, conflict, accomplishment, decay, death and chance' (1991, p. 5). The significance of personal values is apparent from the fact that, despite similarities in institutional values, administrative practice varies considerably from one administrator to another. Some school principals, for example, are more approachable than others, or more caring toward their teachers or more conscientious in working for the good of their students.

Both the institutional and personal values of administrators, then, have to be examined. But on what basis can this be done? What are values and where do they come from? To this question we must now turn.

The Nature of Values

The term values has two connected but different meanings. In one sense, values are the things we pursue and consider important in life, the things we *value*. However, in the context of educational philosophy and theory the focus is normally on a narrower category of values, namely, the things that are *worthy* of valuing, the things that are actually *valuable*. This is what we are talking about when we say schooling should have a basis in values or students should be taught values: we do not mean just any values but rather a set of *sound* values.

This distinction – between the valued and the valuable – is the kind of contrast John Dewey was talking about when he said:

> There is a contrast between the natural goods – those which appeal to immediate desire – and the moral good, that which is approved after reflection. But the difference is not absolute and inherent. The moral good is some natural good which is sustained and developed through consideration of its relations. (Dewey, 1960, p. 56)

However, in my view Dewey did not stress sufficiently that we may reflect a great deal and still make a mistake in our valuing; what we approve 'after reflection' may still not in fact be *valuable*.

In this chapter my main concern will be with values in the second sense, things that really are valuable. But how do we determine what is valuable? What are the criteria and processes of such inquiry? This of course is a vast topic; I will focus here on just four key principles. These principles combine procedural and substantive elements: both must be considered in specifying an approach to values.

Human Well-being is the Central Concern of Value Inquiry

By well-being I mean a life well supplied with elements such as survival, health, happiness, contentment, companionship, friendship, love, self-respect, respect from others, freedom, discovery, creation, achievement, excitement, fulfilment, a sense of meaning in life.[1] This list is open-ended: more could be added and perhaps, for some people, some should be deleted. These are basic values, largely ends in themselves; their attainment is what makes life seem good and worthwhile.

At a popular level there is remarkable agreement on what constitutes well-being. We often hear remarks such as: 'If you are healthy and happy and have some friends, luv, that's what matters.' Among philosophers opinion is more varied, but I concur with Morris Ginsberg's view that the disagreement has been exaggerated:

> The philosophers, after the manner of their trade, emphasize their differences from each other. But in their account of the good for (human beings) they move within a restricted circle of ideas – happiness, wisdom, virtue, fulfilment. These are, except on superficial analysis, interrelated, and taking large stretches of social life, none can be attained or maintained without the others. (Ginsberg, 1962, p. 124)

Elsewhere Ginsberg states:

> The basic human needs fall broadly into three groups. They are, firstly, the needs of the body, for example, for food, drink, exercise, rest, sleep. There are, secondly, the needs of the mind, the need to understand, to construct, to appreciate, to be at home in the world. There are, thirdly, what may be called the social needs, the need for other human beings, to respond and seek response. Moral problems, always related to basic needs, emerge into consciousness with the formation of ideals. These are ends which are built up out of the basic needs by a process of constructive imagination, spurred on by disappointments and failures, directly experienced or vividly realized through sympathy with others. (Ginsberg, 1962, pp. 134–5)

(We might note here the similarity between Ginsberg's view of the origin of moral ideals and Dewey's account of how values are formed.)

We Must Not Make Absolutes out of MEANS to Well-being

The values associated with human well-being listed above are to a large extent ends in themselves; people just want to survive, be happy, experience friendship, be fulfiled and so on, for no particular reason beyond the goods themselves. By contrast, wealth, truthfulness, punctuality, hard work and the like are largely means to well-being; they are not particularly important in themselves.

A key error in value theory has been to see *moral* values as absolutes, as ends in themselves, when to a large extent they are simply means. Truth telling and promise keeping are not of absolute value; they are very important, but we need to be flexible in applying them. Sometimes, for example, we must tell a lie to spare someone's feelings or break a promise in order to meet a more urgent need that has arisen.

A similar error has been made in education, where we have often treated correct grammar and spelling, for example, as absolutes or ends in themselves when in fact they are means. Much of the opposition to allowing a transitional phase of 'invented' or 'temporary' forms in grammar and spelling is due to this kind of absolutism.

We Must Recognize the Great Complexity of Values

Human well-being itself is made up of a wide array of end values. When we add to these the things that are valuable as a means to well-being we find that the domain of values is vast, and also extremely complex. A common mistake in the history of philosophy and religion has been to see all value as residing ultimately in a single value: truth or happiness or beauty or love, for example. But in fact no such simple approach is adequate.

Among the categories of values are the following:[2]

- *basic values* such as survival, health, happiness (see earlier list);
- *spiritual values* such as awareness, integration, wonder, gratitude, hope, detachment, humility, love, gentleness;
- *moral values* such as responsibility, courage, self-control, reliability, truthfulness, honesty, unselfishness;
- *social and political values* such as justice, due process, tolerance, cooperation, loyalty, citizenship;
- *intermediate-range values* such as fitness, sporting ability, musical appreciation, good family relationships, ability to read and write, financial security;
- *specific values* such as a bicycle, a telephone, a particular friendship, a high school diploma, a political party, a particular exercise program.

Values, then, represent an extensive, interconnected system, and in arriving at value judgments and decisions we have to adopt a systems approach. In any given situation dozens of values are relevant and must be weighed against one another. There are no simple rules and no absolute values which override all others.

Value Inquiry Must be Democratic

As postmodernists and poststructuralists have shown so clearly in recent times, values vary greatly from culture to culture and from individual to individual. Accordingly, it is inappropriate for society as a whole or particular authorities to tell individuals and groups how they should live. While there may be some people who have a relatively high degree of wisdom in value matters and skill in studying values, everyone must be involved in value inquiry, especially on questions which affect their well-being and that of people close to them.

A common view is that broad principles of right and wrong should be established by experts such as philosophers and theologians, leaving ordinary people to work out the practical details. However, I accept Richard Rorty's claim that the production of knowledge (including moral knowledge) is everyone's business even at the most fundamental level. We must reject the 'trickle down' view of value inquiry and see everyone – academics and ordinary people alike – grappling with both general principles and practical questions. As Rorty says:

> ... the intellectual ... is just a special case – just somebody who does with marks and noises what other people do with their spouses and children, their fellow workers, the tools of their trade, the cash accounts of their businesses, the possessions they accumulate in their homes, the music they listen to, the sports they play and watch, or the trees they pass on their way to work. (Rorty, 1989, p. 37)

Valuc inquiry is not something that can be carried out separately – in the mind or in the study – by a specialist and then used to unlock the secrets of life for ordinary people. Everyone must get into the act of value inquiry.

Values and School Renewal

This conception of values has many implications for educational leadership. However, before addressing these directly I wish to sketch an approach to schooling based on this conception of values. This will help clarify the context within which the educational administrator's role is played out.

The School Curriculum must be Explicitly Linked to Well-being

Schools are constantly advocating values: intellectual, social, moral, economic, political. Too often, however, these values are taught as absolutes, without adequate reference to human well-being. As a result the teaching of values is often quite ineffective. Students fail to see the importance of what is being advocated, and they are certainly not initiated into a lifelong inquiry into how to promote human well-being. Rather they are placed in the position of reacting to a series of seemingly arbitrary adult pronouncements.

Marilyn Cohn and Robert Kottkamp, in *Teachers: The Missing Voice in Education*, argue that schools today are in urgent need of a more 'meaningful' mode of learning, one which makes a connection 'to the rest of the individual learner's life'. In outlining the findings of their recent extensive study of teachers and schooling, they state:

> In our conception of meaningful learning, learners are intentional human beings with particular historical, cultural, family, and academic backgrounds that they bring to the classroom. It is essential therefore that the individual learners see some purpose, use, interest, or benefit in the material, and find some opportunity to explore the material actively at their ability levels. (Cohn and Kottkamp, 1993, p. 225)

What is particularly interesting in the Cohn and Kottkamp study is that the great majority of teachers – not just a few progressives – saw this as the direction in which schooling *had* to go if the current problems of student rebellion and apathy were to be overcome (ibid., p. 245). Accordingly, to those who say that the school does not have *time* for extensive consideration of values (as one of the members of Ontario's Royal Commission on Learning said to me recently) the reply must be that we have no choice. Students are no longer willing just to work for marks or, more generally, just do what they are told; they must see the purpose of what they are learning in terms of human well-being, now and in the future, for themselves and others.[3]

The School and Classroom Must Embody a Way of Life
Characterized by Well-being

Students should actually experience a high level of well-being in school. This is important if only from a humanitarian point of view. In a world often characterized by loneliness, insecurity and even violence for many students, the school should as far as possible be a contrasting context of friendliness, care and meaningful activity. Given the amount of time young people today spend in school, it is appropriate that they should experience it as a good way of life and not just preparation for the future.[4]

Such an approach is also important from an educational point of view; the most effective way to learn values is through personal experience. For example, instead of just *saying* that females are as able and important as males, we have to create a classroom in which this is patently obvious and where the advantages of equal relationships are experienced. Instead of just *teaching* that community life is important, we have to build a classroom and school community where the benefits of close human relationships are apparent. In this way, students learn in detail what is meant by 'gender equality', 'close community' and so on. They also learn through direct experience how to 'do' these things; they learn the practices as well as the concepts.

The Approach to Values in School Must be Democratic

In line with what was said earlier, teachers and students should learn values *together* instead of one group imposing its solutions on the other. As Roland Barth says in *Improving Schools from Within*, the school should be 'a community of learners, a place where all participants – teachers, principal, parents and students – engage in learning and teaching. School is not a place for important people who do not need to learn and unimportant people who do' (Barth, 1990, p. 43).

Values and Leadership in Education

Based on the preceding discussion we may say that the role of educational administrators with respect to values is to *participate with* teachers and students in establishing a curriculum and a school and classroom life which promote values learning and the well-being of those involved in and affected by schooling. But what room does this leave for *leadership*? Given a democratic approach to value inquiry and school renewal, in what sense can administrators be described as leaders in value matters?

To begin with, I think we can still talk of leadership in values, but in a significantly different sense from the traditional one. The type of leadership that is appropriate might be described as *reciprocal leadership or contextual leadership*. The term 'leadership' typically implies that the one leading has greater knowledge or wisdom than the one(s) led. And this is a very important idea, one which unfortunately has sometimes been neglected by 'soft', 'progressive' or even 'critical' pedagogues. Every time we go to the dictionary, for example, we are appealing to someone else's superior knowledge. In everyday life time and again we go to a consultant, teacher, friend or acquaintance because of their superior 'authority' – and hence capacity to 'lead' us – in a matter of importance. But the crucial point to recognize is that this leadership is contextual; it depends on the particular case. It does not mean that *in general* the other person has superior insight; on other matters they may well come to us for advice. The leadership, then, is not one-way but rather reciprocal.

Now it may be true that certain people, on average, have more value insight than others. However, even if this is the case it is difficult to see what practical significance it has. For one thing, the research and calculation involved in establishing who is on average superior in values is so great that we could rarely be sure we had carried it out adequately. Secondly, and even more to the point, since values insight is contextual, it does not matter who across the board has more of it; what matters is who has more insight (and in what respects) on the question in hand. This is something it is not safe to judge beforehand, since value inquiry can take surprising twists and turns and bring us to entirely new territory. Accordingly, to say that in value matters of type x an administrator – vice-principal, principal, superintendent of curriculum or ministry official, for example – will definitely know best is risky.

Another consideration is that no matter how much general knowledge and experience an administrator may have in a value area, the individuals affected by judgments and decisions in that area will have particular knowledge and concerns which go well beyond the insights of the administrator. Hence, there is no escaping participatory inquiry into a value question. For example, a school principal after years of experience, reading and reflection may have deep knowledge about what kind of reading program will bring most satisfaction and personal development to Grade 6 students. But it would be foolhardy indeed to prescribe in detail the program, the mode of pursuing it and the particular life issues to be considered, disregarding the interests, concerns, needs and preferences expressed by the students and identified by teachers who have personal knowledge of the students. Curriculum development in value areas (perhaps in all areas) should be a joint enterprise of administrators, teachers and students.

It should be remembered, moreover, that the selection of an educational administrator is based on a wide range of considerations. While the writings of Hodgkinson, Greenfield, Sergiovanni and others have made us much more aware of the importance of ethical vision and value insight in administrators, a particular administrative appointment may be made because of a person's special capacity for community building, public relations, fund-raising and careful 'management' in a somewhat restricted sense. The staff of a school or school board should constitute a team; if this is so, not all outstanding qualities need reside in one person. *Leadership in values*, in the sense I have given to this term, may in a particular school come more from members of the teaching staff and student body than from an administrator, although obviously administrators have to play their part in the values arena.

It is true that administrators should in some sense be good at facilitating value inquiry. They must know how to ensure that it takes place in the school. But facilitation may take many forms, including at times 'getting out of the way' so others have greater freedom to contribute. The facilitation an administrator provides in value matters may include making time available for value inquiry in the school and ensuring that people (staff, students, parents and others) who have special interests and abilities in particular value areas have the support they need to 'take a lead'. Being a good facilitator in values does not require having superior value wisdom, any more than being a good basketball coach requires being able to play basketball better than all (or any) of the members of one's team.

It is sometimes said that a major part of the role of educational administrators is to model good values. However, I believe this idea has all the same problems as the notion of the administrator as *the* values leader. Of course administrators should 'set a good example', but no more than anyone else in an educational community. A heavy requirement of values modelling places educational administrators under too much pressure, and can even lead to their pretending to have virtues they do not have, which does nobody any good. It also implies that administrators have in general better values than those 'underneath', something I have argued is not necessarily the case. Finally, and most importantly, too strong a requirement to model good values can hinder administrators in their own value development. All learning involves experimentation and risk taking, and if administrators are required to have already solved their value problems so they can model the correct solutions – if they are not permitted to express their doubts, fears, concerns and problems – it will be very difficult for them to grow beyond their present level. Somewhat paradoxically, administrators will be better able to help students in value development if they are co-learners with them rather than value 'leaders'.

Having said all this, however, we must not forget that educational administrators have been *placed* in a 'leadership role', just like the captain of a team, the chair of a meeting, or the conductor of an orchestra. Certain initiatives and decisions are expected of them simply by virtue of this appointment. They are 'it', so to speak, and people will look to them to ensure that certain things are done. But the implications of this should not be exaggerated. As I have argued, their having been appointed as administrators does not mean that they must be – or must be seen to be – wiser in value matters than others. Rather it means they must *see to it*, in one way or another, that extensive value learning (including their own) takes place in schools and that the well-being of students, teachers, administrators, parents and others affected by schooling is promoted to a significant degree in and through the school.

Notes

1 This list is taken, in part, from Beck, 1990, p. 2.
2 This paragraph is taken, with slight modifications, from Beck, 1993, p. 24.
3 A tendency in this direction even down to the elementary school level was noted by Carl Bereiter over 20 years ago: see Bereiter, 1973, pp. 84–7.

4   Jane Roland Martin has argued that because of the reduced emotional and other support children experience today outside the school, the school must become more 'homelike': see Martin, 1992, Chapter 1.

References

BARTH, R. (1990) *Improving Schools from Within*, San Francisco, CA: Jossey-Bass.

BEREITER, C. (1973) *Must We Educate?*, Englewood Cliffs, NJ: Spectrum/Prentice-hall, pp. 84–7.

BECK, C. (1990) *Better Schools: A Values Perspective*, London: Falmer Press.

BECK, C. (1993) *Learning to Live the Good Life: Values in Adulthood*, Toronto, Canada: OISE Press.

COHN, M. and KOTTKAMP, R. (1993) *Teachers: The Missing Voice in Education*, Albany, NY: SUNY Press.

DEWEY, J. (1960) *Theory of the Moral Life*, originally 1932, New York: Holt, Rinehart and Winston.

GINSBERG, M. (1962) *On the Diversity of Morals*, London: Mercury Heinemann, pp. 124, 134–5.

GREENFIELD, T. (1991) 'Foreword', in HODGKINSON, C., *Educational Leadership: The Moral Art*, Albany, NY: SUNY Press.

MARTIN, J.R. (1992) *The Schoolhome*, Cambridge, MA: Harvard University Press.

RORTY, R. (1989) *Contingency, Irony and Solidarity*, Cambridge: Cambridge University Press.

14   The Future of Public Education

Lynn Bossetti and Daniel J. Brown

There has always been a preoccupation with millennium thinking, and with the year 2000 just around the corner, the future looms very near. Almost any current magazine or professional journal has at least one article dedicated to the future and the impending transformation to a new age – the Information Age or the Post-modern Era. For some, the future is slipping away from them and for others it is like a brick wall that they are about to hit dead-on (Brand, 1995). These various perceptions of the future are contingent upon our conception of time, our values and beliefs, and whether we think the future is getting better or worse. Depending on one's point of view, the future of education has different priorities. For example, there is the value-free/technological view of the future where futurists extrapolate trends, often based on technology and economics, to create a scenario of the probable future. For this perspective, the future is determined pretty much by events happening now, and is based on the presumption 'that the future really depends on forces that are beyond human capacity to control in any significant way. The enduring image of the future left by all such writings is one of irreversible technocratic trends remote from whatever social and political capacities ordinary people might retain' (Livingstone, 1983, p. 181).

The message being that we need to 'see the handwriting on the wall' in order to change our ways so we can compete and survive in that probable future state. Proponents of such perspectives encourage us to become part of a 'learning culture' so we can adapt to the autonomy of technological change (Senge, 1990). They view the future of persons as agents of economies (Lanning, 1994). There is little discussion regarding the desirability of that future state and the impact of these trends on the everyday life of people; rather the concern is to address the needs of business and the state. As a consequence, such a conception of the future appears beyond the control of the common person, thereby encouraging us to be reactionary, to capitalize on these trends (reap now, sow later), and to permit the prophecy of the business and industry sector to reign. This perspective is rooted in the life of the global economy, profit and productivity. It has little concern for the everyday life of the common person and certain necessary human needs such as love, relationships, good and meaningful work, and the reproduction and maintenance of life. Education is about preparation of individuals to adapt to the changing requirements of the global labour force, and to live with uncertainty (Emberley and Newell, 1994; Lanning, 1994).

There is another group of futurists that is concerned with probable and preferred futures. Their perspective is explicitly morally and ideologically based. They take the proactive, 'sow now and reap later' perspective and are very much concerned with responsible action, the maintenance and enhancement of life on the planet, and the creation of a more civil and just society (Bowers, 1993; Kincheloe, 1995; Purple, 1993). People in this group conceive of time as a deep flowing process in which centuries are minor events and that much was decided before we were born. They are concerned with the need to look at the handwriting on the wall to see what will happen if we do not change our ways now to steer the course to a more desirable future. Our ideas about public education spring from our images of the future, therefore education is concerned with preparing children for meaningful participation in that future. This group believes that the only possible guarantee of the future is responsible behaviour in the present (Berry, 1977), and therefore they are concerned with creating a public education system that prepares children for a desirable future and addresses moral character, democracy and civic responsibility.

The Post-modern Condition

Throughout history, education has reflected the ideals of the society in which it is embedded. At one time it was dominated by the church, then by the state, and now it is influenced increasingly by other external forces such as business and industry. After a long period of religious influence in order to maintain society, education became a public enterprise in the service of the state. It was seen as the vehicle by which the underprivileged could gain access to the benefits of the affluent. Public education was designed to not only disseminate knowledge, but to also produce qualitatively better human beings. Today, both government and business view education as the engine that will drive economic and social prosperity in an increasingly competitive global marketplace. Hence, the demands placed upon the public education system are for accountability for high learning standards and quality programs that equip students to compete in the global marketplace.

However, in an increasingly pluralistic and metropolitanized society, the continuation of a public education system that can accommodate the diverse educational needs and value orientations of a heterogeneous community becomes problematic. This is because there is a lack of consensus regarding the role and purpose of schooling in society.

The problem is made more complex because of the ubiquity of change and uncertainty that pervades the post-modern era. Since 1965, the hippie movement, student unrest, the free speech movement, the women's movement, the green movement and the peace movement all provided counter cultures that emerged and grew with intensity, challenging our traditional notions of what it means to be white and middle class in western society. We are in a period in history in which we are forced to be free and to make choices, whether or not we are prepared to make them. We can select from a variety of alternative cultures, religions, lifestyles and beliefs. However, we are unsure of what constitutes the status quo or where to find a set of criteria, a single philosophy or an agreed-upon-view to help guide us in our choosing. With choice comes the responsibility and consequences of our good or poor choosing. The feeling is akin to the experience of Alice in Wonderland when she fell out of control down an endless tunnel until she arrived in a world where nothing made sense anymore.

At the heart of the controversy over public education in a democratic society are the tensions between majority rules and minority rights on the one hand, and public and individual interests on the other. The issue is 'who should control the socialization of children'? The problem is manifested in the debate over private schooling, charter schools and the extent of parental choice in the education of their children. What does this lack of consensus in how children should be taught, the increase in parental voice and choice in education, and the influence of business and industry mean for the structure and governance of public education in the near future?

This chapter is based on the simple premise that ideas and not just events will influence the schools of the future. As public education slowly changes, voices are heard that draw from different visions on how life should be lived and thus how schools should be governed and organized. If ideas are as potent as we think they are, then it is incumbent on those concerned with education to clarify and order the many disparate concepts expressed into some meaningful clusters so their implications may be explored. We make such an attempt in this article, albeit a very modest one, drawing upon the literature and our experiences with educational administrators and policy makers in Canada.

We provide an overview of three value positions that dominate much of the public discourse on education. For convenience, we call them the egalitarian, libertarian and communitarian views. They are essentially clusters or groups of values which are largely compatible within clusters but at variance between clusters. We believe that this trichotomy is a tentative but useful framework to make sense of the dissonance surrounding public education heard today. After a discussion of its components and their interrelations, we emphasize one perspective, the communitarian view, since we consider it in ascendance and thus deserving further elaboration. Some implications of the trichotomy for educational policy are then considered.

Three Value Positions

The Egalitarian View

We begin this overview with the position that emphasizes equality. Its core unit of analysis is a society and the large groups within it. The relative power of these groups are compared usually on the basis of their sex, race or social class. Relations are fundamentally conflictual so there is something of a war of group against group; they are pitted against each other in a struggle for control and resources. The intellectual basis of the egalitarian view may be Marxism feminism, or post-modernism, all of which tend to be critical of many institutions.[1] Current champions of the egalitarian view include Michael Apple (1991a, 1991b) and Charol Shakeshaft (1989), although many others come to mind. The general ideal is often a welfare state which provides security throughout life and does so via the extensive provision of centralized government services using bureaucratic organizations to effect their aims.

Uniformity is a natural and intended outcome since variation in services is seen as a detriment to the basic desire to provide a 'fair shake' to all regardless of their origins. Justice, then, is seen as a means of overcoming past oppression and relies on redistribution of wealth, as advocated by Rawls (1970). While researchers study subjugation, imperialism and decolonization, social activists call for a classless society, participatory democracy, affirmative action, social justice, voice, and most often, rights legitimated by the Charter of Rights and Freedoms. Advocates optimistically provide 'hope for the hopeless'. The egalitarian view, with its sense of widely-shared values, has its heroes and heroines, such as Thomas Jefferson, Franklin Delano Roosevelt, Tommy Douglas and Maude Barlow. It can also claim substantial victories in Canada during the last 60 years, including: Medicare, pension plans, unemployment insurance, growth in the union and women's movements, the environmental movement, human rights acts and antidiscrimination policies in universities. Most importantly, public education is a clear manifestation of its ideas in action.

The egalitarian view of *homo sociologicus* (attractive to certain philosophers and sociologists) suggests a person who largely reacts to the circumstances surrounding him or her. It does not escape criticism, however (Hayek, 1973). As the dominant cluster of ideas that directed public policy in Canada for the last several decades, it is now associated with a large public debt, big government, bureaucracy, rigidity, inefficiency totalitarianism at the macro level. It also accompanies unresponsiveness, the status quo, political correctness, individual irresponsibility and something of enslavement at the micro level of society. Its worst exemplar is probably Joseph Stalin who was a leader of a society based on apparently egalitarian principles. However, another cluster, which we have labelled libertarian, offers some ideational balance.

The Libertarian View

The core element within the libertarian view is the individual, always seen as a separate entity pursuing his or her own interests. The guiding concept that is said to explain a great deal of this individual's behaviour is his or her rationality. He or she is smart enough to find the means to achieve desired ends and weigh the attendant costs and benefits. Fundamentally, relations between people are competitive as they find the best way to achieve their goals. 'Life is what you make of it.' The intellectual basis for the libertarian view may be called modernist and Adam Smith is seen as its founder. Current champions are Gary Becker (1993) and Milton Friedman (1962), to mention two. The dream is often a capitalist state that is most able to create wealth through greater productivity and efficiency, but that offers no security, each person contributing to and benefiting from the free market which is driven simply by supply and demand. Hong Kong and Singapore come to mind. Such conditions of social life are seen as very empowering to individuals and thus justice is focused particularly on the recognition and protection of property rights and entitlement, as asserted by Nozick. A natural product of this optimistic view of the triumph of human ingenuity and invention is that there will be both winners and losers. We are all investors and consumers. While students of libertarianism study decentralization, deregulation, anarchy and entrepreneurship, activists 'on the right' call for competition, liberty, accountability, responsibility, self-help, choice and academic freedom using the traditions of free societies as a source of legitimation. Government does not control society; it only steers. The main force for governmental policy in Canada in recent times, the libertarian view has its heroes and heroines, such as John Rockefeller, Margaret Thatcher, Lee Iacocca, Preston Manning and Ralph Klein. It can claim some victories, such as the election of conservative governments around the world, free trade, maintenance of a free press, freedom of speech, association, and travel, the growth of small businesses, the new Russia, and a preoccupation with the public debt and the reduction in the size of government in Canada. Regarding the topic of education, libertarians often call for educational reform via choice and sometimes request aid to private schools.

As with the egalitarian view, the libertarian position with *homo economicus* (a rather smart and self-sufficient individual attractive to many economists and political scientists) has received ample criticism which is merely highlighted here. Often seen as reactionary, it is admonished to be encouraging of greed, result in the uneven distribution of wealth, to deny opportunity, to be responsible for poverty, to be harmful to the environment, result in excessive individualism, be substantially uncaring, and generally be sociopathic in overall orientation (Schwartz, 1986). Persons may be free but they are also 'free to starve' in the competition of individual against individual. Its worst exemplar is probably Clifford Olson, who demonstrated his freedom from society's constraints. As sketched in this article, the egalitarian and libertarian views clearly coincide with the traditional left and right wings of the political spectrum. But there is an alternative.

The Communitarian View

The principle unit of analysis in the communitarian view is the group which is usually small, such as a family, clan or a collection of people who have come together for common cause (shared values). Their guiding concept is often their common origin or destiny, their place in the social universe. Relations among group members are usually cooperative within the group but may be quite competitive with other groups. The intellectual basis of communitarianism is advanced by MacIntyre (1981). It is also demonstrated by example, such as Muhammed's Koran, since the orientation is pre-modern (in contrast to a modern or post-modern position). Recent champions of the communitarian view include Amatai Etzioni (1993) and James Coleman (1990). For many proponents, the ideal society is perhaps an ethnic state or one that is organized into small groups and provides community-based services, as exemplified by Canada's Native peoples. Such a social organization may be seen as primordial and have its basis in ancient structures. It offers not optimism but the natural integration of all parts of life as illustrated by the orientations of many peoples in third world nations. Under communitarian rules, justice is largely based on the individual's contribution to the group. There is a great deal of social capital which persists across generations, illustrated by the expression, 'Bless the King and his relations; keep us in our proper stations.' Traditions and customs are maintained actively. Government intervention is often unwelcome. While researchers study extended families, places of worship, symbolism and personal identity gained from group membership, advocates call for a return to basic values, the need to exonerate the common good, cultural rediscovery, family values and the maintenance of contact with the past. Heroes and heroines are specific to each group and examples include Pope John Paul, Martin Luther King, Queen Elizabeth, Mother Teresa, Chief Maquinna and Lucien Bouchard. Recent successes which the communitarian view can demonstrate are the election of politicians with a cultural base, a resurgence in religion, the rediscovery of cultures (such as Native and Celtic), the near success of the referendum by the separatist French in Quebec, and innumerable local community actions.[2] As for public education, communitarians ask for more parental influence and the establishment of charter or traditional schools. They may also request aid for religious or band schools.

While both old and new, the conununitarian view and *homo anthropologicus* (with the emphasis on culture or subculture attractive to anthropologists and historians) receive their share of severe criticism. Detractors insist that its thrust is a return to a dark age of ethnocentrism, fundamentalism, imperialism, censorship, exclusion and oppression. Groups are seen to put up walls, engage in sectarian strife, pursue strictly tribal interests, be subject to authoritarian rule and thus become undemocratic. Some consider this view to hold a fatalism as demonstrated by the followers of Jim Jones, one of its worst exemplars. The individual becomes lost and subservient to the group.

Relations Between Clusters

Having presented the three positions, we can explore some of their articulations by demonstrating the genuinely adversarial exchanges among them, beginning with the relationship between egalitarian and the libertarian views. Since they are quite hostile to one another, they find the unreality of each other's underlying assumptions easy to criticize. The egalitarian says, 'There must be some rules for even a market to exist.' 'What about those persons who are not by any means rational adults, such as children and the unwell?' Rather than address these grave questions, the libertarian chooses the offensive and asks: How can you hope to improve the lot of humanity if you assume people (and thus you yourself) are not rational?' 'Why do you use oppressive means to relieve oppression?' The libertarian bemoans the egalitarian's lack of understanding of incentives, while the egalitarian worries about increasing inequities in western societies. However, there are instances when one view actually works to achieve the aims of the other. For instance, in order for poor people to be helped, an efficient governmental organization is sometimes required. Otherwise, the resources to help the disadvantaged are wasted. Thus, it is possible to use the language and concepts of economics (based largely on the libertarian view) in the service of equality.[3] Another example is exactly the one given by the egalitarian: 'government as umpire' is at least necessary for markets to survive and not to degenerate into physical conflict. Yet, the communitarian says, 'Both of you are missing the point. People are not just lost in mass society or merely individuals, they are always members of groups, which is where their loyalties lie. Neither of you has a sense of history or tradition.'

The libertarian and communitarian have a similar dispute. The libertarian will say, 'Your restrictions on individual behaviour are dysfunctional and result in crushing the human spirit. Your rules are arbitrary and you can provide no universal justification for them.' In response, the communitarian asserts, 'There is so much more to life than just proclaiming your individualism and achieving personal success. What are your real priorities?' And 'How do you think you chose your goals in the first place? Where in your frame of reference do they come from?' The libertarian rankles at his/her loss of freedom while the communitarian insists that excessive freedom is a curse. Yet, there are some examples in which these two views are dependent upon one another. The communitarian's groups actually rely on the confluence of individual interests when people work together, thus forming social bonds. And when the libertarian wishes to unite with others to achieve social action, he or she must rely on the ability of organizational norms to achieve even economic success, as shown by the Saturn story. Here the egalitarian interjects, 'But what about the welfare of the whole, not just your separate individual or group interests?' 'How can you ignore the concern for the commonwealth?'

The egalitarian and communitarian also have their quarrels. When the egalitarian attacks, he or she may remark, 'It is your customs and traditions that have resulted in the oppression of so many different kinds of people worldwide.' 'You would return us to a time of gross social injustice and conflict as witnessed by the Serbs and Moslems in Bosnia.' In response, the communitarian ignores these important points by going on the offensive. 'You claim that all people should be equal, but in practice, you are still selective in your endless quest for new rights. For instance, reverse discrimination is still discrimination.' 'Actually, your plan is to replace a traditional social order with an inverted one, likely more oppressive than the original.' The egalitarian insists that injustice will result while the communitarian maintains an opposite definition of justice. Yet, again, the principles of each group sometimes aid the other. Egalitarians find great comfort in their ability to raise the consciousness of disadvantaged groups to produce a solidarity and a willingness to take action for social justice based on the identification with the large group. Some groups with a strong communitarian basis are able to use legislation inspired by social justice to further their aims, as shown by blacks in America. But the libertarian asserts, 'How can you not acknowledge that individual invention and rational action is a central part of the means to achieve your goals? Why must you always interfere in the lives of ordinary people?'

The aforementioned arguments and examples show how the three value clusters are chiefly antithetical to each other but at times rely on contrary principles to effect their aims. Some readers will recognize the clusters in the cry of the French Revolution. While they remain rough composites of many perspectives within each

Figure 14.1   Three values behind educational governance

Attributes	Egalitarian	Libertarian	Communitarian
Assumptions			
Unit:	societies	individuals	groups
Key Concept:	inequality	rationality	origin/destiny
Relations:	conflict	competition	cooperation
Basis:	post-modernism	modernism	pre-modernism
Examples			
Schools:	public schools	private schools	parochial schools
Services:	government provision	free markets	community-based
States:	welfare state	capitalist state	ethnic state
Strengths			
Basic:	fair shake	power of self	primordial
Justice:	anti-oppressive	entitlement	contributory
Outcome:	security	productivity	social capital
Criticisms			
Intention:	uniformity	insecurity	restriction
Outcome:	slavery	arbitrariness	fatalism
Example:	Stalin	Olson	Jones

of them, the clusters illustrate generally shared views of social existence. When the advocacy of one cluster is compounded by ignorance of appreciation of the initial positions of others, misunderstanding is guaranteed. A simple depiction of the three value clusters might be a triangle with the egalitarian appropriately on the left, libertarian situated on the right, and communitarian on the bottom to depict its antecedent status. Figure 14.1 presents an approximate sketch of some of the dimensions of this explication of the three views. Since the communitarian view has received less attention in the literature and is becoming more important as we observe developments in education, we shall focus on it further.

Clearly, the 'new kid on the block', the communitarian view (which is both new and old) offers an alternative to the usual left–right choices among the values used to guide social policy. People are no longer required to choose between statist or individualism. Rather, the need to have a clear social identity (to belong to a group) is asserting itself, we believe. This need may be very basic to most people. After all, when Lucy's three-million-year-old bones were dug up in Ethiopia (along with those of her family), it was apparent that she was very much part of a social group. It is most unlikely that she considered herself an individual or that she dreamed of rectifying injustice on a mass scale.[4] Individualism did not become an alternative until markets became active about 500 years ago. Calls for equality were seldom heard before two centuries ago. Current conditions in Canada seem ripe for communitarian assertions, sometimes dramatically and on a large scale. For instance, the Native peoples, the French in Quebec, and the Chinese in British Columbia all draw great strength in their collective identity, the power of their cultures to heal and prosper, and the faith that their ethnicity will sustain them. They also raise questions about the ideal of cultural maintenance, the geographic implications of group identity and issues of language use. Naturally, their successes can produce a sense of isolation, misunderstanding and even conflict. The basic question, of course, is how much can group welfare be emphasized over the interests of Canada as a whole? We believe that it is possible to permit even such large groups a great deal of latitude providing there is sufficient tolerance and respect of natural differences. Once centrists, pragmatists and political opportunists become aware of this possibility, communitarian principles will be reflected in legislation and policies. The position holds for small groups as well, including those who make up the students, families and neighbourhoods surrounding public schools.

Implications for Future Schools

The trichotomy of values may be used to understand many of the discussions pertaining to public education. If the antithetical nature of the clusters is taken seriously, then it is not possible to attain an ideal public school. If one value is emphasized, it will damage or even trample the others. For example, an egalitarian school may offer equal opportunity but cannot deliver a high level of excellence or solidarity. A libertarian school may stress achievement but will not provide fully equal access or achieve extensive community. A communitarian school will strive for integration but will not offer complete equality of opportunity or achieve notable excellence. However, there are many possibilities for compromise. It must be possible to achieve some balance among the extremes. One way of making education more balanced is to adopt structures of governance and administration which draw their principles from all three clusters rather than emphasize one greatly to the detriment of others.

Public schools in Canada were born in the egalitarian tradition and remain in it today (Phillips, 1957). It is the status quo. Schools aspire to serve the entire society and are financed by public dollars. Virtually guaranteed clientele and the sole institution of schooling in many places, conventional public schools try to teach common values and emphasize equality of educational opportunity but suffer from a multiplicity of goals. They are required to follow provincial curricula under the constraints from union contracts, board policies and legislation. Their teachers are usually unsupervised, have a very high level of job security and receive ample compensation. However, the same teachers are subject to overwork, brought about by frequent changes in policies and demands for services which are not educational in nature. When the trichotomy is considered, it evokes suggestions for the ways in which public schools may be improved by adopting libertarian or communitarian principles and characteristics.

We suggest that public schools are being asked to change in one of two ways: either to adopt elements of the libertarian tradition or the communitarian one. That proposal indicates that the coexistence of the three value sets is possible and even desirable. If so, policy makers will need to generate directions at the macro-level that will permit two or more of the value clusters to be espoused and acted upon in districts and public schools.

The initiatives of choice within public education in Alberta and alternative schools in British Columbia are examples of the merging of these two value positions.

In these instances, the government establishes a legislative framework that defines goals and outcomes for public education for the common good, and provides the opportunity for individuals and communities to act in their own interest in determining how best to achieve those goals and outcomes through selection of curricula, methods of instruction and norms that govern student behaviour. In the following examples of changes in public education we consider how the clusters of values may find a balance.

Charter Schools

Calls for charter schools in Canada are largely requests for more parental choice along with demands for greater school freedom, accountability and responsibility (Raham, 1996; Wilkinson, 1994). Clearly, the assumptions of the aim of education is to address the needs of the individual student, largely a libertarian position. The purpose of the school is to serve the child, to best educate him or her for life as an individual. Once parents have chosen charter schools, they are seen to want to participate in their governance and to contribute to their daily well-being. The notion that like-minded parents might flock together begins to transcend the strictly marketplace view of charter schools when these parents with common interest work extensively together for all the children in the school, not just their own (Brown, 1996). When this happens, social capital is generated, as predicted by Coleman (1990), and the social cohesion of charter schools begins to approximate private schools with their emphasis on social goals, in addition to the intellectual ones (Cookson, 1994). Thus, the libertarian aim can turn into a communitarian outcome without direct intention. Marshall and Peters (1990) argue that when the fundamental theoretical unit for the consideration of educational policies is the individual chooser, the concept of community that is produced is a 'collection of individual choosers maximizing economic choices' (p. 51). They are skeptical that self-interest, exercised through school choice, can develop a sense of communal or group interest to allow communal benefits to accrue. Does this eventuality mean a complete departure from the goals of a public school system that was intended to benefit all students, not just those with active, choosing parents? Not necessarily. In the United States for example, a substantial fraction of charter schools have been established for students who require alternative programs, specifically for high-need and at-risk children (Raham, 1996). Consequently, despite the controversy surrounding charter schools, elements of all three value positions are associated with them because they offer parental choice within public education.

Education and Work

Public schools are criticized frequently for their lack of preparation of young people for the world of work (National Commission on Excellence in Education, 1983). Countries, in order to be competitive in what is now a global economy, require workers who are both sufficiently skilled and have the right social habits to perform well for their employers that are often business firms. The employees sell their skills in the labour market. The perspective most closely allied with this problem is the libertarian one, with human capital theory being its main variation (Becker, 1993). One action taken that is in keeping with the libertarian perspective is the use of contract schools (Lawton, 1995), in which districts surrender the schooling of students to private firms. Another development is the growth of school–business partnerships in which students are sent into the workplace for experience (Hoyt, 1991; Mann, 1987; Zacchei and Mirman, 1986).

These arrangements and their foundational assumptions are usefully questioned by those with an egalitarian perspective (Kincheloe, 1995; Lakes, 1992). They point out the bleak and unsafe conditions of factory life and required docility of workers. Rather than a fair exchange among equals in a labour market, they perceive that short-term interests of the business firms can predominate over the long-term interests of the workers. For them, it is necessary to integrate both academic and vocational emphases in school in order to prepare students for their work lives. This arrangement means that graduates will be smart workers, not only skilled in communications, reasoning, problem solving and learning throughout life, but also aware of the social and ethical issues of work and its meaning (Kincheloe, 1995). The curricular implications are for a more contextualized learning and emphasis on the preparation for citizenship.

Curiously, the communitarian view is almost absent from this debate, apart from Rifkin's (1995) admonishment that as work changes, the third sector of the economy (the voluntary sector) will need our contributions to build and rebuild the spirit of goodwill (see also Kahne and Westheimer, 1996). Some questions the communitarian perspective could pose are: How does the students' preparation for work serve the community? Can work be conceived so that the mobility of workers will not destroy the community's social capital? Can we educate our children 'up, but not away?' Again, whose schools are they?

Technology

The future of public schools looks both bright and troubling when the new technology is considered. On the one hand, computers and telecommunications will mean that schooling and learning will take place at any time, anywhere. Distance learning and home schooling will become viable options for students. The use of televised lectures, teleconferencing and video conferencing will imply that all students can have access to very high quality programs and engage in learning with excellent teachers. School sites in a variety of settings will provide the opportunity for many partnerships with business and industry. Teachers will become coaches that assist students in solving messy problems, in selecting materials and facilitating meeting their needs as learners. Students will be in more control of their learning. They will come to the school site only to do that which cannot be accomplished at a distance. Social functions could become part of a seamless web of learning not just in childhood, but lifelong (Halal and Leibowitz, 1994). Libertarian critics of current public education take delight in the promise of open education and its attendant choices, and the demise of the present monopoly over providers of public education.

On the other hand, there is concern about the information-rich and information-poor on the part of egalitarians (Kenway, 1995). Will some parents provide more education to their progeny than others as they purchase time on the Internet? Will this ability not magnify the disadvantages that some of our children now face? Will commercial interests dominate the educational function and saturate it with their marketing messages? Will face-to-face learning decline so that the social aims of schools in building common values are undermined? Again, the communitarian view is not usually present in this debate. Its queries might be: How do we protect our children from the miseducation of the Internet? How do we guide their learning so that it is directed by community norms rather than persons who do not have the interests of our children at heart? How do we maintain our customs and traditions in the face of such competition for children's socialization? Who should control the socialization of children?

Conclusion

The authors hold the belief that through education we can express our vision of how life ought to be lived. If like-minded people know what they want, then by joining others in building children's education through voluntary association for the common good, they can achieve schools that will reflect their visions. Such schools would make their contributions to the entire society, the group which fostered them, and the individual students who pass through them. Future schools will depart from the schools of today in their governance, their relation to work and their use of technology. In short, they will not reflect the same configuration of values as did schools in the twentieth century because we want them to change. It is important to 'sow now, reap later' by holding a desired future in mind so we may steer toward it. Surely we want people who are not just clever workers and adroit consumers, but also cultured, compassionate and courageous human beings. If we do not achieve a morally explicit image of our preferred future rather than simply an adaptation to our fate, civil dislocation may be great (Rifkin, 1995). We need to pull together, to acknowledge our differences, and to build a future for all of us.

Notes

1 For the relation between post-modernism and feminism, see Biesta (1995). A general account of post-modernism is given by Rosneau (1992).
2 See Lappe and Dubois (1994).
3 As exemplified by the work of Henry Levin (1980).
4 See Johanson and O'Farrell (1990).

Lynn Bossetti and Daniel J. Brown

References

APPLE, M. (1991) 'Conservative agendas and progressive possibilities', *Education and Urban Society*, **23**, 3, pp. 279–91.

BECKER, G.S. (1993) *Human Capital: A Theoretical and Empirical Analysis with Special Reference to Education*, 3rd edn, Chicago, IL: The University of Chicago Press.

BERRY, W. (1977) *The Unsettling of America*, San Francisco, CA: Sierra Club Books.

BIESTA, G. (1995) 'Postmodernism and the repoliticalization of education', *Interchange*, **26**, 2, pp. 161–83.

BOWERS, C.A. (1993) *Critical Essays on Education, Modernity and the Recovery of the Ecological Imperative*, New York: Teachers' College Press.

BRAND, S. (1995) 'Two questions', *Wired*, **3**, 11, pp. 28–46.

BROWN, D.J. (1996) 'Schools with heart.' Unpublished manuscript, University of British Columbia, Vancouver, BC.

COLEMAN, J.S. (1990) *Foundations of Social Theory*, Cambridge, MA: Belknap Press of Harvard University Press.

COOKSON, P.W. (1994) *School Choice: The Struggle for the Soul of American Education*, New Haven, CT: Yale University Press.

EMBERLY, P. and NEWELL, W. (1994) *Bankrupt Education: The Decline of Liberal Education in Canada*, Toronto, Canada: University of Toronto Press.

ETZIONI, A. (1993) *The Spirit of Community: The Reinvention of American Society*, New York: Simon and Schuster.

FRIEDMAN, M. (1962) *Capitalism and Freedom*, Chicago, IL: University of Chicago Press.

HALAL, W. and LIEBOWITZ, J. (1994) 'Telelearning: The multimedia revolution in education', *The Futurist*, **Nov–Dec**, pp. 21–6.

HAYEK, F.A. (1973) *Rules and Order*, London: Routledge.

HOYT, K. (1991) 'Educational reform and relationships between the private sector and education: A call for integration', *Phi Delta Kappan*, **February**, pp. 450–3.

JOHANSON, D.C. and O'FARRELL, K. (1990) Journey from the Dawn: Life with the World's First Family, New York: Villard Books.

KAHNE, J. and WESTHEIMER, J. (1996) 'In the service of what? The politics of service learning', *Phi Delta Kappan*, **77**, 9, pp. 593–9.

KENWAY, J. (1995) 'Reality bytes: Education, markets and the information superhighway', *Australian Education Researcher*, **22**, 1, pp. 35–65.

KINCHELOE, J.L. (1995) *Toil and Trouble: Good Work, Smart Workers and the Integration of Academic and Vocational Education*, New York: Peter Lang.

LAKES, R. (1992) 'Where are the intellectuals in vocational education?', *Journal of Thought*, **27**, 3 and 4, pp. 43–55.

LANNING, R. (1994) 'Education and everyday life: An argument against educational futures', *Canadian Journal of Education*, **19**, 4, pp. 464–78.

LAPPE, F.M. and DuBois, P.M. (1994) *The Quickening of America*, San Francisco, CA: Jossey-Bass.

LAWTON, S.B. (1995) *Busting Bureaucracy to Reclaim our Schools*, Montreal, Canada: Institute for Research on Public Policy.

LIVINGSTONE, D.W. (1983) *Class Ideologies and Educational Futures*, London: Falmer Press.

MacINTYRE, A. (1981) *After Virtue: A Study in Moral Theory*, London: Duckworth.

MANN, D. (1987) 'Business involvement and public school improvement, Part 1', *Phi Delta Kappan*, **October**, pp. 123–8.

MARSHALL, J. and PETERS, M. (1990) 'The insertion of new right thinking into education: An example from New Zealand', *Journal of Education Policy*, 5, 2, pp. 143–56.

NATIONAL COMMISSION ON EXCELLENCE IN EDUCATION (1983) *A Nation at Risk – The Imperative for Educational Reform*, Washington, DC: US Government Printing Office.

NOZICK, R. (1974) *Anarchy, State and Utopia*, New York: Fireside Books.

PHILLIPS, C.E. (1957) *The Development of Education in Canada*, Toronto, Canada: W.J. Gage.

PURPLE, D. (1993) 'Holistic education in a prophetic voice', in MILLER, R. (ed.) *The Renewal of Meaning in Education: Responses to the Cultural and Ecological Crisis of our Times*, Brandon, VT: Holistic Education Press.

RAHAM, H. (1996) 'Revitalizing public education in Canada: The potential of choice and charter schools', *Fraser Forum*, August.

RAWLS, J. (1970) *The Theory of Justice*, Cambridge, MA: Harvard University Press.

RIFKIN, J. (1995) *The End of Work: The Decline of the Global Labor Force and the Dawn of the Post-market Era*, New York: Tarcher/Putnam.

ROSNEAU, P.M. (1992) Post-modernism and the Social Sciences, Princeton, NJ: Princeton University Press.

SCHWARTZ, B. (1986) *The Battle for Human Nature: Science, Morality and Modern Life*, New York: W.W. Norton.

SENGE, P.M. (1990) *The Fifth Discipline: The Art and Practice of the Learning Organization*, New York: Doubleday Currency.

SHAKESHAFT, C. (1989) *Women in Educational Administration*, Newbury Park, CA: Sage.

WILKINSON, B.W. (1994) *Educational Choice: Necessary but not Sufficient*, Montreal, Canada: Institute for Research on Public Policy.

ZACCHEI, D.A. and MIRMAN, J.A. (1986) *Business-education Partnerships: Strategies for School Improvement*, Andover, MA: The Regional Laboratory.

15 Future Directions for the Study of Values and Educational Leadership

Pauline E. Leonard

The chapters that comprise this volume stand as testimony to the substantial and increasing number of critics of traditional organizational theories; particularly those either explicitly or implicitly promoting conceptualizations of leadership, decision making, and policy as value-free. Two decades ago, Scott and Hart (1979) sharply criticized those traditional bureaucratic organizations where management tends to be 'heavily weighted toward the expedient by people who have been trained to consider value questions as impractical, even foolish' (p. 40). In the field of educational administration, Thomas Greenfield (1979) warned that 'we should begin to regard with healthy scepticism the claim that a general science of organization and administration is at hand' (p. 12). Similarly, Christopher Hodgkinson (1978) informed us that leadership is a function of self-knowledge and values, and he continues to pursue that treatise via his contributions to this publication in Chapter 1.

In this opening chapter, Hodgkinson amplifies the shortcomings of a science of administration, reminding us that 'science itself stops short at the edge of voluntarism, at the frontiers of conscious choice'. He distinguishes between administration and management: '... the former opening upon the limitless horizons of philosophy, the latter upon the restricted field of vision right and proper to science and technology'. Accordingly, he critiques two deep-seated, grand assumptions embedded in administrative theory: we are all honourable, and authority and leadership legitimize power. These 'presumptive fallacies' serve to 'divorce the administrator from problems of ethics, morals, values ... leaving in their place only problems of technique, of managerial efficacy and efficiency'. Hodgkinson underscores the connection among the concepts of will, power and administration, arguing that administration *is* politics. Hence, leadership involves understanding the full spectrum of values from the self (V_1) through to the cultural (V_5), in order to perceive and ameliorate value conflicts. This process is necessarily both conscious and non-reactive and, therefore, demands that the leader have a knowledge of self. To facilitate self-revelation, Hodgkinson calls for an 'education of the will'. In this way, he asserts, leadership involves an appreciation of the entire range of values through 'an independent V_1 interpretation' – which may ultimately result in 'a triumph of the will'.

As Telford (1996) suggests, reconceptualizing leadership to include values, politics, power and the leader's triumphant will alerts us to its 'moral connection'. It is this moral connection which is reflected in much of the recent discussion, debate and research in educational administration literature. For instance, in relation to the works contained herein Begley (in Chapter 4) declares: '*The debate has not abated, it has intensified!*' That moral dimension of educational leadership is particularly significant in this postmodern epoch: 'given the character of the times . . . educators and those interested in education will increasingly be making moral judgments in a world where traditional ethical guidelines are often of little assistance in the matters at hand' (Ryan, in press).

A continuing quest to better understand the nature and function of values and the manner and situations in which educational leaders attempt to resolve value conflicts characterizes many of the ideas presented, analyzed and evaluated by the contributing authors of this text. Some of the overarching themes which have emerged are those concerning:

- determining 'altruistic attitudes, values and beliefs' (Starratt), and a 'morally explicit image of our preferred future' amidst 'global and national turbulence' (Carlin and Goode);
- considering 'the criteria and processes of value inquiry' (Beck);
- acknowledging and understanding the *contextuality* of moral leadership (Ribbins, Evers, Lakomski);
- recognizing and critiquing the power relationships embedded in language use (Ryan);
- clarifying, examining and addressing the relevancy gap between academic and practitioner perspectives on values (Begley);
- viewing the perception, construction and use of time as a lens for examining what we value (Lafleur);
- understanding the paradox of leadership couples (Gronn);
- analyzing the barriers to collaborative leadership (Leonard).

All of these themes re-affirm the importance of responding to the connection between leadership and its moral dimension.

This concern for and interest in the moral dimension of leadership should not be construed as an affront on the current moral state of educational leaders. Deliberations about moral leadership do not imply that today's educational leaders are uncaring or amoral. 'Indeed, it can be argued that in the case of educational administrators and other educators, good intentions are not the problem. Most of those who chose careers in schools appear to be rather altruistic and committed to an array of good outcomes for students' (Willower, 1994, p. 469). Nevertheless, Willower does shed light on the difficulty for leaders: 'The real problem is negotiating the maze that separates good intentions from desired results (p. 459).' Furthermore, given the complex nature of values, the variations in value orientations embedded in competing educational ideologies, and the multiple choices which confront educational leaders in their daily school activities, 'uncertainty rather than sureness' (Ryan, in press, p. 1) is often the prevailing norm. Continued discourse among academics, researchers and practitioners are warranted. Future discourse on values, however, requires more clarity, coherence and relevance to administrative practice if closing the relevancy gap is to be a realized goal (Begley, in Chapter 4).

A challenge to achieving value clarity, coherence and relevance is related to the dichotomous nature inherent in attempts to define the concept. Garforth (1985, p. 55) suggests that the word 'value' is frequently used to signify worth. If something has worth then it is choiceworthy. For example, *objects* such as clothes, vehicles, and money may be considered to *hold* value. However, values such as *happiness* and *contentment*, considered to be affective (Rokeach, 1973, p. 6) in that they imply a state of mind (Garforth, 1985, p. 55) and values such as *courtesy* and *kindness* considered to have a 'behavioural component' (Garforth, 1985; Rokeach, 1973) in that they refer to conduct, are not objects holding value but abstract notions of value. What follows is a bifurcated understanding of the concept of value: a person may value; or, an object or abstraction may hold value. In the former, values connote subjectiveness in that the worth of the value (e.g. money, happiness, kindness) is perceived or held by the individual. With regard to the latter, value is used in the objective sense in that it may be used to indicate the thing that is being valued (e.g. money, happiness, kindness). In other words, value can refer to the values that a person subjectively perceives or holds, or it can refer to the object or abstraction that is being valued. This may not be a problem when discussing concrete notions such as money, cars or clothes; however, when considering abstractions like peace, truth or respect, the distinction between subjectiveness and objectiveness is an important one. Beck explains the distinction this way:

> The term values has two connected but different meanings. In one sense, values are the things we pursue and consider important in life, the things we *value*. However, in the context of educational philosophy and theory the focus is normally on a narrower category, namely, the things that are *worthy* of valuing, the things that are actually *valuable*. This is what we are talking about when we say schooling should have a basis in values or students should be taught values: we do not mean just any values but rather a set of *sound* values. (1996, p. 2, original emphasis)

When undertaking value research or engaging in discussions of educational values, it is important to be aware of variations in value positions; it is also important to understand the problems inherent in polarizing these differences.

Contextual Considerations

Concomitant with the rejection of a general science of organization that embraced views such as Taylor's principles of scientific management and Fayol's general principles (Shafritz and Ott, 1996) is the acknowledgment of the importance of *context* in administration and decision making. Again this raises the issue of moral leadership. For example, Evers (in Chapter 5) puts forth the query: 'How is ethical leadership in educational contexts possible?' In addressing his own question he reminds us of the futility of searching for universal moral rules. Lakomski (in Chapter 3) supports this view stating, 'Generality, insofar as it can be obtained, would be a matter of the coherence of accounts in a *specified* context.' Evers goes on to claim that moral leadership and ethical knowledge are gained in the same manner as practical knowledge, 'through learning from experience in complex, shifting, context bound circumstances'. Similarly, in outlining a 'three-level approach to the study of leaders, leading, and leadership', Ribbins (in Chapter 8) also accents the importance of context. His call for more research into the praxis of both the leaders and the led within a variety of contexts underscores the necessity of grounding theory in action and provides us with another direction in our plan for future contributions in the area of values and leadership. The ultimate goal, however, is not to develop a prescription of values, for, – as Begley (in Chapter 4) points out – 'the processes of valuation in school leadership situations are much too context bound to permit this quick fix'. Instead, a reasonable goal is to help future leaders become reflective in their practice – in other words, to develop values, sophistication and self-knowledge (Hodgkinson, 1991).

Multiple Realities and Common Ground

In addition to recognizing the impact of context, is the need to realize that systems of values (Rokeach, 1973, 1979) may vary from one individual to another. It is the different ordering of these value systems which accounts for 'the richness and variety of individual differences in behaviour, attitudes, ideologies, self-preservations, judgment, evaluations, and rationalizations' (Rokeach, 1979, p. 49). Therefore, given the multitudes of different ways a relatively small number of values can be ordered, it is little wonder that value conflict is the 'normal human condition' (Hodgkinson, 1991, p. 102). It is also apparent that clarifying differences in value positions involves an attempt to navigate the many subtle complexities, the network of nuances and the gradations of differences associated with the varied positions. Multiple meanings and variations in interpretations have significant implications for schooling in general and educational leaders in particular. For example, when educators and other stakeholders debate and discuss educational values related to such issues as multicultural education, character education, caring schools, zero-tolerance policy, technology education, peace studies, cooperative learning, this question arises: Do participants in the discussion perceive these concepts as means values or end values? Put another way, is the educational value considered to be the end-purpose to schooling, or is it a means to achieve the end-purpose? For example, should character education be an overarching educational purpose? Beck (1993, p. 3) suggests that 'being moral should be seen not as an end in itself but rather as a *means* (original emphasis) to the good life, for ourselves and others'. He reiterates this position in Chapter 13, stating that a 'similar error has been made in education'. The question is then, should character education be an end in and of itself, or is it a *means* to an end. The answer is an important one because it can help clarify educational purposes and curriculum orientations.

Undoubtedly, clarifying the differences in interpretations of means and end values is a real challenge for educational leaders. This is commonly recognized to be due, at least partly, to the fact that we live in an increasingly pluralistic society comprised of different religions, ethnicities and social groups. The result is that there are potentially – and indeed probably – disparate value orientations among educational stakeholders. Educational leaders need to be fully aware of this disparity. However Bossetti and Brown (in Chapter 14) point out that the challenge is made more complex because of 'the ubiquity of change and uncertainty that pervades the post-modern era'. The question arises regarding whether or not there are any absolutes in educational settings today. If there are, then next to be asked is, whose absolutes are they? How, and by whom, can these absolutes be decided upon? Carlin and Goode (in Chapter 11) propose that schools and families 'play a vital role in enculturing tomorrow's citizens and leaders into the values and meanings that constitute our essential humanity'. They also emphasize the importance of moral leadership for the fulfilment of this role. The implication is that there may be some educational values that everyone can agree upon as basic. These would be common conceptualizations of what is desirable, rather than a promotion of particular group interests and desires. A corollary following from this position is that it is incumbent on moral leaders to facilitate the understanding of and differentiation between educational values that are desirable and those that are motivated by self-interests.

Holistic Leadership

Perhaps an equally important missive to consider is that leadership does not necessarily reside in one individual. In fact, the developing trends to democratize and decentralize educational decision making embodies a holistic approach to leadership – 'the idea of expanding opportunities for teachers, parents, and other local groups to play a role in guiding their schools' (Duke and Canady, 1991, p. 130). More succinctly put, there is no limit to who can be a leader (Telford, 1996). Beck (in Chapter 13) supports this notion and states that, 'having been appointed as administrators does not mean that they must be – or must seem to be – wiser in value matters than others'. Traditional forms of leadership, where the administrator is seen as the omnipotent arbiter of values, no longer work well in pluralistic societies. Leadership in a holistic sense involves, as Starratt describes in Chapter 2, 'engaging people in the recreation of their work and their work environment, and indeed in the more intentional work of the continuous creation of themselves as individuals and as a community'. This important process would necessarily mean valuing the 'wide variety of languages that show up in schools' (Ryan, in Chapter 7). While Ryan discusses the significance of respecting language diversity primarily in relation to students and curriculum, his message also has implications for collaboration and shared decision making. He reminds us that not all language is equally valued and 'power relationships have favoured it [standard English] over other languages'. Given the importance of language as a 'vehicle for voice', attention should be given to promoting respect for diverse forms of language and dialect in the interest of equalizing power in the values negotiation process.

Moral leadership, then, necessarily involves the democratic process of collaboration, and negotiation among participants in the educational community. But there is more – as is advocated by Shakotko and Walker in Chapter 12. They argue that leadership involves 'an artistic, imaginative dimension' and then proceed to present a model 'through which the imagination is engaged in moral reasoning'. Important 'poietic' resources for educational leaders engaged in moral discourse are *perspective, metaphor, narrative, the fine arts* and *irony*, all of which leaders can creatively employ in their facilitation of moral decision-making processes. For them, the ultimate goal is that educational leaders be guided by a 'practical wisdom which incorporates both reason and imagination in a creative praxis'.

Lafleur (in Chapter 10) also has something to say about imagination in his discourse on the effects of time. He posits that 'organizational time is character-istically monochronic, future-oriented, compartmentalized and calendar based'. In relation to the effects of time on aspects of schooling, Lafleur proposes a challenge to revisit and re-evaluate both the purposes and organizational structure of schools. In his words, 'stretching our understanding of time can create possibilities and enable educators to make leaps of *imagination*'.

Future Directions

As the nature and importance of fundamental value orientations as an influence on administrative decision making receives increasing attention in the literature, there is an emerging contingent need to clarify aspects of the discussion. In today's mushrooming pluralistic societies, administrators are becoming 'increasingly sen-sitive to values issues' (Begley, 1996, p. 405) where there are no 'straightforward solutions' (Ryan, in press). Right resolution requires sophistication about the nature of values (Hodgkinson, 1991, 1996). However, considering the high level of ambiguity that is embedded in understanding the nature and function of values, value finesse may not be easily attained. Therefore, it is necessary to revisit and enhance our efforts to clarify and cohere dialogue in the area of values and leadership. The contention is that a better understanding of varying and competing terminology embedded in value inquiry is helpful for understanding the challenge that administrators face as facilitators of value-laden decision making among educational stakeholders. There is also the need to acknowledge the contextual ambiguity enveloping educational leaders engaged in the practice of moral leader-ship where there is a concomitant recognition of value pluralism. Consequently, a better understanding of the implications that multiple meanings and interpretations related to value theory have for the practice of moral leadership is of fundamental importance.

Although some might consider these matters to be the exclusive domain of ethical philosophers and academic researchers, others would disagree. Walker's (1994) study of the notions of ethical among educational leaders suggests that it is important to examine practitioner knowledge, understandings and interpretations in this area. This means it is necessary to examine educational settings to better appreciate emergent multiple meanings and realities related to context, time, and language. Questions to be asked are abundant. For example:

- Is it necessary for all participants involved in collaborative decision making – which often gives rise to value conflicts – to not only arrive at shared values but to begin with shared conceptualizations of the nature of values?
- How do leaders facilitate shared decision making when stakeholders subscribe to different value orientations and hold different and often subconscious interpretations of value theory?
- How can leaders facilitate the process of arriving at the 'common good'?
- What is the nature of the relationship between language and power in the process of achieving common ground?
- What is the role of the imagination in moral leadership endeavours and how can the imagination be cultivated?
- Can reconceptualizations of time enhance creativity and imagination and by extension inform moral leadership? If so, how?

This challenging (but not exhaustive) list of questions and the partially formed answers provided in this book have very definite implications for future directions in the study of values and educational leadership. In the wake of such queries – and coupled with the preceding ruminations – comes the compelling recognition that value-oriented inquiry must continue to stimulate and evoke critical dialogue and debate. Failure to meet the challenge will almost certainly cause us to fall short of even approaching the ideal of moral leadership in the encumbered world of the educational practitioner.

References

BECK, C. (1993) *Learning to Live the Good Life: Values in Adulthood*, Toronto, Canada: OISE Press.

BECK, C. (1996) 'Values, school renewal and educational leadership.' Paper presented at the 1996 Toronto Conference on Values and Educational Leadership, Toronto.

BEGLEY, P.T. (1996) 'Cognitive perspectives on values in administration: A quest for coherence and relevance', *Educational Administration Quarterly*, 32, 3, pp. 403–26.

DUKE, D.L. and CANADY, R.L. (1991) *School Policy*, New York: McGraw Hill, Inc.

GARFORTH, F.W. (1985) *Aims, Values and Education*, Hull: Christygate Press.

GREENFIELD, T.B. (1979) 'Organization theory as ideology', *Curriculum Inquiry*, 9, 2, pp. 97–111.

HODGKINSON, C. (1978) *Towards a Philosophy of Administration*, Oxford: Blackwell.

HODGKINSON, C. (1991) *Educational Leadership: The Moral Art*, Albany, NY: Suny Press.

HODGKINSON, C. (1996) *Administrative Philosophy: Values and Motivations in Administrative Life*, London: Elsevier Science Ltd.

LAKOMSKI, G. (1987) 'Values and decision making in educational administration', *Educational Administration Quarterly*, 23, 3, pp. 70–82.

ROKEACH, M. (1973) *The Nature of Human Values*, New York: The Free Press.

ROKEACH, M. (1979) *Understanding Human Values*, New York: The Free Press.

RYAN, J. (in press) 'Beyond the veil: Moral educational administration and inquiry in a postmodern world', in BEGLEY, P.T. (ed.) *Values and Educational Leadership*, Albany, New York: SUNY.

SCOTT, D.K. and HART, W.G. (1979) *Organizational America*, Boston, MA: Houghton Mifflin.

SHAFRITZ, J.M. and OTT, J.S. (1996) *Classics of Organization Theory*, New York: Wadsworth Publishing.

TELFORD, H. (1996) *Transforming Schools Through Collaborative Leadership*, London: Falmer Press.

WALKER, K.D. (1994) 'Notions of ethical among senior educational leaders', *The Alberta Journal of Educational Research*, **40**, 1, pp. 21–34.

WILLOWER, D.J. (1994) *Educational Administration: Inquiry, Values, Practice*, revised edn, Lancaster, PA: Technomic Publishing Company, Inc.

Notes on Contributors

Clive Beck is Professor in the Department of Curriculum, Teaching and Learning at the Ontario Institute for Studies in Education of the University of Toronto, Ontario, Canada.

Paul T. Begley is Associate Professor and Head of the Centre for the Study of Values and Leadership in the Department of Theory and Policy Studies at the Ontario Institute for Studies in Education of the University of Toronto, Ontario, Canada.

Lynn Bossetti is Associate Professor in the Faculty of Education at the University of Calgary, Alberta, Canada.

Daniel J. Brown is Professor in the Faculty of Education at the University of British Columbia, Vancouver, British Columbia, Canada.

Paul Carlin is an Education Officer with the Australian Principals Centre which is housed within the Faculty of Education at the University of Melbourne, Parkville, Victoria, Australia.

Colin Evers is Associate Professor in the Faculty of Education at Monash University, Clayton, Victoria, Australia.

Helen Goode is an Education Officer with Catholic Education Office, Melbourne, Victoria, Australia.

Peter Gronn is Associate Professor in the Faculty of Education at Monash University, Clayton, Victoria, Australia.

Christopher Hodgkinson is Professor Emeritus at the Faculty of Education, University of Victoria, British Columbia, Canada.

Clay Lafleur is a doctoral student in the Department of Theory and Policy Studies at the Ontario Institute for Studies in Education at the University of Toronto, Ontario, Canada.

Gabriele Lakomski is Associate Professor and Reader in the Department of Educational Policy and Management within the Faculty of Education at the University of Melbourne, Parkville, Victoria, Australia.

Pauline E. Leonard is Assistant Professor in the Department of Educational Administration at the University of Saskatchewan, Saskatoon, Saskatchewan, Canada.

Peter Ribbins is Professor and Dean of Education for the Faculty of Education and Continuing Studies at the University of Birmingham, England.

James Ryan is Associate Professor in the Department of Theory and Policy Studies at the Ontario Institute for Studies in Education at the University of Toronto, Ontario, Canada.

Don Shakotko is a doctoral student in the Department of Educational Administration at the University of Saskatchewan, Saskatoon, Saskatchewan, Canada.

Robert J. Starratt is Professor in the School of Graduate Studies in Education at Boston College, Chestnut Hill, Massachusetts, USA.

Keith Walker is Professor in the Department of Educational Administration at the University of Saskatchewan, Saskatoon, Saskatchewan, Canada.

Index

accent, 115–16
accountability, 96
action cluster, 208
Acton, Lord, 9, 129
administrative conservatorship, 142
administrative values, 223.
aesthetics, 202, 203–5
alternating time, 173
ambiguity, 207, 218, 251
antecedent-effects model, 38, 39
Anthony, S., 118
Apple, M., 234
Argyris, C., 46, 47, 183
Aristotle, 203
Arnold, M., 10
Arrow, K., 73
artificial neural networks, 75–7, 79
Ashbaugh, C.R., 59
attitudes, 55–6
axiology, 12, 19

backward mapping, 154–5
Bakhtin, M.M., 215
Baldwin, P., 189
balkanized culture, 101
Ball, S.J., 197
Barker, G., 190
Barnard, C., 141, 155, 159, 160
Barth, R.S., 59, 228
Bass, B.M., 154, 157, 159, 191
Bateson, M., 219
Beare, H., 189
Bebeau, M., 218
Beck, C., 54, 59, 60, 102, 182, 223–31, 247, 248, 249, 250
Beck, L.G., 22
Becker, G.S., 235, 242
Beckett, D., 216
Begley, P.T., 1–3, 15, 51–69, 175, 247, 249, 251
Berggren, D., 206

Berry, W., 233
Bloom, A., xiv
Bloom, H., ix
Blum, L., 219
Bolman, L.G., 39, 177
Bossert, S.T., 38, 40
Bossetti, L., 232–45, 250
bounded rationality, 62
Bourdieu, P., 112
Bowers, C.A., 233
Bowers, D.G., 41, 42, 44
Bradley, R.T., 142
Brand, S., 232
Bredeson, P., 217–18
Bridges, E.M., 38, 39, 40
Brown, D.J., 232–45, 250
Brown, K., 86, 89, 92
Brown, R.H., 202, 205, 206
Brubacher, J.W., 182
Bruner, J., 24
Bryman, A., 143, 161, 162
Buechner, F., 213–14
bullying, 151–3
Burns, J.M., 25, 140–1, 159, 191, 192
Butler, M., 86, 87, 91, 92, 94–6, 99

Cadwell, B.J., 194
Campbell, E., 175
Campbell, J., 189
Campbell, R., x, xi
Campbell-Evans, G., 59, 85, 99, 102
Canady, R.L., 250
Carlin, P., 187–200, 247, 250
Case, C.W., 182
Cavanagh, R.F., 99
Chaplin, C., 214–15
charter schools, 241
Churchland, P.M., 46, 48, 78–9
Churchman, 184

civil society, 189
codes of practice, 71–2
cognitive aesthetic, 202
cognitive economy, 47
cognitive perspectives, 61–5
Cohen, B., 54
Cohen, M.D., 177
Cohn, M., 227
Colebatch, T., 190
Coleman, J.S., 236, 241
collaboration, 84–105, 219–20
collegiality, 91–2, 98, 100, 103–4
committee structure, 89–91, 95, 99–100
commons, 9–10
communitarian view, 236–43
community, 29, 57
compatibility, 92
competence, 28
competition, 100–1, 102
complexity, 70–81
computational models, 74–5
conflict avoidance, 101, 102
Confucian thought, 70
Conley, D., 182
Conlon, D., 162
Connell, W.F., 156–7
consensus, 60, 61, 64, 66
consequence, 60, 61, 64, 66
constellation-of-traits theory, 40–1
constructivism, 62
context, 70–81, 125–39
contextual leadership, 228, 229
contextual variables, 141
contingency theory, 43
Conway, D.W., 7
Cookson, P.W., 241
Coons, A.E., 42, 46
Corbin, J., 144
corporation, 12–13
Corson, D., 106, 111–22, 171
couples, 142–3, 154, 157–61, 163
Courville, L., 12
Cousins, J.B., 59
Covey, S., 181–2
Cox, E., 189
creative ambiguity, 207
creative leadership, 192
creative rationality, 206
creativity, 201–22

Culbertson, J., x
cultural relativism, xiv
cultural time, 173, 174
culture, 57
Cummins, J., 114, 119, 120
cyclical time, 173, 174

da Costa, J.L., 103
Darling, J.R., 141, 142, 143, 144–61
Davies, R., 207
de Mirabeau, Comte, 14
De Montaigne, M., 11
DePree, M., 193, 202
Deal, T.E., 39, 177
deceptive time, 173
decision making, 73, 74, 194
    imagination, 219
    shared, 93–4, 95, 96, 99, 101, 102,
        197–8, 252
delegated authority, 150
Dellar, G.B., 99
democracy, 13
Dewey, J., 224
dialogical approach, 182–3
direct effects, 38, 154
distance learning, 242
Dorfman, P.W., 154
Drucker, P.F., 192
dual control, 161
Duke, D., 202, 203–4, 205
Duke, D.L., 103, 250
Duke, P., 214
Dwyer, D.C., 38, 40

Eckersley, R., 188
Edwards, J., 117
Edwards, V., 121, 122
egalitarian view, 234–5, 237–43
Elmore, R.F., 154–5
Elvins, R., 195
Emberley, P., 232
empiricist theory, 44
empowerment, 28, 29, 32, 33, 96, 112
enduring time, 173
English, F., 211
environmental capital, 189
Eraut, M., 216
erratic time, 173
ethical knowledge, 77–9

ethical leadership, 70–81
ethics, ix, 203
Etzioni, A., 236
Evans, R., 177
Evers, C.W., 14, 44, 64, 70–81, 248–9
  coherentism, 49
  contextuality, 247
  functional relationships, 48
  Greenfield's argument, xi–xii
  neuro-scientific explanations, xiii
  personal preference, 54
  semantics, 59
Executive, 62, 63, 64, 66
existential self, 56
experienced time, 173, 174
explosive time, 173

facilitation, 230
facilitative leadership, 94, 99, 252
factivity, 203
fascism, 13
Feather, N.T., 183–4
Fiedler, F.E., 43
Fiegl, H., xi
financial capital, 189
Fine Arts, 212–13
Finkelstein, S., 150, 160, 163
Fitchett, W.H., 161
Flanagan, O., 78, 79
focused time, 173, 174
forward mapping, 154.
Foster, W., 70, 216
Fraisse, P., 171
Frankena, W.K., 54
fraternal-permissive role, 160
free will, 16
freedom of will, 10–11
Friedman, M., 235
Friedrich, C.J., 150
friendships, 114–15
Frost, P., 155
Fulghum, R., 206
Fullan, M., 25, 101, 178, 179
functional relationships, 48

Gaarder, J., 17
Gardner, H., 127
Gardner, J., 205–6, 212, 213

Garforth, F.W., 248
George, A.L., 160–1
George, J.L., 160–1
Getzels, J., x, xi
Gibb, C.A., 40–1, 47
Giddens, A., 172, 178
Giles, 117
Gillingwater, D., 143
Gilson, E., 202–3
Ginsberg, M., 224–5
Giroux, H.A., 175
Gleick, J., 215
goal orientation, 39
Goldstein, T., 114, 121
Goode, H., 187–200, 247, 250
Gouldner, A.W., 159
Grace, G., 199
Graen, G.B., 158, 163
Greene, M., 212
Greenfield, T., xi–xiii, xv, xvi, 15, 125–6
  Boethius, 129
  moral order, 142
  personal values, 223
  science of organization, 246
  Theory Movement, xi–xii
  training, xv
Greenfield, W.D., 195–6, 216, 218
Griffiths, D., x, xi
Gronn, P., 14, 126, 140–67, 202, 247
group, 56
Guare, R.E., 32
Gurr, D., 202
Gurvitch, G., 173

Hahn, Kurt, 145–6
Halal, W., 243
Hall, 172
Hallinger, P., 37–9, 40, 43, 47
Halpin, A., x, xi
Halpin, A.W., 42, 46
Hambrick, D.C., 150, 160, 163
Hampshire, S., 201
Handy, C., 176
Hargreaves, A., 101, 172, 178, 179
Hart, W.G., 246
Harvey, D., 177
Hawkings, S., 173
Hayek, F.A., 235
Hays, E., 215

Heath, S., 122
Heck, R.H., 37–9, 40, 43, 47
Hemphill, J.K., 40, 42, 43, 46
Henry, A., 120
hidden curriculum, 180
hierarchical leadership, 163
hierarchical organization, 70
hierarchical relationships, 157–8
Hodgkinson, C., xvi, 1, 54, 55, 138
  analytical model, 60, 63
  integrated model, 64–5
  leadership model, 70
  moral outcomes, 216
  moral primitives, 142
  motivational bases, 56
  praxis, 125
  reflection, 249
  science of organization, 246
  semantics, 59
  sophistication, 251
  training, xv
  transformational leadership, 103
  value audit, 183
  will, 6–21
Hodgson, R.C., 143, 158, 160
holistic leadership, 250–1
Hone, B., 156
honesty, 92–3, 97, 102, 103, 104
Howe, W., 38
Howell, J.P., 154
Hoy, W.K., 45
Hoyt, K., 242
Hughes, M., x–xi
Hughes, P., 187
human capital, 189
hypothetico-deductive theory, 44, 48

Ibrahim, A., 116
ideology of correctness, 115
image control, 97–8
imagination, 201, 209, 211, 213, 216–20, 251, 252
indirect effects, 154
information processing theory, 62–3, 66
institutions, 112
interdisciplinary collaboration, 219–20
irony, 213–16, 218
isolation, 100

Jermier, J., 140–1, 150, 154, 162, 163
Johansson, O., 61
Johnson, M., 179, 206, 208–11

Kahne, J., 242
Kantianism, 73–4
Kasten, K.L., 59
Kearney, P., 201
Kenway, J., 243
Kerr, S., 140–1, 150, 154, 155, 162, 163
Kets de Vries, M., 202, 216
Kidder, R., 181
Kierkegaard, S., 213
Kincheloe, J.L., 233, 242
Kipling, R., 17
Kluckhohn, C., 54, 180–1
knowledge-based economy, 23
Korman, A.K., 42–3
Kotter, J., 191
Kottkamp, R., 227
Krantz, J., 142, 143, 150, 158

Labov, W., 119
Lacey, R., 128
Ladson-Billings, G., 120
Lafleur, C., 170–86, 247, 251
Lakes, R., 242
Lakoff, G., 179, 208
Lakomski, G., 14, 36–50, 248
  artistic flair, 202
  contextuality, 247
  Greenfield's argument, xi–xii
  neuro-scientific explanations, xiii
  personal preference, 54
  semantics, 59
Lang, D., 59
language, 106–24, 252
Lanning, R., 232
Lawler, E.F., 41, 42
Lawton, S.B., 242
Leader Behavior Description Questionnaire (LBDQ), 37, 42, 45
leader-follower reciprocity, 159
leadership, 15, 101, 103, 187–200, 223–31
  context and praxis, 125–39
  couples, 142–3, 154, 157–61, 163
  criticisms, 36–50
  ethical, 70–81
  facilitative, 94, 99, 252

holistic, 250–1
moral, 22–35, 250–1, 252
poietic, 201–22, 251
substitutes, 154, 155, 156, 157, 160–1, 163
transactional, 25–8, 33, 159, 191, 192
transformational, 25–6, 30–2, 33, 103, 191, 192
transitional, 25–6, 28–30, 33
Leadership Opinion Questionnaire (LOQ), 42
learning organization, 177
learning process, 23
least-preferred co-worker score (LPC), 43
Lee, G.V., 38, 40
legitimacy, 9–10
Leibowitz, J., 243
Leithwood, K.A., 59, 62, 63, 64, 65, 102
Lemay, S., 114, 115, 118, 120
L'Engle, M., 206
Leonard, P.E., 84–105, 246–53
Lepani, B., 188
Levinson, D.J., 143
libertarian view, 235–6, 237–43
Lichtenstein, B., 218–19
Lingis, A., 15
linguistic metaphors, 58–60
linkage model, 47–8
Livingstone, D.W., 232
logical positivism, ix–x
long-term memory, 62, 64, 66
Lubeck, S., 172
Lucy, J., 111
Luther, M., 120

McCullough, J., 120
McGuinness, I., 143
MacIntyre, A., 209, 210, 236
Mackay, H., 187–8, 194
MacKenzie, S.B., 140, 163
McLaughlin, B., 114
McMahon, S., 115, 118
McMorrow, W.J., 195
MacNamara, R.S., 8, 12
Maguire, M., 197
maintenance metaphor, 217
malaise, 11–14
Mann, D., 242
Marland, M., 127

Marsh, D.D., 178
Marshall, J., 241
Marsick, V.J., 177
maternal-nurturant role, 160
mediated-effects model, 38
Medley, J.D.G., 156
Meindl, J.R., 161
Menschenkenner, 16
mentoring, 96–7
metaphors, 58–60, 142, 208–9, 217
micro-political time, 172
Mill, J.S., 72
Mirman, J.A., 242
Miskel, C.G., 45
Mitfühlung, 16
Molino, J., 203
monochronic time-frames, 172
Montgomery, D.G., 62, 63
Montgomery, E.H., 142, 143, 146–61
Moore, G.E., 78
moral ambiguity, 207
moral character cluster, 208–9
moral connection, 246–7
moral dilemmas, 218
moral dimensions, 22–35
moral guidance, 70
moral knowledge, 71–5
moral leadership, 22–35, 250–1, 252
moral outcomes, 216
moral perception, 219
moral reasoning, 72–5, 209, 211
moral reciprocity, 159–60
moral sense, xiv
moral values, 181, 225, 226
Morrison, D., 120
Mortimer, J., 127
Mortimer, P., 127
motivational base, 56, 60
multi-perspective, 127–9
Murdoch, I., 201, 219
Murnighan, J.K., 162
Murphy, J., 177, 192–3

narrative, 209–11
Nattiez, J., 203, 204
naturalism, 78, 79
naturalistic coherentism, xii, 49
naturalistic fallacy, x, 78
negativity, 117

negotiation, 101–2
neo-feudalism, 13
neural networks, 75–7, 79
neuro-scientific explanations, xiii
Newell, A., 72
Newell, W., 232
Nietzsche, F., 7, 9, 10–11, 14, 15
noetics, 203
norm of reciprocity, 159
Nozick, R., 235

obligation cluster, 208
Olson, C., 236
open question argument, 78
openness, xiv
organization, 57
Ormrod, J.E., 62
Ott, J.S., 248

paternal-assertive role, 160
patois, 117–18, 121
peer coaching, 96
Perrow, C., 41, 42, 43
personal values, 223
perspective, 205–7
Peters, M., 241
phenomenological time, 172
Philips, S., 113
Phillips, C.E., 240
Phillips, K., 202
phonetics, 58–9
physical-symbol system hypothesis, 72
Pierce, C.S., 203
Pitcher, P., 202
Pitner, N., 38
Podsakoff, P.M., 140, 163
poietic leadership, 201–22, 251
poietics, 203, 204
political time, 173, 174
political values, 226
polychronic time-frames, 172–3
Popper, S.H., 217, 219–20
Porter, L.W., 41, 42
positivist theory, 44
postmodernism, 14, 175, 176–8, 233–4
power, 6, 7–9, 10, 15, 77, 111–12, 129, 252
preference utilitarianism, 73
principle, 60

problem-solving, 64
professional development, 96–7
prolegomenon, xii, 126
proleptic time, 173, 174
Purple, D., 233

Raham, H., 241
rational values, 66
Rawls, J., 74, 235
Reagan, T.G., 182
reciprocal leadership, 228
reciprocal-effects model, 38, 39
reciprocity, 155, 159
recuperation, 14–15
reductionism, xiii
reflective practice, 182
reflective time, 173, 174
Reich, R.B., 188
Rein, M., 206, 219
Rejai, M., 202
Renihan, P., 206
Report of the National Education
    Commission on Time and Learning,
    178
restructuring agenda, 22–5
retarded time, 173
Ribbins, P., ix–xvii, 125–39, 141, 142,
    161, 162, 247, 249
Richardson, E., 128
Rickford, J., 120, 121
Ricoeur, P., 206
Riffel, J.A., 187
Rifkin, J., 242, 243
Riorda, G., 103
Roberts, N., 142
Robinson, V.M.J., 77
Rokeach, M., 175, 181, 183, 248, 249
role rehearsal, 159–60
ronin, 13
Rorty, R., 212, 226
Roth, G., 7
Rottier, J., 102
Ryan, J., 106–24, 247, 250, 251

Sartre, 17
Saul, J.R., 9, 12–13
Scandura, T.A., 158, 163
Schon, D., 206, 219
Schon, D.A., 182, 183

school renewal, 227–31
Schopenhauer, 7
Schwab, J., xi
Schwartz, B., 236
Schwartz, E., 178
Scott, D.K., 246
Seashore, S.E., 41, 42, 44
Seerveld, C., 201
self, 23–4, 56
self-discipline, 156
self-interest, 9, 60, 61
self-knowledge, 246
self-mastery, 16, 17, 18
self-preservation, 7
Selznick, P., 141, 142, 159
semantics, 58–9
semiological tripartition, 203
Senge, P.M., 103, 177, 232
Sergiovanni, T.J., 14, 39, 59, 103, 181,
    193–4
Shafritz, J.M., 248
Shakeshaft, C., 234
Shakespeare, W., ix
Shakotko, D., 201–22, 251
shared decision-making (SDM), 93–4, 95,
    96, 99, 101, 102, 197–8, 252
Sherratt, B., xv–xvi, 128
short-term memory, 62
Silins, H.C., 191
Simon, H., x, 8, 52, 62, 72
situational favourableness, 43
Slattery, P., 172, 176
Smith, A., 235
Smith, B., 218–19
social capital, 189, 190, 241
social values, 226
socio-political time, 173
Socrates, 213
Solomon, P., 118
Southworth, G., 128
speakers, 155
speaking consciousness, 111
Speicher, B., 115, 118
Spencer Chapman, F., 146
spiritual capital, 189
spiritual values, 226
Sproull, L.S., 177
Squires, J., 175
staff room, 91

Starratt, R.J., 22–35, 190, 192, 247, 250
Statement of Ethics, 71
steering committees, 28
Steffy, B., 211
Steinbach, R., 59, 64
Steinbeck, J., 207
stereoscopic vision, 206, 207
Stigelbauer, S., 25
Stogdill, R.M., 40
Stout, R., 216
Strauss, A., 144
Strike, K.A., 54
sub-rational values, 58, 63–4, 66
substitutes, 154, 155, 156, 157, 160–1, 163
survival metaphor, 217
Swain, M., 114, 120
syntactics, 58–9
syntax, 55–6, 59, 112, 115

teacher compatibility, 92
teacher efficacy, 97–8, 101, 102–3
team teaching, 84, 87–9, 96–103
technical-rational time, 172, 173, 174,
    178–9
technological time, 173, 174
technology, 242–3
Telford, H., 246, 250
Terry, L.D., 142
Theory Movement, x–xii, 45
theory-in-action, 183
thought, 111
Timbertop, 141–67
time, 98–9, 170–86
time in advance of itself, 173
Times Educational Supplement, 155–6
Toohey, K., 116, 118, 119, 121, 122
Torbert, W., 218–19
trace dimension, 203
transactional leadership, 25–8, 33, 159,
    191, 192
transcendent self, 56
transcendental, 57, 213
transformational leadership, 25–6, 30–2,
    33, 103, 191, 192
transitional leadership, 25–6, 28–30, 33
transrational values, 58, 60, 61, 64, 65, 66,
    70
tripartite value model, 183
trust, 92–3, 97, 102, 103, 104

Turner, F., 212
Turner, M., 179

unit discipline, 155
unitary traits theory, 40
utilitarianism, 72, 73

value-added leadership, 61
verifiability principle, ix–x
vertical line relationships, 157–8
Vicker, G., 6
Vico, G., ix
vision metaphor, 217
Vlastos, G., 213
voice, 111
voluntarism, 6

Waldrop, M.M., 177
Walker, K., 201–22, 251
Walsh, C., 111, 113, 121
Watkins, K.E., 177
Weber, M., 7–8, 125–6
Weiss, C.H., 198
well-being, 224–5, 228

Westheimer, J., 242
Wheen, F., 161
Wilkinson, B.W., 241
will, 6–21
Willeford, W., 214
Willower, D.J., 14, 51, 54, 247
Wilson, E., xiii
Wilson, J., xiii–xv
Winer, B.J., 42, 46
Wittich, C., 7
Wong, K.C., 70
work, 241–2
worth, 111
Wragg, T, 138
Wyatt, T., 195

Yukl, G., 47–8

Zacchei, D.A., 242
Zainu'ddin, A.T., 161
Zaleznik, A., 143
Zeitgeist, 13
zone of indifference, 160
zone of uncertainty, 176